Innocent Weapons

THE NEW COLD WAR HISTORY
Odd Arne Westad, editor

MARGARET PEACOCK

Innocent
WEAPONS

The Soviet and American Politics

of Childhood in the Cold War

THE UNIVERSITY OF NORTH CAROLINA PRESS
Chapel Hill

© 2014 THE UNIVERSITY OF NORTH CAROLINA PRESS

Publication of this book was supported in part by a generous
gift from Catherine Lawrence and Eric Papenfuse.

All rights reserved. Set in Minion and Scala Sans by codeMantra.
Manufactured in the United States of America.

The paper in this book meets the guidelines for permanence
and durability of the Committee on Production Guidelines for
Book Longevity of the Council on Library Resources.

The University of North Carolina Press has been
a member of the Green Press Initiative since 2003.

Library of Congress Cataloging-in-Publication Data
Peacock, Margaret.
Innocent weapons : the Soviet and American politics of
childhood in the Cold War / Margaret Peacock.
pages cm. — (The new Cold War history)
Includes bibliographical references and index.
ISBN 978-1-4696-1857-9 (cloth : alkaline paper)
ISBN 978-1-4696-3344-2 (pbk. : alkaline paper)
ISBN 978-1-4696-1858-6 (ebook)
1. Children and politics—Soviet Union—History. 2. Children and politics—
United States—History—20th century. 3. Children in popular culture—Soviet Union—
History. 4. Children in popular culture—United States—History—20th century.
5. Cold War—Social aspects—Soviet Union. 6. Cold War—Social aspects—
United States. 7. Cold War—Political aspects—Soviet Union. 8. Cold War—Political
aspects—United States. 9. Soviet Union—Politics and government—1945–1991.
10. United States—Politics and government—1945–1989. I. Title.
HQ784.P5P43 2014
305.230947—dc23
2014017084

FOR MY CHILDREN
Amelia, Sylvia, and Mira

Contents

Figures

Innocent Weapons

Introduction

For Soviet and American populations in the late 1940s, the fate of the Cold War was tied to the fate of the young. In the Soviet Union, the slogan "Thank you, Comrade Stalin, for our Happy Childhood!" became a rallying cry for resurgent Soviet power. It symbolized the nation's recovery from the Great Patriotic War, and the apparent gratitude of the population to Stalin for making their joy possible. At the same time, in the United States, images of safe and happy children like Little Ricky Ricardo and Beaver Cleaver splashed across America's televisions and newspapers. They established a vision of an abundant middle class, united in its commitment to democracy and the "American Way." These ubiquitous depictions of protected and joyous Soviet and American children represented an ideal of domestic bliss and national strength. They provided a hopeful vision of an abundant future, and they carried the underlying promise that if domestic containment and security could be maintained in the home, national defense would be assured.

Twenty years later, images like those of Stalin's grateful children and Lucy's Little Ricky no longer occupied a central space in the collective imaginations of their people. Antiwar protesters in the United States now took to the streets carrying pictures of napalmed Vietnamese children, chanting, "Hey. Hey, LBJ! How many kids did you kill today?" In the Soviet Union, the filmmakers Elem Klimov and Tengiz Abuladze created child protagonists who had no parents, no leadership, and showed no sense of obligation to their community or their country. The image of the child, which had once embodied all that the nation could provide and protect, was now an icon for all that the country threatened to neglect and destroy. How did one image supplant the other in such a short period of time? What forces led to this transformation, and what does this visual and rhetorical revolution have to say about the cultural and political worlds that surrounded the Soviet Union and the United States in these pivotal years?

This book is not about real children. It is about how Soviet and American politicians, propagandists, and protesters manufactured similar visions of idealized and threatened children from 1945 until 1968 for the purpose of building domestic and international consensus for the Cold War. It is about how rising contradictions in these images led to a crisis in the late 1960s on both sides of the Iron Curtain over who could best protect the young and whether the ideological crusade of the Cold War was worth the potential sacrifice of the next generation. It finds that the Soviet and American propagandists who produced these images had more in common with each other than they did with their audiences, and it suggests a revision of how we should understand the divides that defined the war itself.

THE COLD WAR was a conflict unlike any before it. Its geographic boundaries were expansive, incorporating Eastern Europe, Latin America, the Middle East, Africa, and Southeast Asia. It offered no battlefields where American and Soviet soldiers could line up against each other to determine a winner or loser. As such, it provided no foreseeable means of achieving victory. It was an indecisive and circumscribed conflict waged through "proxy wars" between communist and capitalist systems in the postcolonial world, through economic and cultural competition, and through each side's ability to win the "hearts and minds" of global audiences.[1] As a consequence, in the late 1940s, Soviet and American leaders began calling upon their respective populations to mobilize in new ways. No American men were sent off to fight the Russians in this war (although they were drafted to fight in Korea and Vietnam, conflicts that many believed were financed from Moscow). Similarly, no Russian soldiers were ordered to move against American infantry (although they did occupy Eastern Europe, the Caucasus, and Central Asia and support a failing communist regime in Afghanistan). No one on either home front was asked to darn socks or ration meat or leave their homes to work in armaments factories as had happened in World War I and World War II. Instead, preparedness in the Cold War entailed a willingness to fight to limited ends on distant battlefields. It meant accepting the argument that enemies were not only difficult to identify but could be anywhere, including the school and the home. It demanded that each citizen develop a new level of personal, daily vigilance against ideological weakness and enemy infiltration in order to protect himself or herself from predators. It meant preparing for a war against which there was no real defense. It also meant accepting the self-proclaimed legitimacy of the state and its policies as the primary means of ensuring the country's protection.

When the Soviet and American governments set out in the early 1950s to articulate their new programs for mobilization to their domestic and international audiences, they turned to the image of the child. There was nothing particularly new about the use of the child as a means to rally populations to war. Whether it was the 1917 U.S. resolution to join the British in the struggle against the Germans, the 1938 Nazi declaration of sovereignty over the Sudetenland, or the Soviet decision to march into Eastern Europe in 1945, government actions had invariably been portrayed by state propagandists and politicians as motivated by a desire to defend the innocent.[2] Hungry, dirty, and orphaned—no other image, except perhaps that of the raped woman, could generate the revulsion and rage required to compel a population to support its government's decision to go to battle in the face of certain horror. As the Cold War began in earnest in the late 1940s, the Soviet Union and the United States continued the same tactics; they used images of threatened children to argue for the mobilization of their domestic populations.

Yet, because of the unique nature of the conflict, state-produced images of wartime youth from these years look markedly different from earlier depictions of imperiled children. In previous conflicts, propagandists customarily portrayed youngsters as the victims of direct attack in the form of beatings, abandonment, killing, and rape. During the Cold War, Soviet and American politicians and propagandists argued instead that their countries' children, and the youth of the world, were being exposed to a new set of dangers that threatened both the child and national security. Leaders portrayed their children as imperiled not by bayonets and storm troopers but rather by ideological infiltration and weakness. This was a serious concern in a conflict that had no foreseeable end and that could very well last until the kids became adults.

Soviet and American politicians, propagandists, and members of the press also conjured new, idealized visions of children mobilized in the home and in the school to fight the Cold War. Whereas traditional depictions of mobilized kids in war had focused on their ability to provide rear support (and in the Soviet case, to fight as partisans), during the Cold War mobilization became a daily responsibility that every Soviet and American child was expected to embrace in his or her everyday life—not through military training, but through education and a commitment to maintaining domestic order. In the Soviet Union, the Pioneer organization portrayed the idealized Soviet child as patriotic, diligent, mobilized in the home and school, and loyal to Stalin and the Communist Party. On the other side of the Iron Curtain, state and private organizations devoted to the welfare of America's youth worked together to create an ideal of the American child. They depicted groups like the Boy Scouts of America in national rhetoric and propaganda as physically and emotionally prepared to defend the United States from the onslaught of aggressive communism and from the threat of nuclear annihilation. They presented America's youth as ideologically and physically capable of resisting communist attack, while appearing actively committed to social equality and the maintenance of domestic tranquility.

In order to defend and mobilize the young, leaders and child-rearing experts argued that children would have to be more carefully monitored and contained. This argument crossed national boundaries and justified the increased legal/professional surveillance of families and communities.[3] In both countries, educators and politicians published an extraordinary quantity of materials on the need for increased federal intervention in educating and raising the young. Lawmakers passed new regulations that more carefully monitored the child and the family and their daily activities. Russian and American sociologists, representatives, and psychiatrists discussed new ways to ensure that law-abiding parents not spoil their children and understand their obligations to raise patriotic youngsters. For both superpowers, the need to defend kids from these threats and mobilize youth for national defense opened the private lives of individuals and their families to increased regulation and surveillance.[4] More than ever before, the child became a tool for the construction of a Cold War consensus that defined and imposed normative behaviors upon domestic populations.

As the 1950s wound down, this ideal of the child transformed in response to the changing rhetoric and needs of the Cold War consensus. The "pursuit of peace" acquired increasing currency in the Cold War culture wars, and as a consequence, the Pioneers and the Boy Scouts, who had once stood as models of domestic order and containment, increasingly assumed another identity as emissaries for international activism and peace. The child, whose place had once been in the home, was now envisioned as an active participant in the international competition for cultural ascendancy. In the Soviet Union under Khrushchev, the ideal Cold War child increasingly discarded the rote learning of the Stalinist era in favor of the creativity and independent thinking that was needed to compete with the United States in the sciences and the arts. Meanwhile, both the Boy Scouts and the Pioneers became committed international advocates for world peace who appeared to be struggling on a daily basis to counter American imperialism or Soviet aggression, various forms of racism, and economic exploitation around the world.

These new images supported both sides' domestic and foreign policies. They bolstered the common belief in both societies that each of their countries had been historically, and remained, a target of outside aggression and invasion. As Tom Engelhardt and Vojtech Mastny have argued, the "circling of the wagons" (in the United States) or the "insatiable craving" for security (in the Soviet Union) had become primary ways of viewing America's and

Russia's defensive and relatively benign relationships with their enemies.[5] The image of the child-under-attack upheld the idea that America's and Russia's leaders were being forced to act, both at home and abroad, out of a compelling need to defend innocence from destruction and freedom from tyranny.

These images also symbolized the ability of these nations to survive. On the Soviet side, state depictions of Russian children engaging in economic and cultural competition with the West helped to portray the Soviet Union as a country that was catching up to the United States in science, material comfort, and culture. They provided visual proof that the Soviet Union was making great strides in recovering from Stalinism and the Great Patriotic War. They projected a vision of the communist model as a successful alternative to the exploitation of American capitalism, and they testified to the Soviet Union's commitment to "peaceful competition" with the West and "liberation" for the postcolonial world. Similarly, American depictions of their children as mobilized for national defense and peace against communist aggression allowed Kennedy, and later Johnson, to present their policies as inherently innocent, unmotivated by imperial designs, and committed to peace, while still keeping the country capable of facing an implacable Soviet foe. When Kennedy, Johnson, Khrushchev, and Brezhnev pursued interventionist policies, they brought the image of the child and the promise of peace along with them. The child served as a way of articulating each state's particular vision of its role in the Cold War and of its assumed identity as the sole force capable of providing a viable, peaceful, and morally upstanding path to political and economic stability.[6]

The image of the Cold War child serves as a map for understanding how the meanings of the conflict were constructed for these two societies during these years. Beginning in the late 1940s, Soviet and American leaders, propagandists, and publicists produced visions of protected, threatened, and mobilized children that were surprisingly similar in their figuration and use. They did this in an effort to influence how their constituencies and their allies would understand the threats that the war posed and the obligations it created. Despite the ideological differences that ostensibly separated the two sides, they used these images in comparable ways to rally their populations behind their domestic and international policies, to pursue popular consensus, and to ensure the preservation of public order. Ultimately, they created a constructed vision of Cold War childhood that was shared across the ideological divide. Regardless of whether one was a Soviet or an American citizen, for those who saw these images and heard these messages on a daily basis, childhood (its defense and its possible destruction) assumed indelible significance as a clear justification for each nation's involvement in the Cold War and a gauge of each side's moral worth and future viability.

In the end, however, those who supported the consensus were unable to control how the child's image was rendered or the meanings that it conveyed. Neither side could ignore or suppress the political and moral contradictions of the Cold War, which became apparent in these images as the decades wore on. American and Soviet citizens, who had been told by their leaders that their nation offered the better protection for the world's young, came into increasing contact with images of embattled African American and Vietnamese children, youth abandoned by a disillusioned society, and kids facing the specter of radiation poisoning and nuclear holocaust. Dissident movements on both sides deployed their own visions of threatened and mobilized youth in order to lay claim to the child's image and to challenge their governments' policies, the propaganda industry that undergirded them, and the Cold War consensus itself. In the Soviet Union, artists, writers, and filmmakers used the period of Khrushchev's Thaw to voice their concerns about the legacy of Stalin, the difficulties of mobilization, and the terror of atomic attack. They created new images of youth who appeared abandoned, traumatized, and demobilized due to the ongoing conflict with the West. Across the Atlantic, American antinuclear groups like the Committee for a Sane Nuclear Policy and Women Strike for Peace took to the streets with their children in tow to protest atomic testing, the arms race, and the escalating war in Southeast Asia. Both of these groups voiced their opinions by manipulating the meanings of the child's iconic image and by redefining the source of the Cold War threat as the state itself. Not only did they bring into question their nations' ability to protect the young, they also exposed the scaffolding of the Cold War consensus. They transformed enemies into victims and victorious memories into shameful episodes and established themselves, not the state, as protectors of the children. The idealized and simplified image of the Cold War child had sown the seeds of its own destruction.[7]

These evolving representations of the child in the Soviet Union and the United States played a vital role in ushering in the collapse of the Cold War consensus. For many, these increasingly contradictory images exposed the uncomfortable ambiguities of the war. They seemed to point to new enemies and new allies that were located in neither the East nor the West, but in the seats of power: the U.S. Capitol building, the Kremlin, and the police stations. Images of idealized, happy youth became symbols of a system that was, at best, out of touch with reality and, at worst, coercively intent on manufacturing consent.[8] Visions of napalmed and abandoned children did not simply reflect a loss of faith in each nation's vaunted mission in the world; in the process of their reproduction, they created that loss and they provided a vocabulary for articulating it.

Understanding how and why the Cold War consensus collapsed is a primary goal of this book. In recent years, historians have taken note of this collapse and have begun to track its causes and consequences. As Jeremi Suri has observed, by the 1960s, rising domestic instabilities in countries around the world forced leaders on both sides of the Iron Curtain to seek détente with each other so that they might focus on restoring order at home.[9] *Innocent Weapons* provides the visual and rhetorical foundation for this story. It offers a glimpse into the contradictory experiences of the Cold War that the Soviet and American populations shared in these years. It not only maps this transformation, but it also helps to explain how and why this containment and collapse happened.

By telling a transnational narrative of the Cold War, this book also seeks to shed new light on the traditional tropes that have historically defined the conflict. The days seem to be waning when this war can be viewed as a struggle between two diametrically opposed ideological systems. Over the last two decades, scholars have increasingly expanded their research into global archives and in the process have forced us to recognize the ways in which Soviet and American leaders sometimes colluded in the shared pursuit of power.[10] They have compelled us to question the role of ideology in determining policy and they have shown how the relationships that existed among the superpowers, Europe, and the postcolonial world shaped the Cold War in unexpected ways. When one reads the story of the Cold War through the lens of the child's image, the ideological differences that seemingly differentiated the Eastern Bloc from the Western Sphere are tempered by the revelation that Soviet and American leaders and propagandists were in fact engaging in similar visual and rhetorical projects in order to sell a war, preserve power, justify policy, and maintain domestic order. These deployments of innocent, threatened, and mobilized youth, which spanned the ideological and geographic boundaries of the conflict, reveal a story in which the producers of these images had more in common with *each other* than they did with their intended audiences. By viewing the Cold War as a dialectic between those who owned the means of image production and the intended consumers of those images, this book suggests that we must reexamine our previous understandings of the divides that defined the war itself. In a conflict that was fought so much on the cultural battlefield, the fact that the consensus-building projects of both sides were so visually and rhetorically similar to each other implies that although their ideologies in this conflict might have been different, the underlying means and goals of leaders, individual actors, and institutions to secure power and legitimacy were not.[11]

This observation could not have been made without the integration of the Soviet story into the cultural history of the Cold War, a project that is long overdue. Much scholarship has been devoted to examining how the Cold War was imagined and experienced by domestic populations in the United States. A number of historians have chronicled how the Cold War was understood by Americans in the 1950s and 60s as an "us or them" struggle, a drive to stop "alien conspirators and foreign invasion," and a call-to-arms to halt "Soviet expansionism."[12] Yet works that seek to compare the American experience with those outside its borders are still scarce. Moreover, while a number of excellent books have been written on Soviet Cold War foreign policy, there is only nascent scholarship on what the Cold War looked like and how it was experienced by normal citizens in the Soviet Union.[13] This has led some historians to infer that the Cold War was simply not a daily experience for the Soviet people. Cultural studies of the Cold War have presented the conflict as "a one-sided phenomenon," to which the Soviet population appears largely oblivious.[14] This was not the case. The story of the Cold War child reveals that Soviet leaders and propagandists did in fact work hard to create a vision of the conflict for both domestic and international consumption in order to construct a consensus for their policies. The threat of ideological infiltration was a constant part of official, daily rhetoric in Soviet Communist Party speeches and the press. These threats were matched by calls for mass mobilization that shaped the ways Soviet citizens led their lives and the world they understood around them.

At its core, *Innocent Weapons* is about the relationship between images and the functions they perform in society. As such, it is a book that borrows its methodology from poststructural semiotics and the study of how coded images can define, calcify, undermine, and traverse people's understandings of the world around them. Just as Roland Barthes studied the meanings of wine in France to expose how bourgeois societies assert their collective values upon each other, these chapters explore the image of the child as a cultural myth, or signification, tied not to a real object, not to children themselves, but to a set of constructed cultural beliefs that can be used to support and undermine the status quo.[15] Politicians, leaders, propagandists, and publicists all deployed the vision of the child in order to organize the world around them.[16] For example, when Soviet television broadcasters showed American children being uniformly jealous of Soviet youth in 1955, they were making a number of arguments concerning the relative affluence of Soviet society in relation to the United States, the lack of concern that American adults ostensibly felt toward their children, the success of the Marxist/Leninist system, and the ability of the Communist Party to provide the leadership and support that Russia's population needed.

Yet, as Barthes would agree, there was no monopoly on the production of images, which could also be used to subvert the consensus, even in the most "bourgeois" and "totalitarian" societies.[17] Frequently, images bore meanings that strayed far from their original intent or were used in ways that were intentionally subversive. Thus, when Soviet filmmaker Tengiz Abuladze created child protagonists on the big screen who had no adult supervision and were forced to survive on their own, he was speaking directly to the idealized, normative vision of the contented, prosperous, and mobilized Soviet child that was being created at the time by the Communist Party. In his films, Abuladze presented the state as a distant force that had abandoned the Soviet child while rendering parents incapable of caring for their young. These many images represented what the semiotician Yuri Lotman might call a "semiosphere" of childhood, made up of multiple voices, expressed in many languages, spanning international borders and ideological boundaries, at times reflecting the intersecting beliefs of large groups, at other times expressing the ideas of only a few or one, and often assuming new meanings through the process of production and reception.[18]

Of the possible images that could be used to map the collapse of the Cold War consensus, the image of the child demands attention. In the 1950s, Soviet and American populations defined themselves more than ever before by their children. Families on both sides of the Iron Curtain were having more kids than they had in the previous three decades. The fastest-growing genres in print were children's literature, followed closely by books and periodicals on parenting. Schools in both countries adopted around-the-clock schedules to accommodate the abundance of children, and almost all commodities, from hair tonic to cigarettes, were sold (at least in the United States) using the young. In 1950, *Parents' Magazine* heralded the "Decade of the Child," and nine years later, the United Nations passed the Declaration on the Rights of the Child. Fifty years ago, Philippe Ariès showed how the variegated meanings of childhood disclose the beliefs and fears of the society around it.[19] Perhaps more than ever before, representations of children functioned as mirrors for the populations that generated them.

Just as American and Soviet culture in the Cold War were shaped and mirrored by the contested vision of youth, so too did the Cold War alter the way that populations on both sides thought about childhood. In the post-war years, new technologies allowed for the mass reproduction of the child's image in television and print in the homes of most Soviet and American citizens. These images created a visual and rhetorical universe that was saturated by the child. The vast majority of these images were generated in order to sell something, whether it was a product or an idea. In the process, childhood became a commodity that was open for trade and also defined by the fact that it was produced for the purpose of being sold. Moreover, as the quantity of images increased, so too did their collective and relational complexity. An image of a happy, white, middle-class American youngster could take on new meanings when placed alongside that of an African American boy who had been lynched for whistling at a girl. A kid drinking a glass of milk or walking home alone from school could become a symbol of anxiety when placed in the context of nuclear pollution and atomic threat. When the dangers of ideological and physical Cold War attack were shown to exist not on a distant battlefield but in the home and the school, the most innocent visions of the child assumed new significance. As these images made their way into the daily visual lives of people on both sides of the Iron Curtain, childhood itself assumed these contradictory meanings. It no longer simply brought to mind visions of innocence and hope for the future. It also signified risk and eschatological end. In the words of Anne Higonnet, children became figures that even in innocence "stow away a dark side: a threat of loss, of change, and, ultimately, of death."[20]

Some clarifications on the terminology and structure used in this book are warranted. This project has intentionally avoided establishing a set age range for identifying and defining "the child." While most adults in the West would agree that people under the age of twelve or thirteen should be classified as children, it nonetheless must be remembered that such categorizations are not "natural" or even commonly shared across societies.[21] For instance, groups that some cultures would designate as "children" might be tried as "adults" in many Western and non-Western courts. Laws on statutory rape often argue that a person is a child until he or she turns eighteen. Those who were eighteen and older who fought in Vietnam in the late 1960s were often called "children" and "boys," despite the fact that we might otherwise see them as adults. The gaze of the West upon its colonies and its racial minorities has a long history of infantilizing entire populations, regardless of their age.[22] In short, what defines age limits for "the child" is not only sociopolitically defined and unstable but also speaks to how a society conceptualizes childhood in general and its own position in the world. Incorporating those groups who were designated as "children" is an important goal of this book, as it offers a category of analysis for understanding the society that gave it that designation. The labeling of a figure as "child" (regardless of whether he or she is three, eighteen, or fifty years old) should be enough to open the doors for analysis.

The term "image" also carries varied meanings in this book. Research for this project has included the exploration of government speeches, presidential memos, films, radio broadcasts, domestic and international publications, reports on audience reception, billboards, protest manifestos, screenplays, poems, KGB records, and news programs spanning fourteen archives, three countries, and four languages. All of these materials are rich media containing both visual and textual depictions of youth that create "images" of childhood. As such, the term "image" does not simply describe a physical likeness or representation of the child in visual form. It relies upon the secondary definition of the word to denote a mental representation, an idea, or a concept that can be conveyed through text, speech, symbol, as well as visual capturing and rendering. Just as René Magritte and Michel Foucault argued that the picture of a pipe and the word "pipe" can both create an image of a pipe (but are not a pipe), so too does this book explore the photos, illustrations, and texts that describe and create images of childhood.[23]

Understanding the meanings of these images cannot be accomplished without also understanding who was creating them. This is not an easy task. The attempted constructions of cultural belief that gave meaning to the image of the child and to the Cold War consensus were produced by a broad and amorphous group of people who existed within this discursive universe. Sometimes they shaped these meanings. Just as commonly, they were shaped by them. Often they were people in positions of power who were capable of attracting the public's eye. Given the different levels of censorship under which these two societies functioned, there were marked differences in who was able to create and disseminate these images in the Soviet Union and in the United States. In the Stalinist period, the Communist Party assumed the role of image-shaper and consensus-builder with little contribution from outside the state apparatus. This remained the case even during the most liberal periods of Khrushchev's Thaw, although, as this book shows, there were opportunities for the manipulation of these images, especially in film and literature. In contrast, the construction of the Cold War child in the United States came from a far more diverse cohort: the government, the media, advertisers, and private groups that actively constructed these images either to support or undermine the status quo.[24] It is the clear intention of this book to show that despite the diversity of groups that produced these images in the United States, they nonetheless generated a set of childhood images that not only resembled those being created in the Soviet Union but also performed (or at least endeavored to perform) the same functions.

In addition, *Innocent Weapons* is concerned with how governments, organizations, and individuals used these images in an attempt to create or undermine a "consensus." In this context, the term "consensus" connotes the widespread efforts that particular people made to instill common beliefs about how to understand and wage the Cold War among viewers, listeners, and readers. As Wendy Wall has noted, this consensus was far more of a facade or an idea than it was a reality.[25] I agree; if there ever was a period of "deep and well-grounded national unity" on either side of the Iron Curtain in the early 1950s, it was very soon subject to increasing revision and sublimation. Even though the consensus was a veneer, it was nonetheless a massive political project undertaken by countless people over multiple generations on both sides of the Iron Curtain. This book is interested in what that veneer looked like and how the image of the child was used to build it and then transgress it. It seeks to show how leaders on both sides of the Iron Curtain thought this image would build a consensus—a consensus that would in turn offer moral legitimacy and certainty in a conflict whose ethical divides were actually terrifyingly murky. It uses the word "consensus" to point specifically to the ideals and beliefs that Soviet and American leaders, propagandists, members of the media, and their supporters seemed desperate to instill in their populations during the first two decades of the Cold War. These ideals included a commitment to the preservation of order, loyalty to the nation and the government that led it, ideological vigilance, a belief in the nation's economic path, and a willingness to subordinate individual needs to the preservation of the status quo.

Organizationally, this book is divided into two parts that by necessity take different approaches to telling the story of the Cold War child. Part One addresses the efforts made by leaders, politicians, propagandists, and advertisers in the Soviet Union and the United States to build a Cold War consensus on the shoulders of childhood. It paints a transnational tableau of youth from 1945 to the mid-1960s. The ideal of the happy and contained Cold War kid that emerged in the Soviet Union and the United States carried the weight of its nation's future. Politicians and propagandists in the early years of the Cold War used images of contented and ordered children to codify the relationship between the state and its citizenry, to legitimize policies of containment, and to establish a basic conceptualization for what was at stake in the conflict and what needed to be done to win it. The book then examines the construction of the counter-ideal of the "Other" child, the child living on the other side of the Iron Curtain who provided a sufficiently harrowing vision of the enemy to justify and legitimize the preservation of the status quo at home. It then looks at the fear of ideological infiltration that pervaded discourse on the child in these years and examines closely how that threat was tied to perceived domestic weaknesses like hooliganism, bad parenting, and the transgression of gender norms on both sides of the Iron Curtain. It finally shows how the child's representation fluctuated with the changing demands of the consensus as the 1960s wore on and the struggle over who could be more peaceful took root.

The purpose of Part Two is to reveal how individual actors in the Soviet Union and the United States deployed the vision of the Cold War child to challenge the normative image of youth and the consensus that it ostensibly bolstered. Because these were specific individuals and groups working outside of the state apparatus, they require a different kind of storytelling. In particular, they demand a deeper, more pinpointed examination of the moments where the child's figuration was most volatile and contentious. This alters the perspective of the book (and the reader) from looking at a broad swath of Soviet and American Cold War consensus building efforts, to examining the intimate details of those actors who chose to use the child to undermine that consensus. For the Soviet example, Part Two explores how filmmakers constructed contested images of the child in the period known as the Thaw, which lasted from 1956 until approximately 1964 and represented a period of limited freedom of expression. Moving back across the Atlantic, the book then shifts its gaze to the far more open (although arguably no more subversive) revision of the child's image that antinuclear movements like Women Strike for Peace and the Committee for a Sane Nuclear Policy undertook in these same years. Finally, the book looks at the most volatile place where Soviet and American consensus-building efforts came into direct contact with each other: Vietnam. It reveals how neither the Soviet Union nor the United States could control the figuration of the child's image as they struggled for legitimacy in Southeast Asia.

By the end of the 1960s, the image of the child had undergone a transformation. On the one hand, it remained a symbol of innocence and victimization, at times demanding the protection of the state and at other times seemingly indicting it for its failure to provide security. On the other hand, it became a vision for a new level of mobilization, as either an advocate for the state or a crusader against it. This change in the child's figuration was caused by the Cold War and the unique demands that it placed upon the next generation. Examining how the image of the child changed in these years—and how the Cold War was conceptualized for various audiences in terms of the young—gives us a far more nuanced understanding of both the image and the event. It gives us a clearer view of how visual and rhetorical images like that of the child served as cultural capital for creating conceptual boundaries in the Cold War. It illustrates the connections that persist between the expression of policy and the use of symbols that carry cultural weight. And it provides a new way of seeing this conflict—not only as a struggle for power but also as a compelling and messy battle for visual and rhetorical preeminence.

I

BUILDING AN IMAGE,
BUILDING A CONSENSUS

CHAPTER ONE

The Contained Child
on the Cusp of a New Era

On 7 April 1949, Svetlana Zhiltsova, the Pioneer delegate to the Eleventh Congress of the Komsomol, waited nervously to take the stage before a packed auditorium of Communist Party leaders. The topic of her speech was the future of the Pioneer organization, which, under the umbrella of the All-Union Leninist Communist Union of Youth (Komsomol for short), was responsible for carrying out Communist Party policies among the population's children and young adolescents. Giving a speech before such an illustrious audience would have been stressful in any year, but this one was especially nerve-racking given that the Komsomol had not held a Congress since 1936 and that little Sveta was only ten years old.

In the previous thirteen years, the country had undergone a massive transformation. It had experienced the trials and horrors of Stalin's purges, which had overturned Soviet society in the pursuit of domestic saboteurs and kulaks, had turned neighbors into suspects, and had left upward of a million people dead. This had been followed by Germany's invasion of Russia in the summer of 1941 and four unimaginably brutal years of death, violence, loss, and starvation. In the years after the war, Stalin and the Communist Party marshaled the population again to rally behind the socialist project and the figure of the *vozhd'*, the great leader. When Svetlana, with her braids tied in bows and her Pioneer tie carefully knotted, took the stage to talk about the country's future and the next generation's ability to defend it, much was at stake. After shuffling her papers and clearing her throat, she declared in a high, well-trained voice that "Soviet children are the happiest children in the world. Today, here, in the Kremlin, we give warm thanks for our happy childhood, for the real and ever-more beautiful future that the Bolshevik Party has offered us, and for our dear and loving Joseph Visarionovich Stalin."[1] This was the period of High Stalinism, when the performance of fealty to Stalin was a prerequisite of citizenship and when the vision of Sveta's happy Soviet childhood not only reinforced Stalin's legitimacy but also provided a Cold

War alternative to the vagaries of the exploitative West. Thunderous applause followed.

That same year, in the United States, a new family show on television, *Mama*, became CBS Network's most popular Friday evening program.[2] It followed the life of a Norwegian immigrant family living in San Francisco at the turn of the century. Although she was not the star of the show, the young actress Robin Morgan, who played the role of the smallest sister, Dagmar, quickly became the viewers' favorite. Week after week, the young Dagmar showed herself to be tough, resourceful, smart, funny, sometimes impetuous, capable of making tough moral decisions even if it meant getting in trouble, and a vital bridge between her Norwegian immigrant parents and her own American culture. Replete with open product promotion for its sponsor, Maxwell House, the show represented the growing wealth and stolid patriotism that ostensibly defined and guided the nation as a whole. It articulated the domestic containment that was America's first line of defense against communist attack, and it reflected the nation's equally strong preoccupation with its children.

The U.S. State Department seconded these sentiments. At the Midcentury White House Conference on Children and Youth, held in Washington, D.C., on 5 December 1950, President Harry Truman stood before American parents and promised them that if they supported his foreign and domestic policies, their children would "live in the most peaceful times the world has ever seen." It had not been an easy year for Truman. In the preceding months, he had approved NSC-68, which called for a tripling of the American defense budget and the expansion of the policy of containment to stop perceived Soviet aggression. He had overseen American intervention in Korea, which by December was nearing a stalemate, and he had struggled to mediate the rising popularity of Joseph McCarthy and his accusations of Soviet infiltration into the highest organs of government. And yet when Truman stood before the delegates at the Conference on Children and Youth, he assured them that with a "good home" and "a better understand[ing of] our democratic institutions," their children would be safe and happy in the years to come.[3]

The voices of Zhiltsova, Morgan, and even Truman were but minor contributors in the chorus of the child that arose in the years following World War II. U.S. representatives from across the political spectrum, Soviet officials, academics, entrepreneurs, artists, writers, and parents, joined in the public refrain arguing that the next generation was poised to enjoy a higher quality of life than any previously known. The Soviet Union pointed to its sacrifice in World War II as proof of its ability to rear the next generation.

Meanwhile, the United States argued that the same war that had demolished Europe had transformed America into a superpower of unprecedented strength and wealth, establishing it as the sole power capable of providing for the children of the world.[4] These images of happy Soviet and American children stood as symbols for a much larger set of cultural and political messages about what defined each country and its mission in the world. They ostensibly bequeathed to the viewer a knowledge of all that was being referenced by them, as if by protecting the part (the child), one was protecting the whole (the nation). They provided a handy way of understanding the gifts that each system had to offer its population and the world. In short, the image of the ideal, contained, Cold War child carried the weight of its nation's future on its shoulders. It was a hagiographic rendering of all that was good and decent and hopeful about its country, and it stood as the only promise of victory in a war that showed no sign of ending.

The Happy, Afforded Child on the Front Lines of the Cold War

The image of the Cold War child can be traced to previously established cultural tropes in the United States and the Soviet Union. In the century and a half before these antagonists turned to youth to promote their policies, they, like most in the Western world, experienced a transformation in their understandings of the relationship between childhood and national identity. The innocence of youth became an ideal that not only defined the nation but also required the marshaling of the state for its preservation. From Tolstoy and Wordsworth to Lenin and Roosevelt, the image of the innocent child came to signify the moral legitimacy of its society. "The prototype of the Soviet Utopia was childhood" and the "success of America's republican experiment" was defined by the young.[5] The child became an icon for the transformative capacity of its country and an emblem of a modern future. It necessitated the increased intervention of the state into the lives of its constituents, and it created common cause for those who sought social change and revolution. By the time the Cold War began, the relationship between the child and the state had become entrenched in the sociopolitical fabric of both superpowers.

Given this, it comes as no surprise that the image of the happy child played a central role in articulating the terms of the early Cold War. In 1947, when Harry Truman declared his intention to assist the Greeks in their struggle against the "terrorist activities" of communists, he did so in part by arguing that 85 percent of Greece's children were tubercular and in need of salvation. When the Marshall Plan poured billions of dollars of aid into European homes and businesses, the U.S. State Department used exhibits filled with happy children to promote the value of the project. In 1948 and 1949, West Berlin children, left hungry and cold, quickly became the most prominent symbols of Soviet tyranny. And when Jan Papanek, the Czech delegate to the United Nations, reported in 1948 on the events surrounding the Soviet-led communist coup in Czechoslovakia, he emphasized the forced and contrived exuberance that had been demanded of the country's children even as it lost its popular leaders. At the same time in the Soviet Union, the image of the happy child quickly became the most prominent symbol of its country's swift recovery from World War II. When the Korean War began in 1950, Soviet condemnation of the United Nations focused on the fate of Korean children left slaughtered while its populace struggled for unification. Five years later, when Nikolai Bulganin announced the creation of the Warsaw Pact to a rapt outdoor audience in Warsaw, Soviet television cameras jumped back and forth from Bulganin, to happy, clapping children, to Marshal Ivan Konev (the new commander of the Warsaw Pact forces), and back to the children now chanting his name.

For the Soviet Union, the most important role played by the image of the happy child was as the recipient of Stalin's benevolent care. When thousands of people across the Soviet Union and the communist world gathered to celebrate Stalin's seventieth birthday on 18 December 1949, many of them articulated their gratitude and patriotism through the vision of the joyous child. Farm and factory workers pledged to double, triple, and quadruple their production levels in order to ensure the future of the nation's children. Vyacheslav Molotov hailed Stalin as "teacher, leader, and favorite friend" to the children of the world. The newspaper of the Young Pioneer Organization, *Pionerskaia pravda*, heralded Stalin as the "first defender of youth and world peace."[6] Meanwhile, the Academy of Sciences declared that "Stalin's statements," in regard to "the case of capitalist encirclement, [had given] to the Bolshevik party, to the working class, to the next generation, and to all toilers of the Soviet country a great perspective and clarity of goals."[7] Emphasizing all of this, children standing in long lines around the central podium delivered flowers to Stalin and Molotov while *Komsomol'skaia pravda* reported that 2,000 Pioneers aged nine to fifteen had organized a ball with the theme "Thank you, Comrade Stalin, for our happy childhood."[8]

Stalin's birthday celebration provides a window into how the party leadership, the press, and sizable portions of the population used childhood to engage in the Cold War. Throughout the second half of 1948 and the first half 1949, images of young German children going hungry as a consequence of the Berlin blockade had splashed across the world press. The American pilot Gail Halvorsen had become a household name as the "candy bomber" or "Rosininbomber" who dropped sweets and bubblegum tied to little parachutes to the trapped German children. Six months after the blockade was over, the Soviet leadership moved decisively to reassert Stalin's position not as the captor of children but as their savior. Amid sweeping declarations of fealty to the leader, party delegates depicted the Cold War as a conflict that demanded Stalin's leadership as a way to protect the young from the ravages of the West. In the wake of Stalin's victory against the Nazis in what was being promoted as a quick recovery from the ravages of the Great Patriotic War, Stalin seemed to have proven himself as capable of leading the country against American aggression. At the birthday celebration, a young Nikita Khrushchev announced that "the great Stalin," while educating his cadres and protecting the next generation, "has taught us a sharp intransigence toward the slightest appearance of alien bourgeois ideology."[9] These depictions hinged on the idea that by protecting the happy childhood of the Soviet utopia, the entire nation could be defended. They codified the relationship between Stalin and Russia's citizenry, established one of the crucial cultural battlefields on which the Cold War would be fought, and revealed what was expected of the population to fight this war in the years to come. For everyone in the Soviet Union, the state and its supporters argued, uncritical loyalty to the leader would provide the key to future happiness and national security.

The connection between Stalin and the ideal of Soviet childhood was of Cold War importance in the late 1940s and early 1950s. In art, literature, and the press and in numerous speeches, the image of the child linked the indebtedness of the population to Stalin to the happiness that he could provide them. Without indebtedness there could be no happiness. Children provided the perfect vehicle for articulating the two sides of this equation, appearing both grateful and happy as living symbols for the Soviet Union's reassuring future. In paintings like Boris Vladimirsky's 1949 *Rozy dlia Stalina* (Roses for Stalin) and Nina Vatolina's 1950 poster *Spasibo rodnomu Stalinu za schastlivoe detstvo* (Thank you, dear Stalin, for our happy childhood), renditions of Stalin standing among happy children created what Rachel Rosenthal has called "a comforting intimacy between the leader and his proletarian body politic."[10] The image of the joyous, admiring child mirrored Stalin's ascendancy to power, it manifested the creation of a "symbolic order" that placed Stalin in a ritualized, beatified space, and it testified to the consummate happiness of the larger national family that was supposed to be flourishing and peaceful as a result of the country's turn toward Marxism-Leninism-Stalinism. As Catriona Kelly has noted, the period from the mid-1930s to Stalin's death in 1953 marked "the real heyday of 'happy childhood.'"[11] Within the context of the Cold War, these ubiquitous images of happy and well-cared-for children offered a vision of a mythical Soviet family and future, with Stalin as the father of each child working to defend his kids from American attack. This familial mythos presented an ideal of "domestic containment" that demanded the compliance of the populace and that, in the words of Elaine Tyler May, "was bolstered by a powerful political culture that rewarded its adherents and marginalized its detractors."[12] As Georgi Malenkov put it in a 1950 lecture to the Department of Propaganda and Agitation, "The continued happiness of our children in the face of resurgent war depends on our shared struggle for peace and support for Stalin."[13]

Across the Atlantic, the ubiquitous image of the happy American child also assumed Cold War significance. Joyful American kids were everywhere in the 1950s. Between 1946 and 1964 75 million American children were born (in contrast to 50 million between 1920 and 1945). Young, white, male GIs came home from war to find a booming economy coupled with incentives to get married, buy a house in a suburb, and have children. The major television networks dropped their old dramas and began airing programs for kids like *The Lone Ranger*, *Disneyland*, *Mama*, *Sky King*, *Lassie*, *Howdy Doody*, and *Kukla, Fran and Ollie*. All of these programs featured children who faced reasonable challenges that could be solved with the help of their communities and their nation. *Life* magazine, which carried an average of fourteen images of children in each of its issues from 1949 until 1963, offered regular feature articles on American children that reported predominantly on the happiness and carefree innocence of the young.[14] Feature stories offered snapshots of the happy lives being led by children in places like "Rocket City," California, where youngsters could play while their fathers carried on weapons research. "The bomb leaves rocket-like clouds of dust," one such caption from 1948 read, showing boys joyously dragging an old practice bomb along an automobile rut.[15] Such visions testified to the harmless joy of children under the protective umbrella of a powerful nation. While a far more diverse group of television producers, publishers, advertisers, and politicians manufactured these visions in the 1950s, the image of the child that they produced nonetheless bore striking resemblances to those being constructed on the other side of the Iron Curtain. The absence of the Stalin figure in American culture did not preclude the widespread figuration of the child as a loyal and happy citizen enjoying the benefits of "The American Way."

СПАСИБО
РОДНОМУ СТАЛИНУ
ЗА СЧАСТЛИВОЕ ДЕТСТВО!

Figure 1.1 Nina Vatolina, "Spasibo rodnomu Stalinu za schastlivoe detstvo!" (Thank You, Comrade Stalin, for Our Happy Childhood!), 1950. © Fine Art Images.

As in the Soviet Union, the American child became an important tool in the "manufacturing of consent" for the Cold War.[16] American leaders and the press made the argument that popular domestic mobilization was required in order to maintain the defense of the family and the nation against communism. Like in Stalin's Russia, where the cult of personality required an embracing of the mythos of the Stalinist family and the preservation of domestic order, Eisenhower's policies necessitated domestic compliance and the maintenance of the status quo at home. Eisenhower accomplished his move from the "limited commitments of Taft Republicanism into the virtually unlimited commitments of Reagan Republicanism" by creating a "consensus at home that has been unsurpassed by any other President after 1945."[17] His legacy of opposing revolutions wherever they might occur (whether in Iran or Guatemala, and regardless of their democratic underpinnings) required the cultivation of a public consensus that would accept covert military actions and would support poorly articulated "advising" programs like Vietnamization.[18] Eisenhower's Cold War policies demanded the development of a consensus-building project that would accept this new, circumscribed, and often morally ambiguous conflict as a part of the traditional mythos of the American fight for truth and justice in the world. As Eisenhower stated in his inaugural "Chance for Peace" speech in 1953, the world's expenditure on weapons represented not "the spending of money alone," but "the hopes of its children." The tying of youth to the fate of the nation was not new, although arguably it had never been used in such abundance and with such profligate abandon until the 1950s.

In the selling of the Cold War consensus, whether in the East or the West, a happy childhood was contingent upon an afforded childhood. No country or its government could be seen as legitimate in the twentieth century if it could not show that it took care of the wants of its children. The connection between the state and the material welfare of the child had begun in earnest at the turn of the century with the rise of child-saving programs intent on limiting child labor and the exploitation of the young. To leading figures as seemingly disparate as Theodore Roosevelt and Anton Makarenko, such experiments represented a "manufactory of citizens" that would provide the foundation for a revolutionary future and would bolster the country's reputation in the eyes of the world.[19] In the 1920s in the Soviet Union and in the 1930s in the United States, the role of government in providing for the young was codified in law. By the 1950s, populations on both sides of the Iron Curtain widely believed that the legitimacy of the state was connected to its ability to provide material comfort for the next generation.

This relationship assumed heightened significance when the Cold War began. It became a means for establishing the preeminence of capitalism or communism and a way to create popular compliance. For many, the Cold War was a struggle between two diametrically opposed systems that were defined largely by differing approaches to political economy.[20] As the Soviet historian Julie Hessler has argued, "The success of an economic system was to be judged not on the basis of its coal and steel output but on its ability to provide consumers with an ever increasing complement of goods."[21] A victory in the Cold War would mark triumph for an entire economic system. Likewise, the success of capitalism or communism would theoretically mark conquest in the Cold War. Moreover, if the population on one side or the other could be convinced that only its system was able to ensure the material well-being of its kids, then the afforded child would go a long way toward creating consensus for a myriad of policies that might otherwise seem unpalatable.

Toward these ends, Soviet and American leaders frequently and explicitly connected the happiness of the afforded child to the economic system that supported it. In the Soviet Union, abundance was not a luxury enjoyed by many. In the late 1940s, the Stalinist state offered material wealth only to those adults who had shown their commitments to the Soviet project, like the Stakhanovites who surpassed their production targets through herculean efforts or the pilots who broke flight records. While the rest of the populace was expected to live lean, the one group that was not excluded from abundance was the child, who, according to Soviet rhetoric, could be denied nothing. In the words of Catriona Kelly, the preservation of the young "was a legitimating sacred value" that offered security for the next generation in return for compliance from the rest of the population.[22] Pioneer meetings and literature promoted the happy abundance of children at summer camps with the promise of three good meals, clean sheets, and wholesome fun. Domestic tourism offered "beautiful beaches and luxurious resorts," frequently showing pictures of children enjoying the abundance of the centralized economy in brochures and pamphlets.[23] The embracing of material gain under Stalin did not represent a "great retreat" from the original intentions of the Revolution, as Nicholas Timasheff argued years ago. Instead, the promise of abundance legitimized the planned economy, the state ownership of the means of production, and the role of the vanguard in leading economic development.[24] In the context of the Cold War, production capacity became a manifestation of a successful revolution.[25] This was reflected in the fact that most Soviet advertisements in the Stalinist period were not interested in selling products so much as they were intent on selling the capacity of the state to acquire and produce those goods for the young. Indeed, given that so much of the promise of abundance was just that—a promise and not a reality—the state's ability to provide for the young was crucial in the continued preservation of the Revolution and the Soviet project.

The importance of material well-being as an emblem of Soviet success became even more pronounced in the Khrushchev era, as the population increasingly demanded access to more goods. Families began moving into private flats, and their growing comfort became a sign of national growth and social solidarity for a system that was finally following through on its promises. In interviews, mothers and children spoke glowingly of the toys and the new washers and dryers now housed in their individual flats—all provided courtesy of the state.[26] Steadily, as each broadcast and publication attested, standards of living were improving. Not only were material goods available, the press argued, but produce, bread, meat, and butter were also provided at heavily subsidized prices.[27] All of this was enshrined in the Third Party Program that was adopted at the Twenty-second Party Congress, where

it was declared that the Soviet Union would now set itself upon the "historically important task of achieving in the Soviet Union a living standard higher
than that of any of the capitalist countries."[28] Individual pay would rise, as
would the production of consumer goods, in addition to education, medical
treatment, pensions, child care, and the free use of public amenities.

Soviet leaders worked to show families that they were just as capable of
acquiring and consuming a wide variety of goods as their counterparts in the
United States. In order to encourage consumption and to get out the message of state care for the populace, Soviet publishers and advertisers used the
image of the child. As Helena Goscilo has observed, "Children comprised
a high percentage" of people in advertisements in the 1950s.[29] Throughout
these years, kids appeared in women's magazines and in daily newspapers
smiling over ice cream, jars of fruit, and a whole variety of clothes and domestic items. The image of the child-made-happy by the acquisition of goods
became a symbol of personal consumer accumulation that reflected the gifts
of the state and the legitimacy of communism. One telling article published
in *Izvestiia* in 1959 showed a mother and daughter making pel'meni in a modern kitchen with white cabinets and a marble countertop. "Our kitchens," the
caption read, "are just as good as America's."[30] Such advertisements, which
explicitly targeted women and their concerns over the material well-being
of their families, connected production to the actual aggregation of goods by
the individual family and then placed that aggregation in the larger context
of Soviet material parity in the Cold War. Such consumption helped to resus-
citate the concrete promises of Marxism-Leninism and to establish the Soviet
Union "as a modernizing power committed to democratism."[31] Through the
child, the Soviet leadership made the argument that their citizens, by virtue of
the society that cared for them, did not have to be impoverished like the West
and could look forward to an increasingly abundant future. These advertisements not only helped to push the sale (or at least the promised sale) of con-
sumables, but they also attempted to produce a sense of material well-being
that would establish compliance with the state and counter rising concerns
over the emergence of a "consumer gap" between the East and the West.

Soviet leaders and advertisers from the 1930s on promoted a particular
vision of affluence that was contingent upon a specific kind of acquisition.
Goods were not to be acquired for the sake of simple accumulation or sentimentality but instead for *kulturnost*, which implied the careful accumulation of goods as a part of cultured living. In the context of the Cold War,
when the availability of material goods increasingly served as a barometer
for each side's success, it was *kulturnost* that separated and elevated Soviet

consumption from its more "conspicuous" American corollary. In the post-Stalinist period, *kulturnost* entailed a rejection of the population's historical indebtedness to Stalin in exchange for a new embracing of tasteful acquisition that would still make consumption somehow less conspicuous and more mindful. Just as the state began to follow the American practices of tracking consumer data and ordering goods according to their popularity (so that supply could meet demand), they also argued for a revised mind-set toward consumption that would promote a more refined and discriminating appraisal of goods. As the graphic artist Nikolai Zhukov declared in the pages of *Novyi mir*, this reforming of popular taste would be an important part of the formation of Soviet society and would be vital in helping those in the communist world to "establish their own style of material culture."[32] Again, the child became the means for teaching such a lesson. One radio broadcast exclaimed triumphantly in 1959 that modern, "well-lit" apartments were being built at a breakneck pace, "planned with an eye for spaciousness; with a desk set up in the living room for little Katia."[33] This purchasing and careful use of modern goods was new and beneficial, especially for the young, but it was not unmanaged or conspicuous. Not only did this approach seemingly differentiate it from the United States, but it also provided an alternative path to material comfort and a way in which Soviet citizens could show their willingness to participate in the Cold War. Children became the tool through which this message was sold and the purpose for which it was fought. Their ability to secure material comfort because of the system that supported them served as another brick in the building of the consensus.

Ties among childhood, consumption, and the manufacturing of consent also manifested in the United States in these years. Beginning in the late 1940s, American leaders argued that the unprecedented wealth generated by World War II offered the best future to the young. As Oscar R. Ewing, the Federal Security Agency administrator, reported to President Truman in October 1950, it had been "a year of hard-earned progress in most of the things that make life worth living,"[34] Kids, who, like their parents, had been forced to economize in the days of war and rationing, could now be seen enjoying new toys and entertainment with increasing amounts of money at their disposal.[35] Thanks to national subsidies and the GI Bill, a number of U.S. representatives and members of the press declared that the next generation was poised to enjoy a higher quality of life than any previously known. "Culture, cars, and kids—they are the symbols of the new American society," the foreign correspondent William Attwood wrote in *Look* magazine in 1955.[36] Like in the Soviet Union, the afforded child implied success for an entire nation.

Not only did the United States seem to have the wealth to offer its young (by virtue of the gifts of capitalism), but it also appeared to understand its moral obligation (thanks to its ideological fortitude) to meet the needs of the family and the next generation. As Tom Hayden, the future author of the Port Huron Statement, would write of his childhood in the 1950s, "For Americans who had come through the embattled thirties and forties, it was a time of respite, when one could finally sit back and enjoy the good things in life, and raise one's children well."[37] This was a simplified vision of American abundance that for many bore no resemblance to reality. But it was an ideal that appeared with such frequency that it became the norm.

In contrast to the Soviet Union, where the state was responsible for promoting consumption, a far larger and more diffuse group of politicians, businesspeople, and advertisers placed themselves at the front lines of the Cold War consumer battle. They mobilized the image of the child in ways and quantities that no society had seen before. Advertisers in the West had been using children to sell their wares since the nineteenth century, but it was not until the postwar economic boom and the baby boom that followed that children became icons of modern consumerism.[38] Children's increasing centrality in the lives of American families meant that the percentage of advertisements depicting them increased.[39] Advertisers used images of kids in an average 11 percent of all advertisements in *Look* and *Life* magazines between 1950 and 1964.[40]

In order to sell their products, advertisers periodically made the argument that the purchasing of their goods would protect the young and help in the struggle against communism. Sometimes they made this argument explicitly, as when the Douglas Aircraft Company printed a photograph of a young German girl holding up a glass of milk that had been delivered to her by American pilots during the Berlin airlift in 1949. "Flying Douglas Aircraft almost exclusively, Yankee crews have poured over half a million tons of supplies into Berlin since last June." Cups of milk appeared to be falling from a sky littered with planes. Similarly, thirteen years later, the Advertising Council and the Magazine Publishers of America launched a campaign to sell U.S. savings bonds using images of innocent children placed against visions of Soviet oppression and censorship. Major magazines ran each advertisement for a month in the spring and summer of 1962. The ads carried headlines like "What's Nice to Have, Hard to Save, and Essential to Your Future? (Besides Money)." Showing a picture of an American girl in the arms of her father next to the famous photograph of Khrushchev banging his hand on the podium at the United Nations, the caption read, "You couldn't purchase freedom for her at any price. But you can help Uncle Sam protect it by putting your dollars into Savings Bonds."[41] Another headline from March 1962 read, "How to Protect Your Children's Future . . . as You Save for Your Own," showing a picture of two youngsters playing next to a photograph of an angry Khrushchev. The caption read, "Will they have freedom in their future? Wishing won't help but buying Savings Bonds will."[42] Savings bonds became modern-day indulgences through which American families could save the eternal souls of their children. The freedoms of the "American Way" became a kind of "life-style branding" that attracted consumers not to the product but to the life that the product seemed to enable.[43]

Even more than in the Soviet Union, these advertisements sought to create a fear that could be alleviated only by the purchasing of the products. For instance, in 1951, the Bowman Trading Card Company printed a series called "The Children's Crusade against Communism," producing the forty-eight-card set in the months following Kim Il-sung's invasion of South Korea. Each packet offered a piece of bubble gum along with a card that bore a vision of life under communist rule. In effect, each card featured a different fear; pictures of ghost cities left in rubble from Soviet nuclear attack, illustrations of all the leaders of the communist nations, images of families standing amid the debris of their shattered homes, and children watching as their parents were arrested for listening to Voice of America. Card thirty-five showed a terrified family standing under the shadow of a policeman, with a description on the other side of the life one could expect in a communist country. The card, which was available for purchase at local dime stores for pennies, declared that the daily routine of the communist family "insists on absolute obedience to their leaders and following communist doctrine." Harking back to the first Children's Crusade of the thirteenth century, these cards provided not only a visual portrayal of the enemy but also a way to mobilize for a war whose front lines were not easy to find. Children could not march to Russia as they ostensibly had marched to the Holy Land 800 years earlier. For them, the best path of the crusade lay in the embracing of fear itself, a willingness to purchase a product, and a subsequent disposition to support whatever measures American leaders needed to take to defend liberty. As with the U.S. savings bonds, and as with the purchasing of tasteful furniture in the Soviet Union, Bowman turned buying bubble gum cards into an act of citizenship and mobilization.

While these examples were explicit, a far larger group of advertisers in the United States used the child to sell their products in ways that tapped into the desires of the American public to ensure the security of their young.

These ads pushed a wide variety of products, and they inevitably promoted the message that safety for the next generation could be purchased. Johnson and Johnson produced images of children fixing each other's wounds with the slogan, "Mommy always says you're safe when you use Johnson and Johnson."[44] Similarly, the Prudential Company ran a series of advertisements in *Life* magazine in 1949 using the slogan "The future belongs to those who prepare for it." This slogan, which would become a catchphrase for individuals as diverse as automobile tycoon Jim Moran and Malcolm X, started as a pitch to sell Cold War financial security to the American public. Each ad featured a new scenario that would seem familiar to the average, white, middle-class American family: two parents tucking their kids into bed, a sister and brother tugging on a wishbone after dinner, a young couple coming home with a new baby, a father and son building a fire. "You want the best for your children," one ad began, "that they will have friends, happiness, and above all, a fine, secure future." Security was the key—a security that on the surface could be found through the accumulation of money but that was clearly contingent upon an entire sociopolitical system to make it happen. As George Lipsitz, Ellen Seiter, and others have observed, consumption in the 1950s, particularly when it was tied to childhood, connected the priorities of the Cold War to those of capitalism. It tied the freedom of spending to the freedom provided by democracy, offering emancipation to women by "liberating" them from their kitchens and authority to fathers by giving them the ability to be providers "in an increasingly administered and institutional society."[45] It held up the possibility of classlessness through equal access to goods, as when the magazine *House Beautiful* claimed in 1953 that the one-level homes being built resembled the leveling of America's class structure.[46] It furnished a solution through spending for how to be a good parent, a good citizen, and a defender of capitalism. Moreover, as in the Soviet Union where *kulturnost* represented a popular way to mobilize for the Cold War, American advertisers granted the possibility of participating in a particular kind of virtuous and rational consumption as a way to live a cultured American life. As Lawrence Glickman has noted, radicals and conservatives worried equally over the effects of conspicuous consumption upon the population, both for its anesthetizing effects on the masses and for its tendency to "level society to the lowest common denominator."[47]

While the advertisers who produced these images came from a broader array of backgrounds than their counterparts on the Soviet side and while their primary goals may have been to generate profit, the cumulative result of their efforts was similar to those found in the East. In the process of using the child in the context of the Cold War to sell consumption, American and Soviet advertisers established consumerism as a gift of the sociopolitical system that surrounded them. They juxtaposed the vision of their own prosperous children against that of communist or capitalist deprivation. They mobilized Cold War youth to create, in the words of Lizabeth Cohen, a "Consumer Republic" that conflated the ideal of "abundance" with that of "freedom." In effect, they offered a path to citizenship and mobilization through purchasing. They were not just selling economic capital—they were selling social and cultural capital as well. Ultimately, they played a vital role in the construction of Cold War consent—one needed to buy these goods and embrace the consensus if one hoped to protect the children. Likewise, one was compelled to defend the young and the consensus if one wanted to have access to goods. And finally, one was required to protect the young and one's consumerism if one wanted to retain the popular consensus. Consumer goods, childhood, and the Cold War consensus converged to create a network where any two of these commodities could be used to sell the third. Economic, social, and cultural capital were all open for trade and were all for sale.

This confluence is not surprising given that the efforts to construct the Consumer Republic and the Cold War consensus, whether in the United States or the Soviet Union, had much in common. Both had to be sold to the public by those who were capable of manipulating popular culture. Using the image of the afforded or threatened child, these image producers rallied a population to "buy into" the consensus and the idea that purchasing equaled citizenship. In the pursuit of consumption and consensus, both sides sought to create a population that would feel grateful for the amenities that their way of life offered. Both worked to convince their populations that the needs of the nation matched the needs of the family and the individual. Not only were the Consumer Republic and the Cold War consensus produced for the purpose of being sold, but they were also self-perpetuating in that they created the needs that they ostensibly satisfied. Finally, both provided visions of their societies that were facades. The image of the happy and afforded child was a thin patina covering the existence of children living in poverty.

And yet the afforded child was arguably more important for this conflict than it had been for any before it. Cold War kids were not just useful for legitimizing each side's economic path (and for selling products along the way). They were also vital in the international propaganda wars of the late 1950s. For the United States, perhaps nowhere were the politics of the afforded child brought more to the fore than at the American exhibit at Sokolniki Park in July 1959. Historians have traditionally (and with good reason) looked to the now-famous "Kitchen Debate" as the crowning achievement of the American exhibit. In fact, the cultural Cold War had been in full swing for years by this time, but many came to see the debate that happened between Khrushchev and Nixon over the implications of having a washing machine in every home as a seminal moment that changed the battlefield of the conflict and determined its path for decades to come.[48] This was a showcase for American abundance and economic solvency that in the words of Khrushchev was at the heart of "economic competition."[49] In the early phases of the American planning for the exhibition, organizers knew that the Soviet public would not be swayed by evidence of efficient industrial production and growing nuclear capacity. They understood that the best way to entice the population would be to depict the United States as "dynamic," "free," "progressive," and "peace-loving," with a deliberate emphasis on consumerism and the rewards of the American system.[50]

Although it is seldom discussed in modern histories of the exhibition, one of the largest exhibits at Sokolniki was a children's playground. It consisted of an abstract sculpture made of four huge aluminum shapes standing on slim legs perforated with large holes through which Soviet children could squeeze themselves. It had a spiral slide made of a modern polymer, various perforated cubes, a large plastic hippopotamus accompanied by smaller plastic hippo calves, a six-person seesaw, and a skewed set of monkey bars that swirled up and down for climbing. This playground represented a consumerist and contained ideal that was intentionally foreign to Soviet children. Such difference presented a message to the Soviet populace that American children played in better, more modern, and more enlightened environments than Soviet youth. In the Soviet Union, where the communist system was ostensibly required for cultured consumerism to happen, the presence of this modern playground was indeed threatening. And for parents there was nothing more troubling than the knowledge that one's own children could not play as well as American children could. Thus, in 1958, *Time* magazine reported that Russian women were most impressed with the playground and the "spectacular wedding sequence." "We used to have that long ago," said one wistful spectator. "But not anymore."[51] Ironically, the Sokolniki playground was also foreign to American kids. One news report quietly admitted that, in fact, no comparable playground existed in the United States.[52] This structure was the first of its kind largely because it existed to meet an ideal of an afforded life, not a reality.

At its core, the exhibition was a testament to the idealized vision of the abundant American family and, without question, of the American child.

Figure 1.2. A scale model of the playground that was used at the Sokolniki exhibit. It was first unveiled at the Association for Childhood Education International on 2 April 1959 in St. Louis and was built by Creative Playthings, Inc.

The centerpiece of the entire exhibition was a 50,000-square-foot glassed-in pavilion that displayed American items ranging from sporting goods to art, books, and musical instruments. The items that were displayed with the most frequency, however, were domestic goods, particularly clothes, food, and toys. As Harold C. McClellan, who was a Los Angeles industrialist and the organizing force behind the exhibition, proclaimed, "It is almost like a great bazaar of the conveniences that the American family enjoys."[53] Domestic policies and trends were borrowed and transmuted from foreign policies so that the containment of the family became a building block for the containment of communism. Yet, as the Sokolniki exhibit shows, this process of borrowing semiotic and rhetorical meaning could go in both directions. When McClellan and Eisenhower sat down to construct a golden pitch to sell the "American Way" to the Soviet populace, they turned to the trappings of domestic Cold War containment. What they produced was an idealized vision of American Cold War society, not as particularly free or peaceful, per se, but as contained and wealthy, with all its baubles. They presented to the Soviets the very vision of domestic normativity that was being projected at home in order to promote the Cold War consensus.

This explains the centrality of the family and the child in the imagery of the exhibition. At Sokolniki, American ascendancy over the Soviet system could have been defined by a number of common American visual tropes: the open road heading west (symbolizing freedom of mobility and individual destiny), the vibrancy of the independent press (symbolizing freedom of speech), the relative openness of the electoral system (symbolizing political freedom within a civil society), the power of the American industrial giant (showing that the United States could compete with the Soviets in heavy industry). Yet the images that held center stage were those that symbolized consumerism and happy domesticity in the American family. If domestic containment did represent a way for Americans to fight the Cold War at home, then this exhibition in Russia did not just present visions of American containment to the Russian populace, it also revealed to the Russians that the Americans were armed with a dizzying array of domestic weapons, not the least of which was the ability to provide great playgrounds for their young. The playgrounds and kitchens and wedding scenes were there to show the Soviet populace and its leadership that the United States was buying into the Cold War consensus and was indeed fighting this war at home.

On both sides of the Iron Curtain, the image of the afforded child and the consumption that the child required served as visual weapons in the economic and cultural battles of the Cold War. For domestic consumers, wealthy kids represented their own system's ability to provide. They equated consumerism with citizenship and mobilization. When these images of abundance were exported, they became clear manifestations of their nation's ability to offer a particular kind of cultured consumption to all who decided to follow in their path.

Defensive Mobilization and the Prepared Child

The youthful happiness and abundance of the Cold War child existed in tandem with a deep-seated belief that preparedness for defense was crucial to the next generation. Beginning in the early 1950s, leaders on both sides of the Iron Curtain reminded their populations of their obligations to protect the home from invasion. Not simply innocent and joyous, American and Soviet children became instructional tools for each side's efforts to prepare the home and the nation for potential attack. They embodied a new ideal that had the capability for survival. Such depictions helped to create the idea that this was a war against which the population could defend itself. They offered a vision of a future that would persist even in the worst of scenarios. They provided security and a chance to mobilize when there were no ramparts to man.

In the Soviet Union, propagandists continued the long tradition of arguing that Soviet youth were prepared to defend Russia against capitalist encirclement. In the one month of March 1949, *Komsomol'skaia pravda* published no fewer than ten articles that mentioned the struggle of Soviet youth for "defense against the United States." Essays and speeches constantly called upon children and adolescents to join in the campaign to "defend the demo cratic world against warmongering."[54] As Cold War tensions rose in the summer of 1949, *Pionerskaia pravda* informed its readers that Soviet children, as the "builders of peace and culture," would "stand against the aggressive plans of those who would wage war."[55] It was this rhetoric that sent many in the U.S. State Department and in the press scrambling to their typewriters with apparent proof that the Red Menace was indoctrinating Russian children to be soldiers and was spreading the communist message abroad.[56] Yet this language spoke far more to the child's commitment to domestic defense and order than it did to any larger ideological mission.[57] For readers in the United States, stock rhetorical descriptions of Stalinist children committed to "defense and peace" seemed to imply that the next generation was manning the ramparts, but such calls to mobilize against capitalist encirclement did not mean that the Soviet leadership sought to train aggressive youths for a communist crusade. Instead, they reflected the mandate to create physically fit and disciplined kids at home who could promote an image of the Soviet Union as primarily happy, well-ordered, affluent, and prepared.

The images of well defended Soviet children that were being produced in stunning numbers in the early 1950s support this contention. Since the opening of the Soviet archives in the 1990s, historians of Soviet foreign policy have largely agreed that in the early years of the Cold War Stalin was far more concerned with establishing defensive buffers and the demilitarization of Germany than with the promotion of an aggressive ideological campaign for communism.[58] How better to articulate a defensive foreign policy to a population than by promoting an idealized image of children who are well contained and defensively mobilized within the home and within the larger Soviet family? The process of raising, fostering, and believing in the existence of happy, prepared Soviet children became another means by which domestic populations could mobilize for the Cold War. Within the family, the community, and the nation, "containment was the key to security."[59] The lesson conveyed in these images was that only by embracing a carefully prescribed array of attributes and behaviors could the nation survive.

Stalinist portrayals of defensively mobilized children can be seen most clearly in the literature produced by the Local Anti-Air Defense (MPVO), which was the organization most responsible for mobilizing the nation's youth against potential Western aggression. MPVO had been founded in 1927 to train reserves for the armed forces. Twenty years later, it boasted a membership of over 13 million children and adolescents, all of whom were supposed to receive varying levels of military training at state-of-the-art air-fields and archery ranges. MPVO published pamphlets and articles in the early years of the Cold War that provided instruction on a variety of conventional civil defense topics. Bearing titles like "Always at Your Post," "The Infantry Battalion," and "Defending the Front," MPVO brochures argued for the continued vigilance of each child against capitalist encirclement. They generally featured images of children of about eight to thirteen, wearing uniforms, bearing compasses and maps, and seen hiking and skiing across difficult terrain.[60] In one such three-page pamphlet entitled "The Insidious Methods of the Secret Service of the Imperialist Governments and the Problems of Raising the Vigilance of Soviet Children," boys and girls approximately eight to fourteen years old appeared sitting in the classroom, digging ditches, and hiking on a trail.[61] In the accompanying text, young readers were reminded of the role that Soviet children played in ensuring the "defense of the motherland." They were then directed to "listen to the lessons of Stalin who instructs us to remain vigilant."

This pamphlet and many reports like it presented a prescribed and largely conventional message concerning what was at stake in the Cold War and what was needed of the population. They argued that American imperialism around the world could be combated only through the mobilization of the country's youth for the causes of national defense.[62] Although Stalin had prohibited open discourse on nuclear defense, by 1962 the state was publishing pamphlets with titles like "How to Defend Oneself against Weapons of Mass Destruction" ("Kak zashchishchat'sia ot massovogo porazheniia").[63] Soviet citizens and their children were told that their survival would happen as a "collective endeavor" through "active, state-led effort."[64] Children invariably could be found participating in evacuation scenarios that portrayed the mass survival of the population. These images of children, rendered both as the beneficiaries of the state's care and as disciplined, nonmilitarized citizens, presented a vision of how the Cold War was to be understood by the general populace as well as international audiences. They argued that the mobilization of the country's children for "defense and peace" against the United States was inherently self-protective, requiring physical and ideological discipline at home and in the public sphere.

A similar story of collective, defensive mobilization played out in the United States in these same years. As Ellsworth Augustus, the president of the Boy Scouts of America, put it in 1955, "Our children cannot be protected anymore from the threats they face around them every day. . . . Preparedness is more important today than ever before."[65] Youth groups worked throughout the 1950s to conceptualize the Cold War for the American public as a defensive struggle that, although daunting, could nonetheless be won through mobilization at home and in the community. At the forefront of the effort to construct an ideal American child sat organizations like the Scouts and the YMCA. These groups, which received sizable government support and funding, created an image of the ideal American youngster who was not just patriotic, physically fit, God-fearing, and respectful of authority but also well-educated in the sciences, devoutly anticommunist, defensively mobilized for nuclear disaster, committed to capitalist humanitarianism, unperturbed by the possible psychological traumas of the atomic bomb, and dedicated to the maintenance of domestic order.[66] As Representative Peter Rodino remarked to his colleagues in 1954, "Scouting has the ability to teach a boy how to take care of himself and how to not be afraid, even in the most unimaginable circumstances."[67] In 1959, Boy Scouts handed out over 375,000 home emergency handbooks across the country in an effort to keep the populace "up to date" on its civil defense policy.[68] With the addition of the Emergency Preparedness Badge in 1962 (a little late by many people's standards, but ironically right on track with the Soviet switch to open nuclear civil defense policies), boys were given specific instructions on what was required to "prepare for emergencies, both conventional and nuclear."[69] The obligations for the badge included participation and leadership in local civil defense exercises and the spreading of awareness of civil defense issues among members of the community.[70]

Years before their Soviet counterparts were reading up on how to defend themselves from weapons of mass destruction, the Boy Scouts appeared prepared for the possibility and the consequences of nuclear attack.[71] These images of mobilized boys reflected the nature of Cold War mobilization in America. They affirmed the nation's apparent willingness and ability to defend itself from atomic assault; they helped to create the sense that a sizable portion of the next generation was well-informed, well-trained, and not traumatized by the possibility of a nuclear emergency. "A good scout is a prepared scout," one 1959 pamphlet on civil defense declared. "If we all work together, we can help our families and our communities to be prepared as well."[72] The Scouting motto "Be Prepared" had now been refashioned as a motto for Cold War preparation.

Like the Soviet Pioneers, these images of American Scouts participating in civil defense drills provided a vision of nuclear survivability to their nation—a vision that largely ignored the existential issues presented by the threat of the thermonuclear holocaust. For example, in a 1962 directive to Scouts on how to prepare for a nuclear emergency, the authors informed their readers that "no one can predict the future or control how other countries or political leaders might use their weapons. There is no need to be especially alarmed. There is a need for preparation and awareness."[73] The booklet went on to instruct Scouts on the varieties of warning signals, the importance of learning evacuation routes, the need for fallout shelters, and the importance of storing sufficient supplies in case of attack. "Such measures will help to create a safer environment for you and your family," the pamphlet concluded, thereby making the argument that collective mobilization could lead to collective safety. In Scouting literature, generals like Lewis Hershey spoke of civil defense as a means for career advancement. Others conceptualized it as a kind of sport, as when Terry Brennan, who was then the head football coach of the University of Notre Dame, explained the need for nuclear civil defense in a speech to Scouts at the Philmont camp in the summer of 1956.[74] He argued that "scouting, football, and civil defense have a lot in common. And, as everyone knows, it is a good defense that wins the game." With no further explanation offered about what "offense" would entail in a nuclear attack or how his envisioned "defense" would work, Brennan strove to do exactly what the now-famous nuclear preparedness film *Duck and Cover* had tried to achieve. He made nuclear defense seem tangible, animated, and sporting.[75]

Visions of defensive mobilization have thus far focused on boys, or implied such a focus. Yet in the 1950s, the standard image of the idealized Cold War child was frequently a girl. The Soviet Pioneer was far more likely to be depicted as a girl than a boy, even though gender distinctions were seldom articulated openly. In an examination of images in the cover pages of the main Pioneer journal, *Pionerskaia pravda*, 60 percent of the time girls appeared in the constructed space of the ideal Soviet child. These girls could occasionally be seen embracing traditional gender roles like cooking and child care, but they were also pictured as engaging in civil defense activities, physical competitions, and social projects that were "male-dominated" by Western standards. Like the young Svetlana Zhiltsova, who gave the opening speech at the Komsomol Congress in 1949, girls dominated youth-generated public discourse in the early years of the Cold War. Disproportionately, they were the recipients of Stalin's fatherly gaze in hagiographic paintings of these years. They were far more likely to be cited in Pioneer and Komsomol documents for their achievements, particularly in school. At the same time, depictions of "problem girls" as sexually promiscuous and disrespectful of their parents and their community appeared with a rarity that was noticeably different from common visions of young male hooligans in these years. This girl-centered phenomenon is by no means absolute, but it is telling. In contrast to earlier visions of mobilized girl-children during the Great Patriotic War, which presented young women like Zoya Kosmodemyanskaya as combatants whose bodies were sacrificed for the preservation of the Motherland, girls after the war became icons for innocence, preservation, and the ordered, defensive mobilization of the population for the Cold War and the High Stalinist project. Girls became the figurative bride for the Stalinist marriage between the leader and his feminized, infantilized population. In an age when the destroyed male form was, in the words of Lilya Kaganovsky, a "model of bodily obligation" for supporting the "dominant fiction of Stalinism," the image of the intact girl-child presented an acceptable corollary, an ideal subject that was still whole but nonetheless posed no threat to Stalinist power.[76] In an age when domestic mobilization revolved around the defensive containment of the population, the subjected, outwardly identified, innocent girl-child was arguably less problematic as a vessel for constructing consensus than was the boy who had the capacity for challenging the normativity of the Stalinist body.

The frequency of the ideal girl-child in America in these years is more difficult to discern. Politicians, propagandists, parents, advertisers, and youth leaders in the United States produced such large quantities of images from such diverse sources that it is difficult to draw conclusions from the study of them. There are some telling signs, nonetheless, that point to a similar trend in the United States in the 1950s. For instance, in a detailed study of images of children in *Life* magazine from 1945 to 1955, whether one is referring to children in advertisements (where girl-children appeared 61 percent of the time) or in articles and photo-essays (where girl children appeared 52 percent of the time), the disproportionate appearance of girls is worth noting.[77] Girls tended to appear in advertisements targeting fathers and their responsibilities (to buy life insurance or wear the right hair tonic). They appeared to exist comfortably within their designated gender roles of future mother, consumer, and provider. At the same time, as the 1950s wound down, they also became symbols for the obligations of parents to provide their girls (as they had their boys in the past) with creative toys and good shoes for play and exercise—all for the purposes of creating a generation of strong future Americans capable of facing the outside world and the communist menace.

Perhaps the place where the Cold War containment of the girl-child can be best seen is in the activities and initiatives of the Girl Scouts of America. Like the Boy Scouts, the Girl Scouts embraced defensive containment with energy. In 1951, the Girl Scouts created the Institute on Volunteering and Defense, which concentrated on how Girl Scouts could help to "win the war and preserve a way of life—the democratic way, which is in danger because of the totalitarian threat." The meeting defined the current struggle as two-pronged: first as a fight between ideals and "philosophies of life," and second as a physical war of "offense and defense."[78] Like the Boy Scouts, the Girl Scouts envisioned themselves as playing a central role in marshaling the country's population to act upon these dual threats. While the Boy Scouts focused on the logistics of managing populations in civil defense drills, the Girl Scouts prepared to care for children, utilities, water supplies, and refugee rooms (the organization encouraged girls to find "secret hiding places" as a way to cultivate their interest in equipping these rooms).[79]

Ironically, while the Girl Scouts organization was willing to promote the differentiation of gender roles in childhood mobilization for the Cold War, it also used these campaigns to assert its own power in a nonprofit world that was largely dominated by male organizations like the Boy Scouts and the YMCA. The Girl Scouts reminded the country's population repeatedly throughout the first two decades of the Cold War that with thirty-nine years of experience and a membership of over 1.2 million girls, they were uniquely positioned to provide an ideal for girls that could meet the country's needs.[80] The Girl Scouts organization was not just a congressionally mandated tool for the construction of a Cold War consensus among the nation's girls and their parents; it also used the pursuit of that consensus as a means to construct its own legitimacy. Like in the Soviet Union, the frequency and importance of the image of the girl-child suggests a connection between femininity and the Cold War, particularly in the 1950s. While dangerous female sexuality came to be seen as a threat to national security, as Carolyn Lewis and Elaine Tyler May have noted, innocent, protected, largely prepubescent, contained girl-hood became a prime vessel for the domesticated ideals that characterized Cold War mobilization in the early years.[81]

Conclusion

In both the Soviet Union and the United States, the ideal of the happy, afforded, and defensively mobilized child became a building block for the containment of populations. These images of protected, prepared, and patriotic children provided a scopic regime, or visual trigger, for the larger Cold War in the early 1950s that helped to define the cultural and conceptual boundaries of the conflict for populations on both sides of the Iron Curtain. The myth of the ideal Cold War child in the 1950s—seen as defensively mobilized, protected, frequently feminized, and prepared for the challenges to come, inhabited a visual and rhetorical space that paralleled the larger policies being pursued by each side's leaders and propagandists. As children's historian James Kincaid has noted, the myth of childhood again and again "emptied" children of their own unique identities and histories so that they could meet the symbolic demands made upon them by the adult world.[82] This was the case in the Cold War as much as it was during Kincaid's Victorian era. The ideal child served as a mirror for the ideals that 1950s Soviet and American leaders and politicians (and arguably much of their populace) wanted to project for themselves and their futures. They served as the building blocks for the biography of the Cold War child, which was written both by state power and by "individual appropriations and significations." These images functioned as models upon which adults could ostensibly shape their own biographies and bind themselves to the system that made their lives possible.[83]

In 1932, Reinhold Niebuhr argued that the general public lived in a conceptual universe that was built upon a series of "necessary illusions." These illusions were built on the shoulders of childhood, providing a sense of certainty and moral constancy in a world that was rife with confusion. In the process, these illusions constructed a clear vocabulary for the preservation of the status quo. In these years, leaders on both sides of the Iron Curtain made policy choices that put children and their families in harm's way. They authorized atmospheric nuclear testing. They condoned the forced occupation of Eastern Europe. They propped up colonial regimes in Southeast Asia and Africa. They purged their own populations and allowed entire races to fall victim to violence. The image of the innocent, afforded, and domestically contained child provided a vital foil to all of these contradictions. It built the illusion of the Cold War itself and offered "emotionally potent oversimplifications," which were ostensibly needed in order to keep the populaces working toward the building of a better society, to keep them from falling into inertia, and to keep them from questioning the status quo, which in reality led to deep inequalities in society and in the world.[84]

At the core of these illusions sat a series of visual tropes that transformed seeing into believing. When Americans and Soviets looked upon images of their own protected, happy, afforded children, they were participating in a process of knowledge-building that theoretically provided them with the tools and certainty that they needed to continue on, to avoid apathy, and to fall in line behind their countries' leaders. The pervasive image of the happy child became an integral part of that illusion. And yet this happiness could not have existed in a vacuum. A counter-ideal was needed. An Other was required that would allow the populace to see its own youth in *contrast* to children on the other side, as something not endangered, not suffering, and not living a life of fear.

CHAPTER TWO

The "Other" Child

The construction of the Cold War child was inextricably bound to the formation of social and cultural identities on both sides of the Iron Curtain. But visions of containment could only perform their desired functions if they had a counter-ideal against which they could be compared. In the first two decades of the Cold War, this antithesis came in the form of the "Other" child living on the enemy side, who provided a sufficiently harrowing vision of the enemy to justify and legitimize the war. In the Soviet Union, this meant identifying American youth as cursed by material want and poverty, lost in an ideological vacuum, and impoverished by violent, racist, bourgeois imperialism. In the United States, this meant seeing Soviet kids as bound and roboticized into a state of conformity and inhumanity by an oppressive regime. Both sides engaged their domestic audiences and each other in a wide-sweeping, visual and rhetorical dialogue of victimhood about the enemy's children. Both sides did this in order to identify themselves and their own young as *not* persecuted by a systemically destructive and predatory sociopolitical system. By contrasting positive images of the lives of their own children with representations of the destitution of the other side's youth, politicians, lobbyists, advertisers, domestic propagandists, party members, and educators participated in a campaign of differentiation that defined the cultural currency of the war.

As the Cold War progressed, these visions of suffering children on the other side of the Iron Curtain became more complicated. New and arguably far more disturbing images of the "Other" child emerged bearing traits that were, in the context of the Cold War, potentially to be envied. The discipline of Soviet children became something to be admired in an age in which the war was sure to continue into the next generation on the battlefield and in the laboratory. The seemingly free lives of American youth allowed for a kind of self-expression and creativity that could foster the inventive leaps that were necessary to continue competing. American pedagogues and politicians looked longingly at the high number of disciplined engineering and physics graduates that the Soviet Union seemed to be producing. Similarly, educators and Communist Party leaders in the Soviet Union expressed grudging admiration for the apparently inventive capacities of American youth.

These images of the "Other" child performed important functions in shaping Soviet and American culture. As in many wars before it, the specter of the suffering child reinforced the moral underpinnings of the conflict for domestic populations. It identified the enemy as a predator for children and justified the role of the state as protector of the young. When, in the late 1950s, the perceived discipline and freedom of the enemy's child became increasingly desirable, these images helped to justify increased funding and reforms to both side's educational systems. Yet, at the same time, for many on both sides of the Iron Curtain, this tentative recognition of the "Other" child as having enviable traits represented a fraying of the images that supported the Cold War consensus. It forced each side to question (albeit tentatively) the validity of its own approach to child-rearing and its own leadership. It introduced increasingly problematic visions of both sets of children into the mainstream. It turned education into a Cold War issue in ways that led both sides to question if the state was in fact intervening in the lives of children *for* the children, or for the war.

"American Children Are Starving and Violent"

In the Soviet Union, the official image of the capitalist child in the 1950s was based on historical perceptions of Western childhood dating back to the *Communist Manifesto*. To Marx and Engels, child labor, having emerged from the Industrial Revolution, was an integral part of the capitalist drive to exploit the worker whenever possible. They contended that this exploitation had created generations of children who faced futures of continued violence and destitution.[1] In the Soviet Union, in 1937, the writer Sergei Ostriakov wrote that "in bourgeois societies, the human being absorbs with the mother's milk a consciousness that either you rob another, or he robs you; either you are the slave-owner or the slave."[2] By the time the Cold War arrived, the image of the capitalist child had become an integral part of the Communist Party's larger effort to convince the nation and its neighbors that capitalism was detrimental to the well-being of the young. As the Pioneer organization reported, "In all the capitalist countries the position of the majority of youth since the end of the Second World War not only didn't improve, but quite the opposite, it deteriorated."[3]

The Communist Party and the press often provided proof of the suffering of American youth by contrasting it explicitly to the happiness of the Soviet child. On 4 September 1949, *Komsomol'skaia pravda*, the official newspaper for the Komsomol youth organization, printed a report on the happy work of Soviet children on civil defense alongside a drawing of an American child wielding a gun. In contrast to the joy expressed by the Komsomol and Pioneer members, who "were forever grateful to Stalin," an American boy, aged seven or eight, stood in the middle of a destroyed room, wielding a large weapon (see fig. 2.1). His grandmother sat on the floor holding her bleeding head. A dog lay on the ground with a knife in its belly while the boy's parents hid under the kitchen table. In the foreground sat a gun box with the text "Made in the USA" prominently displayed. The caption read, "Papa and Mama! Come out, I am done playing!" For the young viewer, the connection between the article on page one and the illustration on page two would have been hard to ignore. Taken in context, not only did these contrasting images effectively compare the lives of Soviet youth to those of American children, they also attributed that discrepancy to the careful supervision provided by Stalin.

Labeling the children of the Western world "The Lost Generation," the Soviet press, as well as the Komsomol, the Pioneers, and the Communist Party leadership, argued that the children of America were being raised in a way that would lead inevitably to a loss of interest in life, with, as one Komsomol leader put it, "existence seeming to them instead to be reactionary, dirty, base, and aimless."[4] In stark contrast to idealized images of the Soviet child, a variety of groups and individuals both in the press and in official party meetings described American children as having a hatred for work and an education focused on violence and militarization, with no belief in friendship, love, or the possibility of peace. One pamphlet released by the Komsomol in 1954 for national distribution argued that American children had "no idealism, no target which would inspire them. They are indifferent to the future of their country, and nothing, aside from their own fates, interests them. Everyone is deeply bogged down in a quagmire of drunkenness, criminality, debauchery, and moral wildness [*odichanie*]. Unrestrained, predatory exploitation, unemployment and lack of faith in their future characterize the complete indifference of capitalist society towards the future of the young."[5] By painting a picture of American youth as aimless and disillusioned, the Komsomol rendered them as both victims and objects of scorn.

These depictions continued into the late 1950s and 60s, with increasing reports also appearing on the hedonism of American youth, with their loud music and seemingly uninhibited behavior. Speaking of the American child, one Komsomol leader declared during the Thirteenth Komsomol Congress

Figure 2.1. "Papa i mama! Vylezaite, ia uzhe poigral!" (Papa and Mama! Come out, I am done playing!). *Komsomol'skaia pravda*, 1 September 1949, 6.

Папа и мама! Вылезайте, я уже поиграл!

in 1958 that under the constant onslaught of Western propaganda, the "process of disintegration and demoralization of the youth of capitalist countries and especially the U.S.A. is quickly spreading wider and deeper."[6] This idea of Western contagiousness and of the threat that it posed to Soviet youth would receive increasing attention as it became clear in later years that many Soviet youngsters were attracted to the image of American intemperance and as the issue of domestic delinquency came to the fore.

The Communist Party portrayed the children of America as being alone in an aggressive world, as directionless and bereft of lofty sentiment. The Soviet media throughout the 1950s and 60s returned again and again to the image of the solitary American child who had been left to fend for him or herself with no help from the poorly organized and inherently corrupt youth organizations of America. They argued that American youth groups, instead of providing healthy direction, "busied themselves with rock-n-roll" and with seemingly frivolous activities like "hunting butterflies and turtles." American kids, they claimed, were unable or unwilling to address not only questions of politics, economics, and ideology, "but the defense of the rights of the young."[7] Because organizations were not state sponsored, they had no rights and received no attention from the government. Instead, children and students were portrayed as being forced to recite loyalty oaths in order to receive an education.[8]

With all its wealth, America was portrayed as having failed to provide the necessary physical care that children required. This was the message of a 1955 domestic broadcast on the anniversary of the International Day for the Defense of Youth, which reported to its young listeners on the quality of life that proletarian children faced. "You live in Soviet society," the broadcast began, "where the government constantly worries about its children. Everyone here can study and become what they want to be. Right now it is summer and almost all Soviet children are vacationing either at the Pioneer camps, at children's sanatoriums, or at their dachas." In sharp contrast to this idyllic life stood American children, whose parents were portrayed as being unable to support their families and who were thus forced to go without. "My family is hungry," an American father, Dale Wanson, was reported saying. "My children are sick, but we cannot go to a doctor." American children were depicted as unprotected from hunger and destitution and envious of the Soviet system and the lives its population enjoyed. The report continued: "Many children of capitalist countries know about the Soviet Union and dream about the life that you children lead. They strive to have a life similar to yours." Citing an interview that he had with a young American boy in Washington, the broadcaster reported that the boy only wished "to be the same as a Soviet boy—to be loved, to be smart, and to be healthy."[9] Such depictions of ideological and physical weaknesses on the part of the West painted the children of the Soviet Union as viable living alternatives to the capitalist option.

These campaigns focused on the ideological and material emptiness of white children in America, but there also existed a completely separate body of literature and propaganda in the Soviet Union concerning the lives of African American children, which had begun in the 1930s and then picked up steam as the Cold War and the civil rights movement in the United States became political and cultural backdrops for both countries. One of the earliest and best-known indictments of American racism was Grigorii Aleksandrov's 1936 film *Tsirk* (Circus), which chronicled how a white actress in the United States frantically escapes from a lynch mob with her swaddled, mixed-race child to find a welcoming home in the Soviet Union. It was not until the 1950s, however, that the Communist Party could step away from a movie set and offer domestic and international viewers visions of real, black, American children suffering at the hands of real, white, American adults (and other children). *Pionerskaia pravda*, which was intended for readers under the age of fifteen and their parents, issued a story on American race relations two times a week on average from 1952 until 1959.[10] These pieces treated the passing of seminal cases like *Brown v. Board of Education* with skepticism and continuously indicted the United States for needing to pass such a law in the first place.[11]

Рисунок Н. ЛИСОГОРСКОГО.

— Принёс несколько несчастных долларов, а платить надо ла-
вочнику, за квартиру, за электричество да ещё за содержание Ли Сын
Мана...

Figure 2.2. This *Krokodil* article from 1956 pictured a destitute American family and
carried the caption, "I couldn't bring in enough money to pay the shopkeeper for the
apartment, for the electricity, and to keep the children fed." N. Lisogorskii, "Lishnii rot"
(Another Mouth). *Krokodil*, 10 June 1956.

In 1960, the image of African American children streaked across the world
press and stayed there. Soviet media coverage of the American civil rights
struggle increased threefold. Little Rock was the catalyst. In a discussion of
the events of October 1960, domestic broadcasters at Gosteleradio, the Soviet state radio service, phrased the conflict in terms of American hypocrisy
toward its own citizens: "The dear uncles from the state departments of the
United States appear very anxious about the fate of their black students and
their preparations to hospitably open the doors of their institutions to them.
They are convinced that the young black cannot find a more inviting place
than America. Especially in the United States, they believe that the Negro
can freely receive an education. But where in the United States can we really
discover such celebrated freedom for the Negroes while still not forgetting
the facts of the past few years? Last summer twenty-one Negro students were
denied entrance into a school in Little Rock. This past fall two young Negro
students were lynched. Not long ago the home of a Negro family in Chat-
tanooga, Tennessee, was burned down, while in the town of New Orleans,
members of the school union decided that they would close the state school
in order to stop integrated education between whites and blacks."[12]

Subsequent articles in *Komsomol'skaia pravda* and *Izvestiia* further indicted the U.S. government and its continued violence against black children. One article entitled "Troops Advance against Children!" reported to

Figure 2.3. V. Goriaeva, "Shkola" (School). *Krokodil*, 30 September 1956, 16.

Figure 2.4. This image of the American child contrasted with the Soviet child who, in the words of the Pioneer illustration on the right, "makes friends with children of all countries of the world." The photo of the children in Klan costumes appeared in *Krokodil*, 1 November 1966, 9. The illustration of the Pioneer children was a poster reprinted by the Pioneer organization through the 1960s. © Fine Art Images.

its Soviet readers that national guardsmen were physically keeping African American girls away from the high school in Little Rock.[13] Another article claimed that the Ku Klux Klan was organizing a "savage hunt for Negro children because they plan to attend classes with white boys and girls." Similarly, *Izvestiia* reported that black children were being barred from entering school, threatened with bayonets, and tear-gassed.[14] These portrayals of white American barbarity in newspapers, journals, and radio broadcasts argued to their Soviet audiences that children in America were suffering, impoverished, and far from free.

According to the Communist Party, this combination of ideological vacuity and open violence in the lives of American children had dire international ramifications. The press and the Party argued that white children in the West, because of their bigoted upbringings, were failing to receive the instruction necessary to serve as viable citizens and to function as decent human beings capable of seeing beyond the doom and exploitation that surrounded them. For instance, on 22 May 1961, the lives of two American children were highlighted in a broadcast to young Soviet listeners entitled "Your Young American Contemporaries." In his first exposé, the broadcaster chronicled the life of a white boy whose childhood was marked by disillusionment and apocalyptic resignation. Born from "a hopelessness and catatonic nuclear fear," his life had begun with the "division of the world into two hostile camps. From the newspapers of his country, from the screens of the cinema and the television, from the radio, in school and in his family, they say, scream, and prophesy that his happy [life] will unavoidably perish [*pogibnet*]." But this was only the beginning. "What has been the effect of the Cold War on the children of the West?" the broadcaster asked. "How has the culture of materialism, racism, and emptiness led the children to accept the rhetoric of doom that surrounds them?" To answer these questions, the reporter turned to his second subject, a young girl who, in his words, was "no less cynical" than the boy who came before her. "But she is not angry at the world because she simply doesn't know it and she doesn't want to. In contrast to the heroines of other eras, she is attracted neither by the revolutionary struggle, nor great love, nor motherhood, nor the family hearth, nor art. She is constantly bored, bored until such time as she is distracted. She strives for nothing, she searches for nothing."[15] Note in this poetic language that the traits used to describe these children are similar to the traits used to describe problem children in the rhetoric of the era. This broadcast almost certainly would have had a dual purpose: to create a harrowing image of American life and to warn Soviet children of the possibility of falling into such vices themselves.

It was not just the American child, however, whose life was portrayed as being sadder and less fulfilling than that of Soviet youth. Komsomol leaders and journalists also focused their attention on the suffering of children in the less-developed parts of the world. Not by accident, the suffering countries that the domestic press highlighted were often the same countries in which the Communist Party had vested international interests. A broadcast on Chilean children in 1959, for instance, focused on their exploitation for labor at the hands of American-supported capitalists.[16] The inability of Cameroonian children to study their own history was the subject of a report held on the International Day of the Struggle against Colonial Regimes in 1958.[17] Likewise, the lives of South Korean children who had been left abandoned and homeless in the aftermath of the Korean War were a subject of steady concern. "Hard and joyless is the life of the young Koreans who find themselves under the yoke of the ROK [The Republic of Korea]," one broadcast declared in 1958. "Two million people have become vagrants in the search for a morsel of bread. Approximately forty thousand homeless orphans have been left by parents who died from hunger."[18]

These domestic broadcasts concerning the young of the postcolonial world also explored the volatile topic of the child warrior. At times, this child appeared as an innocent victim who had been forced to carry a gun and fight. At other times, militarized youth appeared as noble crusaders for national liberation. It depended largely on the side on which the child was fighting. For instance, in the broadcast on the Korean War mentioned above, the reporter argued to his listeners that "with the support of the American government, South Korean children find themselves under the constant threat of being mobilized into the ROK army. Those who do not wish to put on the uniform are heatedly pursued . . . with twenty-thousand, five-hundred and thirty-six young people being arrested for refusing to fight . . . some of them as young as seven."[19] In the rhetoric that defined the Soviet Cold War universe, the U.S. government was responsible not only for depriving American youths of any semblance of personal nobility but also for turning defenseless children into youngsters who could now defend themselves in terrifying and deeply unchildlike ways.

Such depictions of ideologically vacuous and materialistic white American youth, besieged black children in the American South, and war-torn youngsters in the postcolonial world all worked in Soviet discourse to contest the claims being made by American broadcasters and publishers that the United States was the defender of freedom and liberty at home and abroad. They also stood in stark contrast to the life that the Communist Party purported to offer its own people and particularly its children.

"Soviet Children Are Robots"

The images of suffering American and foreign kids propagated by the Communist Party in the first two decades of the Cold War bore some striking resemblances to those created, in the same years by American politicians, writers, and journalists, who consistently portrayed Soviet children as victims of direct and abusive state coercion, as impoverished, trapped, militarized, and without much hope for the future. More interesting than the shared figuration of the "Other" in the imagery of the child were the shared functions that these images performed. As with the Soviet images of American children, visions of destitute, robotic Soviet kids provided a glimpse into the menace that seemingly threatened American freedom. It existed as a necessary counterpoint and specter, embodying all that the nation should fear. If the child at home represented a crucial point of identification for the population and its assured survival, then the child on the other side carried on its small frame a nightmarish apparition of a future worse than death. This was the image of enemy childhood that found its way into the collective consciousness of American and Soviet Cold War culture.

As in the Soviet Union, American perceptions of what defined Russian childhood were founded in earlier understandings of Russia's history in the twentieth century. On the one hand, Americans viewed Russian children as the targets of a constant, dogmatic, idealistic, and directed state intervention that was based on a totalizing Marxist-Leninist belief system. Americans who studied the Soviet Union in the 1940s and 50s were fully aware of how important child rearing and education were to early communist theorists like Alexandra Kollontai and Nadezhda Krupskaia. They understood that the ideology of communism was bound up in the belief that children are born decent, good, open to improvement, and flawed only when the poverty and inequality around them make them so.[20] They were also largely aware of the improvements in education that the Soviet Union had experienced since the Revolution. Largely as a consequence of state-led initiatives, literacy rates in the Soviet Union had soared (to a level higher than in the United States). The Communist Party had built summer camps and begun programs for impoverished and homeless children.[21] Yet, at the same time, this image was complicated by a long visual legacy of Russian children as the direct victims of state power and violence. Few could forget the images of destitute and dying children that emerged in the wake of the Russian Civil War (when child mortality rates rose to 50 percent in 1921), the forced Ukrainian famine of the 1930s (although the record of this was slow to emerge), and World War II (when entire provinces of children were killed or displaced).[22] Massive relief efforts, including those organized by UNESCO, the Save the Children Fund, Herbert Hoover's American Relief Administration, and the Crusade for Children, used images of dying and starving Russian kids to solicit much-needed aid from sympathetic American families.

These visions did not disappear as both sides settled into their semiotic trenches in the early 1950s; what did change were the ways and means by which those images were produced, conveyed, and consumed. In the United States, helping suffering Russian children was a constant mantra of the Cold War. In 1951, wealthy individuals and organizations held numerous charity events in the United States for the benefit of Russian kids. The Russian Children's Welfare Society, which had been formed in 1936, enjoyed a resurgence in funding from families like the Chryslers and the Hearsts.[23] In 1953, the American Friends of Russian Freedom appealed to the U.S. population to help fund the delivery of Christmas parcels to families in West Germany that had escaped from The Soviet Union.[24]

Charity for the children of Russia in the Cold War went hand in hand with vitriol directed at the Soviet leadership. Sympathy for Soviet children displaced during World War II turned into anger at a communist system that had failed to protect them and continued to subjugate them. The nature of American sympathy toward Soviet youth changed as well. Just as Soviet rhetoric had argued that American children were raised from the cradle to believe that the world was a scary and aggressive place where only the strongest survived, so too did American popular rhetoric argue that Soviet kids, while deserving of sympathy for their victimization, nonetheless were being transformed at an early age into brainwashed robots capable of betraying their mothers and fathers at the behest of the state. In many ways, the act of sympathizing with these children only intensified the fear that they elicited. Robotic, impoverished, pitiable Soviet children represented the desecration of a sacred innocence and the collapse of the family. They symbolized the worst, the most unspeakable crimes that the enemy was willing to commit against its own young for the causes of ideological orthodoxy and expansion.

This was the image created in a widely published article by Russian émigré Nina I. Alexeiev, whose testimony on living conditions in the Soviet Union was published in *Liberty* magazine on 7 June 1947, was later picked up by the Associated Press, and then was republished in numerous sources, including *Reader's Digest* and the *Congressional Record*, throughout the 1950s.[25] Bearing the title "I Don't Want My Children to Grow Up in Soviet Russia," the article told the story of how Alexeiev and her family had refused to go back to Russia after serving out their term as commercial attachés to Mexico. The front page carried a photograph of a small blonde child smiling as she shook hands with her Soviet teacher. In the background, a banner read, "Welcome New Students." Beneath this happy image, Alexeiev painted a picture of her children's lives that seemed to contradict the happiness portrayed in the front page photo. In describing living conditions in Russia, she stated that as a young person, she had seen "how forcible collectivization wrecked family life and turned innocent, fat, and smiling children in once happy villages into homeless beggars. . . . Hundreds of thousands of 'wild children'—dirt crusted urchins in shredded rags, most of them diseased and depraved—roamed the land, begging, robbing, dying like flies. . . . In the years that followed, I could never accept the propaganda about the 'happy Stalinist life' while all around me I saw half-starved children, their minds and souls maimed by abnormal conditions."[26]

Alexeiev then described the way in which the young of the Soviet Union had ostensibly been indoctrinated "almost from babyhood" with contempt

Figure 2.5. Nina Alexeiev, "I Don't Want My Children to Grow Up in Soviet Russia." *Liberty*, 7 June 1947, 18. © Liberty Library Corporation.

for their own parents. After recalling an incident where a "hoodlum" turned his parents in to state authorities for hiding religious icons, she asked, "What if my own children had been infected with that kind of 'vigilance?'"[27] Her question appeared to be asking American parents what they would do if such "vigilance" was taught to their children.

Central to the fear surrounding Alexeiev's missive was the commonly cited threat of children being "snatched away" from their parents by the state. Alexeiev recalled the "annual mobilization of children from [the age of] twelve [and] up. Millions of boys and girls have been torn from their families and apprenticed as miners or factory hands. . . . In these little slaves, each of us saw our own children." She was probably referring to the system of labor schools where working-class kids were sent from the age of twelve on. They were poorly fed and often held in the camps involuntarily for years.[28] Alexeiev concluded that, "as a mother," she would not be able to "subdue [her children's] natural instincts for truth and beauty in order to fit them into the police state."[29]

Alexeiev's testimony was in many ways accurate. The 1930s, which witnessed the forced famine of the Holodomor and the frenzy of the Terror, was a period marked by the displacement and suffering of millions of Soviet children. Alexeiev's recounting of the denunciation of parents by their young also rang true and referred specifically to the by-then-mythologized story of the young Pavel Morozov, who turned in his father for hoarding grain only to meet his own death at the hands of vengeful relatives. The claims of the "rounding up" of twelve year olds, the forced separation from the family, and the imposed slavery were far more suspect, or at least represented a skewed framing of the state-led activities that most children engaged in during the summers. While the accuracy of this piece may not have been completely established, the function that it was expected to perform certainly was. When this article was published, republished, and discussed in the American press and in official statements on the floor of Congress, it encapsulated both the physical and the psychological threat that communism apparently held for everyone, both inside and outside the Soviet Union.

In the rhetoric of differentiation that defined Soviet children for Americans in the 1950s and 60s, the specter of increasing militarization of the young loomed large. Many Americans, like many Russians, found parallels between old and new enemies as they moved to equate communism with fascism. Speaking to his congregation at the Chevy Chase Baptist Church in Maryland in 1948, pastor Edward Clark pleaded to American parents that they train their children in Christian ideals as the only defense against resurgent fascism, now masking as communism. The crux of his sermon came when he reminded his congregation that both Hitler and Stalin "regimented children to support Nazism and Communism." This sermon, which was given on 14 June, Children's Day, and which was touted as a part of the American Crusade for Children, offered a clear and terrifying warning to American parents who chose not to heed the prescriptions of their leaders to raise law-abiding, politically aware, Christian children.[30] Similarly, in 1950, the historian William Chamberlin denounced in the pages of the *Wall Street Journal* what he perceived to be a commonly held belief among Germans and members of the Communist Party in America that both National Socialism and Communism were good ideas, wrongly applied. These regimes, he argued, were marked by the "high-powered militarization" and "thought control" of the young. Citing the shared suffering of the German people and the Russian people at the hands of the state, he declared that "National Socialism and Communism are not good ideas gone wrong. They are in their very essence bad ideas."[31] The construction of the shared, systemic evils of fascism and communism, both of which ostensibly preyed upon the young, allowed for a continuity of discursive demonization that ultimately served as a foundation for how people were expected to understand the new menace.

To this end, stories abounded in the American press regarding the increasing militarization of Soviet children, particularly in the 1950s. Soviet kids were reported as being made to wear uniforms with epaulets and buckles to school.[32] Reports surfaced that they were being forced to join patrols of "youth control" that included policing Soviet teenagers (who were reportedly "slipping into delinquency," "going to church," and "going astray on alcoholism, brawling, and Tarzan-style hair-dos").[33] In 1957, the *Christian Science Monitor* reported that "armies of school children" were being recruited to "scour the countryside with Geiger counters in a vast search for Uranium ore."[34] Not only did this seem to prove that the Soviet Union was behind in its search for fissionable material, but it also conjured images of helpless children being exposed to radioactivity for the cause of war. This image of Soviet children being actively enlisted into state-regimented obligations clearly brought to mind visions of Hitler Youth (thereby soliciting fear of a resurgent violence) while at the same time casting the young as child soldiers (thereby soliciting revulsion and pity). It is worth remembering that in 1950 the International Children's Emergency Fund, which had been a subsidiary of the United Nations since the end of World War II, was given permanent status due to widespread lobbying for the continuing international need to intervene on behalf of impoverished and exploited children. In 1957 and 1958, while the Soviet Union and the United States were arguing to their constituencies that the enemy was not only incapable of caring for its young but was also turning them into soldiers, the United Nations was drafting a Declaration of the Rights of the Child. This declaration, which was adopted unanimously by all seventy-eight member states of the UN General Assembly in 1959, explicitly forbade the manipulation and exploitation of the young that each side was accusing the other of engaging in. This language of differentiation, this process of envisioning enemy young as violent soldiers *and* as victims, joined the popular rhetoric of universalized childhood that pervaded popular discourse. It provided a Cold War valence to the seemingly apolitical obligation of adults to protect the young. It offered a clear connection between ideology, moral legitimacy, and the importance of the Cold War consensus. As in Russian portrayals of American enlistment of youth, this vision of Soviet-enforced militarization stretched beyond Russian borders to more distant places of conflict in the world. In 1951, the story of nine-year-old Im Sung Nan splashed across American newspapers, ultimately receiving mention on the floor of Congress. As Pulitzer Prize–winning journalist Frank Conniff reported, a young Korean boy had been arrested as a spy by American troops after being sent across the American/Chinese front by the Red Army to gather information on U.S. tank movements. "Little Joe," as the boy was nicknamed in the press, reportedly crossed the border many times a day and reported back to his Chinese and Russian superiors in return for American bubble gum.[35] For the American press and for the politicians who latched on to the story in the months that followed, this tale had all the components that the Cold War consensus required: it put the Soviet Union in Korea (thus confirming Soviet aggression), it indicted the Russians and the Chinese for placing seemingly innocent children in harm's way, and it showed how, in the end, this enemy child had taken incredible risks not for ideology or for the protection of his nation or his family, but for the promise of an American product that itself stood as a symbol not just of America but of the happiness and consumer bliss that American children ostensibly enjoyed (and that this boy wanted to enjoy as well).

These images aroused sympathy for the young and antipathy toward those who would compromise and manipulate them; and they also robbed children from the other side of any potential for reasonable, peaceable behavior as they matured into adulthood. In the United States, the image of the brainwashed Russian child became a symbol of the brainwashed adult. Thus, in 1949, Lieutenant General Walter Bedell Smith, who was Truman's ambassador to Russia from 1946 to 1948, wrote in the *Saturday Evening Post* that the communist leaders of Soviet Russia controlled "the behavior of Soviet citizens from earliest childhood," teaching them to believe "that the capitalist West means to destroy Soviet democracy."[36] "In a country where both parents must work," he continued ominously, "children become part-time wards of the state, and the Soviet state is a careful guardian of its most precious resource." He lamented, "The police-state system molds the minds of its children for the support of a political regime that is basically evil." He then chronicled how the supervision of the child by the schools seamlessly gave way to the supervision of the adult by the secret police, creating an environment that fostered adult resignation and complacency toward the violence perpetrated by the state upon its people.

When a semblance of agency *did* appear in American depictions of enemy young, it was always presented in terms of children breaking the rules and choosing the enemy side. Thus, in a memorable cartoon that was first printed in *Le Figaro* in 1957 and then reprinted in the United States, a group of Soviet children could be seen staring at a vacant television screen as their father entered the room. "What are you waiting for?" he asks the children. And the reply: "For Eisenhower to come on the screen to promise us that our children will all be capitalists."[37]

All of the Western stereotypes about life in the Soviet Union were encapsulated in this cartoon: the broken furniture, the outdated television, the father's Cossack hat, patched cloak, and shoes held together by rags. It was in the children, however, that the message of this cartoon became clearest. They were, for seemingly obvious reasons, captivated by the promise of Western capitalism. The most powerful message conveyed by this image was not that Russian children were poor and living in want, but that their interest and desire for the rewards of capitalism were as much a way of life as was destitution. Just as their poverty apparently defined them, so too did their desire to embrace the promise of the capitalist West.

Or Maybe They Aren't . . . The Image Evolves

In the late 1950s, the image of the "Other" child underwent a subtle but important transformation on both sides of the Iron Curtain. Though in American and Soviet portrayals the enemy's youth continued to be characterized as victims, those captive souls began to assume traits that appeared, at least in part, to be enviable. As we have seen, the American leadership and the Soviet leadership and their supporters consistently defined "Other" children as embodying traits that stood in opposition to those of their own youth at

Figure 2.6. Soviet children wait for the capitalists. J. Primost, "DU BERGER A LA BERGERE" (Tit for Tat). Le Figaro, 5 June 1957, 7.

home. In the Soviet view, American children were unkempt, undisciplined, impoverished, and lacking in leadership, while Soviet kids were organized, well cared for, and an integral part of a much larger national project. In the American view, Soviet children were brainwashed, destitute, and coerced into compliance without outlets for self-expression or creativity, while American kids were imaginative, protected, prosperous, and self-actualized. These identifiers provided handy tools for establishing the legitimacy of the Cold War consensus at home and for demonizing the enemy, but they also left many wondering if there might be aspects of the "Other" child that nonetheless equipped their adversary's youngsters for the Cold War in ways that their own system could not.

This issue rose to the fore most acutely in the field of education, which for both sides represented the state's clearest obligation to the child and its most direct avenue for teaching citizenship. By the mid-1950s, education was in crisis on both sides of the Iron Curtain. The U.S. Congress overwhelmingly passed the American Education Defense Act in 1958 in an attempt to fix an educational system that seemed to be faltering under the weight of the baby boomer generation. In 1960, the American Educational Policies Commission of the National Education Association argued that reforming the teaching of the young, particularly in the sciences, was "the price of survival" in the Cold War.[38] One year later, on the other side of the Iron Curtain, Khrushchev, while speaking at the Fourteenth Komsomol Congress, declared that "the struggle for a creative, deep, and multi-sided education among the young" was crucial for the "construction and survival of the new man in communist society."[39] Such calls for the improvement of education naturally implied inadequacy at home. In their search for how to advance national education, and indeed how to survive, politicians and educators on both sides in the late 1950s looked across the Iron Curtain warily to see if perhaps the other side had discovered a better way to give children the kind of education that would equip them for the modern era. Rote learning (which was associated with the Soviet Union) and progressive, life-adjustment curriculums (which were associated with the United States) became contested pedagogical approaches in both domestic and international debates about the future of education.[40] By the turn of the decade, the Soviet Union began to reject the dogmatic methods of Stalinist education in favor of more pragmatic and progressive practices. At that same time, the United States moved away from the Deweyist models of progressive education toward more dogmatic methods of teaching. Both sides worked frantically to identify the smart children in their midst. In effect, both regressed to a mean. They did so because of the Cold War and, at least in part, because of how they envisioned the "Other" child.

Why did Soviet and American popular rhetoric on the positive aspects of education on the other side of the Iron Curtain not become a part of general public debate until the mid- to late 1950s? In the United States, the answer was Sputnik. While fears about the substandard state of American education had been around since early in the decade, it was not until the launching of the satellite that Americans began looking to the enemy for prescriptions on how to fix the problem. As Robert Divine has chronicled in his study of the crisis that struck America in the fall of 1957, most Americans had previously felt relatively comfortable in the knowledge that their country's science education and scientific research were the best in the world.[41] Most believed that the Soviets would never have been able to detonate an atomic bomb in 1949 had it not been for the work of Soviet spies like Klaus Fuchs, Judith Coplon, and Julius Rosenberg. This time, however, there was no espionage behind the scientific breakthrough that was Sputnik. Few could deny that the satellite was a testament to Soviet ingenuity and that it represented a direct challenge to the common belief that creative, original thought in both the sciences and the arts was necessary in order to make such leaps happen. While Soviet children might seem robotic, they also appeared to be disciplined learners. While they might seem to be terrified into obedience, they also appeared deeply patriotic and well behaved. They gave the impression that they understood the ideological underpinnings of their sociopolitical system and were fully capable of engaging in debates over the values of Marxism. As renowned psychologist Urie Bronfenbrenner warned, "Soviet children of the future will continue to be more conforming than our own. But this also means that they will be less anti-adult, rebellious, aggressive, and delinquent. . . . The streets of Moscow and other Soviet cities [are] reasonably safe for women and children, by night as well as by day."[42]

In an effort to understand how the Soviets had been able to make such apparent leaps in such a short amount of time, large numbers of American educators traveled to the Soviet Union in 1958 and 1959 in order to study the education system and to assess the extent to which the Soviets had moved ahead of the United States.[43] What these educators found led to many sleepless nights. Not only did the young of Russia appear to be well educated in these reports, but they also seemed far less robotic than many had expected, while at the same time exhibiting great discipline and maturity. In one of many widely published reports, Dr. Edward Litchfield, chancellor at the University of Pittsburgh, concluded in 1958 after one year of study that unlike in the United States, where athletes received the nation's admiration, in the Soviet Union, it was the superior student who was "regarded as a hero, not as a grind."[44] The Litchfield report argued that far from being brainwashed, Soviet students read Russian and Western literature, spoke at least one other language, were involved in extracurricular activities like theater and sports, and were interested in world events. Perhaps most disturbing, he claimed that parts of the new Soviet empire were making huge strides in education. In Kazakhstan, for instance, Litchfield reported that the country's population, which only forty years earlier had been almost completely illiterate with no universities, by 1958 had largely eliminated illiteracy and had built twenty-seven universities educating 60,000 students.[45] In June 1958, William Fulbright reported to Congress that the Soviet Union had graduated 70,000 engineers—the corresponding figure in the United States had been only 30,000.[46] Likewise, Dr. Lawrence Derthick, the U.S. commissioner of education, returned from his study of the Russian system to report that "we were simply not prepared for the degree to which the U.S.S.R., as a nation, is committed to education as a means of national advancement. [It is] a total commitment. We witnessed an education-centered economy. The privileged class in Russia is the children."[47]

Figure 2.7. This matchbook was created and distributed by the Chicago public school system as a part of a campaign to prevent children and teenagers from dropping out of school. The back of the matchbook reads, "Nikita Khrushchev can be right about burying our children, because of the drop-out problem."

The Soviets seemed to be getting better at everything, Derthick argued, largely because their culture prioritized education in a way that America did not.[48] "In the U.S.S.R., enthusiasm for education is taken for granted," he lamented in *Look* magazine in October 1958.[49] These reports also had some disturbing things to say about the relative state of American education. While Soviet students appeared to be tackling difficult subjects like physics and calculus, Litchfield pointed out that American students were choosing to study "life adjustment education," which included courses in marriage, choir, and driver's education. The novelist Sloan Wilson, famous for writing *The Man in the Gray Flannel Suit*, argued in 1958 after serving on the National Citizens' Commission for Public Schools that 8 million Russians were learning English, but only 8,000 Americans were learning Russian.[50] Hubert Humphrey seconded Wilson's observations in 1960 when he commented to his colleagues that "the real threat to America's world leadership comes not from Soviet rockets, but from Soviet schools."[51] By 1963, this critique began to apply not only to science education but to the art of indoctrination as well. On the one hand, American leaders in the 1950s and 60s openly rebuked Soviet education for seeing it as "a source of power." Yet they could not ignore the fact that the Soviet Union's apparent attempts to "obtain that power" had resulted in the graduation of 162,000 engineers in 1962 and a teacher-to-student classroom ratio of eighteen-to-one (in contrast to twenty-six-to-one in the United States).[52]

For Americans, the stories of Soviet scientific successes in the classroom implied that the Russians were creating a large pool of potential scientists and thinkers. Not only did it appear to many Americans that the Soviet Union was indoctrinating vast populations within its own empire to follow communist teaching, it was also evidently creating a massive brain trust that could rally around the hammer and sickle when needed. The news of Russian successes in places like Kazakhstan also seemed to increase the possibility that the postcolonial nations of the world might choose the Soviet model as a means to speed up their own development and industrialization. If the Soviets could teach Kazakhstan to read in forty years, imagine what they could do for Angola and Guatemala. Where was the American example of such pedagogical beneficence, Derthick and Litchfield both wondered.

Without a doubt, such widespread praise of the Soviet education system and subsequent condemnation of the American system was neither honest nor realistic. The Russians were not nearly as successful or as confident as they appeared to be in educating their populations. Schools in Central Asia suffered significant shortages. Statistics were inflated and corruption was rampant. Thanks to careful Soviet government control over the American expeditions to Russia, however, the message that came back to the home front was one of astonishing Soviet success, stretching from Belarus to Siberia. Moreover, it is important to remember that the groups sent to evaluate the Russian schools were all lifelong advocates of greater education spending in the United States. By portraying the education of Soviet children in the most glowing terms, they transformed the troubled American classroom into a problem that was as relevant for the Department of Defense as it was for the Department of Education. This in turn increased the odds that the U.S. government would allocate more funding to education programs. In January 1958, Senators William Fulbright, Mike Mansfield, John Sparkman, Joseph Clark, and Lambert Gwinn all made speeches on the floor of Congress arguing that education spending equated to defense spending.[53] Thus, as JoAnne Brown has noted, by capitalizing on Truman's earlier proclamation that "education is our first line of defense," educators gained the legitimacy that such a responsibility afforded them.[54]

The result of all this was significant change in public education across the United States in the late 1950s. Progressivist and life-adjustment curriculums, which had always received only grudging support from the American public before then, were forced out.[55] Educators now paid new attention to programs like the New Math movement, which had been founded by Max Beberman in 1951 but had been largely ignored by mainstream education until 1958. American concerns over education culminated in the passing of the 1958 National Defense Education Act, which mandated that the nation increase the number of science, math, and foreign language graduates that it was producing and start building more schools to accommodate the overcrowding happening as a consequence of the baby boom. The act provided over $887 million over four years to support national security goals and famously required that recipients of the money sign affidavits disclaiming any desire to overthrow the U.S. government. America would abandon its history of progressivism in exchange for the possibility that it could "strengthen the national defense."[56]

A similar story of educational transformation unfolded across the Atlantic in these same years, although the causes for this transformation were different. In the Soviet Union, the education of the "Other" child had remained absent from pedagogical and political discussion before 1954 because there was simply no conceptual room in official Soviet discourse for the possibility that Americans might be doing something right in the classroom. Such a recognition would have required a willingness not only to view bourgeois education in a positive light, but also a kind of critique of socialist, and particularly Stalinist, education, which was out of the question. However, after

Khrushchev's Thaw began in 1956, educators and party leaders quickly moved to debate such issues in academic, educational, and mainstream journals.[57] This happened as a consequence of the much larger, state-sponsored de-Stalinization program, which sought to return to a theoretically purer form of socialism, a form that had ostensibly been repressed in 1928. The year 1956 opened some doors and deliberately left others closed. One of the doors that opened the widest was the issue of Soviet education and the need to reevaluate it in the wake of the Stalin cult. As Khrushchev said in his speech before the Twentieth Party Congress, in naming prizes, holidays, towns, national anthems, and "monuments to the living" after himself, Stalin had claimed ownership of "the whole educational, directional and inspirational activity of the great Leninist Party," and in so doing had deviated from Marxism-Leninism and had debased and belittled the role of the Communist Party. He compared Stalin to Lenin, whom he in contrast characterized as a man who believed in the "stubborn and painstaking education of [the people]." The failure of Stalinist education writ large stood as one of Khrushchev's greatest indictments of the *vozhd'*.

While Khrushchev did not intrinsically tie the Stalinist educational legacy to the mandates of the Cold War, those who followed him did. In the late 1950s and the 1960s, educators and party officials argued that the tradition of rote learning under Stalin had limited the ability of the next generation to become a creative force capable of competing with the West in the sciences and the arts. [58] Historian Boris Kagarlitsky has argued that the Stalinist past, wrought with heavy controls and poor cultural production, left the country in a condition of real worry over the ability of the next generation to be forward thinking and creative.[59] It was true that the Soviets had been the first to put a satellite into space, but the memory of the first American detonation of the Bomb and the knowledge that the United States was ahead in the design and production of atomic weaponry led many in the Soviet Union to wonder how it was possible that an educational system as strong as theirs, which was producing such a large number of engineers and scientists, could be struggling to maintain its perceived lead. Pedagogical documents from the state archives support this contention, although it is important to remember that in the wake of the anti-Stalin campaign, insufficiencies in almost all fields, from biology to machinery to literature and art, were blamed at least in part on the Stalinist past. "The remnants of bourgeois ideology," which had traditionally served as the culprit for substandard performance and educational insufficiency throughout Soviet history, were replaced with "the remnants of Stalinism" as the corrupting force in national education. Not only did this tactic of blame provide an easy scapegoat for unsolved problems in the nation's educational system, but it also offered a means through which educators could express their support for reform and even, at times, use these new criticisms to enact significant changes.

The apparent consequences of Stalinist education, many educators argued, was that Soviet youth lacked the creativity needed to compete in the Cold War—a trait that made it possible for American children to become designers of supercolliders as adults. As one Komsomol leader reported tentatively in 1957, "Soviet education must examine earlier approaches to education that existed before Stalin. American children have been educated in a system that bears some weak resemblances to these earlier methods." In contrast, he argued that Soviet schools had, in recent decades, "inadequately fostered imagination and ingenuity among their students." This threat of a "one-sided education" challenged not only the country's economic development but also the ongoing efforts of the state to imagine its children, and itself, as powerful, adaptable agents in the Cold War crusade. A country of dogmatically educated children presented a problematic image for a nation that was struggling to present itself as culturally and scientifically "forward" and "modern."[60] While such admissions bore little resemblance to the open admiration expressed for Soviet education by people like Derthick and Litchfield, in the Soviet context such a statement was brave indeed.

In 1957, Khrushchev finally articulated at the party level the need for a renewed examination of Soviet education. He declared that educating the nation's youngsters to be effective workers and creative thinkers in the sciences would foster the growth of a generation capable of matching or even surpassing American technological development in agriculture, industry, and the military. With these objectives in mind, he declared that "the current challenges faced by the Soviet Union place before the schools a new, great demand. School must commence with the speedy and creative development of modern science and industry."[61] Earlier, in 1954, urban schools, which had been separated by gender since 1943, had been desegregated.[62] In 1958, a whole series of educational changes were enacted in the Soviet Union that bore noticeable resemblances to progressive educational approaches that had been adopted in the United States in the 1930s and 40s (and had, as we have seen, started to go out of favor in America by the late 1950s). Khrushchev's reforms included an embracing of a kind of "life-adjustment" approach that directed a majority of secondary students into polytechnic schools for specialized training in industry and agriculture. Children who at the age of fifteen did not show exceptional abilities were directed into learning more "productive" skills. At the same time, the 1958 reforms also called for the construction of special schools meant to develop the abilities of students who showed promise in mathematics, the sciences, the arts, foreign languages, and music. While Khrushchev embraced an education program that included the construction of nursery and boarding schools (Internats) for bright children, American private schools began popping up all over the United States to provide carefully manicured curriculums to students whose parents and leaders wanted to make sure that they received an education that avoided the problems happening in the public schools.[63] The alterations that both the United States and the Soviet Union made to their education programs in the late 1950s reveal the porousness of pedagogical knowledge in these years and the extent to which an exchange of ideas over how to think about the education of the child was certainly taking place.

As in the United States, the Soviet Union in the late 1950s and early 1960s attempted a number of new programs that seemed to borrow from the lessons learned by the "Other" child. The Soviet Pioneer organization set up an All-Russia Physics and Mathematics Olympiad to provide development for children who showed real aptitude and to help them decide on a specialty that appealed to them.[64] Educators and Pioneer leaders began to publish papers and articles that acknowledged the need to reach children at as young an age as possible. As writer and journalist Marina Rachko would write of her review of Soviet schools in the early 1960s, "I asked them whether anyone could drive a tractor, had they been to the theatre, did they want to go to the city . . . what was the scariest thing they could remember in their lives. . . . The children vied with their answers. But there was nothing spirited in them. Not a spark of originality. I was sweating but my notepad remained empty. The reaction of the children was instinctive. They repeated what was always said in the newspapers and journals. Their conventional responses didn't even contain funny mistakes or the accidental charms of local dialect. Nobody had explicitly taught them this. They simply imbibed it with their mother's milk, the milk of mothers born in 1937."[65] Similarly, philosopher and writer Lydia Novikova argued that schoolchildren were "exhibiting inadequacies in abstract thinking," which prohibited them from mastering contemporary knowledge.[66] These inadequacies, she believed, were associated directly with a "poorly developed imagination and an underdeveloped ability to operate with symbols and symbolic descriptions." "What will the country do," she asked, "if every year we create highly developed people that are all of the same type? Socialist society must be interested in original individuals capable of revolution in the spheres of science, technology, and the organization of production." She prescribed for the next generation a change in the methods of instruction that would not only allow for creative thought and expression but also foster the kind of imaginative thinking that was necessary for success in the modern sciences. Such a change would satisfy the pressing need to produce smart, innovative scientists, she argued, and it would also permit the "realization of a person's individual potentialities."[67] Meanwhile, a directive sent out from the Central Committee of the Komsomol in February 1963 instructed educators to use only toys in the classroom that were "collapsible, built from various elements, or built from many parts that allow the student to construct different systems and shapes in creative and individual ways."[68] And even these efforts were thought by many to be insufficient. *Pravda* and *Izvestiia* argued as late as 1965 that Khrushchev's push for polytechnical schools had resulted in fewer students successfully finishing high school and that, although the Soviet Union had succeeded in producing a population of qualified engineers, the country was still behind America in the fields of physics, chemistry, and the natural sciences.[69]

Interestingly, the Soviets were also aware of the fact that educators in the United States were paying attention to the traditions of more disciplined Soviet education. For instance, in one report by the Soviet Committee on Children, which was funded by the Komsomol in 1961 to explore the state of American education, the author declared that in America "an educational system similar to ours has arisen that presents a serious danger, and which in the technical sector, for instance, shows that the Americans are increasingly able to compete with the Soviet Union. This has happened because America has 'changed its course' and has begun to strengthen its schools with increasing selections of stronger students and fixed, programmatical teaching."[70] This was written just as scholars like Novikova were arguing that such rote approaches to pedagogy were in fact *not* what Soviet children needed in the classroom.

There is clear irony in the fact that the educational approaches that each side appeared to admire in its enemy were the very same approaches that the enemy was trying to eradicate in itself. Derthick and Litchfield spoke glowingly of the efficiency and discipline brought on by Stalinist education, just as such methods were being altered in the Soviet Union. Likewise, Novikova expressed admiration for a child-centered approach to education that had, by the late 1950s, been largely tabled in the United States. This dialectic over the relative merits and faults of the enemy's education reveals the extent to which educators and political leaders on both sides of the Iron Curtain frequently agreed in ways that had more to do with who they were (as teachers and as politicians) than it did with what they believed (in communism or in

Figure 2.8. The promise of Soviet education is contrasted with American schools in this poster from 1957. The top caption reads, "In the USSR: During the period 1951 to 1955 the number of rural and city schools will increase by approximately 70 percent when compared to the previous five-year period." The bottom caption reads, "In the USA, 1 percent of their budget is spent on education and 74 percent on military spending. There are more than 10 million illiterate children." "V SSSR: V SShA" (In the USSR: In the USA). RGASPI f. m6, op. 14, d. 57, l. 10. © Fine Art Images.

capitalism). The educational debates that emerged in these years between proponents of progressive education and those who supported traditional, rote pedagogical methods were frequently demarcated not by geography or ideology, but instead by methodology and pedagogical allegiances.

Conclusion

Jeremi Suri has noted in his study of American higher education in the 1960s that the reforms undertaken in these years, which were intended to create a "learned citizenry [that] would out-compete its Soviet counterparts," ultimately taught youngsters the skills they needed to become dissidents, to question their own leaders, and to undermine "the domestic foundations of Cold War foreign policy."[71] A "cultural contradiction of the Cold War" emerged, where the act of mobilizing the young for national defense resulted in the defense being compromised. Suri's observations, which focus on the American-sponsored education of university students in West Berlin in the 1960s, pinpoint a moment when young, educated adults found themselves incapable of reconciling what they had learned from their American teachers with the seeming hypocrisy of American policy. Such contradictions were not relegated to higher education or to the United States, however, and they arose not only as a result of improved education, but as a consequence of the evolving image of the "Other" child. Wild American kids and robotic Soviet youngsters assumed the mythologized identity of destroyed children living on the other side of the Iron Curtain. They stood in contrast to the seemingly protected and happy kids at home. Yet, as the years progressed, it became increasingly difficult to ignore the real children within both countries whose protection and happiness were actually imperiled by Cold War policies. These included Native American, Mormon, Pacific Islander, and numerous groups of Soviet kids living near nuclear testing zones, as well as children designated as "retarded" who were used as subjects for radiation experiments.[72] What did it mean when the image of the imperiled "Other" child increasingly resembled your own?

In the early to mid-1950s, the image of the "Other" child had served as a touchstone upon which populations on both sides of the Iron Curtain could construct a Cold War consensus. It demonized, victimized, and militarized the enemy and its children. While leaders and politicians in the Soviet Union produced visions of white American, African American, and postcolonial children in varying states of exploitation, their counterparts in the United States worked to show the dire effects of communism upon Russian and East

European youths. The specter of the "Other" became an archetypal image that for both sides represented a terrifying alternative universe filled with suffering children. Such visions served as prescriptives for those who might be unsure where their allegiances should lie.

Yet, as leaders and propagandists set out to show that they could protect the young and, by proxy, provide national security, they discovered that the vision of the "Other" child was not as simple or as clearly comprehensible as they had previously believed. They found themselves in the uncomfortable position of having to recognize that the "Other" child, while abhorrent and pitiable, might also carry traits that could give it an advantage in the long fight to come. While such acknowledgments were understandable, the process of recognizing the strengths of the "Other" child and the scramble to match those strengths with the children at home opened the door for a cultural paradox that went beyond what Suri has observed in his research. It was the increasingly complicated image of the "Other" child (and its ability to grow up and put rockets in space or think abstractly) that spawned movements on both sides of the Iron Curtain to improve education. As Suri has noted, these improvements, which were originally intended to bolster the Cold War consensus, ultimately provided the young with the tools they needed to see the hypocrisies in their own leadership. But more than this, the very act of acknowledging and complicating the previously reified image of the "Other" child undermined the visual foundation upon which that original image had been built. The "Other" child had, by the late 1950s, become something that both supported and at times undermined the Cold War consensus. Popular beliefs about the "Other" child could not be handily reduced to simplistic metonyms for the apparent suffering and destitution on the other side of the Iron Curtain. These children were not just pitiable, they were threatening, intelligent, and even, at times, loved. This begins to account for the increasing skepticism among populations on both sides of the Iron Curtain about each state's ability to realize the promises it made in the postwar period. These dichotomous images also revealed the muddled nature of the Cold War itself. Ostensibly, it was a conflict that pitted democracy against tyranny, with clear ideological divides between East and West. However, there was always the risk that each populace would start to see the "Other" in a new light, not as violent or robotic, but as similar to itself, with strengths and flaws and shared desires for the future of its children. This created the possibility of viewing the Cold War as a struggle between those who shape policy and those who do not, between those who construct the image of the enemy and those who are expected to believe in it. It was at this point that the divides of the war began to shift.

CHAPTER THREE

Victims, Hooligans, and the Importance of Threat

The image of the child had still more functions to perform in the construction of a Cold War consensus. Back in 1949, at the Eleventh Komsomol Congress, the young Svetlana Zhiltsova had delivered five minutes of care fully constructed and memorized text meant to establish an idealized vision of protected and happy Soviet children. But before Svetlana took her turn at the podium, the first secretary of the Komsomol, P. A. Mikhailov, had made his introductions. Mikhailov's job was to raise the American specter and to position the Soviet child as a target of threats coming from outside and inside the country's borders—threats that could only be held at bay by the protective power of the regime and by the policing and self-regulation of the population as a whole. "At the end of the Great Patriotic War the world split into two camps," he declared in his famously resonant voice. "The anti-democratic camp, under the leadership of the American imperialists, initiated the struggle against socialism and democracy and prepared for a new war. These reactionaries created an atmosphere of war hysteria, scraping together political unions and blocs devoted to war, all directed against the Soviet Union and the democratic countries of the world." Applause rose up from the audience. Raising his hand, Mikhailov continued: "Anglo-American imperialism, in its struggle against the Soviet Union, against all the freedom-loving people of the world, and especially against their young, is not squeamish about the means it uses to reach its goals. Blackmail, extortion, economic and political pressure, bribery, trickery, and lies—these are all characteristics of thieving, imperialistic politics."[1] Finishing his oration, he declared that it was the obligation of the Soviet Union to "vigilantly defend youth from pernicious foreign influences."[2] This language was not new for those at the meeting; the threat of capitalist encirclement had been a mantra of Bolshevik rhetoric since the Revolution. Yet, as Mikhailov knew, old language could serve a new purpose. It could illustrate an enemy and mobilize a population. It could legitimate the culture of containment and the policing of the population in ways that no other imperative could.

On the other side of the Atlantic, the language of Cold War threat against the young sounded surprisingly similar. A sixteen-year-old, Irwin Herman, from the Bronx, declared in October 1949 during a youth forum of New York City public and private school students that communism was a disease that threatened the children of America. In a panel devoted to exploring the question "How Can We Best Meet the Threats to Democracy?" he and his peers cited the tactics of the Communist Party and its curtailment of civil rights, its embrace of totalitarian governments, of war and repression, as the main sources of threat to the young.[3] Such language persisted throughout the 1950s. Five years later, in what was perhaps the most vitriolic articulation of generalized communist threat to the young to come from the U.S. government, Frederick Brown Harris, the chaplain for the Senate, warned his flock that "the hideous face of atheistic world communism at long last is unveiled for all who have eyes to see. It is the most monstrous mass of organized evil that history has known. It is the sum of all villainies. The idealist mask which, from the genesis of this deceptive revolution, covered its cruel sadistic countenance, now has been torn to shreds by heartless policies and designs upon humanity's most innocent and most helpless."[4] The rhetoric of threat upon the child would become a leitmotif that dominated mainstream Cold War discourse and transformed it into an identifying trope for populations on both sides of the Iron Curtain. Lurking just beneath happy visions of domestic youth and scary representations of the "Other" child, sat equally prolific images of children at home, vulnerable to attack.

Much to the dismay of American and Russian leaders, educators, and parents, threats to the young also seemed to come from within their own borders. Oversexualized, spoiled, and apathetic children appeared to be multiplying in the cities and towns. In their search for a cause, concerned adults turned their gazes to their own homes and schools, to substandard education and housing, and to the corrupting and weakening influences brought on by lazy parenting, the media, and the rise of consumer culture. By the time the 1960s dawned, it appeared to many as though society's hold over its children was weakening. More and more kids as young as nine and ten were being institutionalized for violent crimes and status offenses like truancy, running away, and liquor violations.[5] By 1965, the label of "delinquent" or "hooligan" and the deviance it implied had led to a massive upsurge in the number of legal interventions by Soviet and American authorities to stop the "pandemic" of disorder among each nation's young.[6]

This perceived presence of external and internal threat led many American and Soviet citizens to embrace the imposition of their own repression. Threat created a particular kind of perspective on the world, riddled with unseen predators and a loss of individual control over one's environment, which demanded containment and a limiting of the boundaries of acceptable behavior and language.[7] In the words of the late Sharon Stephens, the child represented "the vulnerable domestic core" of society. "Protecting this domestic world from its enemies would then require—and legitimate—a vast national defense apparatus." Childhood was integrally bound to "the ideology of the . . . national security state."[8] Regardless of whether or not these threats were real, they nonetheless performed an important constitutive role in shaping how both populations were expected to understand the nature of the Cold War. They provided instruction on what was needed from the populace in order that they might defend themselves, their children, and their countries. Soviet and American consensus builders used the image of the threatened Cold War child to solidify control over the language of the Cold War. Ironically, these new visions of threat would do as much to undermine the Cold War consensus as they would to support it.

Threats from "Over There"

Images that appear regularly in everyday life, like those of children, can reveal the anxieties of the society that creates and consumes them.[9] When, in the early 1950s, many in the American government and in the private sector claimed that the nation's children were at risk of communist ideological infiltration in their schools and homes, they were articulating a much larger fear regarding the threat of outside invasion into the most protected of the country's domestic spaces. They contended that Soviet ideological and nuclear attack was a possibility for every American, especially its children. American kids became symbols for a new threat that was hard to identify and even harder to combat.

The rhetoric of J. Edgar Hoover best reflected this general sense of attack upon the young. Hoover was the self-appointed protector of America's children throughout the first two decades of the Cold War. As he reported to the Senate in 1959, "Today's youth are tomorrow's future. No one is more acutely aware of this fact than are the Communist conspirators—and no one is more eager to exploit them."[10] Many other state leaders chimed in with the same message. Eugene Anderson, who had been ambassador to Denmark, lamented at the Seventh Annual Convention of Americans for Democratic

Action that "the fundamental threat to us all, and to our children, is and remains aggressive Soviet communism."[11] In 1955, representatives like Daniel Flood, the flamboyant Democratic congressman from Pennsylvania, introduced a joint resolution in the House as a part of his duties in the newly formed Institute of Fiscal and Political Education "to promote the teaching in American schools of the differences between the theories and practices of the American way of life and the theories and practices of atheistic communism."[12] The resolution argued that whereas the "atheistic communist system forcibly takes the children from their parents at an early age and places them in state-controlled schools . . . our youth will be better prepared to withstand the cruel and inhuman treatment they can expect to receive at the hands of their captors if they should become prisoners of war."[13]

The most commonly cited locus for suspected communist infiltration among the country's children was in the schools. Significant scholarly attention has already been given to the dangers that communism was perceived to present to American education in the 1950s and 60s.[14] Without question, the image of the schoolchild was deeply enmeshed in a national struggle to combat covert communist ideological instruction in education. For instance, during the now famous 1952 *Adler v. Board of Education*, in which eight teachers challenged the Feinberg Law that had been used to justify firing them for their suspected communist affiliation, the presiding judges conjured an image of a victimized child under siege as justification for indicting the accused teachers. In writing for the majority when the Supreme Court decided the case by upholding the Feinberg Law, Justice Sherman Minton argued that "a teacher works in a sensitive area in a schoolroom. There he shapes the attitude of young minds towards the society in which they live. In this, the state has a vital concern." He, along with a majority of his colleagues, concluded that "New York has a legitimate police power to protect the schools from pollution."[15]

The rhetoric of communist infiltration in the schools lasted well into the 1960s. For example, at the beginning of his much-reprinted essay "America's Little Red Schoolhouse," Republican congressman Karl Mundt argued that communists were "openly teaching subversion in the United States."[16] Of particular concern to many conservative and centrist politicians was the reversal by the Supreme Court in February 1967 of the Feinberg Law, which had kept "subversives" out of the New York public school system since 1952. The result was a popular vote for a "Sense of Congress" resolution arguing that the Supreme Court decision should be overruled "in favor of the right to self-preservation."[17] Such accusations, which were leveled by Hoover, by the Judiciary, and by the Senate, portrayed accused teachers as predators of

Figure 3.1. A comic from the National Catholic Guild presents an image of communist instruction in America's schools. The Catholic Guild, "This Godless Communism." *Treasure Chest* (1961): 7. Courtesy of Catholic University.

children and attempted to cast them as a source of threat and danger for the country.

Following the lead of Congress, private organizations joined in by portraying American youth as threatened by subversive teachers. Throughout the 1950s and 60s, the American Textbooks Publishers Institute warned parents to be on the watch for "whisperings that your child's textbooks are subversive."[18] Similarly, a number of conservative activists, namely Lucille Cardin Crain, who issued the *Educational Reviewer* newsletter, and Allen Zoll, who was a prolific pamphleteer and the head of the National Council for American Education, took it as their mandate to weed out "subversive" material from public school textbooks and to take aim at progressive education in the United States. Zoll's popular pamphlets carried titles like "The Commies Are After Your Kids" and "Progressive Education Increases Juvenile Delinquency." They actively campaigned against texts like Frank Magruder's *American Government*, which they argued promoted communism by supporting the United Nations Charter and by stating that the U.S. Postal Service was an example of a working socialist system. Such groups were consistently successful in impeding the distribution of so-called subversive books across the country, including works by Mark Twain, Bertrand Russell, and George Bernard Shaw. They undertook these crusades in order to ensure, in Crain's words, that the "historical narrative presented to the child" not only complies with the country's larger views on communism, but also helps to create for its youth an "ideological base that could withstand Soviet influence."[19]

The fear of communism derived much of its power from the threat of loss: particularly loss of private property, civil rights, control over family, and religion. In 1961, the Catholic publisher George Phlaum published a comic book series called "Treasure Chest" with a many-part volume entitled "This Godless Communism."[20] Week after week, the strip sought to educate parents and their children on what life would be like under communist rule. At the beginning of each edition, J. Edgar Hoover wrote a letter reminding his readers that "communism represents the most serious threat facing our way of life." Over a series of ten graphically drawn pages, the comic imagined the invasion and takeover of the United States by communists. The opening frames show a family gathered before a television screen to hear that the United States no longer exists. The family flees to church to ask God's help, only to find that it has been turned into a communist museum and the priests have been sent to labor camps. They try to contact their congressional representatives, only to learn that they too have been removed. The next day, the children head to school to find a new teacher, who informs them that communism will give them "heaven on earth" and that "man has no soul." She encourages them to be heroes by reporting to the authorities if their parents speak out against the new regime. Back at home, the father tells his family, "They've taken away all our rights." Finally, on the following day, the family is torn apart as the father is ordered to report to work at a lumber mill in Wisconsin while his wife remains at a factory in Chicago. When the father asks the party apparatchik who will care for the children while his wife works, the man replies that "the government will take care of children in special schools and nurseries. They will see their mother on weekends." "If I and my fellow Americans had only realized how horrible communism really is!" reads a thought-bubble above the face of the distressed father as his wife is pictured laboring over a lathe and his children are seen abandoned in a large room full of cribs. For the Catholic Guild that commissioned the publishing of this series, the primary loss was that of the church, which represented the first line of defense against communism. After that, the Catholic Guild implied that all the other rights guaranteed to the American citizenry would fall away without much of a fight.[21]

These many expressions of fear reveal the extent to which the perceived danger of communism was enmeshed in a vocabulary of disease in the United States, as the epidemiology of one reflected the fears of the other.[22] For instance, Howard McGrath, who served as attorney general from 1949 to 1952, was known for his remarks concerning the "plague of communism" upon American society. Each Communist Party member, he remarked in a 1950 speech to members of Congress, "carries in himself the germ of death for our society."[23] According to Hubert Humphrey, the Communist Party represented "a political cancer in our society" that threatened to "grow unseen until it was too late to stop it." To Adlai Stevenson, communism was "worse than cancer, tuberculosis, and heart disease combined."[24] One disease threatened the physical body while another menaced the body politic.

Articulations of the communist threat shared a similarity with popular American rhetoric on the frightening menace of childhood polio. Both threats manifested initially in innocuous ways: polio could look like a simple cold while communism might be spread through seemingly innocent petitions and causes. Both "diseases" could be anywhere, a danger unseen and undetectable. Moreover, both crises received vast amounts of public attention and tended to cause panic, with the tempered voices of experts like Dr. Spock (who reminded his readers of the statistical unlikelihood of any particular child contracting polio) and Edward R. Murrow (who rejected the Red Scare) often being drowned out by sensationalist headlines. Finally, in apparently attacking without regard to class or status, both of these "diseases," in the words of David Oshinsky, "mocked the dreams of middle-class culture."[25] As Barbara Holland put it in her autobiography, communism "was more dangerous than Hitler because it was invisible, and everywhere, like polio. Your next-door neighbor might be pretending to be an ordinary person, with kids and a lawn-mower, when he was really a Communist in disguise, and simply living next door to him might infect you, invisibly."[26] All of these images of impending assault upon the young attempted to establish in the minds of the American public an image of the United States as a nonaggressor country that was under siege by an unstoppable menace and helped to establish what would become a national mandate to defend the country, its children, and its friends from the perceived deceptions of world communism.

These images of threat appeared with comparable frequency in the Soviet Union. Public indictments of Anglo-American imperialism found their way into public rhetoric with regularity. This had been the case since the very beginnings of the Cold War, when Stalin declared during his famous 1946 election speech that monopoly capitalism had caused the catastrophe of World War II and the suffering of the Soviet people that had followed. Similarly, a strong language of threat appeared in discussions of supposed Jewish- and Western-influenced conspiracies like those of the Doctors' Plot, when Stalin accused Jewish doctors of widespread assassinations in 1952–53. The Soviet population had become accustomed since the Revolution and certainly the Terror to warnings regarding the threat of ideological deviants in its midst. The articulated risk of American bourgeois influence in the 1950s borrowed from that legacy and provided a linguistic and visual tie to older visions of "capitalist encirclement."

Yet the Soviet rhetoric of threat was different from its American counterpart in one noteworthy way. Whereas the threat of capitalist encirclement was a constant motif in Stalinist rhetoric, it was never articulated as a danger against which the population could not protect itself. There were no comic books published with terrifying stories of life under capitalism. When it came to bourgeois threats to youth, Soviet official discourse made it clear that the Anglo-Americans never had a chance. For instance, in the spring of 1949, the agitation arm of the Communist Party commissioned the writing of nine lectures that were to be delivered to Komsomol and Pioneer groups throughout the country. The focus of these lectures was to be on the struggle to defend peace and socialism by Soviet children as well as the youth of Eastern Europe and the postcolonial world. According to Komsomol records, these lectures had been heard by 7.5 million people by the end of 1950. Even if such numbers were inflated, there can be little doubt that a sizable percentage of kids, teenagers, and adults heard these lectures (which would have been read out loud by a Komsomol or Pioneer representative). All of them uniformly began with a discussion of the capitalist threat faced by the youth of the socialist world.[27] "The entire postwar period reveals how, despite the vain attempts of the capitalist world to undermine the movement of the democratic masses on the path toward democratic socialism, the power of the democratic camp grows and strengthens with each passing day."[28] Discussions ranged from the support of Bulgarian children for the socialist cause to explorations of the growing strength of socialist youth in France (despite the influx of American-sponsored "war materials"). The clear goal of these lectures was to present an overwhelming sense of indomitable defensive solidarity among the youth and children of the socialist and even nonsocialist world. As a result, the capitalist threat was portrayed as an unworthy adversary. "In all facets of the Western world," one lecture concluded, "in Europe and in America, in Asia and in Africa, millions of ordinary people who work in incalculable poverty seek the truth to human life. They seek freedom."[29]

The Communist Party adopted this qualified rhetoric of threat because its leaders knew that in the world of public opinion, threat is a double-edged sword. As useful as these dangers might be in demonizing the enemy, the recognition of such perils, of ideological and physical invasion, especially among the young, had the potential to undermine the Party's claim as protector of the nation. In a country where acknowledging the genocidal nature of nuclear war also meant admitting to the Party's and Stalin's inability to defend the populace (not to mention the fallibility of historical determinism), such conversations were better left muted. Admission of threat could imply an admission of weakness. The American-style rhetoric of direct and terrifying invasion was not a useful device in Soviet Cold War discourse, but a language of vigilant defensibility under the leadership of the Party was. This language of manageable threat became a defining feature of the Cold War in the Soviet Union and was vital in the building of popular consensus. It contributed to what the poet Bella Akhmadulina called the "dream" and the "banality" of Soviet life, all done to shape the political imagination of the Cold War.[30] The population did not need to panic over the capitalist threat as long as it continued to offer support for its government's policies. In the United States, the message was that the new threat of communism now demanded a new response by the populace. In the Soviet Union, the message was that capitalism had always been a threat, and it was only because of the Party and the population's continued support for its leadership that safety could continue to be ensured. Not surprisingly, it would be in the spaces left by these omissions that Soviet writers and filmmakers would work to examine their pasts, and the Cold War, with more honesty.

Although the articulated levels of threat from outside infiltration were different in the Soviet Union than in the United States, the roles that such threats played were nonetheless similar. Both ostensibly provided a vehicle for the continued figuration of the enemy. Both allowed for the construction of a defensive ethos based on a siege mentality. Both constituted a viable justification for the population's continued dependence on the state's protection. Perhaps most importantly, both reflected the dual nature of what it meant to live through the Cold War. One strain of Cold War rhetoric argued that children's lives (like those of their families) were defined by security, prosperity, and great promise for the future. Yet, at the same time, another equally pervasive strain contended that the lives of the young were marked by unprecedented vulnerability, decrepitude, and invasion. These children were one and the same. It is at the collision of these two identities that the genesis for the constructions and collapse of the Cold War consensus can be found. How can a child (or a populace) be protected, vulnerable, joyous, and under attack at the same time? Does one not negate the other? While the production of these images served clear purposes for the manufacturing of public consent, it also presented contradictions that were increasingly hard to ignore.

Hooligans and Deadbeat Dads: Threat from Within

External attack upon the nation's young was not the only danger over which parents needed to worry in these years. Beginning quietly in the postwar era and increasing to a fever pitch by the late 1960s, domestic problems like delinquency, bad parenting, sexual deviance, consumerism, and pervasive media translated into dangers that imperiled not just the children but national security as well. To the dismay of many, a generation seemed to be coming of age whose ability to wage the Cold War was seriously compromised. This was one of the primary reasons that governments on both sides of the Iron Curtain took unprecedented legal steps to intervene in the lives of the young. They did this because it was thought by many that parents simply had no idea how to raise Cold War kids. They also took these steps because the state management of children provided an avenue of intervention into the private lives of the populace that could be used in the construction and policing of the Cold War consensus.

The largest and most discussed crisis for the young in the 1950s and 60s was childhood delinquency and criminality. Hooliganism emerged as a crisis in the Soviet Union in the years following World War II, and particularly after Stalin's death. It is best known as a problem that existed among teenagers, not children. For example, in 1953, a group of Polish adolescents occupied sections of the town of Lodz after hearing rumors that policemen had been beating students.[31] By 1956, convictions for hooliganism in Russia had risen to 200,000 annually from the already-high number of 70,000 ten years earlier.[32] This number would more than double in the following year after the Council of Ministers and the Communist Party Central Committee strengthened penalties for crimes of petty hooliganism.[33] By 1961, hooliganism had become a part of what Vladimir Kozlov has called the "Crisis of Liberal Communism," in which the loosening of censorship led to mass uprisings of young people, first in Krasnodar in January 1961 and then famously in Novocherkassk in the summer of 1962.[34]

It was against the backdrop of that summer, when adolescents were quoted by informants as "cursing Khrushchev as a traitor to the cause of communism," that adults increasingly came to view hooliganism as a threat to the country's younger children and as a danger to national security. In 1962, thirteen years after nine-year-old Svetlana Zhiltsova gave her memorable speech, the Fourteenth Komsomol Congress met. Like their counterparts in the West, delegates gathered to address what they perceived to be a delinquency crisis. Antisocial behavior among the young had been a point of discussion at all the previous thirteen Komsomol Congresses, but this one witnessed a 300 percent increase in references to troubled youth from a decade earlier, not just by Communist Party members, but by teachers and concerned parents as well.[35] On the issue of children, one speaker after another reported that fewer

Pioneers were showing interest in joining the Komsomol, while increasing numbers were following street gangs that delighted in American music, dress, and language.[36] Amid rising evidence that the nation's kids were falling prey to delinquency, the Communist Party, as well as parents and teachers, argued that children were at risk of "falling under the radar" and ultimately compromising the nation's security.[37] As one distraught Komsomol leader announced, "If children, who maintain their spiritless disinterest towards the activities of school and the Pioneers do not take part, and instead disturb the rules of social order, they will become hooligans who threaten our nation and our battle with the capitalist world."[38] At least two educators at the Congress reported that between 15 and 30 percent of youths between the ages of eight and eleven had failing grades in most subjects. "If we do not stop it now, this will lead to hooliganism, which threatens our struggle with the capitalist countries," one particularly concerned speaker commented.[39] For those in the Soviet Union who were aware of the rising juvenile delinquency rates in Europe and the United States, such statistics made these countries uncomfortable bedfellows. The Cold War was not the only reason these issues elicited concern by Soviet adults in the 1950s and 60s. Most historians who have examined the rise of hooliganism in these years have not particularly cited the Cold War as a part of what they see as a largely domestic story of reform and counter-reform on the difficult path to socialism. And yet there can be no denying that the Cold War amplified these fears and gave them international meaning.[40] When childhood experts and Communist Party members brought forth images of hooligan children, they frequently did so in the context of the struggle with the West.

In their search for the sources of this apparent decay in youth culture, they increasingly found that it was not possible to blame all these problems on the Stalinist inheritance alone. Instead, they argued that coddling and negligent parenting provided an explanation for the apparent deterioration of discipline among the nation's children—a conclusion that would be made at the same time by adults in the United States. In 1959, the pedagogue and Pioneer leader Irina Pechernikova described the spoiling and pandering that she was witnessing among parents in the Soviet Union. Using a language that would have been familiar to American writers like Philip Wylie, who was famous for coining the term "momism" in 1942, Pechernikova argued that "some parents try to obtain the love of their children by catering senselessly to their whims, by forgiving everything and not demanding anything." This kind of parental "love," she contended, "can produce nothing but harm." She warned that as a result of this indulgence, children would develop into "egotistical despots, accustomed to a life of idleness and loafing."[41] Later Komsomol documents concurred with Pechernikova's assessment, claiming that such "moods of dependency" (*nastroeniia izhdivenstva*) among children led inevitably to a loss of desire to attend university or to work. They argued that children would fail to defend the nation, would lose their ideological strength, and would simply conclude that life is "gifted" to them—"based entirely on the hard-earned money of their parents."[42]

Not only did spoiling parents produce lazy children, sociologists and party members contended, they also threatened to produce a generation that had no discipline and could not control their own impulses. This was the argument made by Tigran Atarov, a sociologist who stated in 1959 in a Komsomol document that the tendency of parents to "satisfy their children's wishes immediately" had rendered children from a very young age incapable of controlling their sexual urges. In a fashion similar to other contemporary reports on hooliganism and parasitism, Atarov was forced to look not only to bourgeois influence, but also to rising consumerism and bad parents within the nation for the causes of the deviant conduct that he witnessed. "Since [these youths] never lived under a capitalist system," he reasoned, "their undesirable behavior can only be explained by incorrect education and bad influences in the home and in the adult environment."[43] This assertion reflected a newfound willingness among sociologists, child experts, censors, and even party leaders to see the causes of delinquency as coming from homegrown weaknesses and inefficiencies.

Just as destructive as spoiling parents, many Soviet child experts argued in the early 1960s, were adults who chose to avoid their parenting responsibilities because of drunkenness or general apathy. This problem was of particular concern to Soviet youth leaders, who in the wake of World War II were faced with a vast shortage of men in the nation who were physically and emotionally capable of mentoring the next generation. For instance, the educational theorist Stal' Shmakov focused on the lack of supervision and parenting that the young faced at home. "So many of our boys are developing without supervision or a father figure and, while they require care, love, and attention, what they need most is firmness, reasonable demands, and courage. The Pioneers of today are tomorrow's adolescents who have a harder task to face while actively participating in new endeavors."[44] Party newspapers like *Komsomol'skaia pravda* and *Pionerskaia pravda*, as well as the satirical magazine *Krokodil*, constantly highlighted children and teenagers being indulged or abused by overprotective mother-hens and drunken, violent fathers. In almost all of their articles, the suffering or delinquent child was a

Figure 3.2. The caption from this *Krokodil* illustration reads, "Busy Hands. . . . As soon as our Sasha has grown up, we are going to vote wholeheartedly for the reform of the school," a commentary on Khrushchev's push to rebuild the schools and the perceived damage that the country's coddling parents were doing to that program. *Krokodil*, 20 December 1958, 5.

young boy who had been transformed into a weak, feminized baby or had been abandoned, made drunk, or beaten by a father who was often pictured in a uniform and sick with alcohol. The popular press portrayed the mother as refusing to allow her son to grow up because of her constant spoiling and the father, regardless of his own suffering, as refusing to play his role as the shaper of the next generation. As a result, boys in particular were portrayed as either weak and sickly—reliant too much on the comforts of their mothers' care, reluctant to work, and uninterested in the affairs of state—or, in the words of sociologist Liudmila Kovaleva, violent and chaotic—inhabiting the "sad streets that reverberate with the cries of hurt children, cursing, police whistles, and the sound of running feet."[45]

Across the Atlantic, many American leaders, parents, and scholars were too busy worrying about the impact of rock music, alternative dress, and bad language upon their own young to revel in this newfound Soviet anxiety. American concern over delinquency had become a topic of official concern since Democratic senator Claude Pepper had convened hearings on the physical and educational fitness of Americans in 1943. This concern only deepened as the Cold War continued.[46] Eleven years later, Sidney Yates, a Democratic congressman from Illinois, would state while speaking at the annual meeting of the Young Men's Jewish Council, "The nation has a real problem on its hands, for which the causes are many and for which there is no single remedy."[47] J. Edgar Hoover, who was the self-proclaimed authority on threat, put it even more bluntly when he wrote, "I see in the juvenile delinquent a threat to the very core of what it means to be American. . . . Dangerous parts of the next generation have lost all respect for law and decency."[48] Just as in the Soviet Union, the problem of children threatened and made delinquent by internal weaknesses dominated public rhetoric.

Whether or not America actually experienced a rise in childhood delinquency rates in the 1950s remains a topic of debate among historians. As James Gilbert points out, in terms of sheer numbers, the country did experience an increase in juvenile and childhood crime from the early 1950s to the mid-1960s.[49] For example, the New York City Police Department reported a 400 percent increase in arrests of children under the age of sixteen between 1950 and 1964.[50] Similar national reports show a 29 percent rise in criminal cases for children between the ages of ten and fourteen.[51] In 1966, James Symington, the chair of the President's Committee on Juvenile Delinquency, argued that "17 percent of today's 10-year-old boys will be brought before juvenile court. . . . That estimate reaches 40 percent in some urban ghetto areas."[52] Yet it is worth keeping in mind that these numbers did not always reflect changes among a controlled group. Thanks to the baby boom, youth populations were on the rise all over the country, and the types of activities designated as "criminal" changed significantly in these years. Thus, while criminal cases for children rose 29 percent between 1950 and 1964, the population of children overall grew by 33 percent.

Regardless of whether or not American childhood criminality actually was on the rise, we can be certain that many people from across the social spectrum believed that it was. As in the Soviet Union, politicians, sociologists, and writers cited as a primary cause of these issues the existence of coddling and negligent parents who were failing to do their part in raising the next generation to meet the rising Cold War challenge. J. Edgar Hoover argued that many of America's children had "been pawns in the buck-passing tactics of those parents who shirk their responsibilities to the country's youth."[53] The press depicted overindulgent mothers as "nagging nellies" who smothered their boys and girls with material goods. While psychiatrists had been making such arguments since the turn of the century, the image of the spoiling mother did not become popular until 1942, when the writer Philip Wylie coined the term "momism" in his best-selling book *Generation of Vipers*. Wylie argued that frustrated, smothering mothers were making their sons weak and passive while encouraging their daughters to emulate them and their overbearing ways.[54] Using a language that would have seemed familiar to many social scientists on the other side of the Iron Curtain, Wylie championed the belief that the best mothers were the ones who remained detached from their children's lives and instead allowed them to be hardened by their fathers and by the world around them. He in turn combined his belief in the weakening of the next generation with his virulent hatred of communism to build the popular argument that the negative effects of momism, particularly upon boys, would seriously compromise the nation and make it susceptible to enemy attack. By the 1950s, in the words of Erik Erikson, there had developed "a manifest literary sport in books decrying the mothers of this country as 'Moms.'"[55]

Fathers fared no better in popular assessments of their child-raising abilities. Instead of portraying American fathers as neglectful, drunk, and damaged by war (as in the Soviet Union), sociologists, psychiatrists, legal authorities, and the popular press often portrayed the traditional patriarch as soft and weak, made apathetic by postwar affluence, overbearing wives, and the emasculation of the modern workplace.[56] Such men were frequently identified as the causes of the apparent apathy and disrespect that the next generation seemed to exhibit toward its elders. In December 1957, for instance, the well-known Brooklyn judge Samuel Liebowitz (made famous for his defense of the Scottsboro Boys in the 1930s) made a direct connection between the impotence of fathers in the home and the increase in childhood delinquency that he witnessed every day in his court. "How many parents have stood before me after I have sentenced their children to prison and asked, 'Judge, what did I do that was wrong? I sacrificed for home. I gave him a good life, put him through school.' It's not what they did, it's what they did not do. They did not put father in charge of the family but let him surrender his rightful and needful leadership to mother. They did not teach their child discipline."[57] For Liebowitz, American fathers had become "losers in one of our greatest tragedies" and, along with spoiling mothers, had created a home environment that was conducive to delinquency.

Tied closely to these condemnations of spoiling and negligent parents were additional concerns about threats to traditional gender roles in American society. For children, aggressive female sexuality and momism, coupled with emasculated male figures in the home, were presented as direct threats to the creation of self-controlling heterosexual boys and girls in America. This was not a new argument; the psychologist, nursery school teacher, and writer Helen Thompson Woolley had argued in 1922 that there was a direct connection between strong mothers, weak fathers, and "sissy" boys.[58] Yet, in the 1950s, this fear was compounded by the threat of communism and its perceived relationship with out-of-control sexuality and homosexuality. As Elaine Tyler May, Robert Dean, and Robert Corber have shown, many people in the government and in medicine "believed wholeheartedly that there was a direct connection between communism and sexual depravity."[59] People who were sexually "normal" were also likely to be politically "normal." During the Red Scare, homosexuals were frequently suspected of communist affiliation because they were perceived to be participating in an activity that disrupted the social and sexual order and also required that they live a secret life that was open to blackmail.[60] Many believed that communism itself was somehow less masculine. This is reflected in Arthur Schlesinger's description of communism as "something secret, sweaty and furtive like nothing so much, in the phrase of one wise observer of modern Russia, as homosexuals in a boys' school."[61]

Just as Tigran Atarov was pointing to the seeming inability of Soviet children to control their sexual urges, so too were American psychologists, politicians, and private citizens arguing that the threats of sexual promiscuity and deviance among the young presented a credible threat to national security. As the historian John D'Emilio has pointed out, many conservatives in the United States believed that the very same leaders in the American government who had allowed the West to "lose" China and Eastern Europe to the Soviets had been "sissies" as children.[62] Just as these men had "feminized everything they touched" and had "sapped the masculine vigor that had tamed a continent," so too did the current generation of boys appear to endanger the country if they were allowed to become weak and feminine. These paired threats of homosexuality and communism were not reserved for boys. As one group wrote to the Johns Committee in Florida in 1963, "Lesbianism, which has been promulgated and perpetuated by many female teachers, has now infiltrated, or is now being practiced by school girls aged 12–18. . . . Certainly, this is not only fertile ground in which to breed communism, but it's also against the very grain of marriage, normal life, and manhood."[63] Girls and boys who were not given explicit instruction on how to fulfill their traditional gender roles were seen to be placing "the security of the nation at risk."[64]

Underlying much of this domestic threat lay the unmistakable footprint of conspicuous consumerism. Parents were spoiling their young with excess goods, and their kids were becoming hooligans as a consequence. American and Soviet children appeared to bear the burden of the very affluence that made them exceptional. In the Soviet Union, amid the increasing attention that the leadership was paying to the importance of consumer culture, a palpable sense of discomfort over the nature of consumption emerged. While Marxism-Leninism certainly accepted the materialist interpretation of history, the pursuit of "stuff" still reeked of capitalism. As historian Victor Buchli has noted, "The spectre of pre-revolutionary *petit-bourgeois* consciousness and its concomitant understandings of domesticity" (that petit-bourgeois consumerism inhibited the realization of socialism) loomed very large in the mid-1950s and the 1960s.[65] At the center of this concern lay the child, whose socialist future depended on its country's ability to achieve the higher standard of living that was demanded by the Communist Party while at the same time avoiding the pitfalls of unfettered consumption. "We must watch that our children learn the right lessons from our development," one Pioneer leader wrote in 1963. "There is a clear potential that they could lose their perspective on what socialist culture means."[66]

Leaders on both sides expressed anxieties about the effects of such prosperity upon a generation that had not experienced the trials and scarcities of the Great Depression and World War II. In 1954, Senator Jacob Javits and Harry Gideonse, president of Brooklyn College, were arguing that "freedom is not a byproduct of the conveyor belt and the advertising business." Gideonse would lament that the country had forgotten the lessons of America's founding fathers who had prioritized the life of the mind and a commitment to moral growth over the accumulation of wealth (something both men already had in abundance). Such an "exclusively economic view of freedom," Javits contended, hindered and ultimately threatened the ability of the nation to remain "inner directed" and committed to a free society.[67] Similarly, J. Spencer Gray, a member of Eisenhower's Committee on Youth Fitness, asked his readers in 1960, "Can it be that we as a people have put too much stock in material success for its own sake, and that our offspring today reflect this worship of success to the exclusions of countless other values many of us of an earlier generation were taught to venerate?"[68] Not only did this preoccupation, as Gray and Javits argued, potentially obscure the priorities of patriotism and free thought, but it also threatened to create a generation of youth who did not understand the nature of personal sacrifice and had instead grown "soft" on the fruits of their parents' labor.

As a part of their concern over American materialism, politicians and members of the American public turned their attention to the rising influence of media and popular culture upon the next generation.[69] Concerns over uncontrolled media were not new in the United States in the 1950s. They had a way of erupting whenever popular culture underwent changes that seemed to differentiate the generations. This was the case during the silent film craze of the 1920s and when the popularity of dime novels took off in the 1930s.[70] Yet, for many in the postwar era, the press, the radio, and the television presented threats to children that the country had never seen before. As members of Congress from across the political spectrum would argue throughout the 1950s, the media had the potential to present a negative image of the United States abroad, and it ran the risk of corrupting the minds of the young at a time when shoring up national patriotism and maintaining domestic order were more important than ever. The impact of media on children was the subject of Fredric Wertham's 1953 best-selling book *Seduction of the Innocent*, in which he chronicled his efforts over the course of three years to "trace some of the roots of the modern mass delinquency."[71] Wertham's sensationalist book documented case after case of child delinquents who seemed to be mimicking actions that they had seen on the television or, in particular, in comic strips. Horror comics, which were popular from 1948 until 1954, showed images of children killing their parents and peers, sometimes in gruesome ways—framing them for murder—being cunning and devious, even cannibalistic. A commonly cited story was that of "Bloody Mary," published by Farrell Comics, which told the story of a seven-year-old girl who strangles her mother, sends her father to the electric chair for the murder, and then kills a psychiatrist who has learned that the girl committed these murders and that she is actually a dwarf in disguise.[72] Wertham's crusade against horror comics was quickly joined by two Senate subcommittees in 1954, at the heads of which sat Estes Kefauver and Robert Hendrickson. They argued to their colleagues that the violence and destruction of the family in these comic books symbolized "a terrible twilight zone between sanity and madness."[73] They contended that children found in these comic books violent models of behavior and that they would otherwise be law abiding.

J. Edgar Hoover chimed in to comment that "a comic which makes lawlessness attractive . . . may influence the susceptible boy or girl."[74]

Such depictions carried two layers of threat. First, as Wertham, Hoover, and Kefauver argued, they reflected the seeming potential of modern media to transform "average" children into delinquents.[75] Alex Drier, popular NBC newscaster, argued in May 1954 that "this continuous flow of filth [is] so corruptive in its effects that it has actually obliterated decent instincts in many of our children."[76] Yet perhaps more telling, the comics, as well as the heated response that they elicited, also reflected larger anxieties about what identities children should assume in contemporary America. As in the case of Bloody Mary, these comics presented an image of apparently sweet youths who were in fact driven by violent impulses and were not children at all. "How can we expose our children to this and then expect them to run the country when we are gone?" an agitated Hendrickson asked his colleagues in 1954.[77] Bloody Mary, like the uneducated dolts of the Litchfield report and the spoiled boys of Wylie's conjuring, presented an alternative identity for American youth that seemed to embody a new and dangerous future.

In the early months of 1954, Robert Hendrickson argued to his colleagues that "the strained international and domestic situation makes it impossible for young people of today to look forward with certainty to higher education, to entering a trade or business, to plans for marriage, a home, and family. . . . Neither the media, nor modern consumerism, nor the threat from outside our borders creates a problem child. But they do add to insecurity, to loneliness, to fear."[78] For Hendrickson these domestic trends, along with what he called "deficient adults," seemed to have created a new population of troubled and victimized children who were "beyond the pale of our society."[79]

The State Steps In

In response to these many threats, the late 1950s and the 1960s witnessed on both sides of the Iron Curtain an upsurge in state efforts to intervene on behalf of the young. In May 1961, the White House and Congress pushed through an array of acts to provide federal avenues for the management of kids. They passed the Aid to Dependent Children of Unemployed Parents Act in order to replace earlier rules that had refused aid to children if their father (employed or not) was still living in the home. They approved funding for the training of teachers for the deaf and for physical fitness. "There is nothing . . . more unfortunate," as Kennedy put it, "than to have soft, chubby, fat-looking children who go to watch their school play basketball every Saturday and regard that as their week's exercise."[80] At the same time, the increasing belief that rising delinquency rates could be blamed on negligent parenting ultimately helped to justify a new form of state intervention in private life. On 11 May 1961, Kennedy created the President's Committee on Juvenile Delinquency and Youth Crime, which culminated in the passing of the first comprehensive federal Juvenile Delinquency and Youth Offenses Control Act later that summer. In a letter to the Speaker of the House, he argued that the nation was compelled to create the "social conditions that will insure the growth of a skilled and resourceful population of young men and women . . . firm in character and committed to a democratic way of life."[81] The act declared that school dropouts and children from broken families now required "intensive and coordinated efforts on the part of private and government interests."[82] This act, which dominated government policy toward the management of delinquency for the following twelve years, allocated 30 million dollars toward a wide-sweeping program to include the federal government in the management of the young. It was the first act ever exclusively passed by Congress for the purpose of preventing and controlling delinquency. It involved aggressive casework and targeting children in urban areas where delinquency rates were highest. Funding allowed caseworkers to carry fewer clients so that they could theoretically devote more attention to each. Outreach programs for parents were also adopted that provided for the mass construction of neighborhood centers across America as well as the staff and facilities to provide family psychotherapy and group discussions on child rearing.[83] A number of youth organizations, including settlement houses, the YMCA, and the Boy Scouts, received increased funding, with the express purpose of mobilizing federal money and local initiative in a combined program. The Head Start and Get Set programs were also pioneered in an attempt to put children on an equal scholastic footing by the time they started elementary school in order avoid "the twin disillusionments of failure and feelings of inadequacy" that were thought to encourage delinquency.[84] Congress extended the 1961 act in 1963, with landmark programs like the Mobilization for Youth Project in New York receiving accolades while at the same time being criticized for disrupting local community power structures.

In all of the federal discussions surrounding the 1961 act and its subsequent extensions, the threats of the Cold War loomed large. Kennedy made this clear when he signed the law that September. Amid national headlines chronicling the continued deadlock in negotiations over West Berlin between Dean Rusk and Andrei Gromyko, Kennedy declared, "The future of our country depends on our younger people who will occupy positions of responsibility and leadership in the coming days. Yet for eleven years juvenile delinquency has been increasing. . . . This is a matter of national concern and requires national action. With this legislation the Federal government becomes an active partner with States and local communities to prevent and control the spread of delinquency. Though initiative and primary responsibility for coping with delinquency reside with families and local communities, the Federal government can provide leadership, guidance and assistance."[85] The federal policy of intervening in the lives of children and their parents constituted a reaction to a threat that was derived not only from evidence of internal disorder among the young, but also from the image of the child, seen as endangered by the ideological and physical invasion that had its roots in early Cold War fears.

A similar story unfolded in the Soviet Union in the early 1960s, when the state moved to reclaim control over the lives of the young (and over the images that they projected). Because of Khrushchev's plan to revitalize the nation through mass participation, and because society's emerging disorder in the early 1960s seemed to have its roots in the home, Pioneer leaders and educators as well as lawmakers concluded that increased governmental involvement would have to be pursued behind the closed doors of the standardized, single-family flats that were mass-produced in the late 1950s (the "Khrushchevka").[86] State directives regarding the raising of children in the home increased dramatically beginning in the mid-1950s, as mothers and fathers themselves became criminals when they failed to provide the specific kind of upbringing that the nation directed for its children.[87] From far-reaching civil laws that criminalized petty crimes and domestic disturbances by redefining them as hooligan acts, to parenting manuals giving instruction on how to provide an orderly personal space for one's child (even in the smallest apartment), to camping instructions on how fathers should test their sons by pushing them physically, to directions on how to talk about peer pressure with a budding adolescent, the state sought to gain a foothold in the private home through the image of the threatened child.[88] As one UN delegate from the Soviet Union argued at a meeting on 10 March 1966, "The state should prevent the rising generation from suffering as a result of the errors of its parents . . . when it was clear, for example, that the imposition of certain beliefs on the child could have a harmful effect on him."[89]

The identification of these culprits opened the door for a new cadre of social and legal authorities to determine normative private behavior, not just for children in the home but for parents as well.[90] This was a period marked by "intense state and Party engagement with the terms of domestic life, one that was highly rationalized and disciplined."[91] Whether it concerned "voluntary" enlistment of citizens into housing committees and comrades' courts or instructions on appropriate fathering, the state sought to maintain its hold over the lives of its citizens and, in the words of Elizabeth Wilson, to pursue the "state organization of domestic life."[92] By issuing directives on previously private matters like how to decorate one's apartment or how to provide a study space for one's children, Communist Party leaders, educators, and private citizens endeavored with uncertain success to impose normative behaviors upon a population that had increasingly become atomized and more difficult to monitor.[93] One question that scholars have not addressed is the extent to which the Soviet state sought to lay claim to the management of the private home and its residents for reasons related to the pursuit of a domestic Cold War agenda. Most Russian historians have viewed the Soviet state's continuing efforts to normalize and monitor private life in the late 1950s and the 1960s as a core element of state socialism—a trait endemic to the attempted and largely unsuccessful totalitarian model. While this certainly serves as a partial answer, the push for "containment" at home also clearly emerged as a popular response to perceived challenges and threats presented by the conflict with the United States.

Conclusion

Were these kids as threatened as everyone seemed to think they were? Was there a massive, coordinated ideological attack being perpetrated against children of either the West or the East? Was delinquency as much of a crisis as people believed it was in the 1950s and 60s? Was the influence of negligent parenting really much different than it had been in previous decades and centuries? The documents, speeches, and newspapers of the period seem to say that the answer is yes, and yet the proof of real threat is tenuous. What is clear is that the image of the threatened child was pervasive in the 1950s. People believed in the threat, and while it may not have been exceptional, the panic over it was. As in other wars that had come before it, Cold War fear, especially when it involved children, was a generative force that shaped how people understood the nature of the conflict itself. For those seeking to control the construction of consensus at home and abroad, for those looking for methods to refashion society, the image of the threatened child promised to mobilize the population and also generated questions about the security of the home that seemingly only the state was able to answer. The child became what Kenneth Pinnow has called a "conceptual tool" for the shaping of state interventions into the lives of the population.[94] It performed a constitutive function. It offered a vision of the enemy when the enemy could not be seen. It necessitated the mobilization of the populace for the cause of defense. Indeed, without that perceived threat, mobilization would not have been possible. In the end, the management of fear was just as crucial as the management of fealty.

This fear over the fate of the young, which sat alongside the continued promises of happiness and wealth, was a shared experience for millions of citizens in the United States and the Soviet Union. Populations on both sides made their way through the 1950s and 60s with this complex vision of the child standing in as a symbol for the nation's mission and plight in the Cold War. It was a part of what they saw and heard every day, and it shaped the way they understood the war and their obligations to it and their leaders. The specter of domestic threat served to build the Cold War consensus and the state's role in defending the child from internal and external threats. At the same time, it also engendered a sense of widespread anxiety on both sides of the Iron Curtain that the state could never quite alleviate. For many, the inconsistencies in these images could not be ignored. In response to this apparent disconnect between the shared visions of innocence and hooliganism, happiness and depravity, politicians in the Soviet Union and the United States worked to create a new vision of the Cold War kid that was not just happy and afforded, but also committed to international activism and the promotion of peace. This new child, it was hoped, would respond to the changing tides of Cold War diplomacy and would provide an answer to the internal weaknesses that had become apparent since the beginning of the war. This child was not as innocent, nor was it a victim of ideological infiltration and internal decay. No longer was it all right for the child simply to stand as an image of containment. Now it had an active and public role to play in the waging of the Cold War.

CHAPTER FOUR

Mobilized Childhood
Responds to the Threat

On 26 June 1960, the Soviet government marshaled the schools, the Pioneers, the Komsomol, and workers across the country to gather for the first annual Day of Soviet Youth. Writers and editors in the Russian press argued that this upcoming holiday was being held in order to honor the peace-loving children of the nation, who were diligently pursuing a better and brighter life for themselves and their compatriots around the world.[1] "This day has been established," announced one radio reporter, "in commemoration of the huge service that our boys and girls give to their motherland. They will face the challenges ahead as fighters for peace."[2] Throughout the day, adults gathered with children in parks, in stadiums, and on the streets—finally meeting, 100,000 strong, in Red Square, where they marched past the Lenin Mausoleum. "The Soviet children not only express their greetings, but are also gladdened by their international peers, who study in the Soviet Union," one Russian reporter announced over the radio.[3] Continuing, he described the young people around him on the streets of Moscow: "Our children devote their talent and their abilities to their work and their studies. . . . [They] think about peace, about friendship, about the future. Every day, [they] convey [*prinosiat*] proof of the vitality and rightness of the politics of the Soviet Union and its leadership in strengthening peace and friendship around the world."[4] Standing in Red Square as the evening sun began to set, the Vietnamese delegate, Nguyen Van Ty, announced that the "boys and girls of Vietnam are happy that together with their Soviet friends they can struggle for peace and higher human ideals."[5]

The evening ended with a stirring speech from Khrushchev, who called upon the Pioneer youth organization to marshal the next generation for the cause of peace. One week earlier, the KGB Chairman, Alexander Shelepin, had warned Khrushchev that the Pentagon was looking for an excuse to launch a preventative war on the Soviet Union. Secretly, Khrushchev was preparing a statement in defense of Cuba in case of an American invasion.

94

Publicly, he was declaring his commitment to peace. "Youth and peace are inseparable," he announced. "We must have peace in order to work, to dare, to love, and to dream."[6] With dove-shaped pins attached to their Pioneer ties, with the flags of the Soviet Union's favored countries flying in the warm, dry evening air of Red Square, and with no images of Stalin on display, these children represented a new way of conceptualizing the Cold War. They conveyed the message that the population was now prepared to take organized, international action for the cause of peace. They promoted a revised imagining of the Cold War as a new crusade for cultural and economic supremacy over the West and for the promotion of national liberation movements around the world that were struggling against perceived American imperialism.[7]

A similar story played out in the United States. Less than two years later, John F. Kennedy stood before representatives of the Children's Bureau at the Statler Hilton Hotel in Dallas, Texas, and delivered a speech on the future of America's children. He declared the importance of youth organizations in working with kids to "further the cause of freedom and peace and dignity throughout the world."[8] This speech fit well with Kennedy's emerging language of popular, organized, and peaceful activism. Thirteen months earlier, he had written the executive order that launched the Peace Corps. In the coming years, the first American delegates in the People-to-People Ambassador program went abroad, while organizations like the Boy Scouts of America embraced new initiatives to widen the international awareness and reach of its members. As the 1960s dawned, it appeared that American children, like their Soviet counterparts, now had a new role to play in the promotion of an American agenda abroad. The days of domestic containment seemed to be waning and a new kind of international activism for the young was on the rise.

In the 1950s and 60s, domestic policy paralleled the foreign policies of Soviet and American leaders. Just as both sides had sought to contain the enemy and create buffers against the possibility of resurgent power in the early 1950s, so too had they encouraged their populations to mobilize defensively in their homes and churches against the possibility of invasion. By the end of the decade, however, it was clear to both sides that containment was not enough. American and Soviet leaders understood how the preclusion of direct confrontation heightened the importance of economic and cultural competition with the enemy. Both sides recognized that domestic containment was creating a population of people who were scared, who had no clear avenues for facing the threat that they saw around them. Artists, filmmakers, and activists were organizing against the very consensus that the state had worked so hard to build in the last decade. Although there is no evidence that it was coordinated, leaders on both sides made a clear and seemingly simultaneous decision that the best answer to the new crises arising at home and abroad would be to encourage their populaces to become activists for their own Cold War consensus—to give their citizens a sense of ownership over the waging of the Cold War at home and abroad, with tangible plans for addressing all the domestic and international problems that both nations were facing, and to make their people feel like they and their children were not simply hapless victims waiting for attack. This did not mean that the image of the contained child would fade. Even if both sides had desired to slough off that image, it was too closely woven into the visual and rhetorical cultures of the people to be wiped away. But there was a change that was marked by the addition of this new vision of mobilization and activism for defense and peace.

The evidence of this transformation is mapped in the image of the Cold War kid, who by 1962 had become an activist for the promotion of government-led peace around the world and a symbol of international legitimacy for each country. This new child would be able to face the multifarious threats that menaced the young, the family, and the nation at home and abroad. He or she would be willing and able to slough off the comforts of domestic insularism in exchange for the challenges and rewards posed by the outside world. To this end, youth organizations assumed responsibility for promoting this new image of the young. They stood poised to respond to all the inconsistencies that the previous images had presented. This child was not a victim of attack; it was the shaper of its own universe. It was an activist, committed to the promotion of peace in the public sphere, all under the careful leadership of state-sanctioned organizations that understood the new role that youth had to play in maintaining the Cold War consensus. The two biggest youth organizations in the Soviet Union and the United States, the Pioneers and the Boy Scouts of America, helped to create this new image and the consensus around it. They attempted to respond to the demands of the era by promoting an image of peaceful mobilization that would unite a population and hopefully quell the rising uncertainty around them.

Building the Better Activist: The Pioneers

As the Khrushchev era dawned, the Pioneer and Komsomol youth organizations became the primary bodies responsible for implementing the transformation of post-Stalinist Soviet culture. They took on the task of teaching a new generation to fight corruption, centralization, bureaucracy, "insincerity," and the strictures of the Stalinist past. Instead of appearing contained, happy, afforded, and innocent within the confines of home and country, they became the vehicles through which a new vision of the Cold War kid could emerge. They promoted a new vision of the child that was an international participant in the Cold War effort, committed to creativity and personal responsibility in work, engaged in a "peaceful competition with the West" and the international promotion of Soviet-led "peace" abroad, and deeply devoted to the rejection of the fraudulence of the Stalin regime.[9] As a consequence, they helped to shape a new vision of the Cold War as a struggle that required the active participation of the entire population. Domestic containment and defensive preparedness were no longer the marks of Cold War mobilization; now international activism for peace and cultural competition became the hallmarks of citizenship. The Cold War kid was not in the home anymore. He or she was in the streets and was calling on the rest of the populace to join in.

Before the new Cold War consensus could be built in the late 1950s, the old one had to be dismantled. One of the first images to disappear after 1956 was that of the youngster grateful to Stalin for his or her joyous childhood. In the place of works like those created by Nina Vatolina, the press consciously worked to produce depictions of Khrushchev standing amid the nation's children, participating in their lives in a manner that would seem more intimate and familiar than had been possible under the grandiose iconography of the late Stalinist period. Take, for instance, a photograph of Khrushchev that was reproduced in *Komsomol'skaia pravda* on 23 June 1958. In contrast to Vatolina's paintings of Stalin standing aloof and preeminent before Russia's adoring youth, Khrushchev was surrounded both above and below by youngsters. All of them could be seen looking at the camera, not at the leader, who in previous years would have served as the point of reference for everyone else in the piece.

Unlike in the Stalinist period, Khrushchev in this photograph (and in many others like it) was not depicted in a particularly beautiful pose; he wore a strange smirk upon his face and was in many ways overshadowed by the far more handsome officer to his left. Moreover, it is worth noting that this is a photograph, not a painting. It is rare to find photographs of Stalin that are not posed and carefully constructed. (Indeed, particularly in photography, the Stalinist era is known for its legacy of falsifying images when the details did not fit current historical and political requirements.) Yet this picture of Khrushchev required only one take; the youngsters in the foreground of the photo were not well ordered and instead gave off a feeling of being comfortable and relatively unintimidated by their illustrious guest. One child even appeared

Figure 4.1. Khrushchev poses with officers of the Air Force and with young DOSAAF members. *Komsomol'skaia pravda*, 23 June 1958, 1.

to be showing off, with his hands placed jauntily on his hips. Khrushchev, in contrast, looked uncomfortable, and even common. These images of Khrushchev and the children around him, which arguably defined his public persona, suggest a marked change from the Stalinist era in the figurative relationship between the leader and the population. Although images of popular indebtedness to the Communist Party and to its general secretary would remain in place until the mid-1980s, no longer would the leader be placed in the beatified space that had been the standard visual practice before 1956.

The visual and rhetorical rejection of Stalin's benevolent image and the tempering of depictions of the population's gratitude to its leader were only a small part of a much larger reimagining of the Soviet child in the late 1950s. Khrushchev and the Pioneers also constructed a new image of Soviet children as individual, responsible workers who could provide a blueprint for the love of labor that had ostensibly deteriorated under Stalin's coercive rule. During the Stalinist period, the causal connection between the population's labor and its means of livelihood (the connection between the value generated by labor and the goods that can be purchased with that value) had been effectively severed. In its place had emerged the idea that the population's material existence was made possible from gifts generously given by Stalin himself.[10] In the years following 1956, many leaders in the Pioneers and the Komsomol frequently expressed worry that the idea of personal indebtedness to Stalin had helped to inculcate in the next generation a culture of meek compliance, conformity, and "know-nothing-do-nothing-ism" (the same worry that was the preoccupation of educators at the time).[11] For instance, in

1957, an article in the Komsomol magazine, *Molodaia gvardiia*, addressed the issues of independence and self-sufficiency that had ostensibly deteriorated under Stalin's watch. "In the ranks," the article argued, "the Pioneers and the schoolchildren sit under the petty guardianship of the teacher and the counselors [*starshikh vozhatykh*], and often do only the minimum work that is required of them."[12] Khrushchev would express his own opinion on the subject at the Fourteenth Komsomol Congress in 1962 when he stated that "we must direct our attention to the development of young boys and girls, so that they do not become thoughtless drone workers, mere followers, passive observers, or simple well-wishers [*dobrozhelateliami*] of communism, and instead become the right-flank of the army that is building a new society and is facing the challenges to come."[13] This transformation could be felt everywhere—in changes happening in education policy, in the laws being passed to manage wayward children, and in the encouraging of tasteful consumption by and for the young. Childhood had to change to meet the needs of the period.

In response to this seeming passivity among the young, Pioneer work campaigns sprung up across the country in 1956 and 1957. These included nationwide programs to collect scrap metal, clean up urban spaces and parks, and gather newspaper subscriptions and monetary donations for a variety of domestic and international causes. In addition to calling upon the next generation to fulfill its duty as young communist workers, children and youth were also solicited to work in order to learn what one Pioneer leader called "the science of personal responsibility."[14] As *Pionerskaia pravda* put it in 1957 while discussing a recent project for the collection of scrap metal, "When *you* are older, maybe *you* will choose to work in a metal factory. When *you* collect scrap metal, *you* prepare *yourself* for the future."[15] This appeal, which spoke not in abstract terms about the "youth of Russia" doing their duty for their nation but instead to the individual child-reader, the "you," offered a personal reward in the form of training and future employment to those who chose to participate. Statements like these represented a tentative, but nonetheless markedly new, approach to envisioning the child worker not simply as a part of a larger collective fulfilling state quotas, but as an active, individual participant, pursuing a common goal for personal as well as communal reasons.

This new image of the individual worker, Khrushchev and the party leadership believed, would provide proof that the Soviet Union was capable of competing economically with the United States, while at the same time responding to the problematic images of children who were both threatened and threatening at home. As a Pioneer group from Pskov put it in its annual report to the Communist Party in 1958, "In response to the directive of the party to catch up to and surpass the United States in the production of meat, butter and milk, we each commit ourselves to helping. We each hope to be an example for the country and for the world."[16] Such declarations promoted an image of the independent child, who was committed to a shared goal and who hopefully would revitalize a country that was at risk of losing its love of labor. This message ultimately hinged upon the idea that these children were pursuing personal labor for personal reasons that were good for the world, good for the state, and good for the individual.

Images of individual, hard-working, creative youth were also joined in the years following 1956 by a vision of Soviet children as active advocates for international peace abroad. Visions of kids working to provide aid to national liberation movements abroad were staples of Soviet foreign propaganda. They provided tangible proof that each citizen of the Soviet Union, unlike its American counterpart, felt a personal and voluntary obligation to help the less fortunate abroad. Across the country, children could be seen and heard in the press, on the radio, and in official speeches working to support foreign children in the postcolonial world, often likening them to future revolutionaries for the larger communist cause. Beginning in 1956, young Pioneers can be seen collecting donations for the children of Hiroshima, writing letters to American politicians for the cause of nuclear disarmament, enrolling in Vietnamese language programs after school, and expressing their solidarity with children in Latin America, the Middle East, Southeast Asia, Africa, and Eastern Europe. Independent, creative, and peaceful—this revitalized envisioning of the Soviet child under Khrushchev helped to conceptualize the Cold War for its audiences as a conflict that pitted a peace-loving Soviet Union against a United States that aggressively sought war. It contributed to the message that the struggle with the United States was both economic and cultural and that the Cold War required a refashioning of the individual to be a responsible, creative, volunteer citizen. It also presented a positive, almost reassuring, picture of Soviet society for domestic audiences in the Cold War world.

The idealized image of the Soviet Cold War child was best presented in stories and accounts surrounding the most popular of the Pioneer summer camps, Artek. Nestled on the banks of the Black Sea and heralded as the dream summer spot for all Soviet children from eight to fifteen, Artek, and the many camps like it, symbolized the future of the post-Stalinist ethos. It was a place where children could learn the value of hard work and creativity while living surrounded by nature under the careful supervision of the state. When Artek opened its doors to international visitors for the first time in the mid-1950s, the camp became a public showcase for the Communist Party's avowed success in raising hard-working, well-educated children, and in its seeming commitment to promoting Soviet-led peace around the world. Just as the image of the ideal Soviet child could be constructed for the purposes of packaging the Cold War to meet the state's needs, so too could the representation of an entire camp, with its participants, leaders, and even its buildings, establish the role of the Soviet Union in its struggle with the West.

Since its inception, Artek had stood as a model for the Soviet leadership in its search to create the ideal child. Founded in 1925, the first camp had accommodated eighty children with four buildings and a running track. By 1957, its yearly population totaled 27,000. Its grounds covered an area of three square miles and consisted of 150 buildings, three medical barracks, a school, a film studio (Artekfilm), three swimming pools, a sports stadium that held 7,000, and numerous playgrounds.[17] Children swam, studied music and art, learned animal care, canoeing, and archery, and in many ways had a camp experience that was not unlike those enjoyed by young people around the Western world.

Falling in line with the larger priorities set out by the Pioneers and Komsomol, one of Artek's main goals was to reinforce an individual work ethic among the young. Artek children organized and participated in weekly and sometimes daily meetings with workers, collective farmers, teachers, sailors, and young soldiers of the Crimea who were housed in local sanatoriums. There they learned many skills, including rudimentary training in driving a tractor (a relatively prestigious career), farming, welding, and the basics of sailing. On a daily basis, the camp was broken up into smaller cadres of eight to ten children, who then performed service work for treats and camp credits. This activity exhibited many of the most central beliefs of the Soviet system—that physical labor and hard work were vital in the construction of a well-rounded citizen, and that work had value, no matter what kind of work it was.[18] Yet this activity also reflected the new priorities that were beginning to emerge in post-Stalinist society—the idea that individual work is worth individual pay and that satisfaction can be derived not only from a job well done, but also from the personal gain that it generates. In 1957, for instance, the secretary of the Komsomol argued for the continuation of the work-for-pay plan at Artek. "In the end," he argued, "the child will see that earning ten to fifteen rubles is not easy. In this way we can show them how much their clothes cost, their bedding and other items."[19] The notion that the population owed its material happiness to the gifts of the state, while certainly still in place, was nonetheless under revision as children were taught that personal gain could be derived from personal work.

Artek's biggest contribution to the Cold War effort was in its promotion of the child's image as an international activist for peace around the world.[20] Artek's leaders were ranking members of the Communist Party and members of the Komsomol who ranged in age from eighteen to twenty-four and who managed the daily running of the camp. The management of the camp's admissions (getting into Artek was very difficult and usually required some kind of personal connection) and its policies, however, were determined by high-ranking party members within the hierarchy of the Komsomol and Pioneer central organizations. In June 1958, 500 children from Eastern Europe arrived by train for the first official international visit to the camp. During their sojourn, they took courses in science, nature, and art and a class called "Learning about Our Motherland."[21] Like their Soviet counterparts, they slept in well-appointed barracks and awoke each morning to a flag-raising ceremony that placed the Soviet flag above their own national flag on the flagpole. If reports are to be believed, the food ranged from sufficient to "delightful." The days were filled with instruction in outdoor sports and occasionally in history and current affairs, while the evenings consisted of sing-a-longs, talent shows, and movie nights.[22] International visitors and their adult chaperones were usually housed with Soviet youths and Pioneer leaders, who worked and played as one group.

By opening its doors to foreign campers, Artek and the Pioneer organization envisioned numerous benefits for the Soviet Union and its international image. The first and certainly most frequently stated reason was "to strengthen friendship between children of different countries."[23] From the flying of various national flags to the constant invitations to foreign celebrities and dignitaries that the camp issued, Artek presented itself as a flagship for international cooperation.[24] "Culture nights" were often held at the camp, where visitors could present the songs and dances from their home countries. Bulgarian visitors were pleased during a visit in 1960 to find that the kitchen staff had prepared yogurt and Kebabcheta for dinner.[25]

By all accounts, most kids had a great time. Hundreds of thank-you letters can be found in the Pioneer archives expressing what appear to be sincere feelings of appreciation by visiting children toward the Soviet Union for allowing them to come to camp. The genuineness of these letters is of course, difficult to assess, as they were almost certainly prompted by teachers and parents. But the quantity of letters, combined with the general feelings of fondness that former campers continue to profess for the camp, do seem to substantiate the idea that the camp leadership, staff, and campers for the most part worked hard to make their visitors feel welcome. Regardless of the potential array of motives that may have ultimately lay behind the rhetoric of friendship that was generated by the Soviet leadership and press when speaking of these foreign visitors, it would be a mistake not to recognize the feelings of international brotherhood and excitement at the camp level that were often generated when these youngsters visited.

That said, there were strong political reasons for the opening of Artek to the world in 1956. While the camp provided comfort, instruction, and arguably a lot of fun to the children of Europe, Africa, Asia, the Middle East, and Latin America, it also garnered their public expressions of gratitude and indebtedness in the domestic and international press. This was evidenced in the visits of Polish, Czech, German, and Bulgarian children, who, in addition to reporting that they had enjoyed themselves at camp, also brought with them generous and constant promises of their nations' solidarity with the Soviet Union. In July 1958, for instance, the Central Soviet of the Polish Pioneer Organization sent a letter with its young delegates. In it, the organization reiterated its loyalty to the Polish Workers' Party and its commitment to "educate the children in the spirit of socialism and internationalism, not to organize under religion, but instead to educate its members in the path of freedom and peace through persuasion and tolerance."[26] Likewise, Bulgarian delegates professed their "shared target to educate the citizens of socialist society."[27] Unlike the letters written by children that often began with sentences like, "I had such a good time at camp! I really loved the swimming and the shows at night," the official letters, which were obviously written by adults, were political in nature.[28] They positioned the camp as a locus for political education and as an opportunity to exhibit their own official compliance with Soviet policy. They also substantiated the idea that the Soviet Union could provide the leadership needed to create "free" and "peaceful" children, not just in Russia proper, but abroad as well.

Artek was also politically useful as a location where Soviet children could be publicly contrasted to "other" children from capitalist countries. One camp leader, in his report to the Komsomol in 1957, described the "barbaric" behavior of capitalist children upon arriving at camp. "Literally not one of the children from the capitalist countries knew how to tie their tie or put on their clothes. Our children tried to teach them how to make their beds, but they were unable. Then one morning, when one foreign child ran out of the tent, forgetting as always, to make his bed, the Soviet Pioneers made his bed without a word. This action embarrassed the foreign children and their leaders, and they tried much harder to stop their poor behavior."[29] This letter, which was presented to an open session of the Komsomol at the end of the summer in 1957, painted a vivid picture of two very different kinds of children at the camp. On the one hand, there were the Pioneer youths, who exhibited decorum, order, and responsibility. On the other hand, there were the Western children (nationality unspecified), who were disrespectful toward the camp and its generosity and infantile in their mental and physical ineptitude. In another report, a counselor recounted how Western children "absolutely were not trained in physical work and were untidy." "Young women," she claimed, "are only attracted to fashion, paint themselves with different rings and beads, while boys are only concerned with sports."[30] In contrast to the idealized Soviet child, Western children appeared in these reports as oversexed and disorganized. We cannot know why the counselors chose to tell these particular stories of their foreign visitors before the open session of the Komsomol, or if these lapses in decorum even happened at all (the fact that the nationalities of these foreign children are omitted makes for skepticism). We do know that these particular leaders had been assigned to work with international visitors that summer, and that their mandate from the Komsomol had been to agitate (or propagandize) "not through words, but through actions and personal behavior."[31] The first interaction described above seems to illustrate this, as the Soviet Pioneers silently chastised their foreign visitors for not cleaning up after themselves. Equally obvious is the fact that these leaders were participating in a much larger cultural practice of contrasting Soviet children with foreign youths as well as problematic images of hooligan kids at home, all as a way to legitimate the Soviet system.

Artek was used not only to compare Western children to their Russian counterparts and to contradict the image of the problem child at home; it was also envisioned as a place where capitalist children could be converted to supporting the socialist project. One Komsomol leader concluded in the summer of 1957 that campers, regardless of nationality, "within three to four days, all want very much to wear the Pioneer tie."[32] This was especially true, the leader argued, for visiting children from the postcolonial world. He argued that these kids were susceptible to American influence while at the same time open to the message that the Soviet Union supported their pursuit of peace and national liberation. Beginning in 1955, groups from Angola, Nigeria, and Uganda began arriving. In August 1960 a delegation of Guinean children became what one leader characterized as "deeply acquainted" with the experience of a working camp, with its traditions and its rituals. They took part in the mass ceremonies. They played and worked in the carpentry rooms, the libraries, and the "rooms of the heroes of Artek."[33] They also shared barracks with Soviet children, swam with them, and ate with them.

These visits ultimately served important propaganda functions, as their presence in the camp articulated the Soviet official position on colonialism and race, all in contrast to depictions of the "other" child that had become so prolific by this time. The Soviet domestic and international media widely reproduced images of happy African children playing with Soviet youths, usually accompanying those images with discussions of the dire domestic situations in the home country and the exploitation of postcolonial children by the capitalist world over many centuries. These images also served as testaments to the ostensible absence of racism in the camp and in Russia as a whole. While organizations like the U.S. State Department and the U.S. Information Agency were struggling to counter the growing image of a racist America, the Soviet press continued to publish articles depicting Russia as the one nation that had given black African children a chance to play and enjoy modern comforts without facing the possibility of racial assault. "Camp is full of color," one young Pioneer was quoted as saying in an international radio broadcast to Angola in 1961, "but race is one color we do not see."[34] Artek offered the youths of the underdeveloped world an opportunity to witness the benevolence of their Russian benefactor and to rethink their previous "incorrect" assumptions about communism and the Soviet Union. Thus, when a Pioneer counselor assigned to work with African visitors testified to a Pioneer and Komsomol panel in 1957 that "unbridled American propaganda hides the truth about the Soviet Union," she was nonetheless able to reassure the panel by showing that "after Artek, none of the campers wanted to return to Africa."[35] These children, accompanied by hard-working, independent, activist Soviet children, stood as incontrovertible evidence of Soviet domestic strength and international progress in a Cold War struggle where the battle lines were increasingly being drawn along racial, colonial, and cultural divides.

Building the Better Activist: The Boy Scouts

At the national conference of the Boy Scouts of America in the second week of June 1959, the president of the Boy Scouts, Ellsworth Augustus, laid out a call for the United States to intervene on behalf of the next generation: "The nation's youth must be prepared to withstand the ideological, physical, and economic pressures of Communism. . . . Never before has it been more important to develop men who will be physically strong, mentally awake, morally straight and committed to their duty to God and their country."[36] Like their Soviet counterparts, leaders, parents, and politicians endeavored in the late 1950s to create a new child that could meet to the threats that endangered the next generation at home and abroad. The containment and domestic mobilization of the 1950s would have to give way, men like Ellsworth Augustus argued, to a new child who could actively promote a new kind of Cold War consensus. Not only was this child capable of defending the nation against communist attack, he was also well educated in the sciences. He was devoted to capitalism without being consumed by it, decidedly masculine, well supervised, nonracist, committed to the preservation of domestic order, and actively involved in projecting a positive image of America abroad. All of these traits, which came into new focus in the late 1950s, emerged in response to the threats of the previous decade and as a part of the globalization of the Cold War cultural battle that had been growing since the conflict began.

The late 1950s witnessed a noticeable shift in American portrayals of children facing the communist threat. Whereas in the early 1950s, Cold War kids had appeared largely as innocents under attack by a communist menace in the schools and in the homes, by the end of the decade they could be seen taking an active role in seeking out communism beyond the traditional spaces that children usually inhabited. Civic leaders like John S. Gleason, the head of the American Legion, and Cardinal Cushing, the archbishop of Boston, argued to their constituents that "no matter what current settlements may be negotiated with Soviet Russia as the 'other' world power, our children and grandchildren will have to face the challenge of Communist competition throughout their lives. If we have been deceived and bamboozled in the past, it is because, as a nation, we did not take enough trouble to learn about communism."[37] "Americanism" programs subsequently sprouted up all over the country, sponsored not only by local veterans organizations and the Bar Association, but also by public schools like the one in Los Angeles County in 1962, at which the school board resolved to "emphasize [in its curriculum] the positive side of our way of life as well as the dangers facing it."[38] The superintendent argued that the schools had a legal responsibility to develop programs for teaching citizenship and patriotism. J. Edgar Hoover declared to young readers in 1961 in a variety of comic strips that "knowledge is most essential, for it helps us recognize and detect the communists as they attempt to infiltrate the various segments of our society."[39] *Junior Scholastic* got on board with a twelve-part series entitled "What You Should Know about Communism—and Why," in which it promised to "drop the bomb of truth" upon the next generation, thereby protecting it from "dangerous mental fallout."[40]

The new image of the Cold War child was not educated just on communism but on science as well. *Boy's Life* published articles on the topic of

Figure 4.2. "Your Welfare Is Being Overshadowed." *Boys' Life*, September 1956, 63.

science education in almost every edition. The push to address education began in earnest in September 1956 with an article entitled "Your Welfare Is Being Overshadowed."[41] "The critical shortage threatens our future security!" it warned in bold letters. Below this caption there appeared a drawing of four American boys bent over a drafting table holding a model rocket and engineering tools. Their bodies and faces were obscured, however, as a towering shadow of two massive Soviet boots threw them into darkness.[42] The boots, which were as large as the boys' bodies, marched forward, preparing to squash the children beneath their unstoppable weight.

Such harbingers reinforced the messages of educational insufficiency that had been presented by legislators like William Fulbright and Mike Mansfield in the previous decade. They implied that the young were the only ones who could carry on the struggle to win the space race, and they put into stark relief the extent to which America's children were physically threatened by the Soviet space and science program. Notably, the illustrators of "Your Welfare Is Being Overshadowed" chose to draw a Soviet boot as the source that threatened these boys. Why not a Soviet satellite, rocket, or bomb? While bombs and rockets implied immense destruction, they also signified something against which man could not really fight. Four boys standing at a drafting table cannot stop a satellite or a nuclear missile. But men *could* stop other men. And now America's boys were being presented as capable of stopping the men in those boots—the Soviet scientists who were bent on creating objects of indefensible destruction. Those boots represented a mandate for every American who worked in children's services to rally their forces in the human struggle against Soviet technological power.

Within the Scouting organization, programs to promote science education came in the forms of official badges, in outreach projects, and even in the organization's comic strips, which, as the leadership claimed in 1960, "never found it necessary to resort to stories of misadventure, crime, sex, or any questionable material to build its reader clientele."[43] They initiated a new Atomic Energy Badge in 1958, in the same year that the National Defense Education Act was passed. Its requirements were rigorous, demanding that boys understand the meanings and functions of beta particles and neutron activation, that they illustrate the process of nuclear fission and critical mass, and that they construct a homemade radiation gauge, dosimeter, Geiger counter, and cloud chamber.[44] In the same year, the Boy Scouts started new programs, including after-school science clubs in low-income neighborhoods that were adopted as a means to reach bright children who might otherwise be overlooked. Each week, *Boy's Life* featured a new installment in the comic sagas of "Albert Einstein" and "Space Conquerors," where engineering lessons were mixed in with stories of "atom rays" and alien life forms on distant planets. With a membership of over 5 million in 1960, the image of young men actively addressing the science gap offered a needed solution to a decade-long crisis.[45] In the words of one troop leader, speaking at the 1961 National Jamboree, "It is our duty to do all we can to help American education get back on its feet."[46]

The Boy Scout organization, like its Pioneer counterpart, made an attempt to address the nation's delinquency problem by "installing, replacing, and fortifying the core of values" that it believed all children needed to have.[47] The Boy Scouts ventured into parts of the nation that they identified as hotbeds for the growth of delinquency. These areas were marked by substandard, overcrowded housing, low-income and single-parent homes, cultural and linguistic barriers, high population transience, lack of residential leadership, and no organized recreation for children. In other words, they made their way out of the suburbs and back into the cities where predominantly African American and immigrant children resided. Labeled as "vulnerables," the Scouts offered inner-city boys the kind of training that the organization hoped would keep the boys out of jail and also provide proof that the country was addressing its problems and fixing its wayward youth.[48]

By positioning itself as a solution to delinquency in America, the Boy Scout organization pursued its larger mandate to create orderly and patriotic citizens while also opening its doors for increased membership and revenue. Unlike the Pioneers, who were largely funded by the state, the Boy Scouts of America was a private organization, which received large subsidies from the federal government but nonetheless had to find substantial revenue in the private sector. In addition, the Scouts had always struggled with the need to increase membership, a fact that is reflected in the massive amount of literature that was devoted to enlisting boys at all ages. Membership was such an issue that Scout leaders were instructed to use school and county nurse directories in order to call on boys to join. Constructing the image of the Boy Scout as an alternative to that of the childhood delinquent was vital to the survival of the Scouts, not only because it responded to the larger needs of the nation, but also because it gave parents a concrete reason to keep paying dues, buying uniforms, and working in fund-raisers.

The Scouts accompanied these efforts with a similar project to either reform America's negligent and indulgent parents or provide a viable substitute for them in the form of the Scoutmaster. Between the ages of thirty-five and forty-five, with a personal past as a Scout, an above-average income, a wife and children of his own, a good education, and a steady churchgoing record, the model Scout leader was envisioned as one who could assume responsibility for a boy's maturity into manhood when the mother and the father were not willing or able to do it.[49] Lord Baden-Powell was established as the ultimate father against whom "regular" dads were to be judged. His son described him as a man who took his family camping on summer holidays, traveled the world with his children, and maintained humility and dignity despite his fame.[50] At the same time, Scouting literature, both public and private, warned repeatedly of the dangers posed by "Dominating Delilahs." One particularly concerned leader wrote in to the main office in 1962 about a mother who had an "aggressive, ambitious, mutinous tendency to try to take over any project."[51] The Scouting organization's response was a "get tough" policy that required having a frank conversation with the mother about her expected role in the troop. President Eisenhower told a similar story of Scouting intervention at the commemorative dinner of the Boy Scouts of America fiftieth anniversary in Washington, D.C., on 1 June 1960. He recounted how he had stepped in to stop his wife and mother-in-law from packing a lunch and setting up emergency transportation for their son when he had resolved to take a solo hike in fulfillment of a badge. "It was important that he do this one on his own," Eisenhower commented to a rapt audience. "Sometimes you have to step in."[52] For the Scouts, as it was in the Soviet Union, delinquency would have to be fixed first in the parents.

The Scouts tied the struggle against delinquency to a campaign of teaching boys appropriate sexual behaviors. Sociologists by the 1950s had begun to view the young boy's liminal sexual body as something that required supervision and control.[53] As we have seen, many in America viewed sexual deviance as a gateway to communism. In response, the Boy Scout literature devoted significant attention to teaching boys to seek male, not female, guidance, to "roughen themselves up," to develop a healthy heterosexuality, and to treat their mothers and girlfriends appropriately. Through officially sanctioned activities, as well as informal, sexually suggestive rituals, Boy Scout troops worked to instill and codify in each of their members a sense of masculine power that was closely bound to issues of national security and strength. In particular, the organization worked to create a new population of boys who would grow to become men capable of assuming their obligations as white collar workers in America (even if it meant putting on the "gray flannel suit" to join the "lonely crowd"), while still maintaining their physical strength and adventurous spirit.[54] The Scouts pursued this program of sexual acculturation through efforts to decrease female influence in boy's lives and to emphasize the importance of fathers and leaders. The organization instructed these fathers and leaders to teach boys how to control their sexual appetites in man-aged, heterosexual ways. As the 1968 Boy Scout Handbook made clear to its readers, "The morally straight boy will become a heterosexual man."[55] It was the boy's duty to remember the power for good that was possible if his sexuality was channeled toward reproduction in wedlock. "As a young man, you are capable of becoming a father," the handbook instructed. "God has given you this very high trust. . . . When you live up to the trust of fatherhood your sex life will fit into God's wonderful plan of creation. It will ensure that you and your children will grow up in freedom and honor."[56] Just as Cold War culture denounced homosexuality as an invitation for communist infiltration, so too did it demand heterosexual behavior from the next generation of young men.

As with the Pioneer organization, these visions of intelligent, nondelinquent, straight boys worked to create a new kind of American child that could cure the troubles of the next generation and also stand as an international icon of American democracy and national defense. For the Scouts, this meant countering images of American racism while projecting a vision of global, peaceful mobilization with the noncommunist nations of the world. Not surprising, for many in the U.S. government, the childhood image that was most damaging to American prestige abroad was that of racist American youth, which as we have seen, the Soviet Union was more than willing to exploit in its own domestic rhetoric. Despite the many efforts that were made by politicians in the North and the South to prove that the civil rights movement was infiltrated by communists and that the Soviets had their own troubled race record, a number of senators and congressmen argued increasingly in the 1950s that the slow pace of race reform was destroying America's image abroad. Marlon Wright, adviser to the U.S. Commission on Civil Rights, argued in 1960 that the names of Little Rock, Arkansas, and Tuscaloosa, Alabama, now evoked "sordid memories. In all countries the names are familiar. They and the train of ideas of which they are the core contribute to the picture we present to the rest of the world. . . . You may be sure that the peoples of Asia and Africa know what is happening to their brethren in this country. The Russian propaganda machine sees to that."[57] In a similar vein, Jacob Javits argued in the *New York Times* in 1963 that the whole world had stood witness when "mounted State troopers in Little Rock, electric cattle prodders in hand, rode headlong into a crowd of Negro demonstrators, trampling children in the process."[58] In these descriptions of African American youth, the physical threat, which came from antisegregation forces within the country, translated into a threatening image for the nation as a whole, which risked condemnation in the court of international opinion.

Like Wright and Javits, the Scouting leadership argued that the image of the ostracized, segregated, African American boy projected a damaging vision of America abroad and also posed a grave threat to the maintenance of order at home. Many feared that African American boys, if not correctly integrated into society, could be lost to the chaotic and angry side of the civil rights movement—or even worse—succumb to the attractions of socialism. The majority of segregationists and integrationists in America agreed that a violent path toward integration would lead to national weakness and disorder. But while the segregationist solution to this threat was to scrap integration altogether, integrationists made a powerful argument that the only way to avoid violence, and even leftist influence among the African American population, was for the country to guarantee civil rights for all. For the Scouts, "creating a smoother path" for the most part became policy, as the organization worked to create a sociocultural map for how integration could be handled without violence and to rebuild the image of American humanism abroad.[59]

In the end, international, political, and moral pressures drove the organization to take a deliberate, if slow, approach to bringing African Americans into the Boy Scouts. This was not an easy task, and the organization had a lot of catching up to do. In 1945, there were only 20,000 African American Scouts out of a total membership of 2 million. Integrated troops and packs did not exist in the North or the South, and African American membership was dropping each year. In 1947, the National Council was not able to meet the goals of its "Thousand for One" Campaign, which had set a target to enlist 30,000 African American boys by the end of the year.[60] By 1958, as the slow rate of school desegregation in the South sparked widespread unrest in the civil rights movement, the Boy Scouts struggled to project a moderate voice for progress and reform. Boys like Marvin Higgins, who was awarded the God and Country Medal for religious work in Athens, Alabama, were highlighted in Scouting magazines. Photographs of troops often included both African American and white boys. Scouting publications also paid particular attention to the patriotic duties being performed by black troops in their communities.[61] And in a massive campaign that included the creation of a full-time staff trained in "ethnic recruiting," Scouting representatives from the National Interracial Service traveled throughout the nation's twelve regions working to make connections with the black community through churches, schools, the National Urban League, and the Frontiers of America.[62] Their efforts to reach out to the country's African American children reflected a desire to protect the young from, and indoctrinate against, the threat of communism and radicalism while simultaneously pursuing a path to integration that did not threaten the maintenance of domestic order. As one annual report noted, "The harmony of the races and the usefulness of the Negro of tomorrow very largely depends on the leadership of the Scouts."[63]

Yet, despite these improvements, integrated troops remained few and far between well into the 1970s, and while the Scouts made admirable efforts to provide an example of how integration was possible, underlying racist assumptions persisted. One report in 1950, for instance, issued by the Committee on Interracial Activities, made explicit efforts to impose "white" levels of hygiene on African American recruits. "Sanitation and health of one group vitally influences the health of every other," it argued. "The Negro needs to be taught all we know about how to live."[64] The Boy Scout organization's efforts to write a map for integration faced the same quandaries that the rest of the nation did—how to transform the idea of equality into a functioning reality and how to project an image of racial fairness in the midst of increasing tension.

The Boy Scouts were far more successful in projecting a positive mobilized image abroad in the program for World Scouting. While the Pioneers brought international delegates to Artek as a symbol of Soviet generosity and communist solidarity, the Boy Scouts established the "World Brotherhood" program in order to create for American boys, for the general public, and for the world the sense that they were part of a much larger effort to uphold the ideals of capitalism and Western democracy. Domestically, World Scouting fostered the idea that the United States was not alone in its Cold War efforts. Internationally, it attempted to establish America as a part of a global consensus committed to a shared cause.[65] The perceived power of the Scouts to build friendships around the world was evidenced by the many ways in which the U.S. government inserted itself into the efforts of the Scouts. In May 1959, the government acknowledged the work of Scouting when Arthur Schuck, the chief executive of the Scouts, received the Freedom Foundation's highest award for "helping to bring about a better understanding of the American way of life." Schuck joined J. Edgar Hoover and Herbert Hoover as the third recipient of the award, which carried with it a mandate to "continue to strive to make this a world of peace and happiness."[66]

World Scouting has a history as old as Scouting itself. It began in 1910 when Scouting in England was adopted by a number of countries in Europe and the Americas. The first official international Scouting event was held in 1920 with the first World Jamboree in Kensington, England. The event hosted 8,000 Scouts from thirty-four countries. Lord Baden-Powell, who was declared the Chief Scout of the World, articulated the mission of World Scouting when he said, "If it be your will, let us go forth from here fully determined that we will develop, among ourselves and our boys, a comradeship through the worldwide spirit of the Scout brotherhood."[67] International connections among the Scouts were severely tried during World War II but were reestablished in 1947 with the American creation of the World Friendship Fund, a grassroots corollary to the Marshall Plan whereby 300,000 Scouts collected nickels and dimes for the purpose of assisting Scouting organizations in war-torn and underdeveloped countries.[68] By 1957, the World Friendship Fund, working under the theme "Good Turn with the Long Reach," was delivering an average of $50,000 per year to the development of Scouting outside the United States.[69] The Boy Scout organization gave heavy attention to funding drives like I.C.B.M, which stood for Intercontinental Brotherhood Missile Envelopes, as a means to promote Scouting abroad.[70] The organization made similar efforts to promote international connections through individual Scout projects and pen pal exchanges. In 1952, it established the World Brotherhood Badge, which required the aspiring Scout to draw a map of the nations in the world where Scouting existed, to describe how one might identify another Scout while in another country, to learn the stories of at least three national heroes of other lands, to carry on a five-minute conversation with a native speaker in a foreign language, and to correspond with a Scout from another country.[71] As with the internationalization of Artek, such actions created bonds between Scout troops, and they also ostensibly connected countries in a pact of shared belief and practice. As Nadezhda Krupskaia, Lenin's wife and a founder of the Pioneers, said of the Boy Scouts, "When we speak of boy-scout activity, we all understand very well, of course, that however attractive it may be, it is meant to bring up the growing generation as loyal servants of kings and capitalists."[72] When the aspiring Scout drew out his required map of all the countries that had Scouting, what he produced was a map of the Cold War. The support or rejection of Scouting in a nation literally drew the line between communism and capitalism.

The event that best signified the international bonds of World Scouting was the World Jamboree, which was held in the United States for the first and only time in 1967, in Farragut State Park, Idaho. A record number, 12,017 Scouts and leaders from 107 countries, participated in the weeklong event. The Jamboree received unprecedented international attention, including the issuing of Farragut Park Jamboree postal stamps in countries as far away as Mozambique and Liberia. With the U.S. State Department providing free visas to all international attendees, the delegates arrived on 1 August to find that the park had been completely transformed from a dismal, U.S. Navy training station into a world village. Each delegation was offered its own barracks. At the center of the camp flew the flags of each Scouting country. The carefully constructed menu included midwestern staples like brisket and potatoes, as well as bratwurst, corned beef hash, and enchiladas (which, in 1967, constituted exotic cuisine). With a schedule that would have seemed familiar to campers at Artek, daily activities included a "skill-o-rama" intended to test boys' acuity in riflery, orienteering, and survival skills. They participated in aquatics lessons and competitions on the banks of Lake Pend Oreille. They undertook a conservation program for thinning underbrush and clearing trails in the surrounding Coeur d'Alene Mountains and participated in mixed-troop trail adventures. They saw what one boy from Abilene, Texas, called a "real old west rodeo." The most memorable event for many was the "friendship game," which had been popular at the previous World Jamboree in Greece and involved every camper attempting to match his own lettered placard with other Scouts' placards to spell out a phrase and then march into the main arena together as a group.[73]

The aims of the Boy Scout organization at the World Jamboree were noticeably similar to those expressed by the Pioneers at Artek. In the months before the event, Gerald Speedy, the national director for the Scouts, argued to his colleagues that "all we do and say there [in Idaho] will be a kind of definition of freedom for some countries which have long had it, and still others which may be about to lose it. It is not too idealistic to expect that several hundred boys encamped at the jamboree will one day become the leaders of their countries."[74] Reflecting the idea that the Scouts were a kind of greenhouse for the development of democratic leadership, and making indirect reference to Vietnam, which was, in his opinion, on the verge of losing its "freedom," he continued to argue that "the world's future rests in the hands of its youth. We must understand with increasing clarity and intensity of feeling our awesome potential to influence the way in which tomorrow's men will think and act as we influence the qualities of mind and spirit of today's youth."[75] Speedy and his colleagues sought to position the Jamboree as a testament to American benevolence and brotherly love for the people of the world and perhaps to promote a vision of the entire "free world" standing behind the United States and its policies in Southeast Asia.

Hoping to reflect these ideas in visual form, the Boy Scouts of America commissioned Norman Rockwell to paint a work of commemoration for the Jamboree. Having begun his career as an illustrator for *Boy's Life* in 1912, Rockwell had painted themes of the Boy Scouts all his life. Although he is rumored to have struggled to find a subject and composition for the painting, he finally settled on representing the moment when six Scouts have successfully matched their placards during the friendship game and are marching into the

Figure 4.3. Norman Rockwell, "Breakthrough for Freedom," 1967. Courtesy of Brown & Bigelow.

arena. In a tableau that most Socialist Realists would have found familiar, an American Explorer Scout occupies the foreground of the painting as he walks a half step ahead of his international peers, one of whom is wearing the South Vietnamese Scouting uniform. Similarly, behind the group, the American flag is also positioned closest to the viewer, followed by the flags of America's neighbors and allies. Entitled "Breakthrough for Freedom," the painting simultaneously encapsulated the ideas that Scouting transcended national borders without eradicating them and that the United States had a leading role to play in the "march" being undertaken by these boys and by their countries.

The message of world brotherhood and shared mobilization conveyed at the World Jamboree was also articulated in the forms of mythmaking and storytelling that the Scouts embraced in the late 1950s and 1960s. Young "freedom fighters" in Eastern Europe were common subjects of Boy Scout stories and publications—first coming from Czechoslovakia in 1952 and later from Poland and Hungary in 1956 and 1968. For instance, a commonly told and frequently repeated story of international brotherhood emerged in 1961 and 1962 around the life of Richard Frantisek Hrdlicka, called "Dick" by his American friends, who allegedly joined the antifascist underground in Czechoslovakia in 1943 at the age of ten and then the rebellion against the Soviets at the age of twelve. In this story, which appeared in *Boy's Life* and was also referenced in campfire-story booklets given to troop leaders throughout the 1960s, Dick was defined not by his nationality, but by his status as an international Scout and by his actions taken in the face of communist aggression.[76] As the story went, on a March night in 1939, just after the Nazis had rolled into Prague, Dick joined his underground troop in the lighting of night campfires that "burned in the mountains and glens of Czechoslovakia, as thousands of Scouts, forbidden to wear their uniforms, and ordered to fly the Nazi flag, renewed their Scout oath." After the war, Dick was again involved in skirmishes between the communist "hoodlums" and the 20,000 freedom-fighting students who had come to Prague to protest repression under Soviet rule. Dick took to the mountains, as Scouting, and the freedom that it represented, again went underground. After returning to Prague under the condition that he join the Komsomol, Dick again put himself at great risk by passing out anticommunist literature in his school. Finally he was able to escape to France and then to Kansas, after the American Scouts of Region 8 secured his airfare and tuition at Friends University in Wichita, Kansas. It is difficult to verify whether the details of Dick's story are true, although Friends University does verify that Richard Hrdlicka did attend sometime in the 1950s. But perhaps the story's veracity is not of real importance. Even if this is but a campfire story, Dick's apparent arrival and integration into America nonetheless functions as an integral component to Boy Scout mythmaking. It presented the boy as someone who spent his lifetime struggling against oppression, and it portrayed the United States as a facilitator in his struggle. The vision of the Scout and of what it meant to be mobilized in the Cold War served as a constant force in the development of this one boy, who was portrayed as having defied the communist system for his beliefs.[77] Dick's story represents the culmination of Scouting's Cold War purpose. Through training and moral instruction, Dick (who had adopted Western ways of thinking and a Western name as well) was imagined as having received the tools necessary to counter communist influence. Despite his nationality, Dick was a member of the world brotherhood and embodied the vision of the new, ideal child because he had overcome such odds as a youngster and had used the lessons learned through Scouting to gain his freedom.

Conclusion

By the late 1950s, a number of sociopolitical forces were at work in shaping the image of the ideal Cold War kid. On the one hand, this shift was a logical extension of international exchange and propaganda programs that had been in existence since the beginning of the Cold War. Harry Truman and Dwight Eisenhower had passed the Smith-Mundt and Fulbright acts, which authorized the U.S. State Department to communicate to international audiences and encouraged educational exchange. They established the Voice of America and Radio Free Europe, organized cultural festivals abroad (often highlighting African American performers), and orchestrated numerous international exhibitions under Eisenhower's 1954 Emergency Fund for the Arts. On the other side of the Iron Curtain, the Stalinist leadership and the Central Committee of the Communist Party had undertaken an extensive exchange and propaganda effort, with an estimated 45,000 Soviet artists and scholars traveling around the world by 1953. It was not until the second half of the 1950s, however, that the Soviet Union and the United States embraced an approach to the waging of the cultural Cold War that included not only the increased use of scholars and artists and the revitalization of "peaceful coexistence," but also the mobilization of the general population that had up to this point been largely "contained" and insulated from the messianic obligations of international Cold War activism.[78] It was here that the new vision of the international child took its form. As Frederick Barghoorn has noted when examining the Khrushchev era, the late 1950s witnessed the "reappearance and growing frequency of 'internationalist' symbols," "a substantial rise in the percentage of attention devoted to 'foreign' as against 'domestic' problems," and "the fact that Soviet concern with and attention to the external world increasingly flowed outward . . . into areas in which previously little attention had been given."[79] Similarly, in the United States, by the early 1960s, Kennedy's administration had begun producing a new visual and rhetorical language that reimagined Cold War mobilization for the population and embraced a new idiom of popular international activism, rising cultural credibility, and the embrace of "peaceful competition." In 1961 alone, Kennedy passed the Fulbright-Hays Act (which extended international exchange), the Foreign Assistance Act (which established the United States Agency for International Development), and launched the Peace Corps.

These new images of idealized children were being shaped in response to and as a consequence of rising contradictions in the Cold War universe. The world that seemed to offer unprecedented wealth and comfort also seemed fragile and out of control, menaced by the largely invisible and indefatigable threat of communism, by poor education, lousy parenting, media overload, and delinquency. The world that seemed to promise security and hopefulness for the future was also confronted all the time by the threat of violence and nuclear holocaust. In these same years, when the Pioneers and Boy Scouts were becoming symbols for their nations' commitments to peace, war seemed more likely than ever. In 1954, the CIA secretly overthrew the democratically elected Jacobo Arbenz in Guatemala. Two years later, Khrushchev authorized the invasion of Hungary after the moderate leader, Imre Nagy, became prime minister. In 1961, Kennedy gave his approval for the Bay of Pigs invasion of Cuba, while Khrushchev ordered the construction of the Berlin Wall. Both men came the closest that they ever would to all-out war over the Soviet installation of nuclear missiles in Cuba. By many people's standards, these were the most dangerous years of the Cold War, and yet they were also supposed to be the wealthiest and safest years for the peace-loving populations of the East and the West.

How could leaders convince their constituencies that things were not as bad as they seemed? How could they show them that they were, in fact, seeking peace even if all the indicators seemed to say otherwise? How could they convince their populaces that everything really was okay? Children were a big part of the answer. While the child remained a symbol of threat, it also became a model for mobilization. In the words of children's historian Joe Austin, the contradictions presented by the image of the child highlighted "the bifurcated social identity of youth as [both] a vicious, threatening sign of social decay and [as] our best hope for the future."[80] But these two images were more than bifurcated; they were also bound together in a causal relationship where one necessitated the other, one cured and fixed the other, and in so doing, supported the social system that enabled that cure. In short, the social order and preparedness that was represented by the Pioneers and the Boy Scouts was necessitated by the hooligans and all the children threatened by communism, capitalism, bad parenting, and substandard education. These visions of besieged and mobilized children helped to establish a conceptual framework for the Cold War at home that lasted well into the 1960s (and arguably into the 1980s). For those who possessed the ability to produce and disseminate these images, these bifurcated visions of the Cold War child performed vital functions. They positioned the United States and the Soviet Union as countries under attack by forces both inside and outside their borders. They legitimated the argument that the mobilization of the entire population was required in order to stave off decline and defeat. They established those who owned the means of image production as the arbiters of culture and sociopolitical legitimacy. And they offered a vision of peaceful leadership that stood in contrast to the brinksmanship that actually marked these years. In this period of uncertainty, a new image of the ideal child represented all that could save the nation from disarray. In this period of great threat, the specter of the problem child symbolized the nation's greatest potential for failure.

Since the beginning of the Cold War, the child had been manning the semiotic barricades. By the late 1950s, images of ideal children, whether as Pioneers or Boy Scouts, stood as cynosures of two systems that were both ostensibly focused on providing security for their threatened children while at the same time mobilizing their young for an active crusade for peace and freedom. Although variations in the portrayal of the child certainly are evident in the Soviet and American approaches, they bore more similarities than differences. In so doing, they engaged in parallel projects devoted to the cultivation of a popular consensus with their respective populations and the world.

Yet, amid these constructive efforts, these semiotic barricades were not without their gaps. In the porousness of the visual world that surrounded the Cold War, the image of the child increasingly lost its ability to hold up the universe that had been built on its shoulders in the previous decade. It turned out that childhood could be just as useful in tearing down the Cold War consensus as it was in building it. Individual groups transmitted, consumed, and refashioned these alternative images as a means to redefine the Cold War struggle and to contest their governments' domestic and international policies. While leaders and their supporters in the Soviet Union and the United States used the image of the Cold War kid in similar ways to defend and bolster the status quo, their detractors also found common cause in the mobilization of youth for the questioning of containment and the Cold War consensus.

II

REVISING AN IDEAL

CHAPTER FIVE

Soviet Childhood
in Film during the Thaw

From 1956 until roughly 1967, the Soviet Union experienced an unprecedented opening in the arts known as the Thaw. During these years, Communist Party leaders urged artists, writers, and filmmakers to discard some of the more onerous shackles of Socialist Realism and explore the "unvarnished" realities of Soviet life.[1] They gave tacit approval to works that highlighted the complicated experiences of ordinary citizens while rejecting the formulaic tropes of the Stalinist era. Previously banned writers like Mikhail Zoshchenko and Anna Akhmatova were reintroduced to the Soviet public. Poet Evgenii Yevtushenko was able to publish his controversial poem "Stalin's Heirs," while Khrushchev personally consented to the publication of Aleksandr Solzhenitsyn's *One Day in the Life of Ivan Denisovich*. Sculptors, painters, and filmmakers like Oleg Vassiliev, Anatoly Basin, and Andrei Tarkovsky produced works that in earlier years would have solicited harsh criticism or arrest.

Khrushchev initiated the Thaw for a number of reasons. He viewed it as an important vehicle through which the country could rebuild its creative strength after years of Socialist Realism's imposed artistic mediocrity. He hoped that it would garner the support of the population while destabilizing conservative elements in the Communist Party. He envisioned it as a program for reform that would help the country decrease bureaucratic corruption. He also saw the Thaw as a way to recast the Soviet Union's image abroad, not as a bastion for censorship but as an advocate for human rights and individual expression.[2] For Khrushchev, the arts were an important avenue for the rebuilding of domestic containment and the international waging of the cultural Cold War. But in order to make the arts viable, the legacy of Stalinism would have to be cleared away and a "new, new Soviet man" put in its place. To this end, Khrushchev directed filmmakers, in particular, to lead the world in making movies that excelled not only in their "wealth of content" but also in their "artistic power and execution."[3]

Yet Khrushchev was not prepared for how filmmakers and writers would use the relaxed censorship of the Thaw to contest his domestic and international policies. In the process of turning away from the stock Socialist Realist narrative of the communist utopia toward a more authentic and individual voice, directors touched on larger themes that were still forbidden. They tackled many of Khrushchev's dearest policies by exploring the social impact of his agricultural reforms, the Virgin Lands project, his educational initiatives, and Soviet involvement in the Cold War. As a consequence, the intended consensus-building goals of the Thaw were supplanted by the careful but deliberate struggle of writers, filmmakers, and artists to tear away the patina from a failing myth, with the mechanisms of its construction exposed before the gaze of the world.[4]

Filmmakers pursued these new themes by turning their attention to images that carried weighted meanings in the lexicon of Soviet iconography. As the historian Alexander Prokhorov has noted, "Two heroes dominate the films of this period: the adolescent and the child."[5] In contrast to the idealized vision of mobilized and peaceful childhood being created in official rhetoric during these years, an amazing number of directors turned their attention to children and constructed young characters that showed a clear disregard for the consensus that their leaders had been so diligently trying to build. These kids had little in the way of ideological conviction. They prioritized their own desires and the needs of their families over their obligations to the state. Far from being supported and loved, they appeared abandoned by the adult world around them as they struggled to survive in a harsh and unforgiving environment.

Sometimes these images of youth worked to support the Cold War consensus; sometimes they did not. While these kids' lives may have been difficult, they did seem to reflect the lasting strength and resilience of the Soviet people in the face of hardship. In a time when the state was encouraging artists to explore the vagaries of real life, the sometimes harsh depictions of the young that appeared on the screen reflected the country's commitment to artistic openness. At the same time, however, these new images of youth also seemed to raise some unavoidable questions about the country's ability and willingness to mobilize for the Cold War. As the ice of Stalinism melted, Khrushchev discovered the underlying current ran against the Cold War consensus. They seemed to show the damage that could be done when state priorities superseded the needs of the individual and the family. Such depictions envisioned a society that had been irretrievably damaged and disillusioned by the ravages of Stalinism and World War II. The children that emerged out of these films were in no position to assume a new "peace offensive." These filmmakers made movies that at times bore little resemblance to the consensus that was ostensibly a founding feature of Soviet society. The multiple meanings that these images carried reveal an era not of collective compliance but of contested perspectives on Soviet society and its future. They provide a window into the often unspoken anxieties of the Cold War in Soviet society during these years. They tell a story of an entire populace that was growing increasingly skeptical about the direction in which their leaders were taking them.

The Cold War in Soviet Thaw film is largely unexplored in current scholarship, largely because manifestations of the Cold War in these movies are subtle and often hidden. Any historian searching for the Soviet equivalent of *Dr. Strangelove* will be disappointed; such films were simply not possible in the carefully censored environment of Soviet moviemaking. Yet upon careful examination (and particularly if one looks closely at the previously uncovered debates surrounding these films during production, which can be found in the Soviet film archives), Cold War resonances are alive and well in the films of this period. As Peter Biskind argues, "It is in [the] 'everyday films,' which seem to shoulder no ideological burden," that evidence of Cold War thinking is best disclosed.[6] Just as American Westerns like *Red River* and sci-fi dramas like *The Thing* could mirror popular ambiguities concerning the battle against communism in the United States, so too could Soviet films reveal underlying doubts about the ability of Soviet society to succeed in its struggle with the West and the heavy price that it was paying for mobilization.[7]

The Cold War appeared in films of the Thaw not simply because filmmakers intended it, but also because these films frequently assumed new meanings through the processes of production and reception. As the famously strong-willed director Andrei Tarkovsky himself admitted, the audience plays an important role in "bringing an image into being" and determining the meanings of what they see.[8] Even when directors saw no Cold War significance in their work, reviewers and members of the Soviet Filmmakers' Union often did. In addition, when we come to these films from a contemporary perspective, with an understanding of how the Cold War was conceptualized officially in the Soviet Union during these years, new messages materialize that we might have previously missed. By unearthing the Cold War cultural messages of Thaw film it becomes possible to "excavate the hidden and not-so-hidden" meanings buried beneath the surfaces of these movies.[9] These meanings show a world that stands in deep contrast to that being mass-produced by the Pioneers and the Communist Party in these same years. Such an investigation not only confirms the significance of the Cold War in shaping how filmmakers and critics viewed the world around them, but it also shows how the party leadership's official conceptualizations of the Cold War, and of the ideal child, were open to revision.

Children of War, Then and Now

The first films that questioned the Cold War consensus were those that reexamined the Soviet experience of the previous war. In earlier years, Stalinist films on the Great Patriotic War had adhered to a carefully monitored set of themes. Popular movies like Fredrikh Ermler's *She Defends the Motherland* (1943) and Mikhail Chiaureli's *The Fall of Berlin* (1949) had focused on the heroic legacy of the Soviet army in expelling the Germans from Russia and on Stalin's personal role in ensuring victory. These early works presented images of Soviet men, women, and children as noble fighters, willing martyrs, and loyal Stalinists. In the words of Denise Youngblood, such films attempted to "cement Stalin's regime," and they reflected the Soviet Union's return in the late 1940s to "strict cultural and social control."[10] By largely ignoring the gruesome realities of the battlefield as well as the physical and psychological trauma that the war had wrought upon the Soviet populace, these films worked to create a mythologized memory of the war that testified to the heroic feats of Stalin, to the role of the Soviet Union in bringing peace to Europe and the world, to the country's quick return to superpower status, and to the popular consensus that undergirded all of this strength and recovery.

When Khrushchev initiated the Thaw in 1956, filmmakers immediately began making a new kind of war film; these movies took an unflinching view of the war experience and its long-term effects on the population. They created characters that were deeply flawed and traumatized by the brutality around them. They largely ignored Stalin's role in the war and instead focused on the personal stories of families and individuals struggling to survive. At a time when filmmakers in the West were still producing their own set of mythmaking movies about the heroic American and British war experiences,[11] Soviet filmmakers forced the camera's eye to explore the war as a brutal event that left an entire continent in ruins, scarred by the horror of what its inhabitants had seen, with a slim chance for a quick recovery. They depicted children, in particular, as traumatized, hungry, vengeful, abandoned, disillusioned, and deeply cynical about the world around them. They portrayed youth as functioning outside of the state's control. They showed the next generation as motivated not by ideological or patriotic convictions, but by fear, vengeance, and personal desires.

For some filmmakers and viewers, these images upheld the state-sponsored view of the Soviet Union as a strong, peace-loving country and presented the sacrifices that had been made by the population during the war to protect the world from Nazi tyranny. They testified to the Soviet Union's commitment to peace, and they stood as evidence of the people's strength and resilience in the midst of incredible loss.

For others, these images carried meanings that seemingly undermined the contemporary image of the Soviet Union as a powerful defender of peace. They raised questions about the ability of the generation that had grown up during the war to mobilize again against the West. They showed children who carried little to no ideological conviction. They depicted youth who were far from protected and nurtured but instead appeared as abandoned by the adult world. They also provided a searing statement about the terror of war in general that hinted at the dangers of Soviet Cold War brinksmanship while also indicting the warmongering of the West. At a time when images of strong, peace-loving children were being manufactured to support the state's official conceptualization of the struggle with the West, these alternative visions of Soviet youth as disillusioned, exhausted, vengeful, and unprepared for modern mobilization stood out as challenges to the Cold War consensus.

The first film to reconceptualize the child's image in war was Marlen Khutsiev's *Two Fedors* (1958), which told the story of a young soldier and a boy who struggle to build a family in the wake of World War II. The film begins as the war is ending. A young soldier is heading home when he meets an orphaned child hiding in his boxcar. During their train ride, the two characters realize that they have much in common. Aside from sharing the same name, they are both survivors of the war, completely alone, incapable of sentimentality, and, as one reviewer phrased it, "removed from society through their shared attitudes of loneliness."[12] At a crucial point in the film, the young Fedor gets off the train to meet his "aunt" who ostensibly lives in a nearby town. The older Fedor guesses that there is no aunt and that the boy actually has nowhere to go. As the locomotive begins to pull away, the older Fedor runs after the child, sweeps him up in his arms, and returns him to the train, thereby committing himself to the care of his namesake. As the two characters begin to settle down in their new home, they quickly switch roles: the boy's dirty, almost wrinkled face reflects a practical knowledge and cynical acceptance of the world around him. He cooks, cleans, and makes sure that his older companion gets his vitamins. Meanwhile, the older Fedor loses their ration cards and decides to buy ice cream instead of potatoes (an action that receives a scolding from his young ward).

Big Fedor is childlike in his habits, and he carries a sense of ethics and belief that is largely in line with the consensus being promoted in the 1950s (but is completely naive and out of place in the rubble of the postwar world). This is emphasized when the young Fedor, in an attempt to find food after the ration cards have been lost, steals a chicken for them to eat. When the older Fedor realizes that the bird is stolen, he admonishes the boy for his dishonesty and forces him to throw the uneaten chicken away. In the young Fedor's eyes, and in the eyes of the viewer, this waste of food is more shocking and somehow more morally reprehensible than the theft itself. The established parameters of right and wrong, which the older Fedor couches in terms of communist obligations to the needs of the collective, make no sense to the young boy. While big Fedor holds on to established, Soviet ethics, the child carries with him a different moral compass that places the needs of the family and the self over those of the country and the communist ideal.

Despite his claims of moral correctness, for the majority of the film the older Fedor appears incapable of creating a world that is physically and psychologically safe for his adopted son. On the boy's first day of school, the soldier forgets to pick up young Fedor in the afternoon, leaving the child alone waiting in vain for someone to retrieve him. Little Fedor finally gives up on waiting for his new father. He wanders the streets, staring into shop windows filled with happy mannequins holding hands and laughing, themselves reflecting the false security that the world around him claims to offer. The soldier's reason for missing the pick-up time is that he has met a long-haired girl and has chosen to spend his evening with her instead. Not only does the older Fedor make a choice that compromises the fragile happiness of his younger namesake, but he again takes on the role of child and adolescent as he places his own desires over those of his family. As a symbol of the country's efforts to reconstruct and remobilize, he conveys the message that before the Soviet Union can make the country safe for its children, it must first let go of the traumas of the war and assume its responsibilities to the next generation. Yet such a transformation remains elusive for the older Fedor through much of the film, symbolizing the difficulties that the entire population is experiencing in meeting its duties to rebuild the country.

The climax of the film occurs when the young Fedor runs away, again to "see his aunt." Again the older Fedor chases after him and again he brings him home. This time, however, the roles of the two Fedors do not seem as ambiguous. Upon the boy's retrieval, it appears as though they are a family now. The younger Fedor has a mother and a father. The film seems to promise that the boy will now go to school, that he will fit into the community and into his appropriate persona as a Soviet child. This redemptive ending seemingly sets a path for Soviet reconstruction from the rubble of the war. It argues to viewers at home and abroad that despite the great losses wrought by the war, the country has indeed recovered. As one reviewer wrote in the months after the film's release, *Two Fedors* had shown to the world the "strength of the Soviet people" and their "great capacity for sacrifice and kindness."[13]

Yet the Cold War resonances in *Two Fedors* were ultimately not all positive. As some Soviet critics noted at the time, instead of providing a hopeful image of Soviet communist reconstruction after 1945, Khutsiev showed his viewers a generation of traumatized, non–ideologically driven children and adults for whom current Cold War mobilization seemed highly unlikely. For instance, in the months following the Hungarian Revolt in the fall of 1956, conservative reviewers of the screenplay (the film was in pre-production at this point) accused the film of being too "dark" and claimed that it was inappropriate for the times.[14] The Ukraine Ministry of Culture argued that "the film does not depict our reality, it is pessimistic and uninspiring. You can't tell what country it's set in. If it's ours, then why don't the schoolchildren wear ties? And what sort of hero is this—sullen, taciturn, unsociable? That's not what our people are like."[15] Such accusations reflected anxieties not about the state of the country in 1945 but about how *Two Fedors* might impact the Soviet Union's image in the eyes of contemporary viewers in 1956. Despite its seemingly normative ending, the fact that the film showed children without their Pioneer ties who were "sullen" raised for these critics questions about the strength of the country's ideological convictions and the ability of the state to foster appropriate behavior in the young. As Victor Nekrasov reminded his readers in his review of the film, there had been an entire generation that had left the schools for the front during the 1940s and had returned to find nothing but ashes. He described boys who had spent their childhoods learning to kill and be killed. "And how are they to live now, when such skills are not needed?" he asked his colleagues.[16] In the opinions of these critics, such images questioned the idea of this child becoming the foundation upon which a new Soviet future could be built.

The question of what would become of the children of war was also tacitly approached in the film itself. At one point after the young Fedor has run away for the second time, the soldier turns in anguish to his girlfriend and says, "What can I do? How can I make a future for him?" On the surface, the film seemed to answer the question by showing the reunion of the two Fedors and the construction of their new family. Yet the question that the older Fedor asked was an important one. As Nekrasov noted, it applied not only to the young Fedor but also to all of the children that experienced the war, including the ones who were not lucky enough to be adopted by generous strangers. For those children, survival alone appeared to be a great accomplishment, while the prospects of becoming an idealized and mobilized Cold War kid seemed distant indeed.

The Cold War issues that were alluded to in Khutsiev's *Two Fedors* were reexamined in a more penetrating way in Andrei Tarkovsky's 1962 masterpiece *Ivan's Childhood*, which also set out to portray the terrible realities of war from the perspective of the child. The film, which received awards at the Venice Film Festival, provided the era's most poignant image of lost and unprotected youth. In twelve-year-old Ivan, Tarkovsky created a child who, while heroic, was nonetheless a far cry from the positive and hopeful image of youth that was so central to Socialist Realist film and to contemporary images of Soviet childhood. He was a youngster who had no future, no ideological belief, and no hope for salvation. Ivan, like Fedor, was seen by some contemporary critics as a symbol of the country's inability to reconstruct and remobilize for another war. His disturbing lack of ideological belief was similarly problematic in the late 1950s, as it raised questions about the willingness of the next generation to engage in the contemporary struggle with the West. Ivan also became a focus for heated debates regarding the failure of adults to protect the young from war and how that reflected upon the ostensible commitment of the communist state to defend its children.

Ivan's Childhood tells the story of a young boy who works as a spy in the no-man's-land between the German and Russian fronts during World War II. The film begins with remembered visions of a happy and healthy Ivan running through a field of butterflies to join his mother. This fantasy is quickly wiped away by the sounds of gunfire. In muted grays and low contrasts, the image of a boy with torn clothes and sunken cheeks is revealed. From his darkened hiding place in the interior of a windmill, the frame opens to a desolate panorama of dead bodies and hulking tanks. Tarkovsky's camera follows Ivan from the vantage point of the barren birch trees as he silently wades, alone, into the chest-high frigid waters of the no-man's-land. Finally he finds refuge in a Soviet army bunker.[17]

Ivan's body represents the physical destruction of all war. In the film, by the dim light of a single lamp, he disrobes to reveal a small, fragile, scarred form attached to the face of a world-weary adult. The camera encourages the viewer to be shocked by Ivan's body, just as the ranking lieutenant in the bunker is stopped short at the sight of the boy. "What's that on your back?" he asks as Ivan removes his shirt. Ivan turns as the camera catches a glimpse of a large scar, half covered in shadow. "Answer me!" the lieutenant orders. "It's none of your business. And don't shout at me!" the clearly exhausted Ivan retorts; a universal warning of what is wrought upon the young by war, not just in 1942 but in the Cold War as well. As one member of the Filmmakers' Union stated in 1962, the most striking scene of the film came for him when Ivan first appeared on the screen. "He bears upon his skinny, shivering, hungry, unfortunate shoulders such drama that we need not know how his mother or father died. We are instead confronted immediately with the reality of children and war."[18] Similar scenes are repeated throughout the film in long close-up shots that linger on Ivan's ribs, his arms, and his neck. The camera becomes a witness to the physical effects of war upon the child.

Ivan's bodily destruction is compounded by the fact that he is orphaned, not just by his mother's death, but by the unwillingness of any adult to take responsibility for him. Like Khutsiev, Tarkovsky focuses on the uncertain obligations of adults to care for the next generation and the effects of such uncertainties upon the young. With his family long since dead, Ivan spends the majority of the film in the company of the young Lieutenant Galtsev and his ranking officer, Captain Kholin. The two men engage in an ongoing debate over what should be done with the boy. At first, their concern for Ivan appears almost parental. For instance, when Ivan arrives in the bunker at the beginning of the film, Galtsev draws him a bath, provides him with dry clothes, and tenderly carries him to bed. Later, when Ivan is met by the older officer, Kholin, he is showered with kisses and expressions of concern over his diminishing weight. Later in the film, when the men decide to send Ivan away from the front to a military school where he can be safe, Ivan runs away in protest and leads the men in a search to find him. Like the older Fedor's rescue of the younger Fedor in Khutsiev's film, Galtsev and Kholin retrieve Ivan from the rubble of a burned-out village. They attempt to express to him why he must leave the front. Kholin says to him, "Can't you understand, silly, that war is for grown men?" Yet Ivan provides a number of reasons for why he should not be sent away. He argues that he is useful in the field. He reminds the men that adult scouts have been killed in the past because they were too big. "Besides," he states, "I'm alone. You know I have no family left." When Kholin announces that Ivan must go nonetheless, the boy yells, "You're not my dad to decide!" After a long pause, Kholin retorts, "Shut up, or I'll spank you. You're my pain in the neck." Such fatherly words bring a smile to Ivan's tear-soaked face. They imply that Kholin is perhaps beginning to see himself as a guardian for the boy, and they give the viewer a sense of security in knowing that Ivan will be cared for, even if he doesn't want to be.

Yet unlike the younger Fedor, Ivan has no one to intervene on his behalf. They become the mannequins of Fedor's shop window, the pretention of a caring family. In the end, Kholin's and Galtsev's parental instincts are not as great as their need for Ivan to perform another mission, thus transforming the boy from a symbol of salvation into an image of abandonment. Near the end of the film, while the men and Ivan wait in a ruined church for nightfall in order to begin their mission, Galtsev again makes the argument that Ivan should go to school. This time, however, Kholin provides the arguments against Ivan's departure from the front. He admits openly that he himself is still a child and will not be able to adopt the boy, thereby denying his responsibility as father. "And besides," he argues, "All [Ivan] can think of is vengeance." These arguments are seconded by Ivan, who reminds the men that children are an integral part of the war. When Galtsev again asserts that the boy should leave, Ivan yells at the lieutenant for forgetting about the concentration camps and the suffering of children there. "What are you *talking* about? What?" Ivan cries at Galtsev, his face only inches from the screen.

Ivan eventually returns to the no-man's-land, fading back into the muted grays of the frigid swamp where we had first met him. At the end of the film, Galtsev is seen sorting through German paperwork on Soviet casualties in the rubble of Berlin. He comes across Ivan's photograph next to a report that the boy was captured and hanged.

The image of Ivan carried different meanings for different people in 1962. According to some reviewers, Ivan was a lasting testament to Soviet military might and was representative of the population's willingness to sacrifice everything in defense of freedom. This was the argument made by the film critic and screenwriter Nikolai Kovarskii (who would later write the screenplay for the 1966 film *The Shot*). He declared during the review meetings for the screenplay (which were required by the Filmmakers' Union in order to move on to production) that the themes introduced in *Ivan's Childhood* attested to the "magnificent character of the Soviet people. It is a theme of [the] gigantic responsibility that the boy takes by working on the same level as the adults. . . . It is a theme that touches on the need for calm nerves, a theme of how war can be fought without bullets . . . a theme of how character can win a war."[19] Such an interpretation attempted to fit Ivan into the contemporary heroic war myth that acknowledged the valiant efforts of the Soviet people and deemphasized the image of Stalin altogether. It also attempted to cast Ivan as a lasting testament to Soviet strength in the contemporary era.

Figure 5.1. *Ivanovo Detstvo* (*Ivan's Childhood*, 1962).
Andrei Tarkovsky. Courtesy of Mosfilm

Other reviewers and critics also saw the film as a testament to the Soviet pursuit of peace around the world. Neia Zorkaia has argued, for instance, that Ivan reinforced the state's public image as a crusader for peace. She contends that in the context of the Cold War, Tarkovsky's Ivan can be seen as a well-placed testament to the Soviet desire for peace. "Andrei Tarkovsky always resented political time-serving," she comments, "but he had an acute sense of time, which prompted his new interpretation of a wartime story."[20] Similar sentiments were expressed at the time by American reviewers of the film, who acknowledged its artistic merits but argued that it was, nonetheless, a piece of Soviet propaganda meant to fit into the larger officially promoted image of the Soviet Union as a defender of peace in the world.[21] These interpretations provided by Kovarskii and Zorkaia undoubtedly help to explain why this film made it past the censors and onto the world screen. For many in the Soviet Union, *Ivan* provided a means for remembering the heroic Soviet past and for casting the Soviet role in the Cold War as an ongoing and heartfelt crusade for peace.

Nonetheless, these were not the only meanings that Ivan's image carried. Whereas for some reviewers, Ivan's destroyed psyche and body represented the spirit of Soviet strength and sacrifice, for others it was an image that questioned the presumed concern of the Soviet system for its youth, that exposed the destruction of a generation that had been lost to war, and that revealed the horror of war in general. Just as the positive meanings of Ivan's image seemed to support the state's official conceptualization of the Cold War as a struggle for peace, so too did the more disturbing meanings of Ivan's form seem to question this view by presenting a destroyed and unprotected generation that had no hope for reconstruction and no commitment to peace.

In 1960, while the film's screenplay was undergoing review, the Filmmakers' Union devoted the majority of its heated debates to the decision of the two officers to send Ivan back to the front. A number of members worried that this action would not be interpreted correctly by contemporary viewers, who would not understand why the Soviet Union had allowed the young to participate in war. One union member lamented to his colleagues and Tarkovsky that the film had made every adult in the room feel as though he needed to apologize for what had happened to the country's children. "Yes, it happened," he admitted. "It was so brutal! At the front there were even organizations of schoolchildren who, after three or four weeks of preparation, we threw over to the other side [perebrasyvalis' za liniiu fronta] and used for reconnaissance. We knew it was wrong, and yet we did it. But did we have a choice? And how can we convey this to the people now?"[22] For all of the union members, this film touched upon the rawest of feelings. It harkened back to the terrible things that had been done in the name of war and for the sake of victory, not just to children but to everyone. It also presented an image of adult Soviet behavior that many feared would be misinterpreted by foreign audiences as evidence of Soviet brutality against its own children.

Worries about contemporary misinterpretations of the film also centered on Ivan's terrible fate and what that might say to audiences about the Soviet Union's ability to recover in the aftermath of the war.[23] Some members of the union strongly urged Tarkovsky to rethink Ivan's tragic death. "It would be possible to save the boy!" Kovarskii pleaded in 1960, while the script was still under revision. He argued that such an action would carry an "enormous contemporary subtext." By this, he presumably meant that Ivan's survival, like that of the young Fedor, would provide evidence to modern audiences of the Soviet Union's ability to survive and save its children, even in the wake of unspeakable terror. But the film's screenwriter, Andrei Bogomolov, refused to adopt the redemptive ending. He retorted that such a subtext would not be compatible with his intentions in writing the script. "What were we trying to say in the end?" he asked himself and the others at the Filmmakers' Union meeting where the ending was discussed. "We wanted to say that people who have survived much become dear to each other, and yet because it is war, they do not ever really meet and are left wishing that they could have connected."[24] Bogomolov's comment, although vague, spoke to the inability to recover from such an event. He wanted to avoid any message that might have provided a hopeful view of the Soviet war experience or of the possibilities for recovery. In May 1961, Bogomolov again declared to the members of the Filmmakers' Union that it was his direct intention in writing the screenplay "to show that in all wars, childhood is not possible and that love is not possible. Sometimes, there can be no reconstruction."[25] Writing a heroic narrative of Soviet national strength and vigilance was not Bogomolov's intent. Instead, he and Tarkovsky sought to use the figure of Ivan to reveal the permanent and irrevocable damage done by the war. They also hinted at the potential for similar destruction in future wars. In the final scenes of the film, where Galtsev's voiceover is heard, he asks the viewer, "Won't this be the last war on earth?" On the screen, the records of the dead are pulled from the rubble. The camera pans back to reveal a room filled with records. Black ash, fallout from the bombing of Berlin, descends from the sky and covers the floor as Galtsev is revealed to be the only survivor of the group.

For some reviewers of the film, Ivan's character and motivation proved even more disturbing than his abandonment and death. Ivan is revealed as a child consumed not by a desire for peace, but by a lust for vengeance that supersedes even his own need for survival. In addition to wanting to do his patriotic duty for the war effort, his refusal to go to military school is also explained by his deep and abiding need for revenge. This motivation is revealed in a memorable scene set in the ruined church before the final reconnaissance mission. Standing alone in the darkened room, the young Ivan fantasizes about bringing his wrath upon the German men who killed his mother and friends. Through the beam of his flashlight, he finds writing on a wall written by eighteen Russian soldiers waiting to be shot by the Germans. In their short message, they call upon those still living to avenge them. The boy becomes enraged. Light and dark flash across the screen, revealing Ivan's contorted face, a knife in his hand, a glimpse of his mother, a German army coat hanging on the wall. These images are made more chaotic by the loud sounds of a weeping woman. "You must stand trial!" Ivan calls out into the darkness before collapsing in tears. Scenes like this one revealed the extent of his destructive passion and the traumatic effects of the war upon his psyche. They presented a vision of a generation that had become lost, not only through its inability to move beyond the traumas of the war but through its absence of hope. The historian Josephine Woll has noted that Ivan is a child who cannot be saved. Shots near the end of the film show documentary footage of Goebbels's poisoned children, suggesting the "twin motifs of vengeance and of ravaged childhood." They attest to the fact that "not only our Ivan (and his Russian peers) have lost their [hopefulness and innocence] to war: all children have."[26]

The Cold War meanings conveyed in these images were unavoidable for some Soviet reviewers who saw the film on the big screen. As one critic put it in 1962, Ivan represented a "violation both of normal psychological upbringing and of the world of the child." He argued that "this is not a view of Soviet childhood that we want to promote now. . . . What does this say about the beliefs of our youth and about their ability to build a future?"[27] Such criticism reveals the extent to which Cold War concerns colored the viewing experience, at least for conservative reviewers and state censors. Many reviewers watching this film were acutely aware of the subtexts that such images could carry for contemporary audiences, as Ivan seemed to have rejected the image of the peace-loving and hopeful Cold War kid. These contrasting perspectives on the meanings of Ivan's story constituted opposing views on how to remember the war itself and arguably on the role that the Soviet Union was playing in the current crisis with the United States—as either an advocate for peace or a player in a dangerous game that threatened everyone. On the one hand, the film seemed to support Khrushchev's argument that "peaceful coexistence" was the only possible alternative for the world. Yet, while Khrushchev was making the argument to his population that Soviet children would "manifest the new communist morals of the Soviet people" and would "find their place in life, and combine their fate with the fate of the country," Tarkovsky was creating an image of childhood that was identified not by peaceful mobilization and the construction of a national future, but by vengeance, destruction, chaos, and death.[28] Moreover, while Khutsiev in *Two Fedors* had created an image of a generation whose mobilization for the Cold War was questionable, Tarkovsky created a vision of youth for whom mobilization was impossible. The form of the lost child became a visual manifestation of unspoken fears about the future of Russia's youth and the permanent damage that had been done by the war.

These same images and ideas were revisited again, three years later, when Mikhail Romm directed his pseudo-documentary *Ordinary Fascism*. Romm's work represented the first attempt in the Soviet Union to provide a documentary on fascism and, implicitly, on totalitarianism. It did not tell a story in any conventional sense, although it carried narrative components through its organization of particular images from throughout the Nazi period.[29] The film instead analyzed "the instincts and motives of people who ceded their individuality to become part of a mindless social mass."[30] On the surface, the movie served as a statement against the "psychological vulnerability of the German petite bourgeoisie," but *Ordinary Fascism* also made unmistakable references to both the capacity for similar "group think" during the Stalinist era and the presence of comparable dangers in the nuclear age.[31]

Romm set out in 1960 to analyze the fascist experience using only real footage drawn from 2 million meters of seized Nazi film, which was then supplemented with still photographs taken from Hitler's personal photographer, Heinrich Hoffman, as well as ordinary photographs taken by German soldiers, by Romm, and by other Soviet cinematographers in the last months of the war.[32] After sorting his vast materials into 120 piles separated by theme, Romm, often said to be the grandfather of Soviet Thaw film, sat down to build a series of episodes that would show the process by which a country of seemingly moral, God-fearing, German citizens could become agents of genocide. He then combined these images with his own commentary, which used irony, humor, and outright anger to guide his viewers through a maze of visual allusion and parallel. Like that of Khutsiev and Tarkovsky, Romm's work in many ways revolved around contested images of children. By showing the dual capacities of adults to both care for and destroy youth, Romm explored the potential for collective brutality in all people. Whereas Tarkovsky's *Ivan* had provided a specific portrayal of war's impact upon one fictional child, Romm took the same themes of the "lost generation" and the creation of vengeful youth and applied them to hundreds of portrayals of real children both during World War II and in the years of rising Cold War tensions.

Romm's film in many ways reads like an academic essay. It presents its primary argument in the first ten minutes by pointing out the contradictory identities that human beings are capable of assuming. In the first several scenes of the film, viewers are shown an array of children's drawings of cats. They see footage of students preparing to take exams, mothers pushing baby carriages, and endearing drawings by children of their mothers. Such images reflect the collective humanity and shared love of family that encompasses humankind. Then Romm cuts from a photograph of a Soviet mother holding her child while crossing a Moscow street, to a still of a Jewish mother shielding her child as they are both shot by an SS agent. The camera dwells silently on piles of children's potties that were brought to the concentration camps by mothers who thought there would be a need for them. These images present to the viewer the film's primary questions: What is the process that

Figure 5.2. *Obyknovennyi fashizm* (*Ordinary Fascism*, 1965).
Mikhail Romm. Courtesy of Mosfilm.

transforms loving individuals into soldiers capable of shooting and burning the innocent? How is it that children can be the focus of deep love and also targets for extermination?

For the remainder of the film, Romm sets out to explore how such contradictory identities are possible. He focuses his attention first on the rise of Hitler's cult of personality, spending almost ten minutes chronicling the meticulous binding of a leather-bound copy of *Mein Kampf* as a reflection of the leader's deification in the 1930s. He then turns to examinations of "ordinary life" in Nazi Germany, looking there for the origins of Nazi behavior. Books are burned at Berlin University. Academics are transformed into soldiers in uniform. Romm's voice intones, "These are humans too. But yet they are not really human. They are a mass." Romm's image of the transformed child then hits the screen. In these segments, which are taken from Nazi propaganda films, German children appear cared for, they are well-nourished and happy, they are shown playing hopscotch to the anthem of the National Socialist Party. Yet in contrast to the drawings shown at the beginning of the film, these children display illustrations of tanks, swastikas, and knives. They work diligently to draft a birthday card for Hitler. The child now becomes not just an object of contested concern and destruction, but the first step in creating the fascist identity. These are children who are learning to kill and be killed. These are children driven by hate who will soon become adults.

Romm's study of the fascist transformation culminates in the final chapter, where he shows images of goose-stepping Hitler Youth followed by scenes of young, growling American soldiers armed with bayonets. "This is the final product," Romm announces. These images and this statement convey two messages. First, they represent the end of the transformative path that Romm has been tracing from the joyful drawings of cats and loving parents to the unimaginable acts of the SS. Second, they make an explicit link between the transformation of youth under the Nazis and the transformation happening among the young in the modern Cold War world. At the end of the film, a nuclear bomb explodes, standing as a terrifying portent of what horrors are possible when such transformations are allowed to occur.

But the transformations that Romm sought to trace were not simply relegated to the "bourgeois world." At a Mosfilm viewing of the work in 1963, for instance, Sasha Bovin referred directly to the "Ordinary Stalinism" that was also inferred in the film.[33] More than this, for some critics of the film, Romm's message failed adequately to differentiate between the upbringings that Soviet and Western children were receiving. Not only did it portray kids who were destroyed and incapable of contemporary mobilization (as Khutsiev and Tarkovsky had), it also seemed to argue that the capacity for brutality was present in the Soviet system as well as in the capitalist one. "Where is the Soviet Union in this film to stand apart from these examples?" one member of the Filmmakers' Union asked Romm in 1962. "You should be clearer in showing that this is not possible here."[34] In some ways, Romm answered this question in the film when he tied pictures of snarling boys with bayonets to his commentary: "You think you know war? You don't know war. Here are the children. What do they know about war?" Romm was reminding his viewers that the dangers of transformation into the life of "ordinary fascism" are easily forgotten by the young, in both the East and the West. He was also making it clear that the consequences of such transformations were nothing less than a nuclear holocaust.

Khrushchev's subsequent criticism of Romm's film testifies to the power of the director's critical vision in speaking to modern issues surrounding the Cold War and the arms race. In 1963, Khrushchev stated in a speech before government officials that "there are certain twisted and wrong views on the role of the cinema among screen people. This applies, in particular, to so well-known and experienced a filmmaker as Mikhail Romm."[35] Khrushchev's criticism of the film was not directed toward Romm's representation of German barbarity but with the film's larger message, which spoke to the Soviet role in the Cold War.[36] Romm's film served not only as powerful documentation of the horrors of the Holocaust, but it also provided a stinging commentary about the world's escalating Cold War aggression.

By recasting the image of the child as embattled, destroyed, and made violent by war, Khutsiev, Tarkovsky, and Romm created a new set of parameters for remembering the Great Patriotic War, and they also presented a vision of youth that was strikingly different from the one produced by the state during these years. Far from being mobilized for peace and economic competition, these children appeared to be prepared only for disillusionment and death, with no hope for the future, which promised only more war. In many ways, these images fit into the larger message being generated by the Pioneers and the Communist Party leadership in these years—that the Soviet Union sought peace because it had experienced the horrors of war and sought to never experience them again. Yet in other ways these images stood as new and remarkably persistent reminders that the population had been permanently affected by their experiences, that childhood itself was not possible in war, and that such horror could happen again.

Abandoned Children in the Khrushchev Era

The image of the suffering child was not restricted to the war story. Thaw films set in the 1950s and 60s also used visions of abandoned and disillusioned children to talk about problems that existed in current Soviet society. They explored the legacy of fear and secrecy from the Stalinist era, the suffering of individuals and families at the expense of state policies, and the loneliness and disillusionment of youth. They also became, as Alexander Prokhorov has argued, a way to focus their attention away from grandiose stories about the collective Soviet family, with its national crusades for mobilization and competitive coexistence, toward the single family, with its personal dramas and its individual dreams.[37] Like Fedor and Ivan, children in these films represented a contrasting image of youth, who, instead of being educated, protected, and prepared by the state for the furthering of the country's Cold War interests, were left without state and parental guidance, had a cynical view of society, and were dependent largely upon themselves to carve their own destinies.

The themes of individual drama and abandonment were central to Georgy Daneliya and Igor Talankin's 1960 film *Serezha*. The movie tells the story of a young boy who is adopted by his kind stepfather, a party official, and who is faced with abandonment when his family must relocate to Siberia without him. Unlike the propaganda films that the boy watches in the movie theater on the success of collectivization, Serezha's life is, in the words of Josephine Woll, "far more complex and absorbing than the artifice of the so-called 'actuality' that is presented in Soviet propaganda."[38] On the surface, this film's story of a father who must leave his little boy in order to save a distant communal farm followed the basic tenets of the traditional Socialist Realist narrative by highlighting the sacrifices made by Soviet citizens to further the communist cause. Yet because the movie sought to tell the story from the perspective of one solitary child, it revealed the heart-wrenching and personal consequences of such sacrifices upon real families. This retelling of the Socialist Realist narrative dramatized the conflict between the family and the state and ultimately questioned the value of such heroic sacrifices when they led to the abandonment of children and the destruction of families.

Serezha begins with the entrance of a new father into the family of a widowed mother and her young son. Suspicious at first, Serezha is soon won over by the man when they go into the city to buy a new bicycle. Serezha quickly decides that, like his new father, he wants to be a farm director when he grows up. He is filled with pride when he sees his dad on an official newsreel documenting the successes of the farm. He is later tempted to become a sailor when he sees the amazing tattoos on the back of his friend's father (he even tries to get a tattoo on his own hand) but soon realizes that while the sailor may be adventurous, he is also brutish and not nearly as good a father as his own.

Serezha's hope and innocence are made all the more poignant when the boy realizes that he is soon to be left behind. His father has become so successful as a farm director that he now is being ordered to move to Siberia to fix a failing farm. The parents have decided to leave Serezha because he has a cold and he would be difficult to care for in the distant steppe. Late in the evening before the rest of the family is due to leave, Serezha runs into the room where his father is working and begs him to let him come along. With tears streaming down his face, he pleads, "Please do not go! Please take me with you! I beg you, please!" In the dark of the night, the father takes Serezha on a walk through the woods and attempts to explain to the boy why the family must go.

> FATHER: There's such a word as "must" my boy. Don't go thinking
>   that we like going to Kholmogory. But we must, and we go.
> SEREZHA: But why papa?
> FATHER: Such is life.

At the climax of the film, Serezha stands in the glare of the car's headlight as it prepares to leave. The boy's mother orders him to move out of the way so that the car can pull off. Serezha then steps out of the light and into the dark shadow of the empty house, thereby mirroring his movement away from innocence and hope toward abandonment and loneliness. Serezha's face reflects a deep grief coming from his realization that he is now alone and that the dreams he had held for his new family had been fantasy. While such

Figure 5.3. *Serezha*
(1960). Georgy Daneliya
and Igor Talankin.
Courtesy of Mosfilm.

separations were a reality for many Soviet citizens throughout these years, never before had the personal tragedy of such an event been captured with so much pathos. The resigned little boy standing in the snow represented a transformation of youth that was different from the one observed by Romm, but was no less poignant. Instead of symbolizing the change from innocence to violence, the film captured the boy's metamorphosis from innocence to disillusionment, resignation, and awareness of loss.

At the film's end, Serezha turns his back on the camera and begins to walk away. The visual chaos created by the white snow on the screen is amplified by the loud sounds of the car. Then, just as all appears lost, the father stops and yells to the boy, "You are coming! Get your things!" The joy on Serezha's face reflects the relief felt by every viewer sitting in the theater. As he runs frantically through the house gathering his things, his mother yells to her husband, "What are you doing! We cannot bring him!" But the father cannot bear to leave him behind. "It doesn't matter. I can't do it!" he yells back at her. Serezha and his father tearfully embrace as the car pulls away into the white snow, but not before we, as spectators, have been allowed to feel the profound sense of abandonment that Serezha felt as he stood alone. What we are left with is a sense that, in the end, the boy's abandonment was only prevented by the fact that the farm director was willing to put the needs of his own individual family before those of the state.

In a period when the mobilization of the family and the child was presented as a popular imperative by the state, *Serezha* stood as an example of what state directives could do to the family, and how families ultimately could choose a different path. As one union member put it in 1958, "Serezha's father makes a choice that we all approve of, but it is a difficult choice that will have an impact upon his ability to do his job in Kholmogory. There is a contradiction here."[39] Such contradictions reflected unspoken anxieties about the role of the individual in performing his or her prescribed obligations to society while still living an authentic life that included a devotion to family.

Moreover, *Serezha* presented an image of youth that was different from the ideal vision being created by the Pioneers and the state. The boy appears innocent and hopeful at the beginning of the narrative, but by the final shots he has experienced disillusionment, abandonment, and suspicion of the older generation. It is worth noting that the film's release came during the fortieth anniversary of the Komsomol, when the premier film journal, *Iskusstvo kino*, along with all of the mainstream newspapers, printed articles in almost every edition praising the power of youth and the next generation's role in creating a new, mobilized Soviet future. As Lev Karpinskii wrote, "Soviet youth always were at the frontlines where they struggled for revolution and communism. . . . They have been loved and educated like no children in history."[40] Yet *Serezha* presented an image of youth that challenged the ideal portrait painted by Karpinskii and numerous others. Serezha is almost abandoned by his family, and the love that is finally shown to him emerges only when the directives of the state are set aside.

Serezha's near abandonment is made all the more poignant by the behavior of the mother, who scolds her husband at the end for choosing to bring the boy along. Daniela and Talankin's depiction of Serezha's aloof and sometimes unfeeling mother constitutes a regular theme in films of this period. Consistently, the image of the nurturing mother is absent in films that use the child as the main protagonist. In addition to *Ivan's Childhood*, *Two Fedors*, and *Serezha*, other films such as Alexander Mitte's *Someone Is Ringing, Open the Door*, Sergei Bondarchuk's *The Fate of a Man*, Tengiz Abuladze's *Someone Else's Children*, and Sergei Paradzhanov's *Shadows of Forgotten Ancestors* all involve the story of the motherless child. Again and again, children simply have no protection from the outside world and are even betrayed at times by the one person that is supposed to defend them. In *Serezha*, it is the stepfather, not the mother, who finally capitulates and insists on taking the weeping boy with them to Kholmogory. In *Ivan's Childhood*, the mother represents a memory of a happier time that has been violently and senselessly ripped away. In Abuladze's *Someone Else's Children*, the real mother is never mentioned and is instead replaced by a reluctant babysitter.

The issue of child abandonment and maternal absence was perhaps best explored in Alexander Mitte's film *Someone Is Ringing, Open the Door*, which was released in 1965 to much acclaim. It tells the story of a young girl named Tania who struggles to make a life for herself while living alone in Moscow in the early 1960s. She finds herself isolated, not simply in her apartment, but in her pursuit of a communist ideal that the people around her appear to have discarded. In the mid-1960s, the film raised concerns for many reviewers because it seemed to portray contemporary adults as potential deserters of children. Although they saw Tania as an ideal protagonist, and the film as a way to focus the attention of Soviet youth away "from the Western influences of Dartagnan [sic] and *The Magnificent Seven*," others viewed it as a troubling indictment of Soviet society and its failure to protect and raise the next generation.[41]

In the opening shots of the film, a young girl walks alone in the dark snow to the accompaniment of staccato music. This audiovisual image sets a tone of quiet isolation for the rest of the film. For the first ten minutes, the child consumes the shot. Alone and parentless, she climbs the stairs to her apartment, undresses, sits quietly as she listens to a musical recording, and puts herself to bed. As the camera pulls away, she is seen huddling in a dark room. We learn later that Tania's mother has gone to be with her father, who is a geologist working in the field. Neighbors tend to the child, but for the most part, she is alone. The film's plot centers on Tania's school project to find old Pioneers from the 1920s, to record their stories, and to have them talk at a meeting. Tania travels from apartment to apartment, searching for people who can talk to her about the past. She is mostly unsuccessful in her search. In a veiled reference to the damage of the Stalinist purges and World War II, one woman tells her, "So many people have left. You won't find anyone here." Another man, who was supposed to have been a Pioneer, turns out to be a drunk (played by the rising star Oleg Efremov) and slams the door in her face. Finally, Tania arrives at the apartment of her friend, Gennadi, whose stepfather Pavel, played by Rolan Bykov, decides to help the children in their search. Although he himself was never a Pioneer or a member of the Communist Party, Pavel is the only adult willing to help Tania. He asks the ladies in the coatroom, the woman who sells sausage, and the traffic cop if they know where old Pioneers might be found, but none have an answer. As the film progresses, it becomes increasingly clear that a positive past is going to be as impossible for Tania and Pavel to locate as a happy present. This was 1965, and there was quite literally no consensus to be found. They do finally locate a former Pioneer, who is now a famous violinist. Unfortunately, he proves to be a terrible narcissist who has no memories of the past beyond how amazing he was in it. When he fails to show up at the children's

Figure 5.4. *Zvoniat, otkroite dver'* (*Someone Is Ringing, Open the Door,* 1965). Alexandr Mitte. Courtesy of Mosfilm.

ceremony to talk about his experiences and to perform, Pavel saves the day by mounting the podium to describe a Pioneer that he once knew. He then plays a short, sad song on his trumpet in tribute to the long-lost and absent Pioneer.

Someone Is Ringing depicted a society that had little ideological belief and no concern for the upbringing of the young, with a new generation that cared not for the Soviet past or the future. As Tania and Pavel move through the streets looking for old Pioneers, they repeatedly encounter strangers who mock their project or are simply too busy with their personal lives to hear their questions. When Tania and Pavel finally do find an old Pioneer, he is the opposite of all that they are looking for. He is vain and forgetful, and the embarrassment caused by his failure to appear at the meeting is only mitigated by the intervention of Pavel himself. Pavel's replacement of the old Pioneer at the meeting brings into question the officially promoted idea that the Pioneers, the Komsomol, and the Party are the creators of society's heroes. Ultimately, a non–party member seems to be the only one who can speak on the revolutionary activities of the Pioneers—and he does so by telling an absent man's story. In 1962, during reviews of the screenplay in meetings of the Filmmakers' Union, Alexandr Khmelik, the author and playwright (and father of the screenwriter Maria Khmelik, who later wrote the screenplay for the film *Little Vera*), strongly criticized Mitte for deemphasizing the value of the Pioneers "at a time when their role in society is so important."[42] He suggested that Mitte rewrite the script so that Pavel himself would become the old Pioneer that Tania eventually finds. "This film does not adapt well to current thinking," he argued. Yet Mitte did not significantly rewrite the script. In a period when Pioneers had become icons for Soviet development and peace activism, such a repudiation of the heroic identity of the Pioneers helped to complicate the idealized vision of a mobilized society.

Tania's solitude also provided a commentary on the modern deterioration of the family. In many ways, this film provides an alternative continuation to the *Serezha* story. This time the child *has* been left behind while the rest of the family travels for the father's work. Despite the efforts of the state to create a modern domestic sphere that adhered to the socialist ideal, Tania's abandonment revealed the extent to which the post-Stalinist Soviet home has become a space that "elude[s] attempts to impose order."[43] Reviewers of the film were understandably bothered by the mother's abandonment of her young daughter. Unlike in *Serezha*, where the family plans to leave the boy behind because of his health, Tania's story is far more complicated. As Khmelik asked Mitte during a review of the screenplay, "How can the mother leave? She has no compelling reason to go with her husband. Or, they should take the child with them."[44] Mitte's explanation for why the mother has gone remains ambiguous in the film. In a touching scene, Tania comes to Gennady's home for dinner. Pavel says to Tania, "You must not be mad at your mother. She cannot live without your father. Life is not an easy endeavor. You are already an adult." As in Serezha's rude awakening, Tania must come to terms with the fact that her mother chooses to leave her alone in a cold apartment. Better explanation for her abandonment is perhaps given by Gennady's mother (Pavel's wife), who, although physically present, is equally absent in terms of the attention she gives to her family. She comes home late at night "too weary to greet or smile at her son, let alone embrace him."[45] The absence of both women suggests that they have reached a point where they are incapable of extending love to their own children.

The abandonment is made all the more problematic by the fact that Tania's father is a geologist. In Socialist Realist film and literature, geology, along with piloting, was one of the most common occupations for male heroes. Such men were portrayed as possessing both scientific acumen and physical virility. They traveled to the far reaches of the Soviet Union ostensibly for the sole purpose of furthering the nation's scientific knowledge, economic prosperity, and territorial acquisition. They were presented as adventurers who were also bound forever within the borders of the Motherland.[46] Yet, as in *Serezha*, in order to do his job, the father in *Someone Is Ringing* is seen having to divide his family—a fact that is brought home by the father's complete absence from the film. All that remains is a solitary girl, no more than ten years old, left on her own by a father whose work for the state compels him to leave and by a mother who chooses to be with her husband in the field instead of her daughter at home.[47]

In her life as a Pioneer, Tania also encounters the cynicism, individualism, and distrust that characterize the actions of the young people around her who do not help with the program to find the old Pioneers and instead pursue romantic relationships with each other. Her expectations are focused specifically on her Pioneer leader, Petia, for whom she holds a secret fancy. Yet he also betrays her when he skates with another girl his age and when he does poorly in school and misses his fencing lessons. These children, who range in age from ten to fifteen, about whom many party leaders and educators were busy worrying and writing in these years, present an alternative vision of youth culture and of the adults around them. Far from embodying the collective mobilization that was so central to Khrushchev's image of the Cold War child, these youths are not only left with little parental direction, but they also show no interest in furthering the socialist cause on their own. The behavior of Tania's friends was particularly problematic for some filmmakers. As Filmmakers' Union member Mikhail Korshunov put it during his review of the film, "So much of what the Pioneers do in this film appears sad. They have none of the hope and energy that characterizes our youth."[48]

Similar expressions of contemporary abandonment and childhood disillusionment also appeared a few years earlier, in Tengiz Abuladze's groundbreaking 1958 work *Someone Else's Children*. Serezha's father's departure for Kholmogory had been presented as needed for work, and Tania's father's absence as a geologist had provided some justification for her isolation, but the children in Abuladze's film are not abandoned for "noble" reasons. Instead, they find themselves incapable of securing parents because the adults around them are too concerned with their own interests to take responsibility for raising them. As such, Abuladze's children represented a direct challenge to the assumed stability of Soviet society, they provided an honest examination of the messiness of personal relationships even under developed socialism, and they constituted yet another image that countered Khrushchev's vision of mobilized and protected youth in the late 1950s.

The film was based on a true story reported in *Komsomol'skaia pravda* in 1956, which chronicled a fateful love triangle in Tbilisi that left two children orphaned. In the opening scenes, the children's father is seen arguing with his girlfriend who is in the process of leaving him. The father begs her not to leave, but she retorts that "your children need a mother, and I can't be that. They won't be happy with me and neither will you." The film then jumps to a few weeks later, with the children running wild and unsupervised on the busy city streets. The two children meet a young woman nicknamed Nato, who saves them from a collision with a car and takes them back to their apartment. She soon learns of the sad situation in which these children are living. "Who is watching you?" she asks. "No one," they reply. The house is in disarray. The brother and sister look unkempt and poorly fed. Feeling sorry for the children, Nato cleans the apartment and cooks a good meal for them. The idea then sprouts in the minds of the children that they can solve their father's loneliness and their own need for a mother by working as matchmakers. A large portion of the film is spent on the children's attempts to bring their father and Nato together. The children recycle bottles in order to save money for a gift for the young woman. They drag their father to places in the city where Nato is likely to be. Eventually, the father and Nato do find each other, and against the advice of her aunt, Nato agrees to marry the man and assume responsibility for his two children.

The story seems to end well, when suddenly the old girlfriend reappears. The camera jumps into a montage of shots, first of the father's shocked face, then to Nato, to the image of a doll left drowning in the bathtub, to the children, and finally back to the old girlfriend. As the girlfriend realizes that the father has remarried, she says flatly, "It doesn't matter what we say to each other. Your children have a mother now and this is what matters most." With that, she turns to leave. The father and the young son follow her out as Nato, the daughter, and the camera wait nervously in the apartment for the men to return. Finally, the door opens and the lone boy walks slowly into the apartment. From this point on, the two children carry the narrative of the film, with little dialogue coming from the adults around them.

> BOY: Papa has left. The woman got on the train and waved as the
> train pulled away. Papa ran after her and jumped on the train.
> GIRL: He didn't say anything?
> BOY: No.

Silence follows as Nato and the children begin to realize that their father is not coming back. Later that evening the boy approaches the shocked Nato. Speaking from his own fears of abandonment, he pleads, "Father hurt you. Father hurt your heart. May I call you mama?" But Nato does not answer. Remembering her aunt's words of warning, she runs crying from the house toward the train station, leaving the children alone and orphaned in the apartment. In the next scene, Nato frantically boards a train with the intention of leaving the children behind. The train pulls away. The children run over the tracks after her, yelling her name. In a final, dramatic moment, Nato decides to jump off the now quickly moving train and returns to raise the children that have been left to her.

The father never returns, and the film ends with many questions left un-answered. Nato is a young woman who has no money, no career, and no way to tend to these children alone. She has left her own family to be a mother for these youngsters and will not be able to work and take care of them at the same time. They, in effect, will return to the unsupervised state that they were in at the beginning of the film. Like the final scene in *Serezha*, the father's and Nato's initial abandonment of the children are enough to convey the deep sense of betrayal and fear that these children feel toward their world and the adults in it.

Someone Else's Children received the prize for the best debut film at the 1960 London Film Festival but was panned by Soviet reviewers. *Komsomol'skaia pravda* found it to be too pessimistic and spiritually debili-tating.[49] While Soviet reviewers were willing to admit that the film captured "the real face of children," they, along with the state censors, ultimately declared that the film was a fraudulent imitation of the Soviet socialist world.[50] This image of Soviet life, which was created through the vision of the child, stood in stark contrast to the world being conceptualized by the state. Youth appeared unsupervised, unparented, uneducated, with concerns that revolved completely around their personal desires for family. They represented a repudiation of the Cold War kid and the consensus that he or she ostensibly supported.

Like Tarkovsky's Ivan, Khutsiev's Fedor, and Mitte's Tania, the children in *Someone Else's Children* are survivors who remain, at least to some ex-tent, committed to living their lives by their own rules. All of them carry a poignant awareness of the cruelty around them. They understand that their chance to be children has been taken away from them. They are often defenseless and victimized. Yet they also carry with them a great sense of agency. Ivan tenaciously holds onto his desire for vengeance in the face of adult pressure. Fedor steals a chicken and breaks the law in order to feed his family. Tania remains committed to her Pioneer projects regardless of her loneliness and the ridicule that she receives from her peers. Similarly, the children in Abuladze's film work diligently to form a family for themselves when the adults around them are incapable or unwilling to do it for them. Ivan, Fedor, Tania, and Abuladze's young protagonists reflected the altered priorities of the next generation, not toward the dictates of the state, but to-ward the pursuit of family and personal security. When viewed in the context of the extensive Pioneer efforts that were being made in these years to posi-tion children as domestically "contained" and mobilized for "peaceful com-petition," the absence of such children in Thaw film reflects an alternative conceptualization of Soviet society and of its questionable mobilization for the pursuit of state directives.

Children of the Corn: Delinquent Youth Take the Party to Task

Given the predominance of child protagonists in Thaw film, it is perhaps not surprising that the era's most scathing critique of Soviet domestic and Cold War policies centered on the lives of youth. Elem Klimov's 1964 comedy *Welcome, or No Trespassing* was a seemingly lighthearted film about a boy's adventures at a Pioneer summer camp. When the film hit the big screen, it provided one of the era's clearest commentaries on Soviet life and on Khrushchev's leadership. This was an amazing feat, considering that nine months earlier Khrushchev had delivered a searing reprimand to hundreds of artists, condemning them for creating generational tensions and for airing the country's "dirty laundry." Klimov's work presented an image of a delinquent, unsupervised youth who rejected the Soviet self-image of collective mobilization and yet at the same time was likable and heroic and received support secretly from the majority of the camp's staff. The film celebrated the actions of the irreverent boy and his friends, who subvert the efforts of the camp leader to maintain order and to present a positive image of the camp to visiting dignitaries. In the process, the piece addressed controversial domestic issues concerning Potemkinism and bureaucratic sycophancy, as well as Khrushchev's foreign and agricultural policies. It also recast the image of the hooligan child not as an agent of chaos and unlawfulness but as a force for reason and sanity in a world obsessed with rules.

In the opening shots, the camera reveals a large panorama of a beautiful lakeside. A camp counselor blows his whistle and the children race into the water. As the camera pans out, we realize that although the lake is very big, the children have been cordoned off into such a small piece of beach that they can only stand still and mildly splash each other. In humorous scenes, the grimacing camp counselors and frantic leader attempt to count and recount the children to make sure they stay inside the swimming space. Out of the mass of crowded children emerges the film's young hero, Kostia, who has broken out from the ringed section of beach and has swum to the other side of the lake. The children yell in admiration, but his actions are enough to have him expelled from the camp and sent home.

Recalling the discussion of Artek in the previous chapter, Klimov's image of the Pioneer camp stood in stark contrast to that being created in official Soviet rhetoric in the 1960s. Instead of providing a place where the Cold War mobilization of the young could be exhibited for the world, this camp was re-envisioned as a locus for mind-numbing bureaucratic formality and shallow ideological platitudes. Compare, for instance, the description that Gosteleradio gave to its German listeners of a beautiful day at a Pioneer summer camp in 1960 to that described by Semion Lungin, the film's screenwriter, in 1965: "Following the old traditions of the god of the sea and lakes, Neptune, there will be held today, a great holiday by the beach. There will be music on board our Pioneer ship 'Freundschaft' (friendship), with swimming and games, and sunny weather and of course, lots of happiness. All of this will be done so that the children will remember this day and so that they will become acquainted with events at the camp."[51]

And Lungin's description: "The place for swimming was completely roped in. They counted the children before letting us swim, while we were swimming, and after we were done. They counted us by voice, by our swim suits, by our shoes. If the count of our shoes did not come out right, they counted again. They let us go out into the water in rows with a leader at the head. And for each three rows, there would be another older leader at the head of that."[52] Lungin's memories of his camp experience made their way into the opening shots of the film. They set the stage for the movie's larger commentary on the constructed nature of official Soviet rhetoric and on the altered priorities for Soviet children in the 1960s.

This scene, as well as many that followed, faced intense criticism while under production and official review by the Filmmakers' Union. In his original screenplay, for instance, Lungin had, in the opening scene at the beach, placed a group of local, "uncultured" children on the other side of the bank whom Kostia then befriends. The scene was removed completely by the Filmmakers' Union because it was too problematic to have the hero of the film be represented by a group that was *outside* of the camp—and therefore outside of the Communist Party's control. The decision to make the change was actually made by a group of Komsomol representatives, who were put on the film's review board. Throughout their review, the Komsomol representatives stated repeatedly that the camp's portrayal "blatantly ignored" the fact that the Komsomol organization had already assiduously "addressed the question of establishing formal methods for raising children so that it will be implemented in the camps."[53] A camp like the one created by Lungin "simply does not exist here," they argued. Bureaucratic and verbose, comments like this one would have fit well into Klimov's larger effort to expose the nonsensical and overformalized elements of modern Soviet society. Although Lungin and Klimov would eventually give in and remove the outside children from the distant beach, they did, nonetheless, succeed in having Kostia escape from the cordoned space and thus break free, both literally and metaphorically, from the confines of the camp's control.

The message of *Welcome, or No Trespassing* revolved around three controversial characters—the first of which was Kostia himself. After his unfortunate expulsion, little Kostia sits at the train station, imagining the sorrow that his forced departure will cause his grandmother back home. He envisions her on her deathbed repeating the phrase, "You'll be the death of me. You'll be the death of me." In his mind's eye, he sees her being carted off in a visually hectic funeral procession as the rest of his town's elders look with condemnation toward the guilty boy. This procession, with its hyperbolic imagery reminiscent of Fellini's *8½*, almost led to the film being shelved in 1963, largely because the editor of the film thought that the dead grandmother resembled Khrushchev.[54] Although Klimov denied the similarity (he could do no less), one can see how such an allusion would have carried serious implications for the film's larger message. Instead of seeing a grandmother who had been brought to her deathbed by her precocious grandson, we would instead have to gaze upon the figure of Khrushchev, who was brought to his grave by the exploits and irreverence of the younger generation.

These scenes of the grandmother's death also subverted the official Soviet vision of childhood by questioning the constructed reality around little Kostia. In disjointed sequences, the viewer sees the grandmother's coffin lined with small papier-mâché figures of elephants—the symbol of Soviet kitsch and uncultured consumption, while the funeral procession forms the shape of a question mark as it moves down the street. In Kostia's imagination, the child is no longer flanked by the real world that is supposed to define his culture. Kostia is instead a child located outside the "transcriptions" of the established world—a child whose environment is created by him alone, and which no longer supports the preestablished reality of the Soviet world. By creating a reality that repeatedly does not support the viewer's preestablished notions of what the Soviet world looks like, Klimov questioned its construction altogether and brought into stark relief the cultural and social assumptions that the viewer had toward the life and identity not only of the child but of Soviet culture as well. While sitting on the bench, waiting for the bus, Kostia decides that in order to save his grandmother from certain death, he must go back to the camp and hide there until the session is over. He finds a perfect hiding place underneath the main podium in the center of the camp, and by the next day, a group of his friends have found him and have decided to help him in his deception.

Рисунок Н. СЕМЕНОВА.   КУКУРУЗА:—С такой нянькой я не скоро вырасту!

Figure 5.5. Khrushchev is depicted as the grandmother of the corn in the satirical newspaper *Krokodil*. He wears a nuclear bomb on his lapel and has clothed his child in an endless quantity of Communist Party protocols, feeding it from a bottle of milk (perhaps referring to Khrushchev's failed promises that the corn would actually be used to feed the cows, not the other way around). The caption reads, "Corn, with such a nanny you will not soon grow up." Compare this image to that of the corn at the end of Elem Klimov's film. *Kukuruza*, in *Krokodil*, 10 June 1956, 1.

Kostia spends much of the remainder of the film avoiding detection. His concealment offers a place for childish creativity, hope, and imagination, as the podium is transformed from a center of power to a locus for the subversion of official culture. From this location, he carries out his various pranks, which include the destruction of facilities, the spreading of poison ivy to the entire camp population, and the halting of the end-of-summer festival. Kostia's imagination and hope, which spread contagiously to his peers and come at least in part from his status as a fugitive, are directed not at socially constructive activities, but toward disruption of the status quo and the open humiliation of the camp's leader.

Next to Kostia's irreverence stands the second controversial child in the film, who listens in on the schemes of the other children and then reports back to the autocratic camp leader. By the 1960s, the "sharp-eyed" child had assumed a hagiographic character in official Soviet culture. The child who is driven to tell the truth and to report on others regardless of who they are had become an almost mythical figure in official Soviet culture since the days of Pavlik Morozov's famous reporting of his grain-hoarding father to the Soviet authorities. Yet Klimov's portrayal of the child-mole is far from idyllic, converting the act of informing into a betrayal driven not by ideological belief but by selfish interests. Notably, the child informant's face is never displayed on screen, attaching a sense of shame to an act that up to this point had been portrayed as noble and patriotic by the Communist Party.[55] In his screenplay, Lungin named the conspirator "Sandals" because his or her feet are the only part that we are allowed to see clearly. His description of Sandals' actions after hearing a particularly juicy piece of information is notably germane in that it reflects larger changes in Soviet society's perspectives toward the virtue of betraying one's personal relationships for the sake of the state. "Sandals jumps up like a toad," Lungin describes in the screenplay. "We first see the owner of the sandals' face, but it is so dirty with watery mud and duckweed, that it is impossible to discern its identity. You cannot even tell if it is a boy or a girl. The child informer begins to whistle and call out like a cuckoo bird. Only the soles of the sandals glimmer, while the path beneath remains dirty."[56] Following Lungin's description, Klimov shot only the informant's dirty, unrecognizable face and immaculate feet. Sandals' visage is metaphorically disfigured by treachery and lies, while his or her feet, which presumably must be washed repeatedly throughout the day, remain "clean." Again, the Komsomol had serious issues with Sandals' characterization. "Is Kostia not breaking the rules and creating disorder?" a Komsomol representative asked at a meeting of the Filmmakers' Union. "And do we not want to encourage our youth to speak out when their peers are being dishonest or insincere?"[57] Indeed, these were the messages conveyed by the state in these years. Klimov's decision to shoot the informant in such an unflattering light condemned that message and revealed its moral ambiguities.[58]

The most controversial character in *Welcome, or No Trespassing* is the camp's dictatorial director, whose sole concern is that the camp be ready to put on a good show for the parents and party officials who are coming to visit at the end of the summer. In a letter from the leader of the Repertory Union in 1963, A. Groshev wrote, "The film discredits the older generation and has no positive educational meaning." While the images of the unruly Pioneers needed to be revised, most bothersome in the eyes of the Repertory Union was the image of the camp director, Dinin, who "embodies the grotesque characteristics of the bureaucrat."[59] Committed to his production goals, Dinin can be seen forcing the children to play their violins instead of sleeping and to repeat recitations without water. Filmmakers' Union members present during the film's review were deeply disturbed by the fact that this imbecilic director of the Pioneer camp was the film's only representative of the party leadership. In the opinion of Aleksandr Khmelik, the figure of Dinin implicated the entire Komsomol organization because his foibles were not caused by his own stupidity but by his dogmatic commitment to outdated and nonsensical party rules. "He understands," Khmelik argued, "that he does what he must do—not for the children, but because he has instructions. It shows that the fault is not Dinin's—the fault is with the actions of the Pioneer organization."[60] This comment sparked such a heated debate at the Filmmakers' Union that Khmelik was forced to backtrack on his analysis of the Pioneer organization's culpability in the film. At issue was what the writer A. G. Zarkhi called a "problematic contradiction" in the figure of Dinin. If the director was simply stupid and personally incapable of leading these children appropriately, then the state should be held culpable for allowing such a man to climb the bureaucratic ladder to this high level of leadership. If he was not stupid, however, as Khmelik concluded, that meant that he was not only following the moronic instructions of a Pioneer organization that had no connection with the real world, but the simple fact that he was blindly following these ridiculous instructions reflected on the poor job that the Pioneers, the Komsomol, and the Communist Party were doing in raising intelligent, independent thinkers for future leadership. While Khmelik's subsequent responses sought to mitigate his earlier comments by claiming that Dinin was an exceptional character (that, in fact, the whole thing was simply farcical), Klimov made it clear in the end that Dinin *was* a bureaucratic middle-aged man and that he was "*not* a stupid man."[61]

The entire film combines slapstick humor with open mutiny to create a situation in which the children slowly wrest power from Dinin's clutch. They feign disease in order to prevent the summer production from going forward, which itself is being organized from illegible directions. The children use a pig to dig Kostia out from inside the podium where he has been accidentally locked. Although the pig fails to set Kostia free, it does manage to run wild through the camp with muddied children shrieking after it. As they chase the pig, which snorts and grunts around the center of the camp, the children cry out in an obvious reference to the common saying from the Stalinist era, "Now we are full of joy! Now we have a happy life!" In a critique of Stalinism that arguably went way farther than Khrushchev ever intended, the children chase the Stalin-pig through the camp and leave complete disorder in their wake. While the Filmmakers' Union made no remarks on the resemblance of the pig to any previous leaders (as they had on Khrushchev's resemblance to Kostia's dead grandmother), certainly they all understood whom the pig was referencing.

The voices of the children only get louder as they revolt openly against Dinin, who barges into the camp's movie theater one night and stops the film that they are watching in order to look for the fugitive Kostia. While Kostia hides, having left the podium for the shelter that is provided by the theater's darkness, the children chant "Kino! Kino!" for the film to be restarted. In this metaphorical image of the film, the movie being watched by the children represents a point of contention and expression, just as the larger movie does for the filmmaker.

At the movie's climax, the parents and party officials arrive for the camp's long-awaited production. The day ends with a parade of the symbols of the Soviet Union's agricultural accomplishments. As custom dictated for a harvest parade, the prettiest girl would be chosen to be the Queen of the Fields. In earlier years, her royalty would have been symbolized by images of Great Russian wheat. In this parade, however, she was to be the Queen of the Corn. In a direct reference to Khrushchev's short-sighted agricultural initiative to bring corn to the Soviet Union, the children erect a great parade float in the shape of a corncob. Of course, it is the young Kostia who pops up out of the top of the corncob at the end of the parade, after hiding there all day.

Klimov's openly irreverent use of the corncob represented many levels of dissent within Soviet society over the ways in which Soviet policy, and particularly the Cold War, had impacted the country over the past decade. In May 1957, Khrushchev had initiated a campaign to overtake the United States in the production of meat, butter, and milk. After seeing the abundant fields of corn in the American Midwest, he had decided to fix the problem

Figure 5.6. Kostia emerges from the corncob, in *Dobro pozhalovat,' ili postoronnim vkhod vospreshchyon* (Welcome, or No Trespassing, 1964). Elem Klimov. Courtesy of Mosfilm.

of fodder production for livestock by growing corn, especially since capital investment was unavailable. Traditional crops were stopped. Climate restrictions and silage requirements were ignored. Quotas were imposed. Private lots were taxed and restricted in order to encourage communal production. By the period from 1960 to 1962, it had become obvious that the corn project had failed. In some places, as much as 70 to 80 percent of the land did not come to harvest. Herds were actually cut and meat production declined sharply. These lean harvests led to mass grassroots revolts across much of Russia through the 1950s and 60s. Spurred on by the need for "meat, milk, and butter," peasants from Grozny to Krasnodar rose up in revolt. While political dissatisfaction and anticommunism were seldom the reasons for these uprisings, because of the antagonism between capitalism and communism, these strikes were nonetheless often interpreted by the state as "a direct attack on the Soviet system."[62] Klimov's reference to the corncob, especially as its head was split open by Kostia's triumphant arms, represented an explicit criticism not only of Khrushchev's agricultural program but of his willingness to let the Cold War negatively impact his domestic responsibilities to the people.

In the end, the high-ranking party official who comes to witness the camp's summer production proves to be thoughtful, balanced, and aware of the deficiencies in Dinin's leadership. He saves Kostia from humiliation in front of his family and friends and allows for Dinin's exceptionalism as a single "bad seed" in what is otherwise a sound program. It is interesting that the original screenplay did not include these redemptive scenes. The positive party leader, as well as the old Pioneers who accompany him to the show, were included at the direction of the Filmmakers' Union and the Moscow film studio, Mosfilm. Klimov's intended ending had instead involved a basic overthrow of Dinin's leadership by the camp members themselves and Kostia's departure from the camp with a family that is none the wiser.[63]

Without question, *Welcome, or No Trespassing* provided good comic entertainment to an increasingly large moviegoing population as well as solid revenue for Mosfilm. But Klimov's film also posed serious, prescient questions to both the party and the population. How are we raising our children? What are bureaucracy and the culture of conspiracy doing to our hopes for a brighter future? How can we expect to raise a population of strong, forward-looking children when we have no understanding of their real lives and opinions? And in what ways is Cold War competition hurting the population on a daily basis? Klimov's message was not only intended as a criticism of individual, dogmatic leaders; it was also a commentary that focused its eye on the entire population and the culture that had bred such inanity.

Conclusion

Khrushchev's crackdown on the Thaw is thought to have begun with his visit in 1962 to an abstract art exhibit at the Manezh Gallery in Moscow. In a public debate with Ernst Neizvestny, Khrushchev reiterated the Socialist Realist argument that the function of art in society was to depict a "higher reality" to provide inspiration and guidance for the population.[64] His focus quickly turned to film. In a meeting with Communist Party officials in 1964, he expressed his increasing displeasure over what films were doing to the image of the child and the family. "Sons are being told that their fathers cannot teach them how to live and that there is no point seeking their advice. . . . Well, that is a pretty clear expression of the authors' attitude. But haven't you gone too far? What do you want to do—incite the youth against the older generation, set them at odds, sow discord in the friendly Soviet family, which unites both young and old in the common effort to build communism?"[65] Khrushchev reminded his listeners that "the press, radio, literature, fine arts, music, cinema and the theatre are a sharp ideological weapon of our party. And the party is concerned that its weapon should always be in battle readiness and allow no one to blunt its edge, to weaken its effects."[66]

The critiques being made during the Thaw posed a threat not just to domestic stability. Khrushchev also feared the critical openness of the Thaw as something that would "delight" enemies of the Soviet Union abroad. In August 1963, at a meeting with a group of prominent Soviet writers, he stated that "there can be compromises for peace, but none in the war of words and ideas."[67] Khrushchev's feelings about the Thaw had changed, thanks in part to the increasingly important role of culture in the Cold War. The arts in the Soviet Union could no longer be a place for experimentation, as the two superpowers sought to engage each other in a battle of images and cultural identifiers.

Throughout the Thaw, the contested image of the child served as a reflection of Cold War anxieties in Soviet society. As we have seen, in official Soviet rhetoric the image of the mobilized, peaceful, and well-ordered child symbolized the nation's ability to rebuild itself for the future, to stand as a shining example of communist success for the rest of the world, and to compete culturally and economically with the West. In the struggle for domestic Cold War mobilization and international credibility, the successful construction of the Soviet child was crucial. Yet because the image of the child was tied so closely to the country's positive image of itself, the portrayal of cynical, victimized, and irreverent youth represented an affront to the nation's ability to create and maintain stability for children. While Klimov confronted Khrushchev's myopic Cold War policies through his parody of the children's camp, Tarkovsky, Romm, Talankin, Mitte, and Abuladze took a more circumscribed path through their explorations of the troubled state of Soviet society. They showed adults who had abdicated their responsibilities as parents and youth who had become ideologically disillusioned, abandoned, and devoted to the pursuit of personal goals over the needs of the state. They in turn provided an alternative conceptualization of the Cold War in the Soviet Union, not as a rallying point for an entire generation, but as a contributing factor to society's ailments that was worthy of parody and rejection.

CHAPTER SIX

American Childhood and the Bomb

In the fall of 1961, while Andrei Tarkovsky was busy putting the final touches on *Ivan's Childhood* and *Serezha* was still in the Soviet theaters, mathematician and counsel to the U.S. Senate Committee on Atomic Energy James R. Newman made a novel suggestion in the pages of the *Washington Post*. "I make a modest proposal," he began. "Let the children go."[1] Instead of arguing that the children should be eaten, as Jonathan Swift had done 232 years earlier, Newman suggested that America's children be relocated to the Southern Hemisphere, where their chances of survival from an atomic attack were significantly improved. After conceding that national suicide through nuclear war had become an acceptable option for many Americans, he declared sarcastically that children nonetheless were "too innocent and foolish to realize that death is preferable to life under alien creeds." He contended that without children around it would be "unnecessary to yield to niceties, to observe amenities, to nurse the sick, to shield the weak, to spare the infirm." Instead of paying for the upbringing of the country's children, he argued that a small sum could be spent to transport and establish the young at their destinations, while the remainder of the money could be used "in vigorous prosecution of the war." "I am anxious that Wise men consider my proposal," he declared, pointing his literary finger at Kennedy's administration. "Is it feasible? (Less feasible, say, than a journey to the planets?) Is it visionary? (More visionary than the preservation of Freedom by a nuclear war?)" Finally he asked, "Is a country without children worth living in? Perhaps not. In which case some better course must be found."

Newman's satirical essay captured the sense of worry and frustration that many Americans felt in the late 1950s and early 1960s over what they perceived to be an escalating nuclear standoff with the Soviet Union. Like many of his friends in the antinuclear movement, and like the Soviet filmmakers working in studios 9,000 miles to the east, Newman used the victimized image of the child to draw attention to the nuclear threat and to emphasize the suicidal nature of the arms race and American foreign policy. In contrast to the prevailing views of the time, he envisioned the child not as a victim of communist infiltration, delinquency, and poor education, not as a citizen mobilized to defend the United States from invasion, but as a likely casualty of nuclear attack who was endangered by the foreign policies of the American and Soviet governments.[2] Newman's worries were seconded by prominent scientists, humanitarians, religious leaders, and concerned citizens who issued urgent demands in the late 1950s and early 1960s for an end to atomic testing and war planning. They formed a number of organizations whose goals were to halt nuclear testing, push for the normalization of relations between the United States and the Soviet Union, and pressure governments on both sides of the Iron Curtain for the passing of a test ban treaty.

In their attempts to reach a wide audience with their message of needed change in Soviet and American Cold War nuclear policy, national activist groups like the Committee for a Sane Nuclear Policy (SANE) and Women Strike for Peace (WSP) created images of America's youth in their publications, rallies, and speeches as diseased, disillusioned, and defenseless against the threats of nuclear attack and fallout. Although many groups and individuals had previously viewed the child as imperiled by the atomic threat, the antinuclear movement was the first to argue that the source of the danger came not just from Soviet nuclear brinksmanship, but also from the myopic and paranoid policies of the U.S. government as well. For the sake of the country's children, they argued that responsible, nonradical, middle-class adults were obliged to act against the interests of America's foreign policy makers. And as scientists and mothers, they presented themselves as the "natural" leaders of the crusade to ban testing around the world.

In addition to portraying children as threatened by the very government that was supposed to be protecting them, the antinuclear movement also created a vision of mobilized youth that was markedly different from that being disseminated by supporters of the American Cold War consensus. Instead of arguing that children had a role to play in defending the United States from communist infiltration and attack, some in the movement contended that youngsters needed instead to defend themselves and their future by becoming activists alongside their parents. This was particularly true for WSP, which was famous for bringing large numbers of children to its rallies and Senate hearings. By taking their children along with them, these women not only blurred the lines between their own domestic and public obligations, but they also created a revised image of the mobilized American child, prepared not for a war against communism but instead for a struggle against internal governmental forces that had put them at risk. Like the filmmakers who were working in the Soviet Union during these years, antinuclear groups in the United States used images of threatened and mobilized children to complicate and at times subvert government policy and authority. They showed youth who had placed their own safety and the needs of their families over the directives of the state.

SANE and the Image of Threatened Youth

In the spring of 1957, Norman Cousins, a well-known advocate of liberal causes, joined a small group of prominent pacifists in an effort to make American citizens aware of the dangers of continued atmospheric nuclear testing. Cousins and his friends were shocked by the seeming complacency of the American population to the threat around them. As the psychoanalyst Erich Fromm would argue, America's behavior seemed downright "pathological."[3] Years earlier, much of the American liberal population had rallied behind the prospect of ceasing nuclear development, testing, and proliferation. They had thrown their weight behind the Acheson-Lilienthal Plan (coauthored by Dean Acheson and David E. Lilienthal in 1946), which had proposed methods for the international control of atomic weapons and the avoidance of future wars. Yet the plan was ultimately defeated, as the Soviet refused to agree to unrestricted inspections. In the United States, the plan's defeat had led many antinuclear activists to stop believing in their ability to effectively influence American foreign policy.[4] By the late 1950s, Cousins and Fromm had concluded that this sense of collective resignation toward the Bomb and its use had led to a lull in activism and a return to the escapes of daily life in American society.[5] We now know that the state of the American progressive movement was not as abysmal as Cousins and Fromm thought. As Julia Mickenberg has shown in her study of children's literature in the 1950s, liberals in the United States did find "circumscribed" avenues for expression, even at the height of the McCarthy era.[6] Nonetheless, for Cousins and his colleagues who remembered a time when the progressive movement had enjoyed widespread public influence, it seemed to them that the country had given up on the possibility of influencing state policy and was in denial over the potentially life-threatening effects of the nuclear arms race.

Amid this sense of resignation in the late 1950s, Cousins and his friends also sensed that change was in the air. For many in America, the promise of safety provided by civil defense was not as easy to believe as it had been in earlier years. The creation of new bombs and new tests increasingly revealed that even in deep shelters, the occupants would be "quickly barbecued."[7] And even if survival were possible, the realities of shelter living made it seem decidedly uncomfortable in the baby boom era, as American adults contemplated life below ground with their growing families. Much to the dismay of the American leadership, parents also turned their attention to the effects of the atomic bomb in their pursuit of the causes of childhood errantry. They increasingly argued in the 1950s and 60s that the bomb had the potential to create a population of terrified and traumatized youth who would become "nervous" adults, incapable of leading the country or surviving in a postnuclear world. *Today's Woman* put it succinctly when it declared in 1951 that "our children are scared."[8] By 1952, private individuals and government representatives in Washington, D.C., had formed a National Committee on War Tensions in Children with the stated mission to "assess the damage being done to children by nuclear fear." At its first annual meeting, delegates brought with them reports of children refusing to leave their homes without a first aid kit, refusing to take their handkerchiefs off their heads, and clinging to their identification dog tags (which were issued in 1951 to all children in the New York public school system) as "talismans insuring physical safety."[9] "The proof is in the pudding," one agitated delegate remarked to her colleagues at the first committee meeting after reviewing the evidence of childhood trauma. "The bomb is creating fear and the fear is having a big effect."[10]

What would be the long-term effects of the nuclear arms race on the nation's children, many individuals and organizations from across the political spectrum increasingly worried during these years, expressing anxiety over the possibility that the sheer presence of the Bomb could create a generation of youth made anxious by the looming threat and disillusioned by their government's promise of safety. As writer Doris Kearns Goodwin would remember in later years, "Our generation was the first to live with the knowledge that, in a single instant, everyone and everything we knew—our family, our friends, our block, our world—could be brought to an end."[11] While almost everyone in the government agreed that childhood awareness of the Bomb's destructive capabilities was potentially dangerous to the psychological health of the next generation, not everyone was in agreement about what to do about it. The question of how to save youth from the Bomb divided American society between those who argued for the value of civil defense in providing a sense of safety and defensibility to the young and those who contended that civil defense was not only useless, but actually did immeasurable damage to the young by reminding them of the futility of nuclear security. Still others argued that the only way to prevent psychological trauma among the children was to do away with the Bomb altogether.

Fears about the effects of nuclear fallout were also heightened in the late 1950s through the increased publication of reports from the scientific community. In 1956, a report by the U.S. Atomic Energy Commission had demonstrated that radioactive fallout was causing milk to be contaminated with the element strontium 90, a known carcinogen that threatened children whose bones mistook the element for calcium in the growth process. These reports, which came from both governmental and private sources, informed the public that the U.S. government had conducted 119 above-ground tests between 1951 and 1958. Such tests had led to strange and disconcerting events, as when "blue-colored snow" fell for two days in 1954 over the skies of New Mexico and Nevada, causing children to develop reddened faces and swollen tongues.[12] In 1958, scientists discovered that children living near the Hanford Plutonium Plant in Washington State had been exposed to 740,000 curies (about 30,000 times that of Three Mile Island).[13] Scientists linked these tests to rising incidences of thyroid cancer, leukemia, and heart disease.

As Cousins and his colleagues perceived correctly, the potentially harmful impact of nuclear testing on the next generation was an issue that resonated with the American public. No longer did these detonations seem like a distant military practice carried out in the deserts of Nevada and the far reaches of the Pacific. Their effects were immediate and local. They impacted the young. Based on their belief that the American public was ready to rally behind the cause of a nuclear test ban, Cousins and his colleagues founded SANE in 1957, which was supported by a long roster of prominent academics, psychologists, and nuclear scientists, all committed to the idea that a "halt [to testing] now [was] not only possible, but imperative for survival."[14] Less than a year later, they had a membership of 25,000 and growing. They took it as their mandate to increase awareness of the dangers of testing among the American public through a wide-reaching information campaign that would hopefully drive the population to public activism.

From its inception, SANE based its propaganda approach on the image of the victimized American child left physically and psychologically damaged by U.S. and Soviet nuclear testing. In its third major full-page ad in the *New York Times* in the spring of 1958, entitled "Nuclear Tests Are Endangering Our Health Right Now," SANE argued that "we must stop the contamination of the air, the milk children drink, the food they eat."[15] They restated these sentiments both in internal policy documents and in public statements throughout the late 1950s. At the 1957 Third World Conference against A- and H-Bombs, held in Tokyo, one SANE representative announced that she was collecting pictures of babies, asking parents to write on the back of each photograph "Stop nuclear tests for my child's sake." One copy of each photo (200 in all) was then sent to Eisenhower, Macmillan, and Khrushchev.[16] SANE also organized a project whereby 5,000 children delivered C.O.D.s to the White House on Mother's Day, 1958, all the while singing "Sometimes I Feel Like My Genes Have Gone Wrong" to the tune of "Sometimes I Feel Like a Motherless Child."[17] When the students from the SANE student office of Cooper Union College in New York gathered in Manhattan on 23 May 1958 to release a giant "mushroom cloud of dark blue balloons" over the Manhattan skyline, participants stated that they were organizing in order to "remind adults everywhere of the dangers to their children inherent in the continued testing of Hydrogen bombs."[18] Similarly, a year later, at a national meeting in Boston, a SANE speaker argued to his listeners that "there is such a thing as innocence. Children, in general are innocent. That is why, even in war, it is most difficult to justify the killing of children. . . . [Yet] now there is a new massacre of the innocents. Without war, without anger, without intention, atomic tests are gradually destroying their health and their posterity's."[19] Later that spring, physicist Linus Pauling argued that current levels of strontium 90 would result in 100,000 deaths and 140,000 "gross mental and physical defects" in the next generation.[20] "There is no way of washing the sky," Cousins himself argued in 1959, "no way to keep the strontium and cesium from falling like rain; no way to keep it from getting into food and milk and thence into the bones of children."[21]

SANE quickly learned that its child-centered approach to the test ban problem was reaching its audience. Letters flooded into the SANE national office beginning in 1957, applauding the organization for taking the necessary steps to protect the next generation. "The government is like a father who, observing a hawk in the sky, holds his children's heads beneath the water [until] it goes away and they are drowned," one father wrote to SANE in March 1958.[22] "I feel like you are the only ones who are talking about my kids as if they matter," a mother from Illinois wrote in.[23] A couple of months later, a father from Kansas City wrote that "murder smells in any language. Some ancients propitiated the gods by sacrificing the life of one of their children or one of their neighbors. We sacrifice many of our children and many of our neighbors with each major bomb that we explode."[24] Such missives reflected the impact that SANE's message was having on the general public, as well as the centrality of the child in defining how Americans thought about the nuclear arms race at the end of the decade.

Other responses to SANE's tactics were not as supportive but were equally vehement. For instance, a lengthy conversation was conducted over letters between Adelaide Baker, a representative of SANE, and Lewis Strauss, chairman of the Atomic Energy Commission, between 1953 and 1958. Citing a renowned pathologist, Strauss wrote to Baker: "We have a choice of a very small risk from testing or a risk of the catastrophe which might result from a surrender of our leadership in nuclear armament. I have a wife, a son, and three happy young grandchildren. Yet I subscribe completely to our policy. I could not do so if I thought the welfare of my family was threatened more by fallout than by possible nuclear war."[25] Baker responded: "You told me before in your letter about your 'happy young grandchildren.' I know they are as lovely as mine, as lovely as the Russian children Bob Hope pictured when he went on an American-sponsored goodwill tour to Moscow to 'relieve tension.' I don't want any of yours or mine or theirs or the millions of others the world round to be the victims of our stubborn and willful idea of defense for ourselves."[26]

Both Strauss and Baker articulated their perspectives on nuclear testing in terms of the child and its welfare. Strauss made what was a common argument against those who supported a nuclear test ban: he contended that the cessation of testing would lead to a loss of leadership in the nuclear arms race and the subsequent loss of deterrent for the Soviets. Only by building and testing the weapons, he contended, could the United States prevent them from being used and thus protect the country's children from annihilation. Baker's response challenged Strauss's assumption that a deterrent was needed in order to prevent the Soviets from attacking. She did this by acknowledging the Russian love for their children and by recognizing that atomic fallout also threatened Soviet youth. In this historically recurrent debate over means and ends, Strauss and Baker latched onto the image of the threatened child as a moral constant from which state policies could be either justified or rejected.

By presenting the child as a victim of nuclear attack, people like Norman Cousins and Adelaide Baker reconceptualized the Cold War in America not as a struggle against communist infiltration, emotional lassitude, delinquency, bad parenting, and poor education, but as a battle against deadly radioactive elements and those who authorized their creation. Moreover, they challenged the established idea that children were capable of defending themselves from nuclear attack and fallout. As we have seen, the American population had been presented with an idealized vision of mobilized children who seemed capable of defending themselves and their country from nuclear assault and communist infiltration. In contrast, SANE portrayed youth as having no capacity to mobilize against the invisible attacks of strontium 90, cesium, and iodine 131. This depiction of children reconfigured the child's relationship with the Cold War, with the Bomb, and with the American government, presenting the child as a symbol not of national strength and defensibility, but of suicide and betrayal by the state.

The child had not always been a symbol for nuclear annihilation. In the early 1940s, those who knew about the Bomb's existence had argued that the weapon posed the same threats to children as did any similar armament. In fact, as Alexander Weart has observed in his examination of the Bomb as a cultural artifact, scientists and politicians consistently envisioned the Bomb as a new and childlike discovery. The Bomb was couched in a "vocabulary of birth" by the atomic scientists who brought it into the world.[27] Thus, the first sustained chain reaction was described as a "miracle, the birth of a new era." Neutrons were said to "reproduce" in successive "generations." Even the Bomb itself was code-named "Little Boy," and when it was first tested successfully in Alamogordo, New Mexico, on the morning of 16 July 1945, news was sent to the secretary of defense that the "'Little Boy' is . . . husky."[28] In these early years, the Bomb itself had been viewed as a child, with the adjectives of youth used to symbolize novelty and hope.

The era in which the child and the Bomb shared the same conceptual vocabulary was short lived, however. After Hiroshima, images of dying and mutilated children became the world's most pervasive symbol of atomic victimization. Survivors' groups like the Hiroshima Maidens and the Keloid Girls represented for many around the world the irreparable damage that had been done by the Bomb.[29] International attention was given to the twelve-year old Japanese girl, Sadako, who attempted to fold a thousand paper cranes before dying in order to counter the fatal effects of radiation poisoning.[30] While American official rhetoric continued to present atomic science as a positive force in the lives of America's young (primarily as an abundant and clean source of energy) and to argue that mobilization against nuclear war was indeed possible, the child also became a symbol of the debilitating effects of nuclear fear and fallout on the nation. For many, including the members of SANE, the Bomb had created a new sense of global doom that specifically targeted the nation's children. It had created a new way of looking at the next generation, not only as symbols of the future but as emblems of the nuclear holocaust.

By the end of the 1950s, SANE's prestige and influence was on the rise, thanks in large part to its ability to capitalize on the image of the endangered child. It ran nationwide ad campaigns with titles like "No Contamination without Representation" and "H Stands for Humanity," which declared that "because of fallout from the tests that have already taken place no child anywhere on this planet can today drink milk that is uncontaminated by Strontium-90."[31]

It staged major rallies in New York in the spring of 1960 to mark the planned summit between Eisenhower and Khrushchev, with marches and speeches on the nuclear threat to the world's young. Although the U2 incident prevented the summit from happening, the rally for it was very popular, drawing 20,000 participants and illustrious personalities like Norman Cousins, Eleanor Roosevelt, Albert Schweitzer, and Max Born. As Clarence Pickett would write to Cousins on the child-centered approach that SANE had adopted, "We seem to have struck a nerve here."[32] The safety of the children was, by 1960, an issue that many in America felt they could not ignore.

Despite, or perhaps because of, this newfound prestige and popularity, SANE's New York chapter became the target of suspicion for communist infiltration in the late spring of 1960. As had been the case in the education hearings a decade earlier, the contested protection of the child again played an important role, this time as a defense for SANE against an insensitive investigation. At the House Un-American Activities Committee (HUAC) hearing for Henry Abrams, a former member of the American Labor Party and at the time serving as the co-chairman for the West Side New York Branch of SANE, the specter of the child appeared in unexpected ways. Although he never made the argument that his activism was inspired by a desire to protect the young, he nonetheless introduced the image of the child by repeatedly talking about his thirteen-month-old granddaughter who had died the night before his trial was set to begin. In the forty-five minutes before Abrams was sworn in, he and his lawyer, Louis Boudin, made the argument that the hearing should be postponed. "The basis of this request," Boudin stated, "[is] the death of Mr. Abrams' grandchild on Monday."[33] Boudin produced a doctor's note stating that Abrams was "at present under the most extreme emotional tension because of the death of his grandchild yesterday." This tension, the doctor claimed, was almost certain to "aggravate" Abrams's own heart condition. It was then made clear that Abrams's wife was also at the hearing, sitting in the audience, thereby implying that neither grandparent was able to be at home with their daughter and her family, who were left mourning the child's death alone. Neither Abrams nor Boudin ever explicitly accused the conservative subcommittee chair, Senator Thomas Dodd, and his council, J. G. Sourwine, of being insensitive bullies. Nonetheless, the effect of the debate over Abrams's grandchild was to present an image of Abrams and his wife as loving grandparents forced to be away from their family at its darkest moment by men who had no sympathy for their loss. This point was made even clearer by Dodd's unwillingness to even mention the granddaughter in his decision to decline Abrams's motion to postpone the hearing.[34] Although Cousins and his colleagues supported Abrams, they eventually asked Abrams to resign and issued a new directive barring members of the Communist Party from holding office in the organization. They then revoked the charter of the Greater New York SANE Committee. By the end of the year, Thomas Dodd could be heard on the Senate floor complimenting SANE "on the measures it has taken to fight communist meddling." The organization was deeply shaken by the experience, and in the months that followed, a number of members who were "disaffected" by SANE's willingness to dismiss members who had been victims of red-baiting resigned in protest, including Linus Pauling and Bertrand Russell.

As 1961 began, SANE's efforts to draw the world's attention to the dangers of nuclear testing and brinksmanship seemed to many to have been for naught. That June, Kennedy returned from unsuccessful talks with Khrushchev in Vienna and promptly pushed through a massive supplemental military spending bill and a tripling of the draft call. Shortly afterward, responding to the hemorrhaging of people from East Germany and to constant pressure from Walter Ulbricht, Khrushchev authorized the construction of the Berlin Wall. Three weeks later, Khrushchev announced that the Soviet Union would resume atmospheric testing. A similar U.S. announcement quickly followed. The Soviet Union subsequently detonated a 58-megaton weapon that was 30,000 times more powerful than the bomb that had destroyed Hiroshima. The United States, meanwhile, tested a number of weapons underground. The situation only appeared to worsen as 1962 began. Kennedy, who had been under increasing pressure by military and civilian advocates of testing, announced that American atmospheric tests would resume on 2 March. The ongoing talks in Geneva on the limitation of testing seemed to be dead in the water, and SANE seemed to have lost the wind from its sails. "It is natural that many of us should have the most anguished sense of disappointment and foreboding," Norman Cousins wrote in a letter to Homer Jack, SANE's executive director. "Our principal objective has been shattered."[35]

In response, SANE leaders again turned to the image of the child. They decided to undertake a massive campaign to make the American people aware of what awaited them if and when Kennedy resumed atmospheric testing. In January 1962, SANE created a Public Information Committee, whose purpose was to organize a national campaign that would reach the American middle class. In attendance at the committee's first meeting were Homer Jack, Robert Gurney, who sat on the Board of Directors, and a staff member named Ross Goddard. As they discussed the upcoming ad campaign, a secretary recorded their words in shorthand. The following conversation transpired:

DR. JACK: We could put an H-Bomb over Columbus Circle.

MR. GODDARD: For brutality, let's have two-headed babies, pictures of actual areas of devastation. No point in mincing words.

DR. JACK: The child approach seems to have big effect.

MR. GURNEY: Maybe we could draw the bomb with concentric circles. Why can't we take and map and humanize: ground zero, pick out SANE supporters in that area, and get Polaroids of actual families living in these areas?[36]

The three men worked late into the night planning for a deluge of visual and verbal messages on the dangers of Kennedy's decision to resume atmospheric testing.

Although they eventually chose to leave the image of the two-headed babies out of their ads, the Public Information Committee did not abandon the image of the child. They quickly turned to the one man who they believed could best reach the American public and incite it to action, Dr. Benjamin Spock. Spock had become famous in 1946 with the publication of *The Common Sense Book of Baby and Child Care*.[37] Whereas his work had been considered too liberal and out of the mainstream at the time of its publication, by 1962 the pediatrician's advice to mothers that "you know more than you think you do" had become a mantra for modern parenting. Spock would later claim that his move into SANE was precipitated by a realization that he had a responsibility as a public figure to think and speak about "all the children who would die of leukemia and cancer, and of the ultimate possibility of nuclear war."[38] After securing Spock's much-coveted membership, SANE and its Public Information Committee quickly offered the pediatrician a chance to express his views on nuclear testing in a full-page ad in the *New York Times*. Following months of revisions, Spock and numerous editors pared his 4,000-word "manifesto" down to 250 words that epitomized the organization's view of the child in the nuclear age.[39]

The final ad, which was published one day before the United States resumed atmospheric tests in the Pacific, featured a large picture of a concerned Spock looking down upon a small child playing before him. "Dr. Spock is worried" appeared in bold letters at the bottom of the photograph with his letter featured below.[40] In the message, Spock wrote, "I am worried. Not so much about the effect of past tests, but at the prospect of endless future ones. As the tests multiply, so will the damage to children— here and around the world." The ad was reprinted in 700 newspapers in Europe and the United States. In an astonishing manifestation of spontaneous

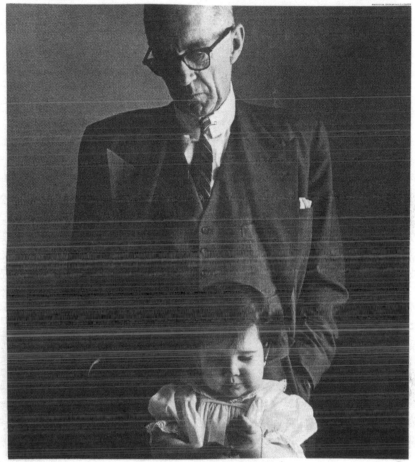

The New York Times.

LATE CITY EDITION

MONDAY, APRIL 16, 1962.

Dr. Spock is worried.

If you've been raising a family on Dr. Spock's book, you know that he doesn't get worried easily.

From the university in Ohio where he works, he sends you this message about the resumption of nuclear testing in the atmosphere:

"I am worried. Not so much about the effect of past tests but at the prospect of endless future ones. As the tests multiply, so will the damage to children—here and around the world.

"Who gives us this right?

"Some citizens would leave all the thinking to the government. They forget the catastrophic blunders that governments have made throughout history.

"There are others who think that superior armaments will solve the problem. They scorn those who believe in the strength of a just cause. They have forgotten that a frail idealist in a loin cloth compelled the British to back out of India.

"There are dangers in any course. I would rather we took small risks today if there is hope of lessening the enormous risks which lie ahead.

"And if I am to be destroyed through some miscalculation I would prefer to be destroyed while we are showing leadership in the search for a cooperative world than while sitting in an illusory fortress blaming our opponents for the lack of a solution.

"In a moral issue, I believe that every citizen has not only the right but the responsibility to make his own feelings known and felt."

—*Benjamin Spock, M.D.*

Dr. Spock has become a sponsor of The National Committee for a SANE Nuclear Policy.

Other sponsors are listed below, with a brief description of what SANE stands for.

If you are worried too about the impending series of nuclear tests in the atmosphere, telegraph or write President Kennedy and your Congressman.

If you would like to do still more, send a contribution to help us run advertisements like this one all over the country. The National Committee for a SANE Nuclear Policy, 17 East 45th Street, New York 17, N.Y.

Figure 6.1. "Dr. Spock Is Worried." Literature 1957–62, SANE Papers, Swarthmore College Peace Collection, DG 58, Series A, box 10.

support, doctors, business owners, and parents reproduced the image in their offices, in shop windows, and on baby carriages.[41] Americans from across the socioeconomic spectrum sent 20,000 copies of it to President Kennedy's office in 1962 alone.

Spock's ad presented a perspective on the country's nuclear future that was significantly different from that being propagated in conservative American rhetoric. In the photograph, the doctor occupies most of the image and serves as its focal point. Having recognized the famous doctor, the viewer's eyes are drawn to follow his gaze as he looks down on the small child below. While the ad was ostensibly about the child, the fact that the girl occupies only one-ninth of the frame suggests that the ad was really about the adult looking at the child and about what the adult (in this case the most esteemed expert on child rearing in the country) was thinking about her. Like SANE's other ads, this photograph was carefully constructed, with the child becoming a symbol for all vulnerable children, and with Spock in effect becoming a mirror for what the viewer should be seeing and thinking as he or she ponders the fate of the world's young.

The prescribed view of the child presented in the Spock ad was reinforced in SANE's construction of a "Peace Shelter" built in the center of Times Square for a rally that was scheduled on the same day the ad was released.[42] SANE constructed the shelter to replicate the familiar semi-mounded civil defense structures that Nelson Rockefeller had recommended to New York residents, with its unmistakable rectangular shape and low ceilings.[43] The shelter required that passersby negotiate themselves around its space, thereby forcing them to acknowledge it tacitly. Before entering the structure, viewers' expectations would certainly have been mixed. Those who knew of SANE's mission might have expected to see statistics on fallout and the futility of civil defense. Others might have expected to see a stocked shelter, replete with canned peaches and a makeshift ventilation system. What they saw instead was a continual loop of projected pictures of children killed in Hiroshima. By placing these images within the physical confines of the very structure that was supposed to provide safety from such horrors, SANE prompted viewers to see the child, the shelter, and themselves in a new way. Not only was the viewer forced to think about what his or her life would be like within the cramped walls of the structures; he or she was also compelled to ponder the shelter's ineffectiveness against the physical horrors of the nuclear firestorm.

But the shelter was only one part of the show. It was barely above freezing on 4 March 1962 as the winds whipped down Seventh Avenue into Times Square. The rally itself began quietly as protestors from SANE, WSP, the

General Strike for Peace, and others marched through Times Square. Then, after an eerie "silent half-hour," the crowd surged forward. Groups walked onto the intersection of Broadway and Forty-sixth Street and sat down in the middle of traffic. As the police vans collected the group, more began to sit down, chanting, "Shame! Shame! Shame!" Many demonstrators had small children with them. One young woman slapped a policeman. Traffic came to a standstill. The police eventually succeeded in dispersing 1,200 protestors and arresting forty-two.[44] That night, the courtroom was filled with the arrested and their friends, many of whom kept their children with them. One of them was Ellen Brooks, a member of WSP, who charged the police with "brutality."

While the public's specific reaction to the "Peace Shelter" has been lost amid reports of the larger demonstrations that were held during that week in March, the national response to Dr. Spock's ad was overwhelming, ranging from positive support to vitriolic criticism. In one letter to the editor in the national tabloid *Star*, an irate reader accused Spock of "exploiting the fears of the fathers and mothers of the country over atomic testing." Whereas Spock had argued in the ad that the cessation of testing did not leave the country susceptible to Soviet attack, the reader stated that the risks of not providing a strong deterrent against the Soviets "endangered the lives and futures of every American boy and girl. They are risks involving the future freedom of American mothers, fathers, sons, and daughters."[45] In contrast, Neil Lee Litvak, SANE's public information director, contended that the ad had "captured the imagination of the people everywhere and is literally sweeping the country."[46] One local chapter leader of SANE wrote into the national chapter in late April that "his whole neighborhood [was] full of Spock-lovers as there were many, many children."[47]

The power of the Spock piece was also made apparent by the number of similar advertisements published by SANE in the following months. In 1962, Dr. James V. Neel, professor and chair of the Department of Human Genetics at the University of Michigan, underwrote a SANE advertisement projecting that 38.4 million children with severe defects would be born if 40 million adults should manage to survive a nuclear war.[48] Another advertisement from August 1962 showed a silhouette of a pregnant woman appearing somber and reflective next to the words "[1.5] million unborn children will be born dead or have some gross defect because of Nuclear Bomb testing." This ad in effect invited two perspectives: one of the woman herself, worrying over the fate of her unborn child, and one of the viewer and the SANE members, collectively worrying over the mother and the baby before them. The support

1¼ Million unborn children will be born dead or have some gross defect because of Nuclear Bomb testing

SANE

Figure 6.2. The small text lists the types of deformities that are possible, including "blindness, deafness, feeble-mindedness, muscular dystrophy, hemophilia, and mental diseases." "1¼ Million Unborn Children Will Be Born," Washington Office 1960–63, SANE Papers, Swarthmore College Peace Collection, DG 58, Series B, box 34.

for this ad was so great that it appeared on subway and train platforms. It was also featured in the U.S. Information Agency Graphic Arts Exhibit to the Soviet Union in 1963 as a last-minute example of how Americans disliked nuclear testing. Ironically, although SANE had created the ad in order to criticize both American *and* Soviet testing, in the hands of the U.S. Information Agency, it transformed into a critique of Soviet nuclear escalation intended for Soviet audiences.[49] Its meanings were altered from their original intent to convey the message that the United States government was actively seeking a cessation to nuclear testing.

As the push for a nuclear test ban treaty grew in its offices, SANE created another ad in January 1963 that showed a picture of three laughing children, smiling brightly above text that read, "*Your* children's teeth contain Strontium-90." As with previous pieces, this ad called upon the viewer to assume the role of concerned adult. The ad was printed in the *New York Times* in the spring of 1963 and was sponsored by the Dentists' Committee of SANE. It delivered a message that would have appeared familiar to most readers of the paper by then, as it presented statistics on the rise in strontium levels among the nation's young and concluded with the statement that, "as dentists, our responsibility to promote life and health compels us to make this public appeal to all governments to cease nuclear weapons tests." Who could argue with the conclusions made by dentists on the troublesome fate faced by American children's teeth?

All of the men who supported these ads, from Spock to Neel to the Dentists' Committee, were presented as experts in their fields whose credibility was beyond reproach. This helps to explain why SANE regularly devoted half of its ad space to listing the names of its sponsors, which included such illustrious men as James Baldwin, Harry Fosdick, Harry Belafonte, Ray Bradbury, and Arthur Penn. At the same time, the ability of each of these ads to place the viewer in the position of a solemn, concerned citizen created a sense that this was not a worry that should be reserved for the country's greatest thinkers. Instead, SANE attempted to compel every adult to assume the same position as its members, regardless of their education or social status.

Central to many of the appeals was the issue of how children consumed radioactive materials, with particular focus on milk. One controversial ad featured little more than a milk bottle with a picture of a skull and crossbones pasted to its front. "Is this what it's coming to?" the July 1962 ad asked its readers in bold letters.[50] The text below read, "Milk is the most sacred of all foods. It is the food of infants and children. No one in the world has the right to contaminate it. . . . The time has come for mothers and fathers to speak up in no uncertain terms. . . . Raise hell; it's time you did." It then suggested to parents that they serve powdered or evaporated milk to children in areas where the fallout of iodine 131 had been particularly heavy. Milk became a signifier for the child, who was thought to be its main consumer. It also became an emblem for the environmental impact of testing and its immediate connection to the health of the population.

Given milk's importance as a symbol of public and environmental health, it comes as no surprise that SANE's ad garnered severe criticism across the country. Five days after the ad ran, Norman Myrick, the director of public relations for the Milk Industry Foundation, wrote a scathing letter to Norman Cousins and Clarence Pickett expressing his dismay "at the terrible prospect this advertisement affords."[51] "[This advertisement] is clearly a violation of the law," he declared. Citing the Federal Trade Commission's guidelines for advertising fallout shelters, he reminded Cousins and Pickett that "scare tactics, such as the employment of *horror pictures* calculated to arouse unduly the emotions of prospective shelter buyers, *shall not* be used. I submit that

Is this what it's coming to?

Figure 6.3. "Is This What It's Coming To?" *New York Times*, 5 July 1962. SANE Papers, Swarthmore College Peace Collection, DG 58, Series A, box 16.

the picture of a bottle of milk carrying the skull and cross bones which is a universal symbol for poison is a 'horror picture' used in order to arouse the emotions of prospective supporters of your organization."[52] Through "fear, innuendoes, half-truths and sly suggestions," he wrote, "you have led people to see our product as harmful to their children, which is completely false." But this was ultimately what SANE *was* attempting to accomplish; they were searching for ways to revise the public's view of its children and their environment. They were working to redefine what was at stake in the president's decision to resume nuclear testing. Myrick was certainly shocked by this tactic, but it was effective, as is evidenced by the subsequent milk boycotts that happened throughout the country that summer.

Despite some setbacks, by July 1963 the path to the Test Ban Treaty had been mapped and approved by both Kennedy and Khrushchev. All that remained was ratification by the Senate. SANE worked intensively to gain the two-thirds approval that was necessary to pass the treaty. In its advertisement, "Now it's up to the Senate . . . and You!" SANE reminded its readers that through this treaty, "present and future generations [would] be spared additional reproductive damage and bone cancer."[53] The campaign, which included a nationwide program of radio, press, and television appeals, was ultimately successful. Whereas public opinion had been almost twenty to one against the treaty at the beginning of the summer, by September a majority of the American population backed the limited Test Ban Treaty. The Senate easily ratified it by a margin of eighty to nineteen.[54]

Through its first five years of existence, SANE leaned heavily on the image of the child as a means to re-envision itself and the world's youth. In contrast to the images of imperiled and mobilized children that were created in other parts of American society, SANE depicted the next generation as victimized by the state in a way that made all other dangers seem inconsequential. Health risks, they argued, came before ideological ones. By reconfiguring the stakes of the nuclear arms race, SANE redefined the nature of the conflict altogether. Instead of seeing the Cold War as a struggle between East and West, or between communism and capitalism, it conceptualized the struggle as one that pitted the American and Soviet leadership against a globally endangered populace.

From SANE's example, another organization arose in the late 1950s that also portrayed its members as authority figures on how best to protect the young: the nation's mothers. This time, however, they would go one step further than putting children in their ads and rhetoric. This time, they brought their children along.

Women Strike for Peace and the Images of Maternalist Politics

On 19 May 1959, a group of white middle-class mothers, many holding babies in their arms, staged a protest at a meeting of a Senate appropriations subcommittee where federal money was being allocated for research on the health hazards of radioactive fallout. "I can assure you," Mrs. Robert H. Harris said, "that a pregnant woman's normal fears are multiplied by the thought that her unborn child might be deformed by invisible particles coming from bombs manufactured and tested by her fellow men."[55] Mrs. Harris and her fellow protesters, who were all members of the Washington chapter of SANE, justified their presence on Capitol Hill in terms of their maternal concern for their children. "I can't tell you what a mother goes through," Harris said to the reporter while holding her eight-month-old daughter on her hip, "when she worries whether she is poisoning her child with radioactivity every time she gives him a glass of milk or a piece of bread."[56]

One month later, the same women again made their way to the Senate building, this time to urge the passing of a bill that would transfer radiation safety controls from the Atomic Energy Commission to the Public Health Service. Dressed in fine clothes indicative of their social status, with numerous children in tow, the women filed into the Senate building to present a petition arguing for more transparency from the government on the effects of nuclear testing on the nation's young. "We are here to express our alarm at the genetic effects of nuclear tests," Mrs. Robert F. Steiner told a reporter for the *Washington Star*.[57] A couple of weeks later, another young mother, a well-known illustrator of children's books, presented a drawing of the petitioning women to the Senate subcommittee chairman, Lister Hill, in commemoration of the event. In the drawing, a group of well-dressed, white, middle-class mothers can be seen standing outside the doors of the Senate subcommittee meeting wiping their children's noses, talking with each other, and presenting their petition to a clerk who is peeking out of the door to invite them in. The illustrator of the drawing was Dagmar Wilson, who would soon become the public face of WSP.

Although drafted two years before WSP's inception, Wilson's drawing provides a window into the maternalist logic of the organization's founders. These women appear well dressed and well mannered, with far more attention shown to their children than to the clerk at the door. In an era in which the "cult of motherhood" and ideas of domestic, "feminine fulfillment" still held sway, these women presented themselves as housewives and mothers who had been compelled to leave the confines of the home for the sake of their children.[58] They stressed, in the words of Adrienne Harris and Ynestra King, "the rights of ordinary mothers to protect children from nuclear death over the rights of governments to kill them."[59] As such, their presence in the hallways of Congress simultaneously solidified their connection to the world of children and domestic life and provided justification for their movement into politics and the public sphere.[60] As Jean Bethke Elshtain has argued, their maternal pursuit of peace became "a crucial trope in [their] construction of identity" and provided a ticket into the world of governmental politics.[61] Although in later years the "motherist" approach posed a number of problems for feminists, who argued that such tactics were based on an assumed subordinate role for women in society, in the 1950s WSP saw itself as participating in an effective and time-tested tradition of female activism.[62]

Like SANE, WSP presented children as symbols of nuclear threat and as rallying points for antinuclear activism. Yet they also took an approach in depicting youth that was markedly different from that seen in SANE's nationwide advertisements. Unlike SANE's admen, who uniformly placed children in carefully constructed photographs taken in studios in front of blank or abstract backgrounds, the mothers of WSP presented their children marching and standing alongside them in real-world environments that sometimes included policemen, bad weather, and social disorder. This image of youth conveyed a far more challenging message than that being created by the SANE national office. In Wilson's 1959 drawing, the youngsters on the one hand appear to be well cared for and sheltered by their mothers; they are uniformly happy as they skip, read, and ask to be picked up. On the other hand, their presence in the hallway (and at the various rallies and public appearances that the organization would organize over the years) also conveys the message that these children, like their mothers, have been compelled to enter the public sphere and to brave its inherent dangers because the Bomb has rendered the home unsafe. Their presence brings into question the state's ability to protect the home and symbolizes the threat of invasion, not from communism or delinquency, but from nuclear attack, radioactive fallout, and state policy itself.

Moreover, the children who participated in WSP protests altered the physical world around them in ways that the SANE advertisements never did. The local Washington SANE chapter and WSP frequently made specific requests to participants to "bring their kids along." As one member wrote to Dagmar Wilson in later years, the presence of the children was undoubtedly instrumental in "making the Senators sit up and listen."[63] But it was not just the simple presence of the children that made them "sit up and listen." It was also the children's behavior. Although there is no evidence showing that these women openly decided to allow their children to make a ruckus while protesting, what transpired at these events seems to suggest that many of them implicitly agreed to let their children "act up" in order to create a certain amount of chaos and to subvert the ordered world around them. These women and their children can be seen acting, in the words of James Scott, "at the very perimeter of what the authorities are obliged to permit or unable to prevent."[64] Thus, in Wilson's drawing, children are not portrayed standing obediently by their mothers' sides in the halls of Congress. Instead, they can be seen turning cartwheels. They skip and crawl on the floor. When the *Washington Star* reported that a group of mothers and children had "turned a congressional hearing into a nursery," one gets the sense that the these children significantly altered the day's regular schedule of business. Through their presence and their irreverent behavior, these children effectively participated in a "ritual of reversal" that made into a carnival these spaces and the people within them.[65] They transformed the congressional environment from a male-centric forum into a nursery, which was perceived by many to be the heart of the home and the world of the child. To be sure, these children and their mothers never sought to break any explicit rules. In later years, they obeyed the police and heeded barricades. Yet through their "childish antics," they transgressed the rules and expectations of the official world around them (to be quiet, to sit still), while at the same time having little fear of punishment or social scorn.

The creation of WSP can be traced back to SANE's decision to purge its communist members in 1960 and to its strict hierarchical structure. However, it was not until SANE refused to take direct action when the eighty-nine-year-old Bertrand Russell was arrested on 5 September 1961 that Dagmar Wilson, Eleanor Garst, and six other members of the Washington branch of SANE officially decided to break away. Russell had been arrested after refusing to leave an antinuclear protest in England. At a late-night meeting, Wilson and Garst resolved to stage a one-day peace strike on the first of November that would involve the nation's women avoiding their daily chores, "on behalf of all the world's children [for] an end to the nuclear arms race." The following day, they issued an announcement asking women everywhere to suspend "the regular routine—home, family, job," and to "visit their elected representatives, and the UN delegates from other countries, to appeal for the future of mankind."[66] In the weeks building up to the protest, the members made thousands of phone calls and wrote numerous letters to friends and famous personalities asking for support. In their letter to Jacqueline Kennedy, for instance, they asked the First Lady to "think what hope would gladden the world if women everywhere would rise to claim the right to life for their children and for generations yet unborn."[67] Meanwhile, some 500 Marin County women in California prepared to abandon housework and "participate in a mass mailing of pro-peace letters to government officials."[68]

At its inception, WSP reprioritized the duties of the middle-class, American mother by linking the need for a test ban with their obligations to the home. "None of our children's problems matter if we can't get this one solved," one mother at the November march was quoted as saying.[69] By redefining their obligations to the child, these mothers were building a new mandate for themselves in the public sphere. While on the surface they seemed to embrace their stereotypical identities as mothers devoted first to the family, they also represented a part of white, middle-class American female culture that, in the words of Joanne Meyerowitz, "was neither wholly domestic nor quiescent."[70] Marriage and family failed to impede these women's involvement with the antinuclear cause and in fact became the primary justification for the movement away from the home.

National participation in the strike and in subsequent rallies was surprisingly large, considering the decentralized nature of the organization and the short amount of time that the women gave themselves to mobilize. During the November 1961 march, women in Detroit exhibited pictures of their own children while pushing baby carriages and holding placards saying, "Testing Damages the Unborn" and "Save the Children." Some 800 women, children, and a dog marched in front of the White House.[71] In Los Angeles, 4,000 women assembled; 600 women gathered in Cambridge, with one little girl wearing a sign that read, "I want to be a mommy someday."[72] Similar protests took place in numerous cities around the country, leading the organization to claim that a total of 50,000 women had participated.[73] Although the accuracy of that number is impossible to verify, there can be no doubt that the success of the November strike led to many more over the course of the next year. In December, WSP published pamphlets presenting new statistics on the levels of strontium 90 in the nation's milk supply. It then issued a memorandum to the secretary of health, education, and welfare containing recommendations for health protection, and a letter was written to President Kennedy declaring that "the women of America are concerned about the contamination *already* in our children's milk."[74] In January 1962, women and their children marched in front of the White House in the pouring rain, while others took up banners on the West Coast and in the Midwest.

From its inception, WSP took an approach in its marches and rallies that was nonconfrontational and yet surprisingly blunt in its criticisms of American and Soviet nuclear policies toward the world's young. Members maintained that their credibility was dependent upon their ability to "look middle-class, ordinary, and lady-like." As Dagmar Wilson noted, it was their intent to emphasize that they were well-behaved women who "did not usually resort to this kind of activity."[75] Their children always appeared with combed hair and appropriate attire. They marched quietly as a rule. Yet at the same time, their approach was remarkably aggressive. For instance, while they always marched in their finest clothes and with their children, they often did so in difficult environments, thereby drawing attention to their cause and to the difficulties they were enduring for the sake of nuclear disarmament. This was the case when 2,000 mothers and their children picketed the White House in a thunderstorm on 15 January 1962. The image of cold, drenched mothers and children marching resolutely in the rain was difficult for the press and the government to ignore. Ironically, the importance of the image of the suffering child trumped the physical well-being of the real children that were in their charge. On this particular day, Kennedy himself attempted to disperse the women by sending a message to them that he had "understood what they were trying to say, and therefore, [that they should consider] that their message was received."[76]

This approach received a mixed response from the American public. A policeman present at a Washington, D.C., march commented to a reporter, "They all want peace. You can't argue with that." A paper in San Diego simply wrote, "The demonstration was orderly."[77] Yet while the women received support from some circles, others argued that WSP was turning mothers and children into communist dupes. One flyer circulated in Portland, Oregon, declared, "Many innocent and well-meaning people—including MOTHERS, God bless them—are being duped by communists and Soviet apologists. . . . We must all remember that CHILDREN UNDER COMMUNISM ARE THE PROPERTY OF THE COMMUNIST STATE."[78] Here, in this dialogue between the marchers and their detractors, lay the crux of the conflict between the vision of the ideal child and the Cold War consensus that it supported and the revision of that image as it worked to undermine that very same consensus. This conflict was complicated by the fact that the Soviet press gave heavy coverage to these various marches, portraying the women and their children as mobilized for peace alongside the Russian population.[79] Despite the fact that WSP uniformly gave equal amounts of protest time to both Soviet and American testing, the Soviet Union's endorsement for its marches left many in the American public uncomfortable and spoke as much to the Soviet consensus-building project as it did to the American one.

Others criticized the organization on the grounds that it was endorsing inappropriate behavior among otherwise respectable women and children. In a particularly angry letter to the editor published in the *White Plains Reporter* in February 1962, one housewife, Frances Strong, declared that "women have always used their sex for these silly 'marches' on Washington, as if being a woman or a mother somehow set them apart from the general American public." Of course, that was the exact argument being made by WSP, an argument that this housewife disregarded, instead labeling the women as "chronic complainers who are always 'off' on any subject which makes news." Continuing, she declared that the organization was handing out false information, did not "trust the government, the experts, or anybody," was being laughed at by American men, and was putting the "American peace effort at risk." "I find any public means of getting attention to be embarrassing and in very bad taste," Strong concluded.[80] This article, which was echoed in less vitriolic terms in other letters to the editor across the country, displayed the risks that WSP was taking in moving its members and their children to the picket lines. The fact that these women embraced their maternal obligations while rejecting their government's expert assurances opened the door for critics who questioned the use of motherhood as grounds for public protest. Women instead became purveyors of "bad taste," based on the argument that no cause justified a woman stepping out into the public arena and drawing attention to herself.

Despite these criticisms, the protests and their heavy use of children continued. In fact, as the threat of resumed American atmospheric testing rose in the spring of 1962, the rallies took on a more serious tone. As noted earlier, WSP joined SANE in New York in March with children in tow, chanting in unison "Shame, Shame, Shame!"[81] A photograph in the *Springfield (Ohio) News Sun* shows a well-dressed woman holding her child while she "awaited her turn as police lifted demonstrators into patrol wagons."[82] At the same time, a number of WSP delegates prepared to travel to Geneva in an attempt to convince the Soviet and American negotiators to settle on a Test Ban Treaty. They issued statement after statement, declaring that they had "one great concern, our children."[83] "We women," another press release argued, "who are a part of the creative force of the world and who are representative of different ideologies and social systems, [gather] to express the hopes and fears of all women in their deep concern for the survival of our children."[84] After they returned to the United States, they intensified their picketing, joining forces with SANE and Linus Pauling to stage nationwide marches. After American atmospheric testing resumed, WSP and SANE called on the nation's mothers to boycott milk, declaring in a press release that "thousands of American mothers will boycott fresh milk after every atmospheric nuclear test." As we have seen, what resulted was an ad war that pitted WSP and SANE against the milk industry. In their efforts to assure the American public that their milk was not contaminated, the milk industry had been publishing articles since January quoting the promises of Kennedy that "the milk supply offers no hazards" and of Edward Teller, who had declared that "fallout from nuclear testing is not worth worrying about."[85]

On 5 December 1962, WSP received a summons to appear before HUAC under suspicion of communist infiltration. Although this hearing was ostensibly about ideological affiliation, WSP made sure in the next weeks to reorient the debate around the figure of the child and who was best able to protect it. This is evidenced in the fact that in the week before the hearing, WSP made careful plans to manage its encounter with HUAC differently than SANE had handled it two years earlier. In public statements, WSP presented its members as simple women who were being subjected to "interrogation" and "fear

Figure 6.4. "Nuclear Tests Cost Lives," September 1961. Literature 1962, WSP Papers, Swarthmore College Peace Collection, DG 115, Series A2, box 1.

tactics" by a committee that "imperils democracy itself."[86] It released a statement to the press one day before HUAC's announcement of the subpoenas, declaring that "with the fate of humanity resting on a push button, the quest for peace has become the highest form of patriotism."[87] The organization wrote an editorial in the *Washington Post* in which it conceded that "it was probably inevitable that this would happen . . . as soon as [we] won any degree of notoriety" but argued nonetheless that its members accepted the "responsibility of the individual in a free and democratic society."[88] They stated explicitly that they had never screened their members according to race, religion, or politics, and had no intention of doing so in the future. Publicly they made no mention of their children or of the damage that this hearing might do to their young. Privately, however, they were making plans that explicitly included their youngsters as a part of their strategy to counter HUAC's accusations. At an emergency meeting of around fifty women from the New

York and Washington, D.C., chapters, members decided unanimously that WSP would stand behind every subpoenaed woman at the hearing, regardless of her ideological beliefs and affiliation. This included providing access to WSP's lawyers and funding. They then distributed a letter to every member of WSP in the United States proposing that each woman send a request to her congressman asking to be subpoenaed as well. They argued that such an act would not only "dramatize the fact that rather than fearing investigation, we welcome it," but would also "give the press just what they need," and might even "result in having the hearings called off."[89] Although no new women were subpoenaed as a result of the letter-writing campaign, the program did succeed in making their position known to every congressman and woman, as well as to the general press.

Crucially, the decision was also made at the emergency meeting to bring children to the hearings. Largely through word of mouth, the women who were scheduled to attend the hearings made plans to arrive with their youngsters in tow. They would, in the words of Amy Swerdlow, transform the hearing into a test of patriotism, waged over each side's "commitment to the survival of the planet and its children."[90] Youngsters would be physically present, thereby creating an environment that would undermine the authority of the congressmen at the hearing and provide living examples of the reason for the women's activism. Ultimately, this approach succeeded in ushering in the "fall of HUAC's Bastille."[91]

When the HUAC hearings began on 11 December 1962, members of WSP occupied all of the open seats in the Old House Office Building. The hearing began with a long opening statement from the presiding chair, Congressman Clyde Doyle: "Excessive concern with peace on the part of any nation impedes or prevents adequate defense preparation, hinders effective diplomacy in the national interest, undermines the will to resist and saps national strength. For this reason, in today's world, intense peace propaganda and agitation in non-Communist nations obviously serves the aggressive plans of world communism."[92] Quoting U.S. Communist Party leader Gus Hall, Doyle reminded those in the audience that "it is imperative [for communists] to bring everyone—men, women, youth, and yes, even children—into the struggle." Amid vague allegations concerning the women's loyalties and the exploitation of their children for the communist cause, the hearing began.

For the remainder of the day, WSP worked effectively to gain control over the hearings. When Doyle conceded that not all peace activists were communists, the women rose and cheered. He then asked the women not to cheer during the hearing, only to see them applaud and stand when the first witness was called. After Doyle asked the women to please not make a ruckus (a request that he would make many times through the course of the day), Blanche Posner, a retired schoolteacher, took the stand. Above the objections and interruptions of the men on the committee, Posner declared resolutely that "this movement was inspired and motivated by mothers' love for children. . . . This is the only motivation."[93] After invoking the Fifth Amendment forty-four times in response to most of the questions asked of her, Posner left the stand in good spirits. Doyle thanked her for her testimony and she replied like only a schoolteacher could: "You are welcome, Mr. Doyle. And thank you. You have been very, very cooperative."[94] The audience broke into laughter as women and children rose to hug her and give her roses. Numerous witnesses followed, all making the same claims to have been drawn to the peace movement out of concern for their children. On the third day, Dagmar Wilson took the stand. On the way to the front, Wilson was stopped by a young woman with a baby on her hip who handed her a bouquet of flowers. Without citing the Fifth Amendment, Wilson presented herself merely as a figurehead for a group of unorganized women who had been drawn together out of outrage and fear over the fate of their young. When asked if she would be willing to admit communists or fascists into the organization, she stated, "If we could only get them on our side." Wilson received a standing ovation. After this, the questioning was quickly adjourned and the hearing officially ended. Amid the cheering and standing ovations, other moments of chaos ensued, as when former FBI agent Jack Levine dashed down the center aisle shouting, "Mr. Congressman! . . . I petition you to discontinue these proceedings before you heap disgrace on the American people!"[95]

The role played by children at the hearing has been largely overlooked in previous examinations of this event. In every picture of the women that was distributed to the national press, children can be seen talking, playing, and crying. Outside the hearing room, baby carriages sat parked near the waiting television cameras.[96] James McCartney wrote in the *Chicago Daily News* that "babies bawled, women cheered. There were hoots and laughs [in] the normally austere, marble columned hearing room."[97] Similarly, Mary McGrory, famed liberal journalist for the *Washington Evening Star*, described how the courtroom had been transformed by the children's presence: "The young crawled in the aisles and noisily sucked on their bottles during the whole proceedings . . . while the ladies used the Congress as a baby-sitter."[98] One newspaper showed a picture of a young toddler being helped out of his coat by his mother. Below the image were the words, "Babies—something HUAC wasn't prepared for."[99] WSP's inclusion of the children and the disruption that they created represented a careful and deliberate delegitimation of the entire proceedings. The presence of the women with their children openly called into question the ability of the congressmen to protect the young or gauge their needs, instead linking the men to the nuclear dangers that they indirectly condoned by prosecuting the women. This connection was made explicit by Bill Galt of the *Vancouver Sun*, who reported that Blanche Posner had managed during her testimony to link Congressman Doyle with "Strontium 90 in babies' milk, leukemia, birth deformation and nuclear holocaust."[100] Moreover, these women, by presenting themselves as motivated primarily by a desire to protect the children, redefined the criteria that determined their own guilt or innocence. The trial transformed from a hearing concerning suspected communist influence into a competition over who most loved their children. Once parental concern became the point of debate, the mothers had little trouble gaining the upper hand.

Over the course of the spring of 1963, WSP worked assiduously toward the passing of the Nuclear Test Ban Treaty. Photographs of children playing at an open fire hydrant in the street were accompanied by the message that this was "the right kind of fallout."[101] A "Disarmament Coloring Book" was distributed to mothers across the country that made the connection between government defense spending and the dilapidated condition of the nation's infrastructure.[102] When the Test Ban Treaty was up for ratification in the Senate, Aileen Hutchinson, a WSP member, pleaded for the "health, safety, and survival of the world's children."[103] Her sentiments were seconded by Senator Maurine Neuberger, who declared that a vote for the treaty would be a vote "that flows from the rational concern of any mother for the welfare of her children."[104] Through the course of WSP's struggle to influence American nuclear policy, images of the threatened and mobilized child played a central role in the organization's articulations of dissent. Children provided a source of legitimacy to women who had previously found themselves relegated to the domestic sphere. They redefined the source of the Cold War threat for many Americans and they identified a new set of national priorities according to which citizens could orient themselves politically and ethically, namely the welfare of the young and the need to protect the next generation from fallout and shortsighted governmental policies. The passage of the Test Ban Treaty in 1963 did not end SANE's and WSP's efforts to reconceptualize the Cold War in terms of the child's contested image. Their focus did change, however, as both organizations recognized that a crisis was in the making in Southeast Asia. After Johnson's bombing campaign began in February 1965, antinuclear activists resumed their use of the familiar image of the victimized child, no longer envisioned as a casualty of American and Soviet atomic brinksmanship, but now as a victim of U.S. imperialism and paranoia in Vietnam. For antiwar activists in the United States, as well as in the Soviet Union and in North Vietnam, the image of the napalmed child became the era's most pervasive symbol of American irresponsibility and brutality in the war. This was reflected in WSP slogans like "Not Our Sons, Not Your Sons, Not Their Sons," "War Is Not Healthy for Children and Other Living Things," and the more incendiary slogan, "Hey, Hey, LBJ, How Many Kids Did You Kill Today?"[105] Meanwhile, SANE, which was now under the leadership of Benjamin Spock and which would soon split over the question of how to find a settlement in Vietnam, led high-profile programs to save war-burned and war-injured Vietnamese children.[106] The centrality of the child's image in public debates about the war was also reflected in the efforts that the U.S. government made to cover up statistics on childhood casualties and in the heated arguments that ensued on the floor of Congress over the extent of childhood injuries and deaths in Vietnam. Democratic senator William F. Ryan from New York spoke no less than ten times in 1967 on the "plight of these children," but Republican senator Jack Miller from Iowa argued to his colleagues that recent visits to Vietnam had "not turned up a single case of a child burned with napalm."[107] Embedded in these debates lay questions concerning American culpability and obligation that had been in place since the late 1950s. Not surprisingly, the struggle over the child's image in the Cold War became a struggle over the young in Vietnam.

Conclusion

The question remains to be asked if these alternative visions of the young actually had any impact on the shape of the Cold War consensus or on the formation of foreign policy. The answer is yes. When Khrushchev and Kennedy reenvisioned youth in the early 1960s as international activists for peace, they were participating in a conversation with these artists and activists. They were attempting to counter the argument that their own policies were endangering the young. When they enacted new laws that offered increasing support and intervention to the marginalized youth of their nations, they were endeavoring to show their own populations and the world that they were in fact able to protect their kids. And when they promoted widespread cultural competitions for the young in New York and Moscow, the message that they ultimately sought to convey was that they could offer a bright future to the next generation. These filmmakers and activists put the idea of "peace" on the table in ways that demanded their leaders' attention. They turned "peace" into a source of political legitimacy that leaders on both sides could not ignore.

Perhaps the best evidence of the impact of the antinuclear movement on its government is the famous "Daisy Spot." Lyndon Johnson's reelection campaign released the ad in 1964. That fall, the advertising firm of Doyle, Dane and Bernbach set out to persuade the American people to vote for Lyndon Johnson in the upcoming election. The firm first proposed an advertising campaign that would focus on Johnson's recent passage of the Civil Rights Act but quickly scrapped the idea after realizing that civil rights was far too volatile an issue for voters in the already-divided Democratic Party. The intrepid advertisers returned to the drawing board and after much brainstorming had a golden idea—they would lionize Johnson as the defender of the nation's children, focusing specifically on his record with the Nuclear Test Ban Treaty, the War on Poverty, and Social Security. In the process, they would paint Johnson's opponent, Barry Goldwater, as a warmongering maniac. In effect, they proposed a reappropriation of the childhood images that SANE and WSP had been mobilizing since the late 1950s, which they of course had appropriated from the consensus builders around them earlier that decade.

A number of memorable, thirty-second television spots resulted from the work of Johnson's admen. One featured a photo montage of poor children in various locales across the country, accompanied by the narrator's reminder that "poverty is not a trait of character. It is created by circumstances. Thirty million Americans live in poverty. So will their children unless the cycle is broken."[108] Another spot centered on an elderly man who pulled from his wallet two small pieces of paper: a photograph of his grandchildren and his tattered Social Security card.[109] Dejected over the difficulties that he and future generations would face without support in their old age, he was shown tearing the card into shreds. This was the vision of life that Johnson presented to the American public if they voted for Goldwater and his campaign to dismantle Social Security.

While Johnson's television spots concerning the War on Poverty and the future of Social Security were well received by the American public, the ads that had the most impact and received the most attention from the press focused on the threat of nuclear war. The most memorable ad, and the one that people remember to this day, was the so-called Daisy Spot.[110] In the television promotion, which aired during an NBC telecast of *David and Bathsheba*, viewers received a vision of their future if it was left in the hands of Barry Goldwater.[111] "One, two, three, four, five, six, seven . . . six," a young girl counts as she pulls the petals from a big daisy. Moving up from her chest, to her face, to the blackness of her pupil, the camera freezes as her voice is replaced by the countdown for a nuclear attack. "Ten, nine, eight, seven . . ." At "one," the landscape is consumed by the familiar mushroom cloud, while the girl, along with the daisy and everything around her, is presumably destroyed. Quoting W. H. Auden, Johnson's voice intones, "These are the stakes—to make a world in which all of God's children can live, or to go into the dark." Finally, the narrator repeats the slogan for the campaign. "Vote for President Johnson on November three. The stakes are too high for you to stay home."

Employing the language of the antinuclear movement, Johnson transformed the once-subversive message of SANE and WSP into a normative program that most Americans were now expected to adopt. Although Bill Moyers would claim in later life that the ad was never meant to vilify Goldwater, in private conversations with the president at the time, he made it clear that "Daisy" had done its job by portraying Goldwater as "a reckless man."[112] Yet the contradictions in the image were unavoidable. On the one hand, this image functioned as a signifier for Johnson's (and the government's) identity as a lover of peace and protector of the child.[113] This was a contained American child in need of defense and protection from threat. On the other hand, the "Daisy Spot" presented an innocent child threatened not just by Soviet attack, but also by the hubris of America's leadership. It exposed the potential for annihilation, all at the whim of whoever happened to be in charge. Johnson's ad was so incendiary that it was pulled after one airing. Arguably, it was pulled not because it indicted Goldwater (muckraking was not new in presidential elections), but because it exposed the volatility of the nuclear standoff and the threat from within.

The American antinuclear movement and Soviet filmmakers during the 1950s and 60s had more in common than one might imagine. While there can be no question that a myriad of discreet and individual forces drove these seemingly disparate groups to use the child's image, we can nonetheless see how they were also driven to create alternative visions of their countries' youth for similar reasons and to similar ends. For instance, both groups existed in an environment where overt criticism of state policy could present great risks. While filmmakers in the Khrushchev era faced the prospect of having their films rejected by censors or even losing their jobs, white, middle-class Americans who were intent on opposing nuclear testing faced the prospects of social scorn and Senate investigations for communist affiliation. Both groups felt compelled to express themselves in ways that could slip by the censors. By presenting the child as their primary protagonist and focus for concern, these groups were able to position themselves as loyal citizens

Figure 6.5. 1964 Democratic National Campaign Spot, "Peace, Little Girl" ("Daisy Spot"). LBJ Library Photo by Democratic National Committee.

whose actions were motivated by a simple and "natural" desire to protect the next generation.

There are also some striking similarities between these two groups' depictions of youth. Both provided a vision of childhood that appeared threatened in ways that the world had never seen before. For Mikhail Romm and Benjamin Spock, the looming threat of the mushroom cloud permanently altered the assumed innocence and hopefulness of youth. Childhood instead became a symbol of potential loss, destruction, and disease. Even the space that children inhabited was changed drastically. Childhood had traditionally occupied what Gaston Bachelard calls the "felicitous spaces" of the home—the loved, nostalgic spaces that society deemed important to defend against threat.[114] These groups altered the location that childhood inhabited, transforming it into a place that promised only false security or even abandonment and death. In the process, they reidentified the source of the threat, not as the enemy outside their borders from whom peace had to be wrested or defense had to be ensured, but as the state itself, whose policies of brinksmanship had created a world that was unsafe for the young.

Each side to varying extents used the image of the child as a way to protest the weakened ability of the parent to protect his or her kids. This was made explicit in the films of the Thaw, where characters like Ivan and Fedor are orphaned and where Serezha and Tania have to reconcile themselves to the fact that their parents' obligations to the state come first. Certainly this is not how children are portrayed in the ads and rallies created by the antinuclear movement. These youths are never portrayed alone and are always surrounded by concerned parents. Yet when WSP took their children to the streets, they were in effect making the same statement that Tarkovsky and Klimov were making: that their government's policies had rendered them incapable of fulfilling their domestic obligations to protect their children and had instead drawn them into the dangers of the outside world.

Moreover, both of these groups contested the notion that the act of mobilization, either for a Soviet-led peace or for an American-led defense against communist attack, provided an effective means to wage the Cold War. They portrayed their children as mobilized in ways that were explicitly different from those proposed by the state. They showed children who were focused on the needs of the family and the individual over that of their governments. They presented visions of youth who could be seen actively rejecting their leaders' policies, whether they were related to the arms race, to agriculture, or to civil defense. They portrayed the young instead as advocates for alternative policies that would ostensibly lead to a brighter future for themselves. Both sides rejected the ideological boundaries of the Cold War consensus by redefining what was at risk in the conflict and by providing new ideas about what needed to be done in order to mitigate the threat. In the end, both sides created an environment where the relationship between the nation's leadership and its youth held just as much possibility for the collapse of consensus as it did for its construction.

Vietnam and the Fall of an Image

From 1964 to 1973, Soviet and American images of the Cold War child clashed in the propaganda battles of the Vietnam War. Information brokers at the U.S. Joint Public Affairs Office (JUSPAO) and at the Soviet State Service for Television and Radio (Gosteleradio) generated vast numbers of pamphlets, television shows, billboards, films, and radio reports that focused on the lives of Vietnamese children. Soviet and American propagandists borrowed heavily from the images of children created in their respective countries in order to present a portrait of themselves as concerned and mobilized for war-ravaged populations in Southeast Asia. They portrayed Vietnamese kids as innocent victims of enemy barbarity, as grateful recipients of Soviet and American care, and, in the Soviet Union, as trained revolutionaries prepared to fight and die for national liberation. They were not the only contributors to this visual cacophony. North Vietnamese propagandists who were working through the Central Executive Committee of the People's Revolutionary Party (called COSVN, or the Central Office for South Vietnam, by the Americans) marshaled these images and remobilized them in their efforts to counter the agendas of both sides. In protest against the visual control, or scopic regime, that Soviet and American propagandists were attempting to create, the NLF presented visions of its own children in order to argue not only that the next generation was capable of fighting off the American menace with or without Soviet help, but that Western policies toward Southeast Asia and their claims to moral legitimacy were bankrupt.

From this visual and rhetorical dialogue surrounding the vision of the Vietnamese child it became clear in the late 1960s that no image, regardless of how seemingly staid or archetypal it appeared to be, could be relied upon as semiotic capital. Visions of mobilized Russian children standing at the ramparts with the North Vietnamese, which fit so nicely into the domestic visual paradigm of the ideal Soviet child, nonetheless could not conceal the unavoidable message that despite Soviet support, the youth of Vietnam, like their parents, were going to have to fight this war without Russian help. Similarly, JUSPAO's efforts to redeem American policies in the region by portraying children (and women) as passive victims of the North Vietnamese rang increasingly false and compromised the argument that populations in the South were capable of liberating themselves from invasion from North Vietnam. JUSPAO's message of American humanitarian concern and defense for Vietnam was made even more problematic by depictions in the world press of lynched children in Mississippi and slaughtered infants in My Lai. Not surprisingly, the North Vietnamese made it a practice to highlight all of these contradictions in their own propaganda. Just as American and Soviet broadcasters worked frantically to use Vietnamese youth to justify their policies in the region and to demonize the enemy, NLF broadcasters were busy using these same images to argue that this was not a war about capitalism versus communism or East versus West. Instead, they argued for a total reconceptualization of the conflict as one that pitted *both* superpowers against those populations who were most vulnerable to state coercion.

Youth, which played such a central role in articulating the semiotic battle lines of the Cold War for American and Soviet image makers, played a part in remapping the conceptual battle lines of the conflict when they were contextualized by the moral and political ambiguities of the Vietnam War. As Soviet and American propagandists would quickly learn, manufactured images of mobilized Cold War youth, even those that seemed to support state policy, were open to alternative interpretations and subaltern constructions by the very groups that were supposed to be their consumers. If there ever had been a Cold War consensus, by 1968 it was gone, and the child had become its greatest symbol of collapse.

The American Message

In 1964, JUSPAO launched a campaign to sell the American message to its Vietnamese audience. Twenty new officers joined the Vietnam office, and funding for propaganda to the region increased dramatically. The American program in Vietnam quickly became the largest propaganda effort in American history, requiring vast expenditure, the attention of thousands of workers, and the use of all possible psychological tactics in the struggle for Vietnam's "hearts and minds." By 1967, Voice of Freedom and Voice of America broadcasts were transmitting seventy hours a day over multiple channels (thus they were producing more than 24 hours of radio each day) to audiences in Vietnam and Cambodia and were heard by 62 percent of the population.[1]

In the press, on radio and television, and in film, workers at JUSPAO delivered a simple set of messages to their Vietnamese audiences. They argued that humanist ideals drove the United States to stop the NLF and their communist beliefs from spreading into the South. They presented the United States as a wealthy country, willing and able to provide a path toward modernization for its allies. As a first step toward freedom, they argued that the Vietnamese people should rally behind the United States and the South Vietnamese government. These messages continued throughout the American propaganda effort and attempted to establish the United States as a benevolent provider and protector of the South Vietnamese people.

Throughout its time in Vietnam, JUSPAO made a concerted effort to portray Vietnamese youth as victims of communist aggression and as beneficiaries of American aid. In July 1965, JUSPAO's planning staff put together a set of recommendations for how the U.S. propaganda effort should exploit NLF atrocities among its listeners and readers. After discussing the effects that various kinds of atrocities could have upon audiences, the authors came to two conclusions. First, listeners and viewers had to be made to understand that NLF brutality was "inseparably linked to the communist system." Second, the most "effective" atrocities were the ones by which the "number of 'innocents' slaughtered was significant or if the slaughter was by its nature particularly abhorrent."[2] As one JUSPAO writer put it, "The demolition by an NLF mine of a bus carrying children is exploitable." Such actions would, in his words "instill fear for the purpose of controlling people's behavior" and would "generate hostility" toward the agents of such "indiscriminate targeting." Children were also useful as tools for evoking homesickness among NLF and North Vietnamese Army (NVA) troops. As a part of what Barry Zorthian, the head of JUSPAO, called the "Born in the North, die in the South campaign," American propagandists endeavored to convince their NLF and NVA readers that their children were suffering without them, that they were certain to die far from the homes of their ancestors, and that the only way to survive was to rally to the United States.[3]

One of the most prominent ways that these images of atrocity and defection manifested to Vietnamese audiences was through the Chieu Hoi program, a campaign meant to encourage the NLF and NVA to defect. Propaganda for Chieu Hoi was conveyed primarily through the dropping of leaflets over areas of South Vietnam loyal to the NLF. Between 1964 and 1968, images of children appeared in 27 percent of Chieu Hoi leaflets dropped by JUSPAO.[4] Considering that over 5,000 different types of leaflets, adding up to 50 billion total, were dropped by the Americans though the course of the war, this represents a significant visual occurrence for audiences in Vietnam. Two kinds of leaflets consistently featured images of children: those based on what

JUSPAO called the "fear appeal" and those founded on the "family appeal." The "fear appeal" involved showing the bodies of dead women and children in order to convince soldiers who sided with the NLF that they were inviting the deaths of their families. As a second and subsequent tactic, leaflets promised that if a soldier reported voluntarily to the Army of the Republic of Vietnam (ARVN) he would receive medical care and rehabilitation and would be able to reunite with his family, thereby constituting the "family appeal."[5] Hundreds of pictures and illustrations depicted families pleading to their fathers to come home, their own survival made tenuous by the absence of their main wage earner. The United States regularly offered families as much as 300 piastras to make such appeals.[6] Other images depicted the bucolic happiness of rural life, with children rejoicing at their father's return, and others showed American soldiers providing medical care to families and their young, kept safe within the confines of the strategic hamlet.

Unfortunately, both the "fear appeal" and the "family appeal" had their flaws. Atrocities often created more fear than hostility among readers.[7] Instead of driving the population to rebel against the NLF in moral indignation, these images encouraged them to side with the enemy in order to improve their odds of survival. In addition, the promise of family reunion was often an empty one. As many JUSPAO workers would admit privately, the United States and the government of South Vietnam (GVN) were largely incapable of reuniting soldiers with their families in NLF-controlled areas. Even worse, a soldier's defection might put his family in danger of NLF retribution.[8] Also troubling was the possibility that these leaflets might encourage South Vietnamese ARVN soldiers, as well as NLF soldiers, to desert their posts for the comforts of home.[9] While it was easy enough to produce these images, it was almost impossible to control the meanings that they carried once they reached their audiences.

By 1967, as the war became more desperate for both the Viet Minh (the communist national independence movement) and the GVN, images of the child-soldier, depicted as brainwashed or kidnapped into forced conscription, also emerged in American propaganda. JUSPAO reported that parents in villages were cutting off their children's trigger fingers in order to prevent their being drafted by the NLF.[10] North Vietnamese children were featured heavily in reports on young Hoi Chanh soldiers, boys and girls who had been conscripted into the NLF army at a very young age and had subsequently defected to the South through the Chieu Hoi program. As one issue of *Vietnam Magazine* declared in 1969, "We have welcomed little boys and girls of 12, 13, and 14 who have returned fully armed. . . . [They had been] abducted, rounded-up, and forced into armed conflict."[11]

GIA ĐÌNH
TRÔNG CHỜ BẠN
CHIÊU HỒI

Figure 7.1. A Chieu Hoi leaflet. The caption reads, "Your family awaits you, Chieu Hoi." Vietnam Archive, Texas Tech University, Lubbock, Texas.

As David Hunt has pointed out in his study of village life during the war, these child-soldiers often were not abductees but had turned voluntarily to the NLF as a way to escape impoverished and abusive homes.[12] JUSPAO assumed that Vietnamese adults carried the same beliefs about the innocence and necessary containment of children in society. These assumptions translated into the formulation of a propaganda tactic. Unfortunately, this tactic did not necessarily resonate with an audience that, whether because of belief or out of necessity, was far more ambivalent about appropriate roles for children in war. Differing cultural perceptions toward children not only informed how JUSPAO shaped its message to its listeners and viewers but also impacted how those messages were received on the ground. This is evidenced most clearly in memoirs of the war written by Vietnamese civilians. Authors like Le Ly Hayslip and Bao Ninh have presented visions of a populace that was frequently forced to disregard the needs of the young for the sake of familial and national survival.[13]

The cumulative effect of JUSPAO's work was to construct an image of America protecting and aiding a largely passive Vietnamese populace from the brutal actions taken by the NLF. JUSPAO established a causal relationship in its broadcasts and publications between the effects of the NLF upon the young of Vietnam and the paternalistic responses of American troops, who provided aid through the pacification program and the corralling of villagers into strategic hamlets. One leaflet from 1965 argued to its Vietnamese readers that, in contrast to the NLF, who "will bring you to their secret zones and kill

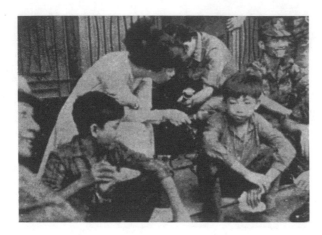

Figure 7.2. "The Returnee." *Vietnam Bulletin*, 1 November 1969, 34.

you brutally," the U.S. army would "take care of your health, cure your sickness, and give you remedy."[14]

Perhaps the most memorable articulation of these themes came early in the war, in 1964, when the U.S. Information Agency teamed up with director/producer Richard Heffron and JUSPAO to make the film *Night of the Dragon* for global distribution. The piece was often played before the feature showing of George Cukor's *My Fair Lady* and received wide distribution not only in Southeast Asia but also in Europe, America, Africa, and Latin America.[15] It told the story of the South Vietnamese struggle to wrest freedom from the NLF. By combining the resonant narration of Charlton Heston with graphic montages of the dead and protracted shots of the brave South Vietnamese, some of which were staged, Heffron was able to portray the United States as resolutely bound to the cause of South Vietnamese freedom, while communism was rendered as an anathema.[16] In the words of Carl Rowan, this film sought "to evoke sympathy and support among world-wide audiences for the Vietnamese cause."[17]

In Heffron's hands, the Vietnamese child became an icon of suffering and hope. In a striking montage at the film's beginning, Heston intones, "Many of the victims did not die from the accidents of war, they were selectively murdered for political example." A collection of photographs follows: a young man on the ground, his throat slit, his elbows bound behind him, a child atop a pile of rubble next to a burned-out bus, a woman's face framed in bangs of blood, a girl's head only tenuously connected to what might be a body, twisted to the verge of decapitation, a mother and child lying dead together. Pausing, the camera finally settles on the dead bodies of two children clumped together in the dirt—their elbows bound. Taken from a distance far beneath the boys, the shot replicates visually the explanation that Heston gives for these deaths: "because they were in the way."

Heffron's film produced seeming verification that American policy in Southeast Asia was, at its most basic, about resisting blind violence and inhuman barbarity. It argued that without American involvement, chaos would reign and the innocent would become fodder for communist warmongering. It also endeavored to justify the American policies of pacification and modernization by portraying well-protected children living in a strategic hamlet. During the day, children can be seen receiving schooling and medical care. At night, Heffron captures the happiness of a festival inside the hamlet, with youngsters laughing and dancing. The festival and the manifest joy of the children are unfortunately cut short by an NLF attack, which forces the children to take cover and the soldiers to man the ramparts. Just as domestic propaganda showed American youth insulated from foreign threats in their homes and schools, so in Heffron's portrayal Vietnamese children emerged as innocent figures within the safe confines of the strategic hamlet.

Night of the Dragon reveals the extent to which JUSPAO broadcasters envisioned the United States as the parent of a juvenile Southeast Asian populace. For instance, during a staged shot of South Vietnamese soldiers crossing an open field, Charlton Heston informs his viewers that the American captain supervising them came to Vietnam because he "can't see a decent future for his children if aggression is allowed to succeed." As the American captain gazes out over his advancing South Vietnamese troops, the viewer is left to wonder which children the captain is referring to: his own young ones back in America or the "children" he is supervising on this open field. Arguably, he is referring to both groups. To the extent that he is concerned for his own children, the global spread of communism presents the most serious risk to the promise of a "decent future." More immediate, however, it is the men walking before him, the "children" of American generosity, whose future is most vulnerable. These sentiments were presented even more clearly by Stanley F. Reed, president of the Reed Research Foundation, who commented to the House of Representatives in 1963 concerning the work of American broadcasting that "these nations remind me of children with their alternating friendships, jealousy of possessions, continual truculence, and petty quarrels. I would like the rest of the world to think we could help each other in the ages to come to give our 'children' a feeling of security and belonging."[18] These expressions of American paternalism continued a larger, much older colonial discourse on the relationship between the Western and the Southeast Asian worlds. They also helped to infantilize and feminize the Vietnamese population in what Lyndon Johnson called "that bitch of a war." On the one hand, they supported the argument that American leadership was needed in guiding newly decolonized countries like Vietnam toward democracy and growth. At the same time, they also reinforced colonial stereotypes about the static, passive, and childlike nature of non-Western populations. As such, they attempted to provide a dominant language for understanding why Vietnam needed what America had to offer.

Despite its colonial undertones and its visual omissions, it would be a mistake to ignore the success of at least some of JUSPAO's tactics on both NLF soldiers and the Vietnamese rank and file. Captured NLF documents attest to the demoralizing effects of the Chieu Hoi program as well as the power of high-budget films like *Night of the Dragon*. As one NLF report declared in October 1966, "Enemy activities . . . demoralize the village and hamlet cadre."[19] Perhaps not surprising, in numerous captured documents dating from 1965 to 1968, NLF propagandists and officials argued that JUSPAO's most effective appeals were those that encouraged soldiers through fear and homesickness to surrender and rejoin their families. As one NLF official put it, "The most common weakness is the ideology of the family and of pacifism."[20] They pointed out that this was a particular problem during holidays, especially Tet, when JUSPAO would increase its leaflet and broadcasting programs in order to exploit feelings of homesickness among the NLF and the NVA.[21] The potency of these programs is also evidenced by NLF efforts to halt defections, by their admission in 1966 that they had not adequately addressed the Chieu Hoi campaign in the early years, and by the strict rules that the NLF and NVA imposed on their soldiers in regard to accessing outside information and entertainment. Cadres were forbidden from listening to spoken enemy broadcasts, and even to music and theatrical programs.[22] For those who showed "defectionist" tendencies, reindoctrination or execution was the remedy.[23]

Yet while these images supported JUSPAO's campaigns to encourage enemy defection, to justify the policy of pacification, and to bolster the idea that America was needed in South Vietnam to protect the innocent, they also compromised the important American message that the Vietnamese should take up arms on their own behalf for the sake of their own national liberation. The Soviets and the NLF would repeatedly argue to their Vietnamese audience that the American presence in Vietnam was one of "reactionary aggression"—that America was exploiting its self-designated role as defender of the innocent in order to justify an aggressive foreign policy.[24] The dependency of the South Vietnamese was arguably useful to JUSPAO and U.S. policy makers in the short term; it justified American military and psychological operations in the region. It nonetheless did little to establish this war as a crusade for national liberation in the South. "The enemy . . . makes [individuals] dependent upon his handouts and money," one security directive from the NLF Propaganda Office (COSVN) argued in January 1967.[25] While JUSPAO embraced this approach in order to justify America's presence in the war, it also undermined the war effort at the grassroots level by encouraging passivity and failing to establish personal connections with the populace.

The Soviet Message

In contrast to JUSPAO's constructed images of youth, the Soviet State Television and Radio Service (Gosteleradio) projected a series of counter-images of Russian, American, and Vietnamese children that embodied the Soviet promise for progress, the horror of the American presence in Vietnam, and the professed belief in the ability of the Vietnamese people to gain freedom on their own. Gosteleradio positioned its own wealthy, educated, activist youth as brothers and sisters of the North Vietnamese. In later years, when it became clear that the Soviet Union would not be sending troops to aid its communist ally, Gosteleradio increasingly portrayed the children of Vietnam as active revolutionaries who did not need Russian help to win the war. This was joined by an all-out condemnation of America and its treatment of African American and Vietnamese youth. As the war dragged on, Soviet expressions of undying unity between the two countries became subject to increasing criticism by the North Vietnamese and the NLF as they realized the limitations of Russian support. As was the case with JUSPAO, Gosteleradio found itself creating images of children that both supported and at times contradicted Soviet policies in the region.

The Soviet propaganda effort in Vietnam began in the late 1950s as part of a larger program to reach audiences in Southeast Asia. Throughout 1956, the Soviet ministers of culture and the radio-technical industry sent regular letters to Khrushchev informing him that current levels of broadcasting were "insufficient." They argued for "smarter" propaganda geared at reaching the cynical ears of populations that were significantly different from populations in Europe and the West.[26] These warnings did not fall on deaf ears. By 1960, broadcasters were transmitting in the native languages of their listeners while new programs like "Peace and Progress," which were targeted at Southeast Asia, grew by more than 250 percent to a total of 2,032 hours per week.[27] In "simple and easy to understand" terms, the internal politics, economics, and culture of the Soviet Union were to be taught to listeners through "radio universities" and cultural education programs.[28] Gosteleradio officials were directed to convey information about Soviet national politics, American colonial interference, the success of the Cultural Revolution, and the "steady help of the Soviet Union to the 'young' nations of the world."[29] They were to deliver the message that the Soviet Union was wealthy, willing to defend the non-European world from colonialism, and deeply opposed to American racism and class difference.[30]

Broadcasts on the prosperity of Soviet children and their families were a steady fixture in Soviet propaganda throughout the 1960s. Proof of wealth, intended to counter stereotypes of Russian "backwardness," came in the form of domestic showcases highlighting the advantages of socialist industry. In interviews, mothers and children spoke glowingly of the toys and the new washer and dryer now housed in their individual flats—all provided courtesy of the state.[31] Steadily, as each broadcast attested, standards of living were improving. Material goods were available, Gosteleradio argued, and produce, bread, meat, and butter were provided at heavily subsidized prices.[32]

Fundamental to these broadcasts was the message that Soviet affluence was different than American abundance—not a form of economic imperialism but a means to gain independence and resist American hegemony. Widely disseminated broadcasts repeatedly argued that the underlying belief structures in the Soviet system enabled youth living under communism to acquire material wealth while avoiding the selfish, apathetic, apolitical consumerism that plagued the Western world. As one 1964 radio broadcast argued, "The capitalists have only one dream—the dream to gain more profit. Children suffer when countries function in this manner."[33] In contrast stood the Soviet Union, whose aims were "to build new factories and new mills, to invent new machines, and to settle new lands so that children can live even better . . . even happier. . . . Not only in our country, but in all the world."[34] Gosteleradio portrayed Soviet affluence as a product of distributed wealth. Even more important was the message that this kind of economic egalitarianism could be exported to the postcolonial world.

Russian children also played a central role in Gosteleradio's efforts to establish Soviet solidarity with the Vietnamese people. As early as 1959, Vietnamese citizens could hear Soviet children expressing their friendship and support for independent nationalist movements. "Dear children of Vietnam— our distant friends," one broadcast began. "I am happy that I can send to you my warmest greetings over the radio. Many of my friends and I have over the past year been exchanging letters with Vietnamese Pioneers. We have learned from them how you live, study, and how you help your elders with their work."[35] As American involvement in Vietnam increased, so too did the volume of such broadcasts. These programs worked to create the impression that Soviet citizens were not far away and not different from their Vietnamese listeners. While Gosteleradio certainly spent time proving Soviet wealth and progress, it also endeavored daily to minimize the political, economic, and social distance between the two countries. As one Soviet boy in 1961 proclaimed over the radio, "We are happy that the youth of Vietnam are moving as one unified rank with the freedom-loving youth of the socialist countries who are all striving to create peace on earth."[36] Five years later, in a radio show entitled "Always Together," Gosteleradio traveled to five schools collecting audio recordings of Pioneer organizations as they expressed their solidarity with the "heroic children of Vietnam."[37] In contrast to the approach taken by JUSPAO, Soviet youth, in the words of one report, "assumed as [their] international duty the obligation to provide concrete help to the youths of nations engaged in nationalist struggles."[38] At the hands of Gosteleradio's spin doctors, aid was characterized as more than simply a geostrategic action; it was an emotional event, born from an ingrained concern for the plight of the common Vietnamese citizen.

Gosteleradio aired broadcasts almost daily on a wide array of children's activities designed to show Vietnam that the Soviet Union was raising youngsters devoted to peace and the eradication of colonialism and racism. Pioneer groups and classrooms constructed "Vietnam Corners," like the one built by School Number Nine in Odessa in October 1966. Just as students had created "Red Corners" and "Pioneer Corners" in past years, now they set aside semi-permanent spaces in their classrooms for materials and documents about the Democratic Republic of Vietnam, with photographs of Haiphong, Odessa's sister city, and the children who lived there. As one reporter marveled, "Here they exhibit letters and gifts. On the table lie books by Vietnamese writers and poets as well as works by Soviet authors about Vietnam."[39] Similar reports highlighted Vietnamese language programs, the publication of a Vietnamese-Russian dictionary, and campaigns like "Young Pioneers of the USSR Aid Vietnam," which was run by the International Friendship clubs of Kiev, Ivanovo, Sverdlovsk, Moscow, and Artek, the summer camp on the Black Sea.[40] Pioneers in these locations collected pens, pencils, textbooks, picture books, drawing paper, and paints and sent them as gifts, with no distinction ever made between North and South Vietnam. Pioneers also initiated a program called "Medicinal Herbs for the Hanoi Children's Hospital," as well as a "Solidarity" movement whereby schoolchildren delivered thousands of pounds of collected herbs and 3 million rubles to Vietnam to build a Young Pioneer palace in Hanoi. In stark contrast to the constructed image of the American child in JUSPAO broadcasting, Soviet youth appeared not only to be the recipients of the gifts provided by a highly developed and prosperous society, but also socially conscious citizens willing to work on Saturdays doing dirty jobs not for themselves or even for anyone within their national borders, but for the sake of their less-fortunate brothers and sisters abroad.

The Soviet child also provided a model for how the Vietnamese could frame their own resistance. From its inception, the Soviet Union had embraced an idealized vision of the child as a revolutionary. While this image had receded somewhat in the early Stalinist period, by the 1960s the image of the mobilized Soviet child, during both World War II and the Cold War, reemerged. In their broadcasts to Vietnam, Gosteleradio argued that Russia's children were living examples of how the youngest in society could contribute to the war. They argued that Soviet youth had experienced the burdens and difficulties of the struggle against foreign imperialists during the Revolution, the Civil War, and World War II, when they "heroically fought against the foreign aggressors and gave all their strength in the name of the Motherland. This is why the Soviet youth, and all the Soviet people, decidedly and uncompromisingly came forward in support of the young of Vietnam, who were needed to stop the American aggressors and expel the American forces from their home."[41] Gosteleradio promised that the Soviet Union not only stood behind the South Vietnamese struggle to wrest freedom from America, but that it would provide a model for the children in Vietnam in their struggle against foreign aggression.

Positive representations of Soviet children supporting the Vietnamese cause were part of a much larger propaganda campaign aimed at contrasting communist success and moral constancy with American exploitation and apathy. Soviet broadcasts specifically targeted images of African American children, to whom the upheaval of the civil rights movement brought international attention. In a 1964 broadcast, one Soviet announcer reminded his Vietnamese listeners, "The Governor of Alabama [George Wallace] and his lackeys, from the height of their official posts, are openly instigating pogroms against innocent children in the American South."[42] In contrast to the assurances made by JUSPAO that racism was a dilemma specific to dwindling populations in the South, Gosteleradio provided an image of an entire nation wracked by hatred and controlled by a violently enforced caste system. "Who are these child-killers?" one broadcaster asked his listeners in 1965. "The semi-official American press asserts that they could be simply renegades of society, moral freaks, but doesn't it seem as though there are a lot of these renegades being allowed in 'civilized' American society?" Broadcasts like these were quick to list the "renegade" actions of America's racist population: George Wallace's election, the survival of Jim Crow, the murder of Medgar Evers, and finally the "six negro children who wanted only to pray."[43] What emerged in these broadcasts was a picture of a sick, amoral American society, littered with the bodies of dead black children.

From the beginning, Soviet accusations of American racism were used to substantiate allegations of U.S. colonialism in Southeast Asia. Images of black children suffering at the hands of American racists were joined by a vast visual and audio record of American abuse of children abroad. As one Soviet broadcaster commented in 1965, "Racist Americans are produced at a young age. . . . When [they] are ten-years-old they are intentionally taught not to see Negroes as human. . . . [Now] they kill thousands of South Vietnamese. . . . It is a terrible, inhumane [chelovekonenavistnicheskaia] logic. But isn't it such a 'logic' . . . which inside America defends racism and outside of it imperialism?"[44] According to Soviet broadcasts, racism was a prerequisite to America's capitalist agenda in the postcolonial world; it was the vehicle by which countries like the United States could pursue their neocolonial programs without facing the moral ramifications of their actions. This meant real danger for nations like Vietnam, Gosteleradio contended. If children in America were being raised to hate a significant portion of their own citizenry, what hope was there for foreign youth?[45]

The barrage of American racist and imperialist images in the Soviet media was staggering. In the large sample of Soviet foreign broadcasts examined for this book spanning the years 1960 to 1968, reports devoted to the United States and to its racial and colonial policies increased dramatically. For instance, in January 1960, foreign broadcasts to Vietnam devoted 25 percent of their reports to the subject of the United States and its racial and colonial history around the world.[46] The remaining 75 percent of broadcasts to Vietnam in that month focused on the Soviet Union's lasting friendship with Asia, its commitment to cultural exchange, its willingness to share Soviet wealth, and its ability to help Vietnam rebuild through agriculture and industry. In contrast, in January 1968, Soviet broadcasts to Vietnam focused 63 percent of their attention exclusively on American racism and colonialism in Southeast Asia (an increase of almost 150 percent), while the remaining 37 percent of broadcasts referred implicitly to the American invasion of Vietnam by dwelling on the efforts being made by the Soviet Union to help those under siege. Of course, these were not always discrete categories, as broadcasts would often cover many subjects at once.

In response to what it considered a fairly clear American imperialist agenda, Gosteleradio used images of dead Vietnamese children in order to solicit revulsion among its listeners, to demonize America's role in the Cold War, to legitimize its own actions against American aggression, and to provide a common enemy against whom Soviet broadcasters and their listeners could unite. Common exposés focused on the bombing of Vietnamese children's schools and hospitals by reckless American bombardiers. "During a regular flight of American pilots over the territory of the DRV [Democratic Republic of Vietnam], barbaric bombing destroyed a children's school in the area of Let-hu, near Kuang Bin. They killed ten children from the ages of three to six years old and two teachers. Many similar schools have also been destroyed. There are no words that can explain in full measure the sadistic actions of the American imperialists, who have lost all notions of human honor, morality, and conscience, who have lost their humanity."[47] Indictments of American barbarity in Vietnam became even easier when the United States undertook campaigns like Operation Ranch Hand, which involved the spraying of toxic chemicals like Agent Orange and Agent Blue over hundreds of thousands of acres of Vietnamese farmland.[48] As one Soviet broadcaster stated to his listeners in 1964, "In the 'dirty war' against South Vietnamese patriots, American warmongers and their friends, while presenting themselves as agents of 'freedom,' again resumed the dropping of poisonous chemical gas over the land of Kai Tau. . . . American pilots hit peaceful populated areas with chemical bombs and bombarded them with chemical bullets. It has been reported that as a result of these barbaric flights, around a thousand peaceful citizens, including about 500 children, have been killed."[49] Just as in its coverage of the American South, Gosteleradio portrayed U.S. involvement in Vietnam as a rape of innocence.[50] Harrowing photographs and reports coming from the world press were reprinted and even described over Soviet foreign radio. "Anyone who looks at these photographs," one reporter declared in March 1964, "cannot ignore the feeling of hatred toward these American executioners, who are committing this bloody injustice upon defenseless children."[51] Because Soviet broadcasts seldom differentiated between North and South Vietnam in their reports, the entire population appeared to be under siege by American forces intent on denying them their much-desired reunification. In stark contrast to Heffron's images of the American captain leading South Vietnamese forces across an open field, Soviet broadcasters painted South Vietnamese soldiers either as traitors or as men forced into conscription, while the citizens of South Vietnam became full supporters of communist liberation in the face of unwanted American pillaging.

In addition to portraying Vietnam's children as unwitting victims of U.S. aggression, Gosteleradio also depicted them as martyrs and warriors facing an ideologically and militarily weak American foe. This message was best summed up in a poem read during a 1965 broadcast to Vietnam:

> The Americans go to Vietnam
> They are headed for some unpleasant work.
> They have children to shoot, villages to seize
> And in the nooses people to string up
>
> . . . .
>
> But for freedom, the young will continue to fight
> Vietnam will not bow its head
> It will tear away the hydra's tentacles
> And it will call to them in Washington
> As the people of the world will all sound the alarm
> And their word will be heard triumphantly and terribly
> "To not return to the history of yesterday!
> To remember, before it's too late" [*poka ne pozdno*][52]

In Soviet broadcasts, the children of Vietnam were not depicted simply as victims. They were envisioned as agents for change. Such children subsequently joined the terrifying mythos of Vietnamese insurgency in the American press. Just as Vietnamese prostitutes could be rumored to carry antibiotic-resistant gonorrhea for the infection of GIs, so too could the most innocent looking of children be hiding a machine gun.

By all accounts, the Soviet propaganda attack overwhelmed JUSPAO. As one American official would admit as early as 1964, the United States had "come out second best in the ideological struggle with Moscow."[53] The aggressive Soviet propaganda program in Vietnam did more than put a dent in JUSPAO's armor, however. It also played an integral role in the pursuit of Soviet foreign policy vis-à-vis the North Vietnamese government and the NLF. These images attempted to conceal the Soviet Union's unwillingness to fight the United States directly while retaining a degree of influence over the communist leadership in North Vietnam.[54] Gosteleradio believed that this program provided a carefully crafted portrayal of the Soviet Union that would condemn the enemy and provide personal legitimacy without demanding real military intervention in the process.

Unfortunately for Gosteleradio, the tactic of masking the Soviet Union's unwillingness to fight with expressions of solidarity only worked for so long. By 1967, the North Vietnamese had come to realize the limitations of Soviet as well as global communist support. As one COSVN executive remarked to his colleagues in an internal policy document, they had "fail[ed] to see all the difficulties and complexities in [their] relations with socialist countries, thinking that these countries will readily and wholeheartedly support the [National Liberation] Front policy."[55] As the NLF and North Vietnamese leadership learned, what drove Soviet policy in Vietnam was only partially related to the cause of national liberation and was equally concerned with Russia's desire to avoid direct confrontation with the United States and to mediate its contentious relationship with China and Korea, whom it saw as threats in the struggle for power in the communist camp. When the NLF turned to build its own propaganda campaigns, it reflected this growing awareness and increasingly portrayed itself not as victim or beneficiary of either American or Soviet meddling, but as self-sufficient warrior driven to defend its homeland.

Despite these setbacks, Soviet-constructed images of children went a long way in building a compelling message of Soviet patronage and solidarity. Victimized by American racism and imperialism and mobilized by Soviet and NLF revolutionary fervor, the kids in these images negotiated the path between the expression and the obfuscation of public policy.

The North Vietnamese Message

In contrast to the heavily financed consensus-building projects of the Soviet Union and the United States stood the massive campaign undertaken by the NLF and the North Vietnamese government to win the loyalties of populations in the North and the South. And, again, the image of the child was central to the NLF's propaganda approach. At the beginning of the war, reports of American atrocities against children were common, but by the middle of 1966, the NLF propaganda office was constructing only one image of the child: that of the warrior. This child, in the words of one North Vietnamese official, represented "the spirit of the Vietnamese people to sacrifice anything for the cause of freedom."[56] More than this, it reflected the specific agendas of the North Vietnamese and the NLF during the war: to inculcate a feeling of hatred among the populace for America and its soldiers, to show the United States the lengths to which the NLF was willing to go in order to win the war, and to establish this crusade first as an inevitable fight for nationalist freedom and only second as a communist class struggle.

From its inception, the North Vietnamese leadership, and especially Ho Chi Minh, considered propaganda to be a "key factor" in their victory over French and later American "colonial" rule.[57] The Central Office for South

Vietnam (COSVN), which was formally established in 1961, initially used the airwaves and publishing houses to attack the corruption of the Ngo Dinh Diem regime. After Diem's collapse on 1 November 1963, COSVN turned its attention to the rising American commitment in the region, claiming to be the sole representative of the South Vietnamese people and the leading force against renewed Western intervention. By the summer of 1965, COSVN was conducting daily broadcasts in Vietnamese, Khmer, Mandarin, French, and English, as well as special programs for American troops in the South.[58] It established publishing branches in every major city. It distributed bulletins and leaflets and placed correspondents in Havana, Prague, Algiers, and East Berlin. At its South Vietnam Liberation Film Studio, COSVN produced feature films with titles like *Telling Blows and the U.S. Imperialists Certainly Will Be Defeated* and *The Vietnamese People Will Certainly Win*.[59] All of these programs received significant funding and attention from the higher echelons of the Communist Party leadership and the Hanoi government. They were distributed widely throughout Vietnam as well as the global socialist camp. They presented well-coordinated messages to their audiences and constructed a markedly different set of images from those of either their American enemies or their Soviet allies.

Images of and ideas about children were central to NLF publishing, radio, and film. In one U.S. analysis of NLF propaganda published in October 1965, evaluators noted that three of the nine geographic areas covered in their study had employed propaganda that "appeared aimed particularly at youth" and the use of children as soldiers and "martyrs" for the NLF cause.[60] These statistics most likely underrepresent the real saturation of the child's image in NLF publishing and broadcasting. Records are incomplete, but the samples reveal that in almost every NLF propaganda document, some kind of reference is made to youth and to its role in engineering the liberation of the populace.

The image of the child in NLF propaganda underwent a transformation in 1966 when reports on suffering children were largely replaced by exposés on young revolutionary fighters who appeared well trained in the art of combat, imbued with revolutionary fervor, driven by hatred for the enemy, willing to take up arms, and ready to sacrifice themselves for the nationalist cause. Broadcasts like the one sent out in September 1965, which declared that U.S. troops had "indiscriminately bombed . . . our kindergartens, schools, and hospitals, and declared war even with the infants and the dead," were rare by 1967.[61] Similarly infrequent by this time were broadcasts that in earlier years had heralded the gratefulness and love felt by the Vietnamese people toward the Soviet Union.[62] Instead, children were portrayed as "combatants" who understood, in the words of one captured NLF document from 1969, "the value of a bullet and a grain of rice."[63] As active participants in the war, children were presented not only as watchdogs for their villages and as support personnel, but "as liaisons and reconnaissance agents" who, as COSVN declared, were now "tak[ing] part in the revolution while still in the womb."[64] By creating a vision of the militarized Vietnamese child, COSVN attempted to depict its nationalist crusade, in both the North and the South, as a moral imperative. The country's young people had no choice but to take up arms in response to clear aggression, they argued. One publication noted in 1969, "Youth of the South, in the face of the extremely savage crimes committed by the American aggressors and the clique of their lackeys, realized that there was no other way than taking up arms to fight and save their country, homes, and their happiness."[65] COSVN strove to unite Vietnamese youth across borders for a shared battle that was not only inevitable but seemingly unwinnable by the United States.

COSVN also used visions of children to prove the ineffectiveness of American policy. Most glaring in this respect were COSVN's portrayals of South Vietnamese children as saboteurs of the strategic hamlet program. In southern villages like Long An and Quang Da, COSVN claimed that "100 percent of the youth, both male and female, joined the guerillas." These troops ostensibly contributed "tens of millions" of working days to the replacement of strategic hamlets with their own version, called the "combat village."[66] Needless to say, such portrayals of Vietnamese children destroying American hamlets seriously challenged Richard Heffron's vision of the contained, passive youth seen in *Night of the Dragon*. Instead of being the recipients of Western care, Vietnamese children became active and mobilized, moving outside of the boundaries established for them by their protectors. They became the very saboteurs that the hamlet was originally built to repel. The problems inherent in the strategic hamlet project were suddenly brought into stark relief, as they appeared to be defending children from themselves. Of course, many Americans were aware of these contradictions. By the end of the war, U.S. soldiers commonly argued that because children were functioning as militants, the killing of civilians was military, if not morally, justified.

The best example of the constructed image of the heroic Vietnamese child can be seen in the stories surrounding the young hero Nguyen Van Be, who became the focus of debates on youth, heroism, and state policy throughout the course of the war. As the COSVN-generated version of the story goes, the young Nguyen Van Be, having grown up in the midst of war, "joined the Revolution and stood with his friends and relatives to free himself and offer his enthusiastic heart to the task of liberating his country."[67] Although "he wished to use a rifle to shoot directly at the heads of his enemy," he was none-theless assigned the less heroic task of transporting weapons to troops at the front. He approached his work with enthusiasm, however, and was "always considered [by comrades and civilians] as one of their children." Be's heroic moment came in 1966, when a fierce battle erupted between his battalion and a platoon of American soldiers. Despite the best efforts of Be's team, it was eventually overwhelmed by the American foes. Be was eventually captured, along with his weapons cache, and, as COSVN reported, was subjected to "all possible savage means to torture him." He remained courageous, and, as one report phrased it, "all the [Americans'] efforts were just like bubbles of soap that were washed away by the flow of a great river." Finally, Be and a fellow plowman were brought to a central location "near My Ann, where the U.S. invaders and flunkeys soon gathered with real proud expressions on their faces." In a moment of seeming heroism, Be signaled to the plow-man to run just as he, "with flashing eyes" and "hateful iron arms," lifted ten kilos of Claymore mines over his head. Shouting, "Long live the NLF and down with the U.S. imperialists!" he smashed the mine on the hull of the armored vehicle and created an explosion that ignited all the other cached bombs, "causing a burst of thunder that shook the world."[68] According to initial COSVN reports, sixteen Americans and ten "flunkeys" were killed in the ensuing chaos, while a number of additional Americans were killed by friendly fire that erupted in the aftermath.

Almost from the moment that the story hit the press, COSVN began hold-ing classes and meetings across the north to study Be's heroism. According to the North Vietnamese, Be represented "the bright example" that could be admired "not only by our youths but by young men throughout the world." Be's actions quickly assumed mythical qualities. One account described him as having "genius arms." Young drama groups reenacted the story of Nguyen Van Be in their local theaters.[69] One report released in May 1967 told its read-ers that although "the mine Nguyen Van Be exploded was an ordinary one," it was, nonetheless, "empowered by magical forces." Because of this empower-ment, this mine "not only destroyed almost one hundred enemies and colos-sal tanks in a second and made a hero out of Nguyen Van Be, it also helped to create a chain reaction that had led to the rise of similar 'copy-cat' heroes around the country."[70] As the years passed, Be became increasingly younger in NLF accounts of the story—initial reports put him at sixteen years old and later reports claimed that he was thirteen or fourteen.

Unfortunately for COSVN, there were numerous problems with the story of the young hero, not the least of which was that he did not appear to be dead and did not appear to be thirteen, or even sixteen, years old. American reports told listeners a different story of the young Be. They argued that he had surrendered to South Vietnamese forces of his own free will and was now participating in the Chieu Hoi program. A damning photo of Be hit the JUSPAO presses, showing Be sitting with a copy of the COSVN newspaper article that recounted his death, apparently visual proof that the entire Be mythos was a product of NLF trickery. JUSPAO identified Be as being twenty-four years old, thereby removing from him the heroic valences of the "child-warrior" and in effect normalizing him as yet another North Vietnamese soldier who had defected to the South in order to settle down with his family away from NLF control.

JUSPAO articles told readers a counter-story of Nguyen Van Be, who had apparently capitulated to the South Vietnamese army of his own volition and was now seeking refuge under American security. Interviews with Be's cousin, who defected later in 1966, reported that within days of Be receiving the posthumous title of "hero" by the NLF, his mother had been invited by GVN forces to visit her son in jail. Fearing for her life, the mother kept her son's existence a secret from her neighbors, only telling her nephew and her husband. The nephew's initial reaction was disbelief, especially since his aunt had apparently been allowed to see her son only from a distance of ten meters. He became convinced, however, when he learned that Be had called his mother and his younger brothers by their pet names. His beliefs were further confirmed when his uncle, Be's father, under orders from the NLF, visited his son and returned to report that he was alive.[71] Rumors quickly spread throughout the Central Nam Bo district where Be's family lived, while the GVN prepared to distribute photographs of the living Be and the NLF mobilized its propaganda network to support its own version of the story. According to the nephew, Be's mother and father were ordered to say nothing and were relocated to another district. When the GVN returned Be to his hamlet for a "visit" later in 1966, many villagers apparently recognized him but, because of fear, told the NLF that they either had not seen him or had not known him.[72] Counter-theater groups, funded by the United States, toured the villages, carrying with them 10,000 song sheets titled "The Truth about Nguyen Van Be." Leaflets were published with photographs of Be's mother with the caption, "I Ought to Know My Own Son."[73] According to Robert W. Chandler, by July 1967 JUSPAO had distributed information on Nguyen Van Be's existence through more than 30 million leaflets, 7 million cartoon leaflets, 465,000 posters, a special newspaper in 175,000 copies, 167,000 photographs, 10,000 song sheets, motion pictures, "and radio and television programs featuring Be, his family, and his Hoi Chanh friends."[74]

The response of the NLF and the party cadres to the Be controversy was to initiate "indoctrination classes" for each individual hamlet. They told their audiences that Be's mother had never actually seen her son and that American plastic surgeons had refashioned a new Be in order to deceive the population. In July 1967, the North Vietnamese Communist Party offered a 2 million piaster reward for anyone who killed the false Be. Internally, they agreed that they would avoid "talking much about Be's family in order to minimize the damage already done by the enemy in case they succeed[ed] in 'buying over' this family."[75] Yet, despite the continued JUSPAO attack on the tale of Be's sacrifice, and despite the fact that Be (or the Be pretender) was carted from one press conference to another throughout 1967, 1968, and 1969, COSVN nonetheless continued to maintain that Be *had* died on that fateful day, and that he was the child-hero against whom all young people should judge themselves.[76]

What is most striking about this story for the purposes of this book is the centrality of this child/man in the North Vietnamese and American struggles to (re)fashion their own images for an uncertain, rumor-heavy population. For COSVN, Be represented the idyllic child-warrior who is driven to make the ultimate sacrifice for the cause of national liberation. As such, his story substantiated its conceptualization of the war as a crusade for which the young were willing to sacrifice their own lives. In contrast, for JUSPAO, the image of Nguyen Van Be, pictured in the exact same pose and with the exact same expression as that rendered by COSVN, symbolized delegitimation, not simply of the North Vietnamese government, the National Liberation Front, and their propaganda effort, but of the imagined child-warrior as well, who was, in its eyes, not a child and not a warrior. In Be's tumultuous story, we can also see the presence of a third group—the nonstate agents in the North Vietnamese villages who are responsible for the spread of rumors about Be's survival. They chose to witness his return to their village and to discuss it among themselves while simultaneously concealing their true opinions from the authorities. For this group, Be's death and rebirth provided a contested visual and verbal space where they could participate in the telling of a story that both defined and at times undermined North Vietnamese legitimacy. Be's mythologized form became open to revision not only by the United States and the GVN, but by the very populations for whom it was supposed to provide inspiration. As was the case for JUSPAO and Gosteleradio, COSVN found that the construction and dissemination of power can become compromised through the inversion of images and narratives, through rumor, and because it is ultimately impossible to maintain control over the flow of information between propagandists and their audiences.

Conclusion

On 1 December 1965, a group of Vietnamese mothers sent an open letter to the mothers of America. In it, they argued that they all had far more in common with each other than they did with their leaders. "No love is deeper than a mother's. We mothers have gone through so many difficulties and hardships bringing up our children. We have taught them to live a clean and honest life, hoping that they will enjoy happiness in labor and peace. How could you resign yourselves to letting your sons be turned by a gang of warmongers into killers of women and children before dying on this far away battlefield or returning with their bodies maimed and their souls stained?"[77]

If the child had once been a relatively stable symbol of national strength and moral ascendancy, by 1965 this simply was no longer the case. On the one hand, the Vietnamese child, seen as a victim, a communist warrior, or a nationalist liberator, worked to justify American, Soviet, and North Vietnamese policies in the war. At the same time, these images carried porous meanings. They helped to question the motivations of the various state powers involved in the war by assuming traits that did not fit their intended mold. When antiwar protesters across the United States took to the streets to ask Lyndon Johnson "how many kids" he had killed that day, they were engaging in a deliberate practice of undermining an image that had once carried on its shoulders the legitimacy of the Cold War consensus. They were not only questioning their leaders' capacity to make decisions on behalf of the nation and the world; they were questioning whether or not those leaders had ever had such a capacity in the first place. On the streets of New York and Berkeley and Hanoi and Moscow, the image of the Vietnamese child mingled with that of the American boy to become a variegated vision of suffering that crossed geographic and cultural divides. As the image collapsed amid the maelstrom of rising domestic unrest, so too did the conceptual borders that defined the boundaries of the Cold War.

Conclusion

In January 1969, *Parents' Magazine* published an article entitled "How Russian Schools Compare with Ours." The cover of the magazine pictured a shadow box holding two girl dolls, dressed in similar garb and each holding a book in one hand and an olive branch in the other. Swirling around them were two ribbons inscribed with the words, "mother," "father," "home," "school," "children," and "living in peace" in English and Russian. Two oval-shaped pictures of the White House and St. Basil's Cathedral hung suspended between them.

This image reflected the astonishing transformation that childhood had undergone since 1945. Whereas in earlier years the efforts of mainstream consensus builders had been to show the differences between children in the East and children in the West, this shadow box conveyed the message that regardless of geographic and ideological position, the people of the Soviet Union and the United States cared and thought about their children in the same way. The article itself concerned a teacher-exchange program that had been sponsored by the American Friends Service Committee, a Quaker organization that arranged partnerships among approximately 150 elementary schools and high schools around the world. American teachers wrote of their experiences as both hosts and guests of their Russian counterparts. For all of them, commonality was the central theme. One teacher commented, "It was really thrilling to discover how many basic attitudes we had in common, in the way we felt about our lives and our families." She remarked that during her exchange, she and her Soviet counterparts had not talked about ideology at all, "not, I felt, because they were avoiding the subject, but because . . . like working mothers everywhere they were concerned with doing their job well and at the same time meeting the needs of their husbands and children." When American teachers visited the Soviet Union, they were impressed by the commitment that the entire community seemed to have to raising the young and the devotion that mothers and fathers seemed to show to their offspring.

By 1969, these were not radical observations. *Parents' Magazine* enjoyed a readership of over half a million. It had been founded in 1923 as the first magazine geared toward parent education and was by this time considered the premier mainstream publication on parenting in America. Clearly, an

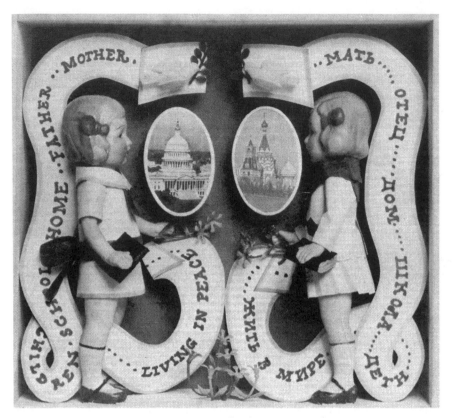

Figure C.1. "How Russian Schools Compare with Ours."
Originally published in the January 1969 Parents® Magazine, 56.

alternative consensus had arisen, and not just among mothers willing to protest nuclear testing and war on the mall in Washington, D.C. The child, who
had once symbolized the generative capacity of those in power to establish
what was at stake in the Cold War and what had to be done to win it, had now
become a negotiated image that supported a plurality of views on what the
Cold War universe should look like.

For many people in the late 1960s, childhood stood as a symbol for the
discredited promises that their leaders had made since the beginning of the
Cold War. Scholars and memoirists have for decades argued that the radical-
ization of the young in the United States, in Europe, and even in Russia in the
1960s was born from a pervasive sense of betrayal over the failed promises
of a bright future. In 1950, a young Tom Hayden had believed in the security and promise of his white, middle-class childhood. Twelve years later, he
began the Port Huron Statement with these reflections: "When we were kids

the United States was the wealthiest and strongest country in the world; the only one with the atom bomb, the least scarred by modern war, an initiator of the United Nations that we thought would distribute Western influence throughout the world. Freedom and equality for each individual, government of, by, and for the people—these American values we found good, principles by which we could live as men. Many of us began maturing in complacency. As we grew, however, our comfort was penetrated by events too troubling to dismiss."[1] This sense of betrayal would not have been so strong or so pervasive if the image of childhood and the promises that it embodied had not been so central to how people understood the world around them. When Hayden wrote out his grievances in his statement of the principles of the New Left, he was speaking for a generation that had grown up on a specific vision of childhood and the subsequent consensus it supported. When that vision fell apart because of internal contradictions, so too did the ideals undergirding it.

A similar story was unfolding across the Atlantic. By 1961, Svetlana Zhiltsova (the young girl who delivered the speech to Stalin at the 1949 Komsomol Congress) had become the host of the Soviet Union's most irreverent youth television program. The show, which was titled *Klub veselykh i nakhodchivykh* (Club of the Cheerful and Sharp-Witted), or *KVN* for short, utilized Zhiltsova's wit and humor to make searing indictments about the Soviet state. In one famous joke from the first season, she turned to the camera and declared, "Если партия сказала "есть контакт!"— значит, будем есть контакт!" which translates to "If the Party said, 'there will be contact!' it means we will have contact!" This joke might have been lost on non-Soviet audiences, but it quickly became a phrase repeated in college dormitories and living rooms in the Soviet Union. The phrase poked fun at the poor workmanship of Soviet industry by referring to the standard call-and-response needed to start a Soviet engine (that couldn't start on its own).[2] It made a work-order sound like an order to eat (est'), thereby taking a jab at the Soviet Union's chronic food shortages. And the line bore a striking resemblance to an old Komsomol slogan that in this context mocked the knee-jerk conformity of Komsomol and youth culture.[3] When Zhiltsova made her guarded joke, she was expressing the feelings of the people around her that the uplifting and hopeful image of a happy childhood, promised by the state, had been an empty one.

The perceived brinksmanship, myopia, and hypocrisy of the world's leaders compounded this sense of betrayal and growing panic over childhood's future. This was the case for the antiwar movement. As Bob Dylan sang in his condemnation of the "Masters of War,"

You've thrown the worst fear that can ever be hurled,
Fear to bring children into the world.
For threatening my baby unborn and unnamed,
You ain't worth the blood that runs in your veins.

For civil rights activists, the duplicity of the state toward the African American youth of the nation seemed irreconcilable. Martin Luther King articulated his hope and his despair for the future in terms of the child when he dreamed in 1963 that his "four little children will one day live in a nation where they will not be judged by the color of their skin but by the content of their character." Similarly, for second-wave feminists, the idea that young girls could hope for equal opportunity seemed ever illusive. The poet Robin Morgan, who as a young actress had embodied the ideal image of the contained American child playing the precocious character Dagmar in *Mama*, described herself as a monster as a consequence of her contained girlhood.[4] For two decades, American leaders and their supporters had argued that both the nation's and the child's future depended on the continued popular support of the status quo. Now that very status quo had become a potential destroyer of the future. Just as parents and magazine editors increasingly noted commonalities with their Soviet counterparts, so too did they begin to take note of the similarities between those who were in power in the West and those who were in charge in the East. This was illustrated most pointedly in the August 1969 edition of the American antiwar newspaper *As You Were*, which argued that if the current situation were allowed to continue, it would not matter if one were in the Soviet Union or in the United States—children would still be "taken from their mothers at birth, as one takes eggs from a hen" and raised to believe the "party line."[5]

By the late 1960s, no one in the world with access to media could avoid the images of children suffering and dying at the hands of the state. Nick Ut's famous photograph of a nine-year-old Vietnamese girl running naked and burned from napalm, screaming down a dirt road, became a widespread symbol of American warmongering. No less infamous was Ronald Haeberle's photograph of women and children weeping before their execution at My Lai on 16 March 1968. One of the most well-known slogans of the antiwar movement asks Lyndon Johnson how many "kids" he had killed that day. In May 1968, author Andy Stapp reported that an estimated 1 million children had been killed, wounded, or burned in South Vietnam.[6] Major newspapers printed weekly reports on child casualties. Meanwhile, the image of Emmett Till's mutilated body after his beating by white men in 1955, the four girls killed in the bombing of the Sixteenth Street Baptist Church in Birmingham, Alabama, in 1963, and repeated visions of children facing violent mobs and hoses in the American South had woven their way into the visual fabric of American culture. These pervasive images became new and unavoidable symbols for not only childhood's betrayal, past, present and future, but also the false assurances of an ordered society, the legitimacy of the state, and the promises of safety that had been a mantra and a justification for the Cold War battle for the past two decades.

This widespread sense of betrayal and fear was not limited to the West. It also erupted in the Eastern Bloc and the Soviet Union, manifesting in unprecedented ways in the wake of the Soviet invasion of Czechoslovakia in 1968. That spring, leaders across the Soviet sphere expressed increasing panic over the state of their youth. On 29 April, N. A. Mikhailov, by then the president of the Soviet Committee on the Press, reported that the Pioneer and Komsomol organizations in Czechoslovakia had disappeared and been replaced by other, unsanctioned youth groups.[7] Nine days later, Leonid Brezhnev, Bulgaria's Todor Zhivkov, Hungary's János Kádár, East Germany's Walter Ulbricht, and Poland's Vladislav Gomulka held an emergency meeting in Moscow to discuss the rising unrest. For all of them, the crisis seemed be coming from the young. As Ulbricht remarked, "Worst of all are the youth. They are running a very sharp campaign."[8] Later, in June, Brezhnev and his colleagues expressed fear at the projected "injection" of 200,000 to 300,000 reform-minded young people into the aging membership of the Czech Communist Party, while at the same time being shocked by continued reports of youths as young as twelve and thirteen turning to hooliganism and outright violence against Soviet representatives in Prague. By August, the Czech Communist Party was releasing declarations calling upon Czech youth to remember their duties to "defend the gains of socialism," while protesters as young as ten took to the streets to remind their leaders through their actions and words that such a consensus could no longer be manufactured.[9]

As had been the case for the previous twenty years, the image of the child served as a measurement of complicity and subversion. At noon on 25 August, eight young Russians quietly sat down on the steps of Lobnoye Mesto in Red Square (a place that had represented state control over the Russian populace since the mid-sixteenth century) to protest the invasion of Czechoslovakia. They carried placards that tied their own fates to those of the young people in Prague who had supported Alexander Dubček's reforms and fought against invasion. "For Your Freedom and Ours," "We Are Losing Our Best Friends," they declared. All but one (who was pregnant) were arrested within minutes. All received prison sentences.

In subsequent months and years, dissidents used the child to articulate the loss of faith that this event and so many years of seeming duplicity had precipitated. For instance, that September, the police chief of Kiev held a meeting with the Consul General of the Czech Socialist Republic, I. I. Gorakom. They met ostensibly to discuss an upcoming exhibition, but Gorakom had another topic in mind. Knowing that his words would immediately be reported to the KGB in Moscow, he accused Brezhnev of acting like Alexander III (presumably referring to the tsar's imperialist policies) and of humiliating the national dignity of 12 million Czech people. As he became increasingly agitated, he turned to the image of the child. "None of your people, none of your soldiers, none of your boys, were killed," he declared. "In fact, some of your soldiers, seeing the injustice of their invasion, committed suicide while the rest were shot by your commissars. You have murdered many of our children . . . and they have been buried with honors. We will never forgive you."[10] Months after the invasion, the KGB was reporting incidences in the Czech countryside of signs appearing in schoolhouses reminding students that "children don't shoot at soldiers."[11] Finally, one of Russia's greatest bards, Vladimir Vysotsky, attempted to articulate the collapse of childhood and the communist dream that he and many of his friends had experienced. The song, entitled "A Ballad about the Struggle," encapsulated the collective sense of loss and betrayal that was felt now by so many:

> Among the melting candles and the evening prayer,
> Among the trophies of war and the peacetime bonfires,
> Lived the children raised on books, who did not know battle,
> Pining away in their small catastrophes.
> . . . .
> We children, not knowing war, tried to understand,
> Mistaking a wail for a war cry,
> Captivated by the mystery of the word "order,"
> The purpose of borders,
> The meaning of assault and the rattle of war chariots.
> In the bubbling kettles of past pillages and turbulences,
> There was so much for our little minds to consume!
> In our childish games we placed our enemies
> In the roles of renegades, cowards, judases.
> . . . .
> But you can't hide away in dreams forever,
> The days for play are short, and there is so much pain!

Go ahead and try to soften the clench of a dead man's palm,
And take over a weapon from a toil-worn hand.
. . . .
If, while hewing your way through with your father's sword
You don't forget the salty tears,
If in a fiery battle you feel the how and why of things,
Then you read the right books!
If you don't eat a measly piece of meat from the knife,
If, your hands folded, you watch from your distant post
And don't battle a scoundrel, a tyrant,
Then you have lived for no reason at all!

For Vysotsky and for many of his generation, the promises of heroism and valor in war, with its rhetorical and visual trappings for the struggle against American imperialism and rampant capitalism, no longer carried weight. Many of those who had been children in the 1950s now saw their own childhoods in a new light and could not reconcile themselves with the contradictions that lay between images and reality. Whatever consensus or willingness to comply that had existed now gave way to a cacophony of beliefs about what the Cold War was, why it was being fought, and who was paying the price for it.

COLD WAR KIDS LITTERED THE VISUAL and rhetorical worlds of the United States and the Soviet Union in the 1950s and 60s. On billboards and placards, in newspapers, speeches, magazine advertisements, and movies they peered out upon a vast population that sought desperately to find some certainty in an increasingly chaotic universe. They offered much to their viewers. In the hands of politicians, party leaders, advertisers, publishers, and political groups, these children became visions of the happiness and security that their own sociopolitical systems made possible. These kids were the lucky ones whose lives appeared to be markedly better than the young who suffered in distant lands across the ocean. They symbolized for their nations the active love of peace and the commitment to freedom and democracy that everyone ostensibly shared. They offered a sense of national direction and moral certainty in a conflict that might otherwise have seemed aimless and rife with ambiguity. They stood as visions of an innocence and purity that were under threat from both an implacable foe abroad and serious risks at home. They made the wages and boundaries of the Cold War seem simpler, and they mapped an ideological divide that was easily demarcated.

Cold War kids also helped to instruct their populations on how to fight and mobilize. Children now had to be raised in ways that would prepare them to take up the torch when their turn came to fight. Ideological infiltration, hooliganism, and poor education presented national security risks that could not be overlooked. For the sake of their long-term defense, the Cold War child demanded a level of monitoring and instruction that parents simply could not provide on their own. Indeed, as leaders and propagandists argued, negligent and coddling parents were often a part of the problem. The only entities capable of providing such protection were the nation's leaders, its youth organizations, and its experts on child development, who worked closely to ensure that the next generation would have the skills that they needed to be able to continue the struggle. These groups became the authorities on how to mobilize the young, and they did so with the widespread support of the populace. In one form or another, all of these groups argued that public consensus was required for the sake of the child's defense. This consensus entailed offering support for not just the domestic and the international policies that leaders adopted, but also the ideological framework of the war itself. In the words of Robert Corber, the consensus demanded that the population buy in "freely and spontaneously" to a "particular vision of reality."[12] Children necessitated their nations' compliance and mobilization. In their threatened and carefully defended happiness, they legitimized the status quo and the people who shaped it.

The construction of Cold War kids was a shared project that crossed the East-West divide. Both sides used these images in order to argue that they were defending an ideal of freedom and democracy that was made possible by the ideologies of either communism or capitalism. Both sides argued that adherence to these ideologies promised a better future for the next generation. Both contended that they were under attack. And both ostensibly required the long-term mobilization of the entire populace in order to survive. Moreover, the methods by which they argued that those ideals could be defended were also similar. For the sake of their survival, both sides demanded the increased surveillance and widespread allegiances of their populations. Both argued in various ways that the ends would have to justify the means— that policy choices could countermand the actual dictates of democracy and freedom in order to ensure the survival of the ideal. The stripping away of individuals' civil rights in the McCarthy era was justified by the larger need to defend the next generation and the country from infiltration and attack. The occupation of Eastern Europe was legitimated by the argument that this was the only way to bring Soviet freedoms to the young people of those nations.

When Soviet and American leaders used images of threatened children and called upon their populations to mobilize for communism or capitalism, it was the promise of, and the threat to, this larger ideal that they were invoking.

Were these advantages and these threats real? Were the Cold War kids really at risk or were they just presented that way in order to create fear and compliance? Were they really happier and better off than everyone else as a result of the sociopolitical system that supported them or was that just another story meant to engender loyalty and consensus among the populace? Most important, what then can these Cold War kids tell us about the role of ideology in this conflict? Does their shared usage as symbolic capital by those in power for the construction of popular consensus and the justification of policy imply that Soviet and American leaders were being duplicitous? Were leaders claiming that they were committed to defending freedom from an implacable foe only in order to conceal other, less idealistic motives for waging this war? Can this war be viewed in poststructural terms as a conflict between those who had something to gain from this conflagration and those who had far more to lose? The argument that the Cold War was not just an ideological conflict is not new. It is not shocking to claim that ideology was only one of many factors in shaping the policies made by those in power in these years. Over the last four decades, historians have chronicled how policy makers on both sides of the Iron Curtain made choices that belied their professed ideological beliefs in exchange for the benefits of economic expansion, defensive buttering, domestic order, and personal power. This history of the Cold War kids seems to support these conclusions. Whether intentional or not, these visions of childhood were born from hypocrisy, symbolizing an ideal and a threat that did not adhere to reality.

This observation suggests a serious shift in how we understand the nature of the Cold War divide. While communism and capitalism might have represented opposing ideologies, the means of achieving and defending them had a lot in common. Both manipulated archetypal images like those of the child in order to simplify the moral underpinnings of the conflict, to legitimate the decisions made by those in power, and to necessitate the construction of a popular consensus. From this perspective, the battle line of the Cold War changes from a vertical one that divided the communist Soviet Bloc from the capitalist American sphere to a horizontal one that pitted those who controlled the means of image and consensus production against their intended consumers. In short, the architects of consensus had a lot more in common with each other than they did with their constituencies. As Kate Brown has noted in her recent comparison of the Soviet and American nuclear towns, the distinctions between their projects were "largely fictional."[13] Likewise, the American people and the Soviet people suddenly appear to have had more in common with each other than they did with their leaders, whose polemicizing rhetoric served only to exacerbate the conflict and put them all in harm's way.

That said, the vast majority of the Soviet and American people and arguably many of their leaders in the 1950s and 60s *did*, nonetheless, see and understand the Cold War as a struggle between two diametrically opposed ideologies locked in a fight between good and evil. If ideology was not the only factor in shaping policy, it was the major factor in shaping popular support for policy. It is here that these images of children can help to explain how the ideological divide was constructed and calcified by wide swaths of the American and Soviet citizenry until it finally became the only issue over which most people thought this war was being fought. In order to build the ideological divide, both sides had to engage in a project that would slowly but steadily mobilize the most powerful images and rhetoric of their cultures. They had to gain control over the meanings of the child's image in order to wield the power that such control bestowed. In the words of Pierre Bourdieu, "the field of cultural production" became "the field of power."[14] This book has sought to understand how people built the ideological divide of the Cold War and how they constructed the consensus that it necessitated. Ideology did matter. It might not have shaped policy as much as many have believed, but it was the reason why most people went along with it.

The story of childhood in the Cold War also discloses how the consensus collapsed. To varying degrees, both countries found themselves over the course of these years betraying their ideals in order to win the war, maintain power, and defend the status quo. The principles of democracy and self-determination were overlooked in both countries. This was the case not just in the Gulag, Hungary, Poland, and Czechoslovakia, but also in the Jim Crow South, Guatemala, Iran, and Vietnam. Over the course of two decades, the image of the child increasingly reflected these inconsistencies. How could American children be the happiest on earth if they were also being attacked by dogs, lynched, and exposed to strontium 90 in their milk? How could Vietnamese children be better off under the protection of the United States if they were also being burned by napalm dropped from American planes? How could Soviet children be joyful if they were abandoned and traumatized by decades of repression, hypocrisy, and violence? How could Czechoslovak, Hungarian, and Polish kids be better off under the protection of the Soviet Union if they were also being invaded and shot by their very protectors? These questions contributed to the destabilization of the consensus. The very images that had been used prolifically to make promises about the safety and hopefulness of the future became the era's most poignant symbols of danger and betrayal. When the sources of stability for the next generation became the sources of destruction and loss, the child transformed from a vision of hope to an eschatological emblem of all that could not be protected. It is impossible to measure the impact of an image this prolific and diffuse, but its Cold War history does seem to offer a cautionary tale for anyone attempting to mobilize long-standing visual tropes for the purposes of consensus building. Even images like that of the innocent child can become volatile when the people who profess to defend the young become the ones who imperil them.

It has not been the intention of this book to lay the blame for the collapse of the Cold War consensus solely on the shoulders of the child's deteriorating image. This story does, however, offer a visual and rhetorical narrative to accompany and complicate existing political and social histories of this era. This project has taken a first leap into the world of Soviet Cold War culture and has placed that world within a global story that chronicles the shared production, consumption, and disruption of public consensus. These images of childhood were not only vital in shaping how people understood the world around them—they also revealed how difficult it was to actually shape the world at all.

Notes

ABBREVIATIONS

BSA   Boy Scouts of America Archive, Irving, Texas

DDE Library   Dwight D. Eisenhower Library, Abilene, Kansas

DOSAAF   Volunteer Society for Cooperation with the Army, Aviation, and Fleet (Dobrovol'noe Obshchestvo Sodeistviia Armii, Aviatsii, i Flotu)

GARF   State Archive of the Russian Federation (Gosudarstvennyi Arkhiv Rossiiskoi Federatsii), Moscow

GSA   Girl Scouts of America Archive, New York, New York

HST Library   Harry S. Truman Library, Independence, Missouri

JFK Library   John F. Kennedy Library, Boston, Massachusetts

LBJ Library   Lyndon Baines Johnson Library, Austin, Texas

RGALI   Russian State Archive of Literature and Art (Rossiiskii Gosudarstvennyi Arkhiv Literatury i Iskusstva), Moscow

RGANI   Russian State Archive of Contemporary History (Rossiiskii Gosudarstvennyi Arkhiv Noveishei Istorii), Moscow

RGASPI   Russian State Archive of Socio-Political History (Rossiiskii Gosudarstvennyi Arkhiv Sotsial'no-Politicheskoi Istorii), Moscow

SANE   Papers of the Committee for a SANE Nuclear Policy, Swarthmore College Peace Collection, Swarthmore, Pennsylvania

TVA   Vietnam Archive, Texas Tech University, Lubbock, Texas

WSP   Papers of Women Strike for Peace, Swarthmore College Peace Collection, Swarthmore, Pennsylvania

INTRODUCTION

1. Appy, *Cold War Constructions*; Hixson, *Parting the Curtain*; Whitfield, *The Culture of the Cold War*; Parry-Giles, *The Rhetorical Presidency*.

2. See, for instance, Nicholas Cull's analysis of the British campaign to solicit American support in World War II. Cull, *Selling War*; Cull, *Propaganda and Mass Persuasion*.

3. Scott, *Seeing Like a State*, 2.

4. Elaine Tyler May, *Homeward Bound*.

5. Engelhardt, *The End of Victory Culture*, 239; Mastny, *The Cold War and Soviet Insecurity*, 23.

6. Latham, *Modernization as Ideology*.

7. Scott, *Seeing Like a State*.

8. Herman and Chomsky, *Manufacturing Consent*.

9. Suri, *Power and Protest*.

10. Gleijeses, *Conflicting Missions*; LaFeber, *America, Russia, and the Cold War*; Westad, *The Global Cold War*; Suri, *Power and Protest*; Kwon, *The Other Cold War*.

11. Campbell Craig and Fredrik Logevall argue in a similar theoretical vein that America's continued waging of the Cold War could be traced not to ideological belief but to the actions of individuals and institutions that had a vested interest in keeping the war going. Craig and Logevall, *America's Cold War*.

12. Engelhardt, *The End of Victory Culture*, 10, 98; Graebner, "Myth and Reality," 20; Wall, *Inventing the "American Way."*

13. Mastny, *The Cold War and Soviet Insecurity*; Zubok and Pleshakov, *Inside the Kremlin's Cold War*; Zubok, *A Failed Empire*.

14. Carruthers, "Review of American Cold War Culture," 956–58.

15. Barthes, *Mythologies*, 58. See also Adorno and Bernstein, *Culture Industry*.

16. Haraway, *The Haraway Reader*, 5.

17. Barthes would make this argument later in life. See Barthes, *Camera Lucida*.

18. Lotman, "O Semiosphere"; Lotman and Uspenskii, *The Semiotics of Russian Culture*.

19. Ariès, *Centuries of Childhood*.

20. Higonnet, *Pictures of Innocence*, 28.

21. There is a difference between how "childhood" as an idea and how the lived experiences of children are studied. The field of children's history (the history of understanding children's lives) has advocated increasing separation in analysis of childhood stages. See, for instance, Hawes, *Children between the Wars*; Calvert, *Children in the House*; Steedman, *The Tidy House*; Clement, *Growing Pains*; Tuttle, *Daddy's Gone to War*; Kelly, *Children's World*; and Ball, *And Now My Soul Is Hardened*.

22. See Klein, "Family Ties and Political Obligation: The Discourse of Adoption and the Cold War Commitment to Asia," in Appy, *Cold War Constructions*. See also Bradley, *Imagining Vietnam and America*.

23. Foucault, "Ceci n'est pas une pipe," 6–21.

24. Fass and Grossberg, *Reinventing Childhood after World War II*, xi.

25. Wall, *Inventing the "American Way,"* 1–10.

CHAPTER ONE

1. "XI S''ezd Vsesoiuznogo Leninskogo Kommunisticheskogo Soiuza Molodezhi, stenograficheskii otchet, 29 March–8 April 1949," RGASPI f. m6, op. 11, d. 27, l. 90.

2. Mitz, *The Great TV Sitcom Book*, 458.

3. "Conference on Children and Youth," *New York Times*, 16 December 1950, 11.

4. Tuttle, *Daddy's Gone to War*, 5; Kucherenko, *Little Soldiers*.

5. Mintz, *Huck's Raft*, 80; Balina and Dobrenko, *Petrified Utopia*, xviii; Tolstoy, *Detstvo*; Wachtel, *The Battle for Childhood*; Gorky, *Childhood*; Creuziger, *Childhood in Russia*; Levander and Singley, *The American Child*; Holl, *Juvenile Reform in the Progressive Era*; Olich, *Competing Ideologies and Children's Literature in Russia*; Mead and Wolfenstein, *Childhood in Contemporary Cultures*; Ball, *And Now My Soul Is Hardened*; Kirschenbaum, *Small Comrades*; Fass and Mason, *Childhood in America*; Kelly, *Children's World*; Zahra, *Kidnapped Souls*.

6. *Pionerskaia pravda*, 24 December 1949; *Izvestiia*, 22 December 1949. Unless otherwise specified, all translations from Russian are the author's.

7. USSR Academy of Sciences, *70th Anniversary of Stalin's Birth*, 1.

8. *Komsomol'skaia pravda*, 20 December 1949, 2.

9. *Pravda*, 21 December 1949, 4.

10. Rosenthal, "Visual Fiction," 1.

11. Kelly, "A Joyful Soviet Childhood"; Brooks, *Thank You, Comrade Stalin*; Reid, *Khrushchev in Wonderland*.

12. Elaine Tyler May, *Homeward Bound*, xxv.

13. Malenkov, "Demokraticheskaia molodezh' v bor'be za mir protiv podzhigatelei voini," 1950, RGASPI f. 1111, op. 32, d. 611, l. 148.

14. I collected these statistics through an exhaustive examination of *Life* magazine in these years. This number is a hard count of each occurrence of a child in advertisements, editorials, and articles.

15. Eyerman, "Rocket Town," 110.

16. Chomsky, *Necessary Illusions*.

17. LaFeber, *America, Russia, and the Cold War*, 147.

18. Eisenhower's propaganda project has been examined in depth in Osgood, *Total Cold War*.

19. Holl, *Juvenile Reform in the Progressive Era*. See also Mintz, *Huck's Raft*, 173.

20. The scholarship on this is vast, particularly for the United States. See Williams, *The Tragedy of American Diplomacy*; Wagnleitner and May, *Here, There, and Everywhere*; Castillo, *Cold War on the Home Front*; Leffler, *For the Soul of Mankind*.

21. Hessler, *A Social History of Soviet Trade*, 2.

22. Kelly, "A Joyful Soviet Childhood," 9.

23. Gorsuch, "There's No Place Like Home," 761.

24. Timasheff, *The Great Retreat*; Siegelbaum, *Borders of Socialism*; Petrone, *Life Has Become More Joyous*; Goldman, *Women at the Gates*; Osokina, *Iranschel, and Bucher, Our Daily Bread*; Randall, *The Soviet Dream World*.

25. Baranowski and Furlough, *Being Elsewhere*, 20.

26. Radio peredacha: "Zavtra mamin den' rozhdeniia," 16 January 1960, GARF f. 6903, op. 23, d. 433, l. 152.

27. Radio sbornik: "Sto voprosov o sovetskom soiuze," 7 February 1961, GARF f. 6903, op. 23, d. 43, l. 12.

28. Communist Party of the Soviet Union, *Programme of the Communist Party of the Soviet Union Adopted by the 22nd Congress*, 31 October 1961, 83.

29. Goscilo, "Luxuriating in Lack," in Balina and Dobrenko, *Petrified Utopia*, 68.

30. Biriukova, "Nasha kukhnia," 23.

31. Reid, "Destalinization and Taste," 178.

32. Ibid.

33. "Teksty peredach napravlennykh v gosdepartament SShA," GARF f. 6903, op. 2, d. 335, l. 23.

34. "Letter from Oscar Ewing to President Truman," 1950, WHCF, OF reel 3, 0086, Truman Papers, HST Library.

35. For a history of the child's experience in World War II, see Tuttle, *Daddy's Gone to War*. For a history of children's consumerism in the 1950s, see Stephen Kline, *Out of the Garden*.

36. Attwood, "A New Look at Americans," 50.

37. Hayden, *Reunion*, 3.

38. Richards, *The Commodity Culture of Victorian England*; Jacobson, *Raising Consumers*.

39. Alexander, "The Image of Children in Magazine Advertisements from 1905 to 1990," 747.

40. Based on my review of *Look* and *Life* magazines from 1950 until 1964, reflecting each instance that any number of children appear inside an advertisement (meaning that regardless of whether two or more children appear in the ad, this occurrence of the child in the ad is counted once). This study largely matches the results found in Alexander's 1994 study, "The Image of Children in Magazine Advertisements from 1905 to 1990."

41. U.S. Advertising Council, "What's Nice to Have," 5.

42. U.S. Advertising Council, "How to Protect Your Children's Future," 91.

43. Lizabeth Cohen, *A Consumers' Republic*, 299.

44. Johnson and Johnson Corporation, "Mommy Always Says You're Safe," 63.

45. Lipsitz, "The Meaning of Memory," 367.

46. From *House Beautiful*, 1953, quoted in Hine, *Populuxe*, 147; Lizabeth Cohen, *A Consumers' Republic*, 125.

47. Glickman, *Consumer Society in American History*, 8.

48. Hixson, *Parting the Curtain*; Reid, "Cold War in the Kitchen"; Oldenziel and Zachmann, *Cold War Kitchen*; Castillo, *Cold War on the Home Front*.

49. Cited in Hixson, *Parting the Curtain*, 180.

50. "Policy Guidance for the U.S. Exhibit in Moscow in 1959" [Confidential], box 7, RG 306, DDE Library. Also cited in Hixson, *Parting the Curtain*, 165.

51. "Russia Comes to the Fair," *Time*, 3 August 1959, 16.

52. "Russian Children to Romp on Latest American Playground Gear," *New York Times*, 3 April 1959, 20.

53. "Transcript of Tape Recording of White House Conference on Moscow Fair," cited in Hixson, *Parting the Curtain*, 175.

54. "Za demokraticheskii mir, protiv podzhigatelei voiny," *Komsomol'skaia pravda*, 27 March 1949, 4.

55. "V zashchitu mira, protiv podzhigatelei novoi voiny!" *Pionerskaia pravda*, 7 July 1949, 2.

56. See, for instance, Hoover, *Masters of Deceit*.

57. "Tematika politicheskikh zaniatii s chlenami DOSAAF v uchebnykh organizatsiiakh obshchestva," Nachal'nik upravleniia orgmassovoi raboty i propagandy TsK DOSAAF SSSR, GARF f. 9552, op. 1, d. 159, l. 72. This book does not deal with the image of the mobilized child during the Great Patriotic War, which did not always depict children as mobilized only for defense. As members of the fabled Molodaia gvardiia (Young Guard), youth could be seen in literature and in film as partisan heroes in their own right, undertaking dangerous missions to weaken the German lines.

58. LaFeber, *America, Russia, and the Cold War*; Mastny, *The Cold War and Soviet Insecurity*; Zubok and Pleshakov, *Inside the Kremlin's Cold War*.

59. Elaine Tyler May, *Homeward Bound*, xxiv, xxv.

60. Predsedatel' TsK DOSAAF SSSR, 16 March 1947, GARF f. 9552, op. 1, d. 23, l. 1–32; Predsedatel' TsK DOSAAF SSSR, "Predsedateliam komitetov DOSAAF soiuzhykh i avtonomnykh respublik, natsional'nykh oblastei i okrugov," 8 February 1950, GARF f. 9552, op. 1, d. 159, l. 11–72.

61. "Tematika politicheskikh zaniatii s chlenami DOSAAF v uchebnykh organizatsiiakh obshchestva," Nachal'nik upravleniia orgmassovoi raboty i propagandy TsK DOSAAF SSSR, GARF f. 9552, op. 1, d. 159, l. 17.

62. DOSAAF literature was examined at GARF f. 9552. The newspapers examined included *Pravda, Komsomol'skaia pravda,* and *Pionerskaia pravda*.

63. Lebedeva, *Kak zashchishchat'sia ot oruzhiia massovogo porazheniia*, 31.

64. Geist, "Scenarios for Survival," 26.

65. Press release from the 49th Annual Meeting of the National Council of the Boy Scouts of America, Curran Theatre and Civic Auditorium, San Francisco, 5–6 June 1959, BSA. Citations from the archive generally include the title, organizational section, date, and page number for the document in question. The indexes for the archives are in the process of being rewritten, and at the moment, the documents do not have specific call numbers associated with them. Instead, they are stored in the archive according to date and the section of the organization that produced the document.

66. Wishy, *The Child and the Republic*, viii.

67. Rodino, "The Boy Scouts of America."

68. Over the course of fifteen years, the American public was at various times told to evacuate the cities upon attack, to stay in the cities and run to a shelter, to go to open spaces, and to stay at home inside bomb shelters of varying sizes, shapes, and strengths.

69. The pressure to create a badge for civil defense began in the early 1950s, but it was not voted onto the list until 1962. "Emergency Preparedness," 1962, BSA.

70. Sherrow, *Encyclopedia of Youth and War*.

71. Rodino, "The Boy Scouts of America."

72. "Train in Family Preparedness and Emergency Living," Ready Unit 3, 1959, BSA.

73. "Nuclear Awareness," 1962, BSA.

74. Hershey, "My Country," 7; speech given by Terry Brennan to Boy Scouts at Philmont, 5 June 1956, BSA.

75. Brennan, "Civil Defense and You," 10.

76. Kaganovsky, "How the Soviet Man Was (Un)Made," 578.

77. I undertook quantitative and qualitative analyses of the images in *Life* magazine from the years between 1945 and 1968. The variables tracked included the number and sex of the children depicted, the kind of piece in which they were highlighted, the messages underlying the images (if this was clear), and, if an advertisement, the kind of product it was attempting to sell.

78. "An Institute on Girl Scout Volunteers and Defense," 1951, Defense—General, box 2/3, GSA.

79. "Defense Institute," 20 September 1950, Defense—General, box 2/1, GSA.

80. "The Place of Girl Scouting in National Defense," 28 July 1950, Defense—General, box 2/3, GSA.

81. Elaine Tyler May, *Homeward Bound*; Lewis, *Prescription for Heterosexuality*.

82. Kincaid, *Child-Loving*, 4.

83. Hellbeck, "Galaxy of Black Stars," 616.

84. Niebuhr, *Moral Man and Immoral Society*.

CHAPTER TWO

1. Edmonds, "Child Labor," 3.

2. Ostriakov, *Chto trebuet komsomol ot komsomol'tsa*, 68.

3. "Predlozheniia o merakh po uluchsheniiu vsemirnoi federatsii demokraticheskoi molodezhi," 1948, RGASPI f. m6, op. 11, d. 121, l. 135.

4. "Soobshchenie," RGASPI f. m6, op. 13, d. 57, l. 89.

5. "Otchet otdela propagandy i agitatsei TsK VLKSM o rabote i materialy k nemy, 1954–1958," RGASPI f. m6, op. 13, d. 57, l. 91.

6. Ibid.

7. Seldom do these accusations specify which youth organizations, occasionally mentioning the Boy Scouts but otherwise leaving it ambiguous. Pioneer groups did, in fact, also hunt turtles and butterflies.

8. RGASPI f. m6, op. 14, d. 111, l. 25.

9. "Peredacha dlia shkol'nikov, posviashchennaiai mezhdunarodnomu dniu zashchityi detei," 31 May 1955, GARF f. 6903, op. 16, d. 288, l. 1–6.

10. This number is derived from my survey of *Pionerskaia pravda* from 1950 to 1964.

11. Dudziak, "Brown as a Cold War Case."

12. A. Putko, "Novaia provokatsiia gosdepartamenta SShA," 14 October 1960, GARF f. 6903, op. 23, d. 10, l. 200–202.

13. Article cited in Dudziak, *Cold War Civil Rights*, 121.

14. *Izvestiia*, 13 September 1957, 4.

15. "Tvoi molodoi amerikanskii sverstnik," 22 May 1961, GARF f. 6903, op. 16, d. 368, l. 1–3.

16. "Peredacha Komitet molodozhnykh organizatsiy SSSR," 1 July 1959, GARF f. 6903, op. 16, d. 308, l. 1.

17. "Peredacha Komitet molodozhnykh organizatsiy SSSR," 12 February 1958, GARF f. 6903, op. 16, d. 303, l. 4–5.

18. Ibid., l. 5.

19. Ibid.

20. Stearns, *Childhood in World History*, 88.

21. Brooks, *When Russia Learned to Read*; Kirschenbaum, *Small Comrades*.

22. Ball, *And Now My Soul Is Hardened*; Zahra, *The Lost Children*.

23. "Dance Aids Russian Youth: Welfare Society Fete Marks Group's 25th Anniversary," *New York Times*, 7 December 1951, 33.

24. "Appeal for Russian Children," *New York Times*, 29 November 1953, 3.

25. Alexeiev, "I Don't Want My Children to Grow Up in Soviet Russia," 18; reprinted in *Reader's Digest*, June 1947, 11. Perhaps not surprising, when *Reader's Digest* reproduced the article, the picture of the smiling child was replaced with an illustration of the head of a scared baby hovering over the Kremlin skyline.

26. Alexeiev, "I Don't Want My Children to Grow Up Communists."

27. Ibid.

28. Filtzer, *Soviet Workers and Late Stalinism*, 53.

29. Ibid.

30. "Children's Day Sermons Urge Christian Life," *Washington Post*, 14 June 1948, B7.

31. Chamberlin, "Good Ideas Don't Go Wrong," 8.

32. "Soviet Children to Don Uniforms," *Christian Science Monitor*, 12 July 1954, 3.

33. "Soviet Youth Patrol," *Christian Science Monitor*, 2 August 1954, 4.

34. "Soviet Children to Hunt Uranium," *Christian Science Monitor*, 12 April 1957, 8.

35. Conniff, "Red Army Using Korean Children," 7.

36. Smith, "Why the Russian People Don't Rebel," 22.

37. Primost, "Du Berger a La Bergere," reprinted as "'Soviet Children Wait for the Capitalists," *Christian Science Monitor*, 5 June 1957.

38. U.S. Educational Policies Commission, *The Central Purposes of American Education*, 9. This document is also cited in Rudolph, *Scientists in the Classroom*, 1.

39. "Vsesoiuznye S'ezdy VLKSM," 16–20 April 1961, RGASPI f. m6, op. 14, d. 115, l. 105.

40. Bronfenbrenner, *Two Worlds of Childhood*.

41. Divine, *The Sputnik Challenge*.

42. Bronfenbrenner, *Two Worlds of Childhood*, 90.

43. Between June 1958 and May 1959, the Department of Education, the National Science Foundation, the Rockefeller Fund, as well as many universities, sent their directors to do comprehensive studies of Soviet education. People who traveled to the Soviet Union in order to study its education system included Lawrence Derthick, U.S. commissioner of education; Dr. Alan T. Waterman, director of the National Science Foundation; and representatives of the Rockefeller Brothers Fund.

44. Litchfield, "Text of Preliminary Report on Higher Education in the Soviet Union."

45. Ibid.

46. William Fulbright, statement in Congress, *Congressional Record*, 16 June 1958, 11244.

47. Speech by Dr. Lawrence Derthick to the National Press Club on 13 June 1958, reproduced in the *Congressional Record*, 13 July 1958, 11075.

48. Various portions of the Derthick report were reprinted no less than seven times by a variety of congressmen and congresswomen in the *Congressional Record* from both sides of the political spectrum.

49. Derthick, "The Frightening Challenge of Russia's Schools."

50. Sloan Wilson, "It's Time to Close Our Carnival," 36.

51. Humphrey, "The Soviet Education Challenge."

52. McCardle, "Education Now Power Struggle in Cold War."

53. See the *Congressional Record*, 15 January 1958, 496.

54. JoAnne Brown, "A Is for Atom," 74.

55. Ravitch, *Left Back*, 361.

56. U.S. Congress, House, *Review of Activities under National Defense Education Act*, 1580; Friedberg, *In the Shadow of the Garrison State*; Hogan, *A Cross of Iron*; Lowen, *Creating the Cold War University*; Schrecker, *No Ivory Tower*; Suri, "The Cultural Contradictions of Cold War Education."

57. "Nekotorye voprosy vospitaniia molodezhi, K XIV s"ezdy VLKSM," 1962, RGASPI f. m6, op. 14, d. 111, l. 50; Korolev, *Razvitie osnovnikh idei Sovetskoi pedagogiki.*

58. For more on this debate, see also Pechernikova, *Vospitanie poslushaniia i trudoliubiia u detei v sem'e*, 7.

59. Kagarlitsky, *The Thinking Reed.*

60. "Nekotorye voprosy vospitaniia molodezhi," K XIV s"ezdy VLKSM," 1962, RGASPI f. m6, op. 14, d. 111, l. 50.

61. N. S. Khrushchev, "Polozhenie TsK VLKSM," 19 February 1963, RGASPI f. m2, op. 1, d. 339, l. 1.

62. Ewing, *Separate Schools*, 1–10.

63. Yelyutin, "Adapting Higher Schools to Contemporary Demands," 68. Khrushchev emphasized that society must "re-shape the system of higher education, draw it closer to production, and link it up with production directly." Khrushchev, "Strengthening the Ties of the School with Life," pp. 3–4, 6–7, 11, 12, cited in Bereday, Brickman, and Read, *The Changing Soviet School*, 92.

64. RGASPI f. m6, op. 14, d. 111, l. 93.

65. Ledkovska, *Russia According to Women*, 79.

66. Novikova, "Vospitanie lichnosti v kollektive."

67. Ibid. See also her earlier work, Novikova, *Iskusstvo i vospitanie novogo cheloveka.*

68. "Polozhenie TsK VLKSM," 19 February 1963, RGASPI f. m2, op. 1, d. 339, l. 1.

69. Benton, "A Personal Report: The Teachers and the Taught in the U.S.S.R." William Benton was assistant secretary of state and U.S. senator, U.S. ambassador to UNESCO and U.S. member of its executive board, and publisher and chairman of Encyclopedia Britannica. This was first published in the *Encyclopaedia Britannica Yearbook* in 1965. Cited in the *Congressional Record*, 17 May 1965, A2423.

70. Sovetskii komitet detei, "Zhguchaia polemika po voprosam narodnogo obrazovaniia," 21.

71. Suri, "The Cultural Contradictions of Cold War Education," 2–3.

72. Stephens, "Nationalism, Nuclear Policy, and Children in Cold War America," 105.

CHAPTER THREE

1. "XI s'ezd vsesoiuznogo leninskogo kommunisticheskogo soiuza molodezhi, stenograficheskii otchet, 29 March–8 April 1949," RGASPI f. m6, op. 11, d. 27, l. 33.

2. Mikhailov, *Otchetnyi doklad na XI s'ezde komsomola o rabote TsK VLKSM*, 33–35.

3. "Students Discuss Communist Threat," *New York Times*, 20 October 1949, 26.

4. Frederick Brown Harris, "Truce of the Bear"; Constantine Brown, "Communist Subversion of Youth," 76; McNees, "Communism Needs You."

5. Zigler, "Early Childhood Intervention," 998.

6. Sealander, *The Failed Century of the Child*, 31.

7. Corber, *In the Name of National Security*, 3; Whitfield, *The Culture of the Cold War*, 12; Elaine Tyler May, *Homeward Bound*; Dudziak, *Cold War Civil Rights*, 13; Dean, *Imperial Brotherhood*; Lewis, *Prescription for Heterosexuality*; Henriksen, *Dr. Strangelove's America*.

8. Stephens, "Nationalism, Nuclear Policy, and Children in Cold War America," 104.

9. This observation is made beautifully by Sutcliffe, *The Prose of Life*, 12.

10. Hoover, "Youth Communist Target," 1.

11. Eugenie Anderson, "Threat of Aggressive Communism."

12. Reece, "The Institute of Fiscal and Political Education."

13. Flood, "Joint Resolution to Provide for a Commission on Communism."

14. Iverson, *The Communists and the Schools*; Caute, *The Great Fear*; Carleton, *Red Scare*; Murphy, *Blackboard Unions*; Foster, *Red Alert*.

15. Justice Sherman Minton, *Adler v. Board of Education of City of New York*, 342 US 485 (1952).

16. Mundt, "America's Little Red Schoolhouse."

17. The case was *Keyishian v. Board of Regents, State University of New York*, decided 23 January 1967. The minutes of the congressional debate can be found in the *Congressional Record*, 20 February 1967, A748.

18. *Current Magazine for Youth*, 15 January 1953, cited in Kahn, *The Game of Death*, 78.

19. *Educational Reviewer* 4, no. 2 (1954): 13, in Lucille Cardin Crain Papers, box 61, folder 10, University of Oregon Libraries, Eugene.

20. Catholic Guild, "This Godless Communism," 7.

21. Smolkin-Rothrock, "A Sacred Space Is Never Empty," 3.

22. Foertsch, "A Battle of Silence"; Beer, "The Epidemiology of Peace and War"; Ogden, "Cold War Science and the Body Politic"; Dean, *Imperial Brotherhood*; Lakoff, "Metaphor and War"; Alcock, *War Disease*; Shimko, "Metaphors and Foreign Policy Decision Making."

23. Howard McGrath (Rhode Island), speech before Congress, *Congressional Record*, 19 April 1950, 130.

24. Hoover, testimony, House Committee on Un-American Activities, 26 March 1947, cited in Schrecker, *The Age of McCarthyism*, 144. See also Humphrey, "Hearings before a Subcommittee on Labor."

25. Oshinsky, *Polio*, 69–72, 161–64.

26. Holland, *When All the World Was Young*, 212; Skolnick, *Embattled Paradise*, 66–67, 71–72.

27. TsK VLKSM, Otdel propagandy i agitatsii, "Spravki otdela ob organizatsii lektsionnoi propagandy sredi molodezhi," June 1950, RGASPI f. m1, op. 32, d. 611, l. 100.

28. Ibid., l. 146.

29. Ibid., l. 175.

30. Akhmadulina, Dutton, and Mezhakov-Koriakin, *Fever & Other New Poems*, 49.

31. Kozlov, *Mass Uprisings in the USSR*, 144.

32. GARF f. R-9401, op. 1, d. 4320, l. 48; GARF f. R-8131, op. 32, d. 5602, l. 37–42; cited in Kozlov, *Mass Uprisings in the USSR*, 138.

33. LaPierre, *Hooligans in Khrushchev's Russia*.

34. Kozlov, *Mass Uprisings in the USSR*, 173.

35. For the Twelfth Komsomol Congress, 19–26 March 1954, see RGASPI f. m6, op. 12, d. 1, 40, 56, 57, 61, 62. For the Thirteenth Komsomol Congress, 15–18 April 1958, see RGASPI f. m6, op. 13, d. 57, 59. For the Fourteenth Komsomol Congress, 16–20 April 1962, see RGASPI f. m6, op. 14, d. 111, 115. Also worth looking at are the documents from the Fifteenth Congress, 18–21 May 1966, at RGASPI f. m6, op. 15, d. 70, 139, 143, 147.

36. Hooligans have a long history in Russian society. The term "hooligan" was first categorized in the 1924 Russian criminal code as a "crime against the individual." It was defined as "the commission of mischievous acts, accompanied by explicit disrespect for society.". In 1937, it was recategorized as a "crime against administrative order," thus turning the act of hooliganism into an offense against the state instead of one against an individual. Ibid., 44. Then, in 1960, it was again redefined in the criminal code (article 206) as a crime against society (a crime against "social order"). Ibid., 76.

37. "XIV s'ezd VLKSM," 1962, RGASPI f. m6, op. 14, d. 115, l. 78.

38. "O rabote pionerskoi organizatsii na sovremennom etape kommunisticheskogo stroitel'stva." RGASPI f. m2, op. 1, d. 321, l. 18.

39. RGASPI f. m6, op. 15, d. 139, l. 10.

40. LaPierre, "Private Matters or Public Crimes"; Siegelbaum, *Borders of Socialism*.

41. Pechernikova, *Pooshchrenie i nakazanie detei v seme*, 3–87.

42. "Nekotorye voprosy Vvspitaniia molodezhi," RGASPI f. m6, op. 14, d. 111, l. 41.

43. Ibid., 82.

44. Shmakov, *Igra i deti*, 39.

45. Kovaleva, *Otsy i deti, seriia 11*, 3.

46. Gilbert, *A Cycle of Outrage*, 32.

47. Yeats, "Help for a Child or Punishment for a Delinquent," speaking at the annual meeting of the Young Men's Jewish Council.

48. Hoover, "Who Is to Blame for Juvenile Delinquency."

49. Gilbert, *A Cycle of Outrage*.

50. New York City Police Department, *Annual Reports* (1950) and *Statistical Reports* (1959, 1964), published by the State of New York.

51. Results reported by the Senate District of Columbia Committee on Juvenile Delinquency, 1953, *Congressional Record*, 6 January 1954, A633.

52. Symington, "Youth, Crime, and the Great Society."

53. Hoover, "Who Is to Blame for Juvenile Delinquency."

54. Wylie, *Generation of Vipers*.

55. Erikson, *Childhood and Society*, 288.

56. As early as 1948, anthropologist Geoffrey Gorer had noted that in "few societies is the father more vestigial than in the United States." Gorer, *The American People*, 54.

57. Liebowitz, "Judge Liebowitz on Juvenile Delinquency," 56.

58. Helen Thompson Woolley, "The Pre-Kindergarten Child," paper given to the Michigan Teachers Association, 3 November 1922, box 117, file 5, Merrill-Palmer Institute Papers, Walter P. Reuther Library, Wayne State University, Detroit; cited in Grant, "A Real Boy," 850.

59. Elaine Tyler May, *Homeward Bound*, 82.

60. Dean, *Imperial Brotherhood*.

61. Schlesinger, *The Vital Center*, 3.

62. D'Emilio, *Sexual Politics, Sexual Communities*, 42–43.

63. Unsigned letter, Records of the Florida Legislative Investigation Committee, 1963; cited in Braukman, "Nothing Else Matters but Sex," 553.

64. Elaine Tyler May, *Homeward Bound*, 87.

65. Buchli, "Khrushchev, Modernism, and the Fight," 161.

66. "Otchet otdela propagandy i agitatsii TsK VLKSM o raboti materialy k nemy, 1954–1958," RGASPI f. m6, op. 13, d. 57, l. 104.

67. Javits and Gideonse, "Ideals and Goals of Citizenship Education."

68. Gray, "Have Our Children Forgotten," 5.

69. The Senate Subcommittee on Juvenile Delinquency was headed at first by Senator Robert Hendrickson but became famous under the leadership of Senator Estes Kefauver, who was eventually responsible for making the comic book industry adopt a self-regulatory ratings code. See Beaty, *Fredric Wertham*; and Nyberg, *Seal of Approval*.

70. Robin Anderson, *A Century of Media*.

71. Wertham, *Seduction of the Innocent*, 1.

72. This story was recounted in detail by Senator William A. Purtell on the floor of the Senate on 16 February 1954, *Congressional Record*, A1196. Purtell was himself working from an article he had read by Irving M. Kravsaw in the *Hartford Courant* entitled "Depravity for Children—10 Cents a Copy," 14 February 1954.

73. Kefauver, "The Menace of Comic Books."

74. Robert Hendrickson quoting J. Edgar Hoover while speaking to the president on the upcoming Philadelphia hearings of the Senate Subcommittee on Juvenile Delinquency, *Congressional Record*, 1 April 1954, 4857.

75. Comic books had served as potential sources of blasphemy as far back as the broadsheets of the 1750s and the disturbing images of Hogarth's *A Rake's Progress* and *Four Stages of Cruelty*. See Kunzle, *The History of the Comic Strip*.

76. Alex Dreier, "Special Report," NBC, 3 May 1954, cited by Congressman Edward Rees (Kansas), *Congressional Record*, 15 June 1954, A4412.

77. Philadelphia hearings of the Senate Subcommittee on Juvenile Delinquency, *Congressional Record*, 1 April 1954, 4857.

78. Robert Hendrickson speaking before the Pennsylvania Citizens' Association of Pennsylvania, 20 January 1954, *Congressional Record*, 24 January 1964, A471.

79. Ibid.

80. Office of the Personal Secretary, 1961–63, Office of the White House Press Secretary, "Remarks of the President at the 50th Anniversary Celebration of the Children's Bureau," 9 April 1962, 2, JFK Library.

81. Executive Order no. 10940, quoted in *Federal Delinquency Program Objectives and Operation under the President's Committee on Juvenile Delinquency and Youth Crime and the Juvenile Delinquency and Youth Offenses Control Act of 1961*, 1.

82. Juvenile Delinquency and Youth Offenses Control Act of 1961, Public Law 87–274, 87th Congress, 22 September 1961, 1.

83. Matza, *Delinquency and Drift*, 13.

84. Kaslow, "Evolution of Theory and Policy on Inner City Delinquency," 33.

85. Office of the White House Press Secretary, "Remarks of the President on Signing S.279, Juvenile Delinquency and Youth Offenses Control Act of 1961," 22 September 1961, President's Office Files, JFKPOF-035-046, JFK Library.

86. Susan Reid describes how the standardization of architecture allowed for public control over the private individual and the way he or she lived his or her life. She states that modern faith in the "regulatory potential of housing" was not "the unique preserve of Soviet planners: the invasive role of architects and other specialists in defining people's everyday lives was part of the modernist project in general, which sought to shunt the messiness of people's lives into a hygienic, rational, manageable, and visible order." Reid, "The Meaning of Home," 145–70.

87. The punishment of bad parents as hooligans in the home became a phenomenon that was locally enforced although not officially sanctioned in the Soviet Union in the Khrushchev era. See LaPierre, "Private Matters or Public Crimes."

88. Ibid.; Field, "Mothers and Fathers"; Fürst, "Friends in Private, Friends in Public."

89. UN Archive, W/CN.4/SR.855, 10 March 1966, 6, cited in Kelly, "Defending Children's Rights, in Defense of Peace," 738.

90. Parents were relying on the normative advice of experts well before the 1950s. For a good history of the efforts of child experts to help parents raise their children over the past century, see Boym, *Common Places*.

91. Buchli, *An Archaeology of Socialism*. As Oleg Kharkhodin points out, "private" is an inexact term in Russian. It encompasses the ideas of *lichnoe* (the individual) and *chastnoe* (personal property). Kharkhodin suggests that it might be more accurate to focus on the collective and the individual instead, with the term *byt*, or "everyday life," in the place of the term "private." Kharkhodin, "Reveal and Dissimulate." See also Kharkhodin, *The Collective and the Individual in Russia*, 300. See collected articles in Siegelbaum, *Borders of Socialism*; Ilic, Reid, and Attwood, *Women in the Khrushchev Era*; and Buchli, *An Archaeology of Socialism*.

92. Elizabeth Wilson, *Women and the Welfare State*; Reid, "Women in the Home."

93. Shlapentokh, *Public and Private Life of the Soviet People*, 153–59.

94. Pinnow, *Lost to the Collective*, 11.

CHAPTER FOUR

1. "Khorosho podgotovimsia k vstreche druzei," 24 January 1956, RGASPI f. 3, op. 15, d. 2, l. 135.

2. Glavnaia redaktsiia propagandy na zarubezhnye strany, radio show entitled, "Otdel zhizni SSSR," and report entitled, "Den' sovetskoi Molodezhi,'" 26 June 1960, GARF f. 6903, op. 23, d. 7, l. 2.

3. Ibid., l. 65.

4. Ibid., l. 68.

5. Ibid., l. 67.

6. Andrew, 38; Glavnaia redaktsiia propagandy na zarubezhnye strany, radio show entitled, "Otdel zhizni SSSR," and report entitled, "Den 'Sovetskikh Molodezh,'" 26 June 1960, GARF f. 6903, op. 23, d. 7, l. 68.

7. Much ink has been spilled over Khrushchev's Cold War policy from 1956 to 1964. John Gaddis has called him "obsequious" and "bibulous," portraying him as a reluctant and uncertain leader, driven to erratic behavior. Gaddis, *We Now Know*, 205–11. Walter LaFeber has characterized him as a "shrewd" and "subtle" man, who attempted to use economic aid to the postcolonial world in order to win hearts and minds. LaFeber, *America, Russia, and the Cold War*, 170–71. Vladislav Zubok and Constantine Pleshakov have characterized him as a man who understood the "ultimate limits imposed by nuclear weapons" but who was also aware of how useful the "nuclear bluff" could be. Zubok and Pleshakov, *Inside the Kremlin's Cold War*, 180–90. See also Taubman, *Khrushchev*.

8. John F. Kennedy, "Remarks on the 50th Anniversary of the Children's Bureau," 9 April 1962, White House Audio Collection, WHA-085-001, JFK Library.

9. "Materialy otdela shkol'noi molodezhi ToK VLKSM k dokladu na XIV s'ezde VLKSM," RGASPI f. m6, op. 14, d. 115, l. 9.

10. This is discussed in detail in Brooks, *Thank You, Comrade Stalin*.

11. "Rezoliutsiia XX s'ezda KPSS po otchetnomu dokladu TsK KPSS," cited in Institut Marksizma-Leninizma pri TsK KPSS, *KPSS v rezoliutsiiakh i resheniiakh s'ezdov, konferentsii i plenumov TsK: 1898–1971*, 8.

12. "Postanovlenie vos'mogo plenuma TsK VLKSM," *Molodaia gvardiia* (28 November 1957): 3–15.

13. "Vospitanie novogo cheloveka—bortsa i stroitelia kommunizma k XIV s'ezdu VLKSM," RGASPI f. m6, op. 14, d. 111, l. 33.

14. "Tol'ko v trude vmeste s rabochimi, s'ezd Komsomola," 17–21 May 1966, RGASPI f. m6, op. 15, d. 139. The emergence of the idea of independence and personal responsibility for work, as well as for one's actions, is discussed in Zubkova, *Obshchestvo i Reformi*, 67.

15. *Pionerskaia pravda*, 15 June 1957. Italics added for emphasis.

16. "Spravka dlia sovetskikh delegatsii," RGASPI f. m2, op. 1, d. 57, l. 4.

17. Artek was actually a group of ten smaller camps, each with its own name: "Lazurny," "Kiparisny," "Morskoi," for example. Four of the smaller camps, "Rechnoi," "Ozyorny," "Lesnoi," and "Polevoi," made up the "Pribrezhny" complex that was built from 1960 to 1964 by a group of architects led by Anatoly Polyansky. They were awarded the USSR State Prize in architecture in 1967 for their work. RGASPI f. m2, op. 1, d. 57, l. 16.

18. As Lenin stated, "All citizens are here transformed into hired employees of the state, which is made up of the armed workers. . . . All that is required is that they should work equally, should regularly do their share of the work, and should receive equal pay." Lenin, *State and Revolution*. See also Lenin, *Tasks of the Youth Leagues*.

19. "Sekretariu TsK VLKSM," RGASPI f. m2, op. 1, d. 18, l. 57.

20. The camp was made officially international in 1958, but it had international visitors as early as 1955.

21. "Otchet sovetskoi delegatsii na mezhdunarodnom seminare 'Destskie i io-nesheskie dvizheniia' v Brioccele," 16–21 June 1958, RGASPI f. m2, op. 1, d. 58, l. 5.

22. RGASPI f. m2, op. 1, d. 58, l. 64.

23. "Pervichnaia razreshenie," RGASPI f. m2, op. 78.

24. Among its illustrious guests were Yuri Gagarin, Indira Gandhi, Urho Kek-konen, Nikita Khrushchev, Jawaharlal Nehru, Otto Schmidt, Lydia Skoblikova, Mikhail Tal, Valentina Tereshkova, and Lev Yashin.

25. From an interview held with Marina Strikalova, who was a Pioneer leader at Artek in 1960, 4 April, 2005, Moscow.

26. "Otchet o komandirovke delegatsii tsentral'nogo soveta pionerskoi organizat-sii imeni V. I. Lenina v soiuz khartserov pol'shi," RGASPI f. m2, op. 1, d. 58, l. 69.

27. "Slovo predostavliaetsia rukovoditelio gruppi Bolgarskikh Pionerov Ivanu Iovchevu," RGASPI f. m2, op. 1, d. 58, l. 82.

28. "Pis'ma detei," RGASPI f. m2, op. l. d. 59.

29. T. T. Koskinen, "Kharakteristika raboty s gruppami inostrannykh druzei po otriadam," RGASPI f. m2, op. 1, d. 17, l. 19.

30. Ibid., l. 27.

31. Ibid., l. 14.

32. "TsK VLKSM vnosit na rassmotrenie vopros o lagere 'Artek,'" RGASPI f. m2, op. 1, d. 17, l. 13.

33. Iu. Kolotilov, "Spravka o prebyvanii v Sovetskom Soiuze delegatsii pioner-skikh rabotnikov Gvineiskoi respubliki," RGASPI f. m2, op. 1, d. 155, l. 46.

34. "Radiosbornik: Sto voprosov i otvetov o Sovetskom Soiuze," 16 March 1961, GARF f. 6903, op. 23, d. 43, l. 116.

35. "Kharakteristika raboty s gruppami inostrannykh druzei po otriadam," RGASPI f. m2, op. 1, d. 17, l. 19.

36. Press release from the Forty-ninth Annual Meeting of the National Council of the Boy Scouts of America, Curran Theatre and Civic Auditorium, San Francisco, 5–6 June 1959, BSA.

37. John S. Gleason, "We Must Teach the Truth about Communism," *Washington Post*, 2 March 1958. Cardinal Cushing's talk, which garnered a huge response on the floor of Congress from at least five representatives, was delivered on 21 June 1959 on channel 4 in Boston. A copy of his talk can be found in *Congressional Record*, 24 June 1959, A5468.

38. Letter from C. C. Tillingham, superintendent of Los Angeles County Schools, to Congressman Clyde Doyle of California, 3 March 1961, republished in *Congres-sional Record*, 10 April 1961, A2365.

39. See, for instance, Catholic Guild, "This Godless Communism," 7.

40. "Facts for Youth," *Junior Scholastic*, 2 February 1962, 3.

41. "Your Welfare Is Being Overshadowed," *Boy's Life*, September 1956, 63. See also articles on how to go to college for free and another direct solicitation for en-gineers, "Wanted: More Engineers," both in *Boy's Life*, December 1956, 11: "You will have the satisfaction of knowing that your efforts are keeping our nation strong and

free through technological progress." Unlike in previous years, "being prepared" now included being prepared for going to college.

42. Boys, in particular, were thought to have the natural ability for math that the nation needed. See "Man and Mathematics," *Boy's Life*, September 1960, 20.

43. "Comic Books and the Boy Scouts," 1960, BSA.

44. Badge Requirements, Atomic Energy Badge, 1958, BSA.

45. Annual Report, 1960, BSA.

46. "Education and Scouting," National Jamboree, 1961, BSA.

47. BSA Research Service Studies 1958, "Scouting in Highly Congested Urban Areas," completed October 1958, 48, BSA.

48. Ibid., 42–45.

49. Shields, "The Men in Your Life"; Pirrung, "Building the Image of the Scoutmaster."

50. Baden-Powell, "The Father I Knew."

51. "Dominating Delilah," *Scouting*, October 1962.

52. Remarks by President Eisenhower at the Fiftieth Anniversary Commemorative Dinner of the Boy Scouts of America, Sheraton-Park Hotel, Washington, D.C., 1 June 1960, 1, BSA.

53. Jay Mechling, *On My Honor: Boy Scouts and the Making of American Youth*.

54. Elaine Tyler May, *Homeward Bound*, 166.

55. Boy Scout Handbook, 1968, BSA.

56. Ibid.

57. Address by Marlon A. Wright before the 1960–61 Leadership Clinic, 17 November 1960, Detroit. Wright was a member of the Board of Directors, chairman of the Southern Regional Council, and member of the North Carolina Advisory Committee to the U.S. Commission on Civil Rights. *Congressional Record*, 24 March 1961, 4755

58. Jacob Javits, "Disgracing America," *New York Times*, 3 September 1963.

59. Annual Report: Interracial Relationships Service, 1959, BSA.

60. Ibid.

61. "Scouting for Negro Boys in the Tennessee Valley," *Speakin' Out*, 7–13 March 1990, 11, BSA. This article tells the history of black Scouting over the span of fifty years. See also the uncataloged folder labeled "African-American History: Involvement with Scouting," BSA.

62. Annual Report: Interracial Relationships Service, 1959, 4–25, BSA.

63. Report of Committee on Interracial Activities, 1950, in "African-American History: Involvement with Scouting" folder, BSA.

64. Report of the Committee on Interracial Activities, 1950, in "African-American History: Involvement with Scouting" folder, BSA; speech, Sixth National Jamboree, Valley Forge, Pa., Marie C. McGuire, commissioner of the Public Housing Administration, 1965, BSA; Proceedings of the 55th Annual Meeting of the National Council of the Boy Scouts of America, Miami Beach, 20–21 May 1965, BSA.

65. "Membership Continues to Grow," Yearly Program Report, 1958, BSA.

66. "Dr. Schuck Given Freedom Foundation's Highest Award," *Boy's Life*, May 1959, 28.

67. Baden-Powell, *International Scouting Yesterday and Today*, 1958, BSA.

68. Jean R. Bader, director of the International Relationships Service, "Thanksgiving and World Friendship," *Scout Executive*, October 1961, 1, BSA.

69. J. A. Brunton, director of the Division of Relationships, "1957 World Friendship Fund International: Good Turn with the Long Reach," *Scout Executive*, December 1956, 1, BSA.

70. "World Friendship—1959," Program Directive, 1959, 4, BSA.

71. "Merit Badge Requirements," 1954, 534, BSA.

72. Krupskaia, *On Education*.

73. "The World Jamboree Is Remembered—The Year in Review," 1968, BSA.

74. Gerald Speedy, "Meeting the Challenges of a Changing World," speech given at a meeting of the home office staff, published in *Scout Executive*, March 1967, 11.

75. Ibid.

76. "Campfire Stories for Troop Leaders," 1961 and 1967, BSA.

77. MacPherson, "Soon I Can Vote."

78. Naima Prevots argues that "Stalin's death had also brought about an increase in cultural diplomacy on the part of the Soviet Union; the amount of money spent on sending artists, writers, and performers to other countries escalated considerably." Prevots, *Dance for Export*, 12.

79. Barghoorn, *Soviet Foreign Propaganda*, 36–38. See also Fursenko and Naftali, *Khrushchev's Cold War*, 23; Zubok, *A Failed Empire*, 175; Ebon, *Soviet Propaganda Machine*, 11; and Osgood, *Total Cold War*, 56.

80. Austin, "Introduction," 2.

CHAPTER FIVE

1. Woll, *Real Images*, 3.

2. In a radio broadcast to the nation on 2 November 1961, Khrushchev said of the Thaw, "The people are waiting and are certain, that the writers and filmmakers in the arts will create a new kind of production in which they will adequately articulate our heroic epoch of revolutionary transformation of society." Khrushchev, "S"ezd stroitelei kommunizma," in a show narrated by P. Brovka, "Radiozhurnal komiteta molodezhykh organizatsii Sovetskogo Soiuza," GARF f. 6903, op. 23, d. 41, l. 57.

3. Institut Marksizma-Leninizma pri TsK KPSS, *KPSS v Rezoliutsiiakh i resheniiakh s"ezdov, konferentsii i plenumov TsK: 1898–1971*, 164.

4. Aksiutin, *Khrushchevskaia "ottepel" i obshchestvennye nastroeniia*; Johnson, *Khrushchev and the Arts*; Burlatsky, *Khrushchev and the First Russian Spring*; Fomin, *Kinematograf ottepeli*.

5. Prokhorov, "The Adolescent and the Child in the Cinema of the Thaw," 115.

6. Biskind, *Seeing Is Believing*, 3.

7. Lacy, "War, Cinema, and Moral Anxiety," 611; Whitfield, *The Culture of the Cold War*, 220.

8. Tarkovsky, *Sculpting in Time*, 20.

9. Biskind, *Seeing Is Believing*, 3.

10. Youngblood, "A War Remembered"; Tumarkin, *The Living and the Dead*.

11. Such films include J. Thompson's 1961 film *The Guns of Navarone*, Darryl Zanuck's 1962 film *The Longest Day*, and John Sturges's 1963 film *The Great Escape*. See, for instance, Pollard, "The Hollywood War Machine"; and Biskind, *Seeing Is Believing*, 52.

12. Varshavskii, "Nado razobrat'sia," 62.

13. Vitalii Gubarev, "Dva Fedora," 3 November 1958, RGALI f. 2453, op. 4, d. 1626.

14. Khutsiev, "Ia nikogda ne felal polemichnykh fil'mov," 195.

15. Cited by Chernenko, in *Marlen Khutsiev*, 9. Also cited by Woll, *Real Images*, 93.

16. Nekrasov, "Slova 'velikie' i 'prostye.'"

17. Merkel', "Snimaet Vadim Iusov."

18. "Pervoe ob"edinenie. Stenogramma zasedaniia Khudozhestvennogo Soveta. Prosmotr i obsuzhdenie fil'ma 'Ivanovo Detstvo', Predsedatel'stvuet—L. R. Sheinin," 1 May 1962, RGALI f. 2453, op. 4, g. 261, l. 19.

19. N. A. Kovarskii, "Stenogramma zasedaniia Khudozhestvennogo Soveta IV tvorcheskogo ob"edineniia—Obsuzhdenie postanovochnogo stsenariia (Ivanovo Detstvo)," 1 August 1960, RGALI f. 2453, op. 4, d. 208, l. 37.

20. Zorkaia, *The Illustrated History of the Soviet Cinema*, 32.

21. Atwell, *Film Quarterly* 18, no. 1 (Autumn 1964): 50.

22. N. A. Kovarskii, "Stenogramma zasedaniia Khudozhestvennogo Soveta 1 go Tvorcheskogo ob"edineniia—Obsuzhdenie postanovochnogo stsenariia (Ivanovo Detstvo)," 1 August 1960, RGALI f. 2453, op. 4, d. 208, l. 39.

23. "Pervoe ob"edinenie. Stenogramma zasedania Khudozhestvennogo Soveta. Prosmotr i obsuzhdenie fil'ma 'Ivanovo Detstvo' Predsedatel'stvuet—L. R. Sheinin," 1 May 1962, RGALI f. 2453, op. 4, g. 261, l. 14.

24. "Stenogramma zasedaniia Khudozhestvennogo Soveta 1-go Tvorcheskogo ob"edineniia—Obsuzhdenie postanovochnogo stsenariia (Ivanovo Detstvo)," 1 August 1960, RGALI f. 2453, op. 4, d. 208, l. 40.

25. "Stenogramma zasedaniia Khudozhestvenogo stsenariia (Ivanovo Detstvo)," 1 May 1961, RGALI f. 2453, op. 4, d. 232, l. 7.

26. Woll, *Real Images*, 141–42.

27. "Pervoe ob"edinenie. Stenogramma zasedaniia Khudozhestvennogo Soveta. Prosmotr i obsuzhdenie fil'ma 'Ivanovo Detstvo' Predsedatel'stvuet—L. R. Sheinin," 1 May 1962, RGALI f. 2453, op. 4, g. 261, l. 1.

28. Khrushchev, "Vospitaniia novogo cheloveka—bortsa i stroitelia kommunizma: k XIV s"ezdu VLKSM," RGASPI f. m6, op. 4, d. 111, l. 1.

29. Belova, *Besedy o kino*, 108.

30. Woll, "Mikhail Romm's *Ordinary Fascism*," 224.

31. Ibid.

32. Romm, *Montazhnaia Struktura Fil'ma*, 301.

33. Fedor Burlatskii in an interview with Grigorii Durnovo, 21 January 2008; cited in Turovskaia, "Some Documents from the Life of a Documentary Film," 157.

34. "Stenogramma zasedaniia," RGALI f. 2453, op. 4, d. 2785, l. 4.

35. Khrushchev, "Vysokaia ideinost' i khudozhestvennoe masterstvo."

36. Ibid.

37. Prokhorov, "The Adolescent and the Child in the Cinema of the Thaw."

38. Woll, *Real Images*, 115. Richard Stites comments on the contrast between the newsreel and the real village: "The cyclical, unchanging nature of the farm life is gently but sadly illuminated in the self-referential scene in which the farmers watch themselves over and over in a documentary production film. The contrast between the bubbling total idyll depiction in *Kuban Cossacks* and the bleakness of *Serezha* is a striking instance of the new quest for cinematic truth." Stites, *Russian Popular Culture*, 140.

39. "Stenogramma zasedaniia," RGALI f. 2453, op. 4, d. 2785, l. 33.

40. Karpinskii, "Prazdnik molodosti."

41. L. Kuravlov, Stenogramma zasedaniia Khudozhestvennogo Soveta Obsuzhdenie literaturnogo stsenariia, "Zvoniat, Otkroite Dver'," 3 February 1964, RGALI f. 2453, op. 4, d. 1420, l. 28.

42. A. Khmelik, "Zakliuchenie," 16 October 1962, RGALI f. 2453, op. 5, d. 1162, l. 17.

43. Reid, "Khrushchev Modern," 235.

44. A. Khmelik, "Zakliuchenie," 16 October 1962, RGALI f. 2453, op. 5, d. 1162, l. 18.

45. Woll, *Real Images*, 214.

46. Kaganovsky, *How the Soviet Man Was Unmade*.

47. Throughout the film, Tania's Pioneer tie is consistently tied the wrong way, which would not have been allowed. Although this might have simply been a mistake on Mitte's part, it is likely that the mis-knotted tie carried some meaning. Perhaps it symbolized further commentary on the lack of parenting that Tania received, or perhaps it carried with it a commentary about the Pioneers and their rules in general.

48. M. P. Korshunov, "Stenogramma zasedaniia Khudozhestvennogo Soveta Obsuzhdenie literaturnogo stsenariia, 'Zvoniat, Otkroite Dver'," 3 February 1964, RGALI f. 2453, op. 4, d. 1420, l. 1.

49. Gerasimov, "Razmyshleniia o molodykh." See also Louis Harris Cohen, *Cultural-Political Traditions*, 274.

50. Gerasimov, "Poddel'noe i Podlinnoe."

51. Iu. Kolotilov, "Information: Internationales Sommerlager für den Frieden und die Freundschaft der Kinder aller Länder," Gosteleradio broadcast, 1960, GARF f. 6903, op. 1, d. 155, l. 7.

52. Semion Lungin, "Avtorskaia zaiavka, *Dobro Pozhalovat'*," RGASPI f. 2453, op. 4, d. 1475, l. 1.

53. N. A. Rudakova, "Stenogramma sovmestnogo zasedaniia Khudozhestvennykh Sovetov tvorcheskogo ob'edineniia pisatelei i kinorabotnikov i tvorcheskogo ob'edineniia 'Iunost'," 7 June 1963, RGALI f. 2453, op. 4, d. 1403, l. 10–31.

54. It was no coincidence that these scenes harkened back to *8½*, considering that the film had been made less than a year before Klimov tried his hand at *Welcome, or No Trespassing*. This point is made by Ian Christie, "Unauthorized Persons Enter Here," 200.

55. Lungin i Klimov, "Stsenarii fil'ma," RGALI f. 2453, op. 4, d. 1476, l. 53.

56. Ibid., l. 57.

57. N. A. Rudakova, "Stenogramma sovmestnogo zasedaniia Khudozhestvennykh Sovetov tvorcheskogo ob'edineniia pisatelei i kinorabotnikov i tvorcheskogo ob'edineniia 'Iunost'," 7 June 1963, RGALI f. 2453, op. 4, d. 1403, l. 10–31.

58. Ibid.

59. A. Groshev, "Pis'mo ot predsedatelia repertuarnogo soveta," 10 May 1963, RGALI f. 2454, op. 4, d. 1483, l. 47.

60. A. G. Khmelik, "Stenogramma sovmestnogo zasedaniia Khudozhestven-nykh sovetov tvorcheskogo ob'edineniia pisatelei i kinorabotnikov i tvorcheskogo ob'edineniia 'Iunost'," 7 June 1963, RGALI f. 2453, op. 4, d. 1403, l. 19–23.

61. Elem Klimov, "Stenogramma sovmestnogo zasedaniia Khudozhestven-nykh sovetov tvorcheskogo ob'edineniia pisatelei i kinorabotnikov i tvorcheskogo ob'edineniia 'Iunost'," 7 June 1963, RGALI f. 2453, op. 4, d. 1403, l. 19–23.

62. Kozlov, *Mass Uprisings in the USSR*, 12.

63. "Pis'mo ot direktorov rukovoditelei IV ob'edineniia" and "Plan dorabotki kinostsenariia 'Dobro Pozhalovat'," RGALI f. 2453, op. 4, d. 1483, l. 23–31. The directors of Mosfilm also wanted Kostia to be caught and reprimanded by the younger counselors, but Klimov refused and maintained that the students and the counselors will "maintain the secret of Kostia"—thus spreading the conspiracy to protect Kostia into the lower administration of the camp. Elem Klimov, "Pis'mo general'nomu direktoru kinostudii 'Mosfil'm' t. V. N. Surinu," RGALI f. 2453, op. 4, d. 1483, l. 43.

64. Bakshtein, "View from Moscow," 332.

65. Khrushchev, *The Great Mission of Literature and Art*, 150.

66. Khrushchev, "Vysokaia ideinost' i khudozhestvennoe masterstvo."

67. "What Khrushchev Told the Writers," *Observer*, 19 August 1963, 3.

CHAPTER SIX

1. Newman, "A Communication."

2. Wittner, *Resisting the Bomb*.

3. Minutes of the Committee to Stop Nuclear Tests, 24 September 1957, DG 58, Series A, SANE.

4. Wittner, *Resisting the Bomb*, 251.

5. Boyer, *By the Bomb's Early Light*, 295. See also Henriksen, *Dr. Strangelove's America*; and Weart, *Nuclear Fear*.

6. Mickenberg, *Learning from the Left*, 8.

7. Newman, "A Communication."

8. "Nuclear Fear," *Today's Woman*, June 1951.

9. Barclay, "Group Plans to Study the Effects of Defense Activities on Children."

10. Ibid.

11. Goodwin, *Wait Till Next Year*, 158. For an examination of the impact that the Bomb had on children's lives, see the politically charged Kahn, *Game of Death*. For a more balanced view, see JoAnne Brown, "A Is for Atom."

12. Lapp, "Fallout—Another Dimension in Atomic Power."

13. Myers, *New Soviet Thinking and U.S. Nuclear Policy*, 25. See also Kate Brown, *Plutopia*.

14. Minutes of Organizing Committee, 1 October 1957, DG 58, Series A, SANE.

15. "Nuclear Tests Are Endangering Our Health Right Now," *New York Times*, 11 April 1958.

16. Conference Notes from Anti Atom—The Third World Conference against A- and H-Bombs and for Disarmament, Tokyo, August 1957, DG 58, Series E, box 34, SANE.

17. "SANE Mother's Day Project," 7 May 1958, DG 58, Series B-3, box 12, SANE.

18. "New York Students Dedicate Balloons," Releases: 1957–58, 23 May 1958, DG 58, Series A, box 11, SANE.

19. "National Meeting, Boston, Mass.," May 1959, DG 58, Series A, box 11, SANE.

20. "Toward a SANE Nuclear Policy," Literature: 1957–62, DG 58, Series A, box 10, SANE.

21. *New York Times*, 29 April 1959; Cousins, "The Debate Is Over."

22. Letter from John Bessor to SANE, 21 March 1958, DG 58, Series B-3, box 7, SANE.

23. Letter from Mary Kirkpatrick of Tuscola, Ill., 2 February 1958, ibid.

24. Letter from James E. Amick of Kansas City, Mo., 24 April 1958, ibid.

25. Letter from Lewis Strauss to Adelaide Baker, 29 March 1958, ibid.

26. Letter from Adelaide Baker to Lewis Strauss, 7 April 1958, ibid.

27. Weart, *Nuclear Fear*, 87.

28. Ibid., 92.

29. Not surprising, it was Norman Cousins who spearheaded American programs to provide plastic surgery and vocational training in the United States for these groups of girls.

30. Sadako completed 644 cranes before dying. SANE commented in internal documents that Sadako's plight had garnered "much comment." DG 58, Series A, box 18, SANE.

31. "H Stands for Humanity," DG 58, Series A, box 11, SANE.

32. Clarence Pickett to Norman Cousins, 27 October 1960, DG 58, Series B, box 9, SANE.

33. U.S. Congress, Senate, Internal Security Subcommittee on the Judiciary, *Communist Infiltration in the Test Ban Movement*, 87th Cong., 2nd sess., testimony of Henry Abrams of the Greater New York Committee for a Sane Nuclear Policy, 13 May 1960, 4.

34. Barbara Deming, "The Ordeal of Sane," *Nation*, 11 March 1961, 200. See also Schrecker, *Many Are the Crimes*, 379.

35. Norman Cousins to Homer Jack, 7 March 1962, DG 58, Series B, box 12, SANE.

36. First meeting of the Public Information Committee, 5 January 1962, SANE Publicity Campaign Notes, DG 58, Series A, box 8, SANE.

37. Spock, *Baby and Child Care*. By Spock's death in 1998, *Baby and Child Care* had sold over 50 million copies and, aside from the Bible, was the best-selling book in the twentieth century in America. It has been translated into at least thirty-nine languages.

38. Interview of Benjamin Spock by Milton Katz, 6 March 1972, cited in Katz, *Ban the Bomb*, 72.

39. Ibid., 75.

40. "Dr. Spock Is Worried," *New York Times*, 24 April 1962, Literature: 1957–62, DG 58, Series A, box 10, SANE.

41. Letter to Dr. Spock published in the periodical "SANE Action," 1 May 1962, DG 58, Series A, box 17, SANE.

42. Meeting of Public Information Committee, 9 March 1962, SANE Publicity Campaign Notes, DG 58, Series A, box 8, SANE.

43. Ibid.

44. "42 Arrested in Times Square in Clashes at Peace Rally," *New York Times*, 4 March 1962, 1.

45. "Is This Really SANE?" *Washington Evening Star*, August 1962, Washington Office, DG 58, Series E, box 34, SANE.

46. Ibid.

47. SANE Publicity Campaign Notes, DG 58, Series A, box 8, SANE.

48. Dr. James V. Neel, "The Effects of Nuclear War," Literature: 1960–62, DG 58, Series A, box 10, SANE.

49. "Seven Years for a SANE Nuclear Policy," *SANE World* 3 (15 April 1964).

50. "Is This What It's Coming To?" *New York Times*, 5 July 1962. See also DG 58, Series A, box 16, SANE.

51. Letter from Norman Myrick to Clarence Pickett and Norman Cousins, 10 July 1962, DG 58, Series A, box 16, SANE.

52. Ibid. Emphasis in the original.

53. "Now It's Up to the Senate . . . and You!" *New York Times*, 2 August 1963.

54. Katz, *Ban the Bomb*, 86.

55. "Mothers Urge Expanded Study of Fallout Peril," *Washington Post*, 19 May 1959.

56. Ibid.

57. "Mothers' Lobby," *Washington Star*, 1/ June 1959.

58. Koven, *Mothers of a New World*, 6; Linden-Ward and Green, *American Women in the 1960s*, xi; Friedan, *Feminine Mystique*.

59. Adrienne Harris and Ynestra King, *Rocking the Ship of State*, 234.

60. Swerdlow, *Women Strike for Peace*, 3.

61. Elshtain, *Women and War*. See also Laville, "Positive Peace," 124.

62. Ladd, *On the Duty of Females*; Howe, *Reminiscences*; Degen, *History of the Women's Peace Party*; Papachristou, "American Women and Foreign Policy," 493–509; York, "The Truth about Women and Peace," 21.

63. Eleanor Garst to Dagmar Wilson, Washington, D.C., September 1962, DG 115, Series A2, box 1, WSP.

64. Scott, *Domination and the Arts of Resistance*, 139.

65. Ibid., 172.

66. "Appeal to All Governments," 21 September 1961, Literature 1961, DG 115, Series A2, box 1, WSP.

67. "Letter to Mrs. Kennedy," 1 November 1961, ibid.

68. "Women Plan 'Strike for Peace,'" *News-Call Bulletin*, 25 October 1961.

69. DG 115, Series A2, box 1, WSP.

70. Meyerowitz, *Not June Cleaver*, 2.

71. *Newsweek*, 13 November 1961, 21–22.

72. *Los Angeles Times*, 1 November 1961.

73. "Report to Women around the United States of America on the Women Strike for Peace, November 1961," 25 November 1961, Washington, D.C., mimeographed flyer, DG 115, Series A, box 3, WSP.

74. Letter to President John F. Kennedy, 1 December 1961, and Report on Health Hazards, Literature 1961, DG 115, Series A2, box 1, WSP.

75. *London Times Mirror*, 4 October 1979.

76. "Message Gets Across," *Washington Post*, 16 January 1962.

77. Ibid.

78. "The Proposed Mother March," September 1961, Literature 1961, DG 115, Series A2, box 1, WSP. Emphasis in original.

79. See, for instance, "U monumenta Vashingtonu," *Trud*, 8 March 1963.

80. "Says 'Women for Peace' Movement Is 'Getting More Ridiculous Daily,'" *White Plains N.Y. Reporter-Dispatch*, 14 February 1962.

81. *New York Times*, 4 March 1962.

82. *Springfield (Ohio) News Sun*, 16 March 1962.

83. "Women Hold 'Peace Talks,'" *Tulsa Oklahoma Tribune*, 4 April 1962.

84. *London Evening Press*, London, Ontario, 5 April 1962.

85. *Washington Post*, 26 January 1962; *New Jersey Herald*, 19 April 1962.

86. Editorial, *Washington Post*, 6 December 1962.

87. "Women Strike for Peace Statement on House Un-American Activities Committee Subpoenas to WSP Participants in New York," Literature 1962, DG 115, Series A2, box 1, WSP.

88. Editorial, *Washington Post*, 6 December 1962.

89. "Letter to WSP Members," Literature 1962, DG 115, Series A2, box 1, WSP.

90. Swerdlow, *Women Strike for Peace*, 100.

91. Bentley, *Thirty Years of Treason*, 951.

92. *Congressional Record*, 17 January 1963, 524.

93. U.S. Congress, House, Committee on Un-American Activities, *Communist Activities in the Peace Movement*, 2074.

94. Ibid. This hearing is discussed in far more detail in Swerdlow, *Women Strike for Peace*.

95. "Ladies' Day," *Newsweek*, 24 December 1962.

96. William May, "Who's Running the Show," *Detroit Free Press*, 13 December 1962.

97. McCartney, "It's Ladies Day at the Capitol."

98. McGrory, "Peace Strike Explained."

99. "Peace Women Baffle HUAC's Masculine Minds," *Pennsylvania Guardian*, 21 December 1962.

100. "It's Not Un-American to Giggle," *Vancouver (B.C.) Sun*, 14 December 1962.

101. "The Right Kind of Fallout," April 1963, Literature 1963, DG 115, Series A2, box 1, WSP.

102. "The Disarmament Coloring Book," Literature 1963, DG 115, Series A2, box 1, WSP.

103. U.S. Congress, Senate, Committee on Foreign Relations, *Hearings before the Committee on Foreign Relations on the Treaty Banning Nuclear Weapons Tests*, 744.

104. Maurine Neuberger, *WSP of New York, New Jersey, Connecticut*, Literature 1963, DG 115, Series A2, box 1, WSP.

105. Small, *Antiwarriors*, 56.

106. "Agony of Vietnamese Civilians," 1967, Washington Office: Vietnam, DG 58, Series E, box 52, SANE.

107. See, for instance, William Ryan's statements on the congressional floor, "Vietnam—Suffer the Little Children," *Congressional Record*, 17 January 1967, A139. Ryan cites an article by Martha Gellhorn by the same name that was published in *Ladies' Home Journal*, January 1967. Miller, "Vietnam Myths," *Congressional Record*, 3 April 1967, 8024. Miller cites an article written by Dr. Howard Rusk, "Reports of Many Children Burned by American Napalm Are Challenged." Citation information for Rusk's article is not given.

108. Video Recording NLJ Ref# MP 983, "Poverty: 60," fall 1964, Records of the Democratic National Committee, 1964 Democratic Presidential Campaign Spots, Video Tape Record 4568, Audio Visual Collection, LBJ Library.

109. Video Recording NLJ Ref# MP 999, "Social Security: 60," ibid.

110. Video Recording NLJ Ref# MP 1001, "Peace, Little Girl (Daisy Spot)," ibid.

111. Memorandum for the Record, June 1992, Daisy Ad, Reference File, ibid.

112. Six days after the ad ran, Moyers reminded the president that "while we paid for the ad only on NBC last Monday night, ABC and CBS ran it on their news shows Friday. So we got it shown on all three networks for the price of one." Memorandum, Letter from Bill Moyers to President Johnson, 13 September 1964, Daisy Ad, Reference File, LBJ Library.

113. Hall, "Bill Moyers Holds a Mirror Up to America"; Memorandum, Letter from Bill Moyers to President Johnson, 13 September 1964, Daisy Ad, Reference File, LBJ Library; "Scenes from the Political Playground: An Analysis of the Symbolic Use of Children in Presidential Campaign Advertising," *Political Communication* 16 (1999): 45–59.

114. Bachelard, *Poetics of Space*, xxxi.

CHAPTER SEVEN

1. W. W. Rostow to President Lyndon B. Johnson, Nationwide Hamlet Survey, 25 October 1967, folder 10, box 02, Veteran Members of the 109th Quartermaster Company (Aid Delivery) Collection, TVA.

2. JUSPAO Planning Staff, "Exploitation of Vietnamese Efforts and Successes," 2 June 1965, box 13, Douglas Pike Collection, Unit 03, TVA, 2.

3. Personal correspondence with Barry Zorthian, September 2007.

4. The Case for Psychological Warfare against North Vietnam, no date, folder 14, box 13, Douglas Pike Collection, Unit 03, TVA.

5. The Diary of a Returnee in Khien Phong Province, October 1967, folder 08, box 01, Gary Gillette Collection, TVA, 1.

6. Consolidation of JUSPAO Guidances 1 thru 22, vol. 1, 1 June 1967, folder 12, box 13, Douglas Pike Collection, Unit 03, TVA, 32. The piastra was worth approximately one dollar in 1967.

7. JUSPAO Planning Staff, "Exploitation of Vietnamese Efforts and Successes," JUSPAO Guidance 6, 2 June 1965, folder 14, box 13, Douglas Pike Collection, Unit 03, TVA, 2.

8. JUSPAO Field Memorandum Number 42, 13 December 1967, folder 14, box 13, Douglas Pike Collection, Unit 03, TVA, 1.

9. JUSPAO Planning Staff, "Exploitation of Vietnamese Efforts and Successes," JUSPAO Guidance 6, 2 July 1965, folder 12, box 13, Douglas Pike Collection, Unit 03, TVA, 1.

10. Analysis of VC Propaganda Activities, 1964, folder 13, box 16, Douglas Pike Collection, Unit 05, TVA, 4.

11. Vietnam Bulletin, 1 November 1969, folder 13, box 14, Douglas Pike Collection, Unit 02, TVA, 1.

12. Hunt, *Vietnam's Southern Revolution*, 15.

13. Ninh, *The Sorrow of War*; Hayslip, *When Heaven and Earth Changed Places*.

14. Propaganda Leaflet with translation, about NLF crimes, no date (1967?), folder 08, box 01, Gary Gillette Collection, TVA, 1.

15. Memorandum from Leonard Marks to LBJ, 19 October 1965, United States Information Agency, 1965, Confidential File, Agency Reports, box 135, LBJ Library; *Night of the Dragon*, 1964, directed by Richard Heffron, MP#103, LBJ Library.

16. "Film and US Foreign Policy: USIA Documentaries in the 1960s," presentation by Nicholas Cull at the 2006 Conference of the Society of Historians of American Foreign Relations, Lawrence, Kansas.

17. Memorandum for the President from Carl Rowan, Director of the USIA, 1 December 1964, United States Information Agency (1964–66), Confidential File, FG266–1-1, box 33, 3, LBJ Library.

18. U.S. Congress, House, Subcommittee on International Organizations and Movements of the Committee on Foreign Affairs, *Winning the Cold War*, 1st sess., 28–29 March and 2–3 April 1963. The Reed Research Foundation was founded by Stanley Reed in 1940. Reed employed American and European scientists in the years during and after World War II to develop technologies in bioengineering and was also active in politics and publishing and lecturing on world affairs to universities and governmental bodies throughout the 1960s.

19. "Psyops in Vietnam," 1 June 1967, folder 12, box 13, Douglas Pike Collection, Unit 03, TVA, 4.

20. Report by the Propaganda and Indoctrination Section, 13 March 1966, ibid., 13.

21. "From a Top Secret Directive on Enemy Espionage and Intelligence Activities," ibid., 11.

22. "From a Circular Issued by the Political Staff Department," ibid., 8.

23. Document 5 and Document 6, no month, 1966, ibid., 31.

24. Ibid., 32.

25. Security directive of the COSVN Current Affairs Committee, 11 January 1967, ibid., 16.

26. N. Mikhailov, "General'noe pis'mo," March 1956, GARF f. 6903, op. 1, d. 495, l. 20.

27. KPSS Otdel Propagandyi i Agitatsii, *Sovetskaia pechat' v dokumentakh*, 50.

28. C. Kaftanov, "O khode vypolneniia postanovlenii TsK KPSS," 29 October 1960, GARF f. 6903, op. 1, d. 624, l. 25–26.

29. Doklad Gosudarstvennogo Komiteta Soveta Ministrov SSSR po radioveshchaniiu i televideniiu, 1962, GARF f. 6903, op. 1, d. 774, l. 20.

30. GARF f. 6903, op. 1, d. 495, d. 624, d. 472, d. 774.

31. Radio Peredacha: "Zavtra mamin den' rozhdeniia," 16 January 1960, GARF f. 6903, op. 23, d. 433, l. 152.

32. Radio Sbornik: "Sto voprosov o Sovetskom Soiuze," 7 February 1961, GARF f. 6903, op. 23, d. 43, l. 12.

33. "Odno muzhestvo ili dva?" 27 May 1964, GARF f. 6903, op. 16, d. 354, l. 5.

34. Ibid.

35. V. Karpov, "Nasha Dela," 24 March 1959, GARF f. 6903, op. 24, d. 138, l. 58.

36. D. K. Khran, "V voskresnom obozrenie," 24 March 1961, GARF f. 6903, op. 24, d. 910, l. 29.

37. N. Osipov, "Reportazh: vsegda vmestse," 5 March 1966, GARF f. 6903, op. 24, d. 2495, l. 68.

38. Glavnaia redaktsiia propagandy: "Maiak," 22 June 1964, GARF f. 6903, op. 23, d. 171, l. 33.

39. S Talitskii, "Druzhba sovetskikh i vietnamskikh rebiat," 11 October 1964, GARF f. 6903, op. 24, d. 915, l. 46.

40. L. Kobolev, Peredacha: "Na uchebu vo Vietnam," 27 February 1966, 9 March 1966, GARF f. 6903, op. 24, d. 910, l. 23, 62.

41. E. Kaznina, "Dobro pozhalovat', poslantsy geroicheskoi molodezhi iuzhnogo Vietnama!" 11 April 1964, GARF f. 6904, op. 24, d. 2080, l. 19.

42. E. Alekseev, "Rasizm—pozor kapitalicheskoi Ameriki i Vietnama," GARF f. 6903, op. 23, d. 136, l. 14.

43. Ibid. It is interesting that four children, not six, died in the bombing of the Sixteenth Street Baptist Church.

44. "Stenogramma zasedaniia komissii po Azii i Afrike," GARF f. 9540, op. 1, d. 34, l. 13.

45. Bradley, *Imagining Vietnam and America*.

46. The majority of the Soviet foreign broadcasts that I examined came from the twenty-fourth and twenty-fifth *opisi* in the Gosteleradio fond (f. 6903) of the State Archive of the Russian Federation (GARF). These *opisi* contain transcripts of Soviet broadcasts to the far reaches of the world, grouped by countries. The sample of broadcasts that I examined ran from 1956 to 1968. I looked at every broadcast that was sent on twenty-four randomly chosen dates for each year. I also looked at every broadcast that was sent for one complete, randomly chosen month of each year.

47. H. Osipov, "Prokliatie ubiitsam!" 4 March 1966, GARF f. 6903, op. 24, d. 2245, l. 33.

48. Cecil, *Herbicidal Warfare*.

49. N. Volntsev, "Novye prestupleniia amerikanskikh zakhvatchikov v Iuzhnom Vetname," 1 January 1964, GARF f. 6903, op. 24, d. 2075, l. 25.

50. In 1964, words like "weak," "soft," and "impotent" start to show up as descriptors of American involvement in Vietnam. The war is now always called a "dirty war," because of both the use of dirty weapons and the violation of international rights agreements signed by the United Nations in 1960 guaranteeing self-determination to the postcolonial world.

51. T. Biriukova, "Svobodu narodu V'etnama," 24 March 1964, GARF f. 6903, op. 23, d. 227, l. 49.

52. I. Lashkov, untitled, 12 April 1965, GARF f. 6903, op. 24, d. 2245, l. 71.

53. "Ideological Operations and Foreign Policy," 27 April 1964, folder 03, box 13, Douglas Pike Collection, Unit 03, TVA, 6.

54. "The Soviet Union and the Vietnamese Conflict," 1 September 1967, folder 03, box 08, Glenn Helm Collection, TVA, 5; "Sino-Soviet Competition in Hanoi," 9 March 1966, folder 13, box 06, Douglas Pike Collection, Unit 06, TVA, 1.

55. "NLF Foreign Affairs And Propaganda Activities," 14 April 1967, folder 18, box 01, Douglas Pike Collection, Unit 06, TVA, 2.

56. T. Biriukova, "Svobodu narodu V'etnama," 24 March 1964, GARF f. 6903, op. 23, d. 227, l. 49.

57. "The Vietnamese Communist Agit-Prop," 1967, folder 12, box 16, Douglas Pike Collection, Unit 05, TVA, 1.

58. "NLF Foreign Affairs," 14 April 1967, folder 18, box 01, Douglas Pike Collection, Unit 06, TVA, 2.

59. "Diplomatic and Psychological Offensive," 2 February 1966, folder 06, box 06, Douglas Pike Collection, Unit 05, TVA, 1.

60. "Analysis of NLF Propaganda for October 1965," 11 November 1965, folder 06, box 13, Douglas Pike Collection, Unit 03, TVA, 1.

61. "Against U.S. 'Psychological Warfare,'" September 1965, folder 06, box 13, Douglas Pike Collection, Unit 03, TVA, 5.

62. Captured Documents, 23 September 1966, folder 1252, box 0029, TVA, 1.

63. "Youth Urged to Emulate Revolutionary Heroes," 15 October 1969, folder 09, box 17, Douglas Pike Collection, Unit 05, TVA, 8.

64. Ibid.

65. "Youth of the South Resolve to Be Heroic," 6 June 1969, folder 09, box 17, Douglas Pike Collection, Unit 05, TVA, 101.

66. Ibid., 100.

67. "Cadres, Party Members & Youths Are Determined to Live and Fight Like Our (Dead) Hero Nguyen Van Be," 1967, folder 03, box 17, Douglas Pike Collection, Unit 05, TVA, 1.

68. "Study of the example set out by Nguyen Van Be," 4 February 1967, folder 03, box 17, Douglas Pike Collection, Unit 05, TVA, 1.

69. "It Is Bound to Achieve the Greatest Results," 21 May 1967, folder 05, box 17, Douglas Pike Collection, Unit 05, TVA, 2–3.

70. Radio Hanoi, 30 May 1967, folder 04, box 17, Douglas Pike Collection, Unit 05, TVA, 1.

71. The story that the nephew tells of his father's visit to see his son is fascinating. He told JUSPAO that before leaving to see Be, the father had been told by

his cadre leader to report back to him in a frank manner on what he saw. When the father returned, the cadre leader was not there, so the father gave his frank report (that it was his son) to another officer. He returned the next day and gave the same report to the cadre leader, who summarily asked him, "Why do you insist on propagating such lies? Are you a spy?" The father was ordered to never again speak of his son and was then instructed to take his wife and leave his village.

72. From an interview with Nguyen Van Be, former platoon leader, political officer, and cousin of Nguyen Van Be, 30 May 1967, folder 04, box 17, Douglas Pike Collection, Unit 05—National Liberation Front, TVA.

73. Hoffer, "Nguyen Van Be as Propaganda Hero of the North and South Vietnamese Governments," 20.

74. Chandler, War of Ideas, 45.

75. "Captured 24 April 1967—Dinh Tuong Province, Subject: Counter Measures against the Enemy's Intent to Spread Distorted Propaganda about Nguyen Van Be," folder 03, box 17, Douglas Pike Collection, Unit 05—National Liberation Front, TVA.

76. The quantity of COSVN materials printed on Be is astonishing and includes, 265 records from the TVA alone.

77. DG 115, Series A, 3, box 2, International Correspondence, 1965, WSP.

CONCLUSION

1. Students for a Democratic Society, The Port Huron Statement, 1.

2. The aeronautic phrase is "   Kontakt!   Est' Kontakt!"

3. The Komsomol phrase is "Partiia skazala—'nada!' Komsomol otvetil—est'!"

4. Morgan, Monster, 81.

5. "Heavy Hint," As You Were 1, no. 7 (August 1969): 2.

6. See, for instance, Virginia Troelstrup, Letter to the Editor, Wall Street Journal, 6 January 1968, cited in Ally 1, no. 2 (April 1968): 2; and Andy Sapp, "Historical Facts about Vietnam," About Face, May 1969.

7. N. A. Mikhailov, "Zapiska predsedatelia komiteta po pechati pri SM SSSR N. A. Mikhailova v TsK KPSS o polozhenii v Chekhoslovakii," 29 April 1968, RGANI f. 5, op. 60, d. 319, l. 43.

8. "Zapis' besedy v Moskve rykovoditelei KPSS, BKP, VSRP, SEPG i PORP o situatsii v Chekhoslovakii," 8 May 1968, RGANI f. 10, op. 1, d. 235, l. 1–72.

9. "Stenogramma soveshchaniia v Varshave rukovoditelei TsK BKP, TsK VSRP, TsK KNSS, TsK PORP I TsK SEPG," 14–15 June 1968, RGANI f. 10, op. 1, d. 236, l. 1–119; "Deklaratsiia Prezidiuma TsK KPCh i pravitel'stva Chekho-slovakskoi Sotsialisticheskoi Respubliki," 17 August 1968, RGANI f. 89, op. 76, d. 77, l. 3.

10. "Informatsiia nachal'nika militsii g. Kieva TsK KPU o besede s general'nym konsulom ChSSR v Kieve po povodu sobytii v Chekhoslovakii," 20 September 1968, TsDAGO (Ukraine), f. 1, op. 25, d. 27, l. 16; cited in Tomilina, Karner, and Chubar-ian, Prazhskaia vesna i mezhdunarodnyi krizis 1968 goda, 343.

11. "Zapiska predsedatelia KGB Iu. V. Andropova v TsK KPSS o podgotovlennoi po pros'be 'nemetzkikh i polskikh druzei' informatsii o deiatel'nosti kontrrevoliutsionnogo podpol'ia v ChSSR," 13 October 1968, RGANI f. 89, op. 61, d. 5, l. 2–60.

12. Corber, *In the Name of National Security*, 3.

13. Kate Brown, *Plutopia*, 336.

14. Bourdieu, *Field of Cultural Production*, 101.

Bibliography

ARCHIVAL SOURCES

Soviet Union

Russian State Archive of Contemporary History (Rossiiskii Gosudarstvennyi Arkhiv
     Noveyshei Istorii [RGANI]), Moscow
Russian State Archive of Literature and Art (Rossiiskii Gosudarstvennyi Arkhiv
     Literatury i Iskusstva [RGALI]), Moscow
  Soviet Filmmakers' Union, Fond 2453
Russian State Archive of Socio-Political History (Rossiiskii Gosudarstvennyi Arkhiv
     Sotsial'no-Politicheskoi Istorii [RGASPI]), Moscow
  Central Committee of the Komsomol (VLKSM) (1918 91), Fond m1
  Central Committee of the All-Soviet Pioneer Organization Named after V. I.
     Lenin, Fond m2
  Committee of Youth Organizations (KMO) SSSR (1956–91), Fond m3
  Anti-fascist Committee of Soviet Youth (AKSM) (1941–56), Fond m4
  All-Russian and All-Soviet Conferences of the Komsomol (1942–53), Fond m6
  All-Soviet Pioneer Camp "Artek" Named after V. I. Lenin, Fond m8
Russian State Library
  Department of Newspapers (OG), Khimki
State Archive of the Russian Federation (Gosudarstvennyi Arkhiv Rossiiskoi
     Federatsii [GARF]), Moscow
  Gosteleradio, Fond 6903
  Soviet Committee for the Defense of Peace, Fond 9539
  Volunteer Society for Cooperation with the Army, Aviation, and Fleet
     (Dobrovol'noe Obshchestvo Sodeistviia Armii, Aviatsii, i Flotu [DOSAAF]),
     Fond 9552

United States

Boy Scouts of America Archive, Irving, Texas
Dwight D. Eisenhower Presidential Library, Abilene, Kansas
Girl Scouts of America Archive, New York, New York
J. Edgar Hoover Archive, Stanford University, Stanford, California
John F. Kennedy Presidential Library, Boston, Massachusetts
Lucille Cardin Crain Papers, University of Oregon Libraries, Eugene
Lyndon Baines Johnson Presidential Library, Austin, Texas
Office of Civil Defense, Department of Defense, Washington, D.C.
Swarthmore College Peace Collection, Swarthmore, Pennsylvania

Papers of the Committee for a SANE Nuclear Policy
Papers of Women Strike for Peace
Vietnam Archive, Texas Tech University, Lubbok, Texas
Douglas Pike Collection

NEWSPAPERS, MAGAZINES, AND JOURNALS

Soviet Union

Iskusstvo kino	*Ogonek*
Izvestiia	*Pionerskaia pravda*
Komsomol'skaia pravda	*Pravda*
Krokodil	*Sovetskaia pedagogika*
Molodaia gvardiia	*Trud*
Novyi mir	

United States

Ally	*New York Times*
Boy's Life	*Observer*
Christian Science Monitor	*Our Sunday Visitor*
Film Quarterly	*Reader's Digest*
Junior Scholastic	*Saturday Evening Post*
Liberty	*Scout Executive*
Life	*Scouting*
Look	*Southern Speech Communication Journal*
Los Angeles Times	*Time*
New Journal and Guide	*Treasure Chest*
New Republic	*Wall Street Journal*
Newsweek	*Washington Evening Star*

SECONDARY SOURCES

Adorno, Theodor W., and J. M. Bernstein. *The Culture Industry: Selected Essays on Mass Culture.* London: Routledge, 1991.

Afiani, V., and Z. Vodopianova, eds. Apparat TsK KPSS i kultura 1953–1957, Dokumenty (seriia kultura i vlast ot Stalina do Gorbacheva). Moscow: ROSSPEN, 2001.

Akhmadulina, Bella. *Fever & Other New Poems.* Translated by Geoffrey Dutton. New York: W. Morrow, 1969.

Aksiutin, I. *Khrushchevskaia "ottepel'" i obshchestvennye nastroeniia v SSSR v 1953–1964 gg.* Moscow: ROSSPEN, 2004.

Alcock, N. *The War Disease.* Oakville, Ontario: CPRI Press, 1972.

Alexander, Victoria. "The Image of Children in Magazine Advertisements from 1905 to 1990." *Communication Research* 21 (1994): 742–65.

Alexeiev, Nina. "I Don't Want My Children to Grow Up in Soviet Russia." *Liberty*, 7 June 1947, 18–23.

Anderson, Eugenie. "The Threat of Aggressive Communism." *Congressional Record*, 83rd Cong., 2nd sess., 1954, A2861.

Anderson, Robin. *A Century of Media, a Century of War.* New York: Peter Lang, 2006.

Andrew, Christopher. *The World Was Going Our Way: The KGB and the Battle for the Third World.* New York: Basic Books, 2005.

Appy, Christian, ed. *Cold War Constructions: The Political Culture of United States Imperialism, 1945–1966.* Amherst: University of Massachusetts Press, 2000.

Ariès, Philippe. *Centuries of Childhood: A Social History of Family Life.* Translated by Robert Baldick. New York: Vintage, 1962.

Attwood, William. "A New Look at Americans." *Look*, 12 July 1955, 47–51.

Atwell, Lee. *Film Quarterly* 18, no. 1 (Autumn 1964): 50.

Austin, Joe. "Introduction: Angels of History, Demons of Culture." In *Generations of Youth: Youth Cultures and History in Twentieth-Century America*, edited by Joe Austin and Michael Nevin Willard, 1–20. New York: New York University Press, 1998.

Bachelard, Gaston. *The Poetics of Space.* Translated by Maria Jolas. Boston: Beacon, 1994.

Baden-Powell, Lord. "The Father I Knew." *Boy's Life*, February 1961, 47.

Bakshtein, Joseph. "A View from Moscow." In *Nonconformist Art: The Soviet Experience, 1956–1986*, edited by Alla Rosenfeld and Norton T. Dodge, 332–37. London: Thames and Hudson, 1995.

Balina, Marina, and E. A. Dobrenko, eds. *Petrified Utopia: Happiness Soviet Style.* Anthem Series on Russian, East European, and Eurasian Studies. New York: Anthem Press, 2009.

Ball, Alan M. *And Now My Soul Is Hardened: Abandoned Children in Soviet Russia, 1918–1930.* Berkeley: University of California Press, 1994.

Baranowski, Shelley, and Ellen Furlough, eds. *Being Elsewhere: Tourism, Consumer Culture, and Identity in Modern Europe and North America.* Ann Arbor: University of Michigan Press, 2001.

Barclay, Dorothy. "Group Plans to Study the Effects of Defense Activities on Children." *New York Times*, 7 March 1952, 16.

Barghoorn, Frederick Charles. *Soviet Foreign Propaganda.* Princeton, N.J.: Princeton University Press, 1964.

Barson, Michael. *Red Scared! The Commie Menace in Propaganda and Popular Culture.* San Francisco: Chronicle Books, 2001.

Barthes, Roland. *Camera Lucida: Reflections on Photography.* New York: Noonday, 1981.

———. *Mythologies.* New York: Hill and Wang, 1995.

Beaty, Bart. *Fredric Wertham and the Critique of Mass Culture.* Oxford: University Press of Mississippi, 2005.

Beer, Francis. "The Epidemiology of Peace and War." *International Studies Quarterly* 23 (1979): 45–86.

Belova, L. I., and M. Romm. *Besedy o kino.* Moscow: Izd-vo Polit. Lit-ry, 1964.

Bentley, Eric. *Thirty Years of Treason: Excerpts from Hearings before the House Committee on Un-American Activities, 1938–1968.* New York: Thunder's Mouth Press, 2002.

Benton, William. "A Personal Report: The Teachers and the Taught in the U.S.S.R." *Congressional Record,* 89th Cong., 2nd sess., 1965, A2423.

Bereday, George, William Brickman, and Gerald Read, eds. *The Changing Soviet School.* Cambridge, Mass.: Riverside Press, 1960.

Berrol, Selma. *Growing Up American: Immigrant Children in America Then and Now.* Twayne History of American Childhood, edited by Joseph Hawes and N. Ray Hiner. New York: Twayne Publishers, 1995.

Biriukova, B. "Nasha kukhnia." *Izvestiia,* July 1959, 23–25.

Biskind, Peter. *Seeing Is Believing: How Hollywood Taught Us to Stop Worrying and Love the Fifties.* New York: Henry Holt, 1983.

Bourdieu, Pierre. *The Field of Cultural Production: Essays on Art and Literature.* European Perspectives. New York: Columbia University Press, 1993.

Boyer, Paul. *By the Bomb's Early Light: American Thought and Culture at the Dawn of the Atomic Age.* New York: Random House, 1985.

Boym, Svetlana. *Common Places: Mythologies of Everyday Life in Russia.* Cambridge, Mass.: Harvard University Press, 1994.

Bradley, Mark. *Imagining Vietnam and America: The Making of Postcolonial Vietnam, 1919–1950.* Chapel Hill: University of North Carolina Press, 2000.

Braukman, Stacy. "Nothing Else Matters but Sex: Cold War Narratives of Deviance and the Search for Lesbian Teachers in Florida, 1959–1963." *Feminist Studies* 27, no. 3 (Autumn 2001): 553–75.

Brennan, Terry. "Civil Defense and You." *Boy's Life,* September 1956, 10.

Bronfenbrenner, Urie. *Two Worlds of Childhood: U.S. and U.S.S.R.* New York: Simon and Schuster, 1972.

Brooks, Jeffrey. *Thank You, Comrade Stalin! Soviet Public Culture from Revolution to Cold War.* Princeton, N.J.: Princeton University Press, 2000.

———. *When Russia Learned to Read: Literacy and Popular Literature, 1861–1917.* Studies in Russian Literature and Theory. Evanston, Ill.: Northwestern University Press, 2003.

Brown, Constantine. "Communist Subversion of Youth." *Congressional Record,* 87th Cong., 1st sess., 1961, 76.

Brown, JoAnne. "'A Is for Atom, B Is for Bomb': Civil Defense in American Public Education." *Journal of American History* 1 (June 1988): 68–90.

Brown, Kate. *Plutopia: Nuclear Families, Atomic Cities, and the Great Soviet and American Plutonium Disasters.* Oxford: Oxford University Press, 2013.

Buchli, Victor. *An Archaeology of Socialism.* Oxford: Berg, 1999.

———. "Khrushchev, Modernism, and the Fight against *Petit Bourgeois* Consciousness in the Soviet Home." *Journal of Design History* 10, no. 2 (1997): 92–109.

Burlatsky, Fedor. *Khrushchev and the First Russian Spring: The Era of Khrushchev through the Eyes of His Advisor.* New York: Scribner's, 1991.

Calvert, Karin. *Children in the House: The Material Culture of Early Childhood, 1600–1900.* Boston: Northeastern University Press, 1992.

Carleton, Don. *Red Scare!* Austin: Texas Monthly Press, 1985.

Carruthers, Susan. Review of *American Cold War Culture.* *Modernism/Modernity* 13, no. 1 (2006): 956–57.

Castillo, Greg. *Cold War on the Home Front: The Soft Power of Midcentury Design.* Minneapolis: University of Minnesota Press, 2010.

Caute, David. *The Great Fear.* New York: Simon and Schuster, 1978.

Cecil, Paul Frederick. *Herbicidal Warfare: The Ranch Hand Project in Vietnam.* New York: Praeger, 1986.

Chamberlin, William Henry. "Good Ideas Don't Go Wrong." *Wall Street Journal,* 5 December 1950, 8–9.

Chandler, Robert. *War of Ideas: The U.S. Propaganda Campaign in Vietnam.* Boulder, Colo.: Westview, 1981.

Chernenko, Miron. *Marlen Khutsiev: tvorcheskii portret.* Moscow: SK SSSR/ Vsesoiuznoe biuro propagandy kinoiskusstva, 1988.

Chomsky, Noam. *Necessary Illusions: Thought Control in Democratic Societies.* Boston: South End Press, 1989.

Christie, Ian. 'Unauthorized Persons Enter Here.' *Monthly Film Bulletin.* London. BFI, July 1987, 200.

Clement, Priscilla Ferguson. *Growing Pains: Children in the Industrial Age, 1850– 1890.* New York: Twayne Publishers, 1997.

Cohen, Lizabeth. *A Consumers' Republic: The Politics of Mass Consumption in Postwar America.* New York: Knopf, 2003.

Cohen, Louis Harris. *The Cultural-Political Traditions and Developments of the Soviet Cinema, 1917–1972.* Arno Press Cinema Program. New York: Arno Press, 1974.

Communist Party of the Soviet Union. *Programme of the Communist Party of the Soviet Union Adopted by the 22nd Congress of the C.P.S.U., October 31, 1961.* Moscow: Foreign Languages Publishing House, 1961.

Conniff, Frank. "Red Army Using Korean Children to Spy on UN Forces." *New Journal and Guide,* 10 February 1951, 7.

Corber, Robert. *In the Name of National Security: Hitchcock, Homophobia, and the Political Construction of Gender in Postwar America.* Durham: Duke University Press, 1993.

Counts, George S. *The Challenge of Soviet Education.* Westport, Conn.: Greenwood Press, 1975.

Cousins, Norman. "The Debate Is Over." *Sunday Review,* 4 April 1959, 26.

Craig, Campbell, and Fredrik Logevall. *America's Cold War: The Politics of Insecurity.* Cambridge, Mass.: Belknap Press of Harvard University Press, 2009.

Creuziger, Clementine G. K. *Childhood in Russia: Representation and Reality.* Lanham, Md.: University Press of America, 1996.

Crowley, David, ed. *Socialist Spaces: Sites of Everyday Life in the Eastern Bloc.* Oxford: Berg Publishers, 2002.

Cull, Nicholas. *Propaganda and Mass Persuasion: A Historical Encyclopedia, 1500 to the Present.* Santa Barbara, Calif.: ABC-CLIO, 2003.

———. *Selling War: The British Propaganda Campaign against American "Neutrality" in World War II.* New York: Oxford University Press, 1995.

Dean, Robert. *Imperial Brotherhood.* Amherst: University of Massachusetts Press, 2001.

Degen, Marie Louise. *History of the Women's Peace Party.* New York: Garland, 1916.

D'Emilio, John. *Sexual Politics, Sexual Communities: The Making of a Homosexual Minority in the United States, 1940–1970.* 2nd ed. Chicago: University of Chicago Press, 1998.

Derthick, Lawrence. "The Frightening Challenge of Russia's Schools." *Look,* 14 October 1958, 5–10.

Divine, Robert. *The Sputnik Challenge.* New York: Oxford University Press, 1993.

Dudziak, Mary. "Brown as a Cold War Case." *Journal of American History* 91, no. 1 (June 2004): 32–42.

———. *Cold War Civil Rights: Race and the Image of American Democracy.* Princeton, N.J.: Princeton University Press, 2000.

Dumančić, Marko. "Rescripting Stalinist Masculinity: Contesting the Male Ideal in Soviet Film and Society, 1953–1968." Ph.D. diss., University of North Carolina at Chapel Hill, 2010.

Ebon, Martin. *The Soviet Propaganda Machine.* New York: McGraw-Hill, 1987.

Edmonds, Eric. "Child Labor." In *Handbook of Development of Economics,* edited by T. P. Schultz and J. Strauss, 3607–9. Amsterdam: Elsevier Science, 2007.

Egorova, N. I., ed. *Kholodnaia voina i politika razriadki:Diskussionnye problemy.* vols. 1–2. Moscow: Rossiiskaia Akademiia Nauk, 2003.

Elshtain, J. B. *Women and War.* New York: Basic Books, 1987.

Engelhardt, Tom. *The End of Victory Culture: Cold War America and the Disillusioning of a Generation.* New York: Basic Books, 1995.

Erikson, Erik H. *Childhood and Society.* New York: Norton, 1993.

Ewing, E. Thomas. *Separate Schools: Gender, Policy, and Practice in Postwar Soviet Education.* DeKalb: Northern Illinois University Press, 2010.

Eyerman, J. R. "Rocket Town." *Life,* 16 February 1948, 110.

Fass, Paula S., and Michael Grossberg, eds. *Reinventing Childhood after World War II.* Philadelphia: University of Pennsylvania Press, 2012.

Fass, Paula S., and Mary Ann Mason, eds. *Childhood in America.* New York: New York University Press, 2000.

Fediaevskaia, Vera, and Patty Smith Hill. *Nursery School and Parent Education in Soviet Russia.* New York: E. P. Dutton, 1936.

Field, Deborah. "Mothers and Fathers and the Problem of Selfishness in the Khrushchev Era." In *Women in the Khrushchev Era,* edited by Melanie Ilic, Susan Reid, and Lynne Attwood, 96–113. New York: Palgrave, 2004.

Filtzer, Donald. *Soviet Workers and Late Stalinism: Labour and the Restoration of the Stalinist System after World War II.* Cambridge: Cambridge University Press, 2007.

Fitzpatrick, Sheila. *Education and Social Mobility in the Soviet Union, 1921–1934.* Cambridge: Cambridge University Press, 1979.

Flood, Daniel. "Joint Resolution to Provide for a Commission on Communism." *Congressional Record,* 84th Cong., 2nd sess., 1955, 1008.

Foertsch, Jacqueline. "A Battle of Silence: Women's Magazines and the Polio Crisis in Post-War UK and USA." In *American Cold War Culture*, edited by Douglas Field, 17–33. Edinburgh, Scotland: Edinburgh University Press, 2005.

Fomin, Valeri, ed. *Kinematograf Ottepeli: Dokumenty i svidetel'stva*. Moscow: Materik, 1998.

Foster, Stuart. *Red Alert! Educators Confront the Red Scare in American Public Schools*. New York: P. Lang, 2000.

Foucault, Michel. "Ceci n'est pas une pipe." *October* 1 (Spring 1976): 7–21.

Friedan, Betty. *The Feminine Mystique*. New York: Norton, 1963.

Friedberg, Aaron L. *In the Shadow of the Garrison State: America's Anti-Statism and Its Cold War Grand Strategy*. Princeton Studies in International History and Politics. Princeton, N.J.: Princeton University Press, 2000.

Fursenko, A. A., ed. *Prezidium TsK KPSS, 1954–1964*. vol. 1. Moscow: ROSSPEN, 2004.

Fursenko, A. A., and Timothy J. Naftali. *Khrushchev's Cold War: The Inside Story of an American Adversary*. 1st ed. New York: Norton, 2006.

Fürst, Juliane. "Friends in Private, Friends in Public: The Phenomenon of the Kompaniia among Soviet Youth in the 1950s and 1960s." In *Borders of Socialism: Private Spheres of Soviet Russia*, edited by Lewis Siegelbaum, 229–49. New York: Palgrave Macmillan, 2006.

Gaddis, John Lewis. *We Now Know: Rethinking Cold War History*. Oxford: Oxford University Press, 1997.

Galumov, E. A. *Mezhdunarodnyi imidzh rossii. strategiia formirovaniia*. Moscow. Izd-vo Izvestiia, 2003.

Geist, Edward. "Scenarios for Survival: Representations of Nuclear War in American and Soviet Civil Defense Manuals, 1954–1972." Master's thesis, University of North Carolina, 2008.

Gerasimov, S. "Poddel'noe i podlinnoe." *Iskusstvo kino* 5 (1960): 19.

———. "Razmyshleniia o molodykh." *Iskusstvo kino* 2 (1960): 22.

Gilbert, James. *A Cycle of Outrage: America's Reaction to the Juvenile Delinquent in the 1950s*. Oxford: Oxford University Press, 1986.

Ginzberg, Eli. *The Nation's Children*. New York: Columbia University Press, 1960.

———. *Values and Ideals of American Youth*. New York: Columbia University Press, 1961.

Gleijeses, Piero. *Conflicting Missions: Havana, Washington, and Africa, 1959–1976*. Chapel Hill: University of North Carolina Press, 2002.

Glickman, Lawrence B. *Consumer Society in American History: A Reader*. Ithaca, N.Y.: Cornell University Press, 1999.

Goldman, Wendy Z. *Women at the Gates: Gender and Industry in Stalin's Russia*. Cambridge: Cambridge University Press, 2002.

Goodwin, Doris Kearns. *Wait Till Next Year: A Memoir*. New York: Simon and Schuster, 1997.

Gorer, Geoffrey. *The American People: A Study in National Character*. New York: Norton, 1948.

Gorky, Maxim. *Childhood*. London: Oxford University Press, 1961.

Gorsuch, Anne. "'There's No Place Like Home': Soviet Tourism in Late Stalinism." *Slavic Review* 62, no. 4 (Winter 2003): 760–85.

Graebner, Norman. "Myth and Reality: America's Rhetorical Cold War." In *Critical Reflections on the Cold War,* edited by Martin Medhurst and H. W. Brands, 20–37. College Station: Texas A&M University, 2000.

Grant, Julia. *Raising Baby by the Book: The Education of American Mothers.* New Haven, Conn.: Yale University Press, 1998.

———. "A Real Boy and Not a Sissy: Gender, Childhood, and Masculinity, 1890–1940." *Journal of Social History* 37, no. 4 (2004): 829–51.

Gray, J. Spencer. "Have Our Children Forgotten or Did They Ever Learn?" *Herald of Winchester,* 5 May 1960, 5–8.

Hall, Jane. "Bill Moyers Holds a Mirror Up to America." *Los Angeles Times,* 12 November 1989, 4.

Hans, Nicholas A. *The Russian Tradition in Education.* Westport, Conn.: Greenwood Press, 1973.

Harasymiw, Bohdan. *Education and the Mass Media in the Soviet Union and Eastern Europe.* New York: Praeger, 1976.

Haraway, Donna. *The Haraway Reader.* New York: Routledge, 2004.

Harris, Adrienne, and Ynestra King, eds. *Rocking the Ship of State: Toward a Feminist Peace Politics.* Boulder, Colo.: Westview, 1989.

Harris, Frederick Brown. "The Truce of the Bear." *Congressional Record,* 83rd Cong., 2nd sess., 1954, 2390.

Hartman, Andrew. *Education and the Cold War: The Battle for the American School.* New York: Palgrave Macmillan, 2008.

Hawes, Joseph M. *Children between the Wars: American Childhood, 1920–1940.* New York: Twayne Publishers, 1997.

Hayden, Tom. *Reunion: A Memoir.* 1st ed. New York: Random House, 1988.

Hayslip, Le Ly. *When Heaven and Earth Changed Places.* New York: Plume, 1993.

Heath, Shelby, Anne Wolf, and Shirley Brice. "Living in a World of Words." In *The Children's Culture Reader,* edited by Henry Jenkins, 406–30. New York: New York University Press, 1998.

Hellbeck, Jochen. "Galaxy of Black Stars: The Power of Soviet Biography." *American Historical Review* 114, no. 3 (2009): 615–24.

Henriksen, Margot. *Dr. Strangelove's America.* Berkeley: University of California Press, 1997.

Herman, Edward S., and Noam Chomsky. *Manufacturing Consent: The Political Economy of the Mass Media.* New York: Pantheon, 2002.

Hershey, Major General Lewis B. "My Country." *Boy's Life,* July 1956, 7–8.

Hessler, Julie. *A Social History of Soviet Trade: Trade Policy, Retail Practices, and Consumption, 1917–1953.* Princeton, N.J.: Princeton University Press, 2004.

Higonnet, Anne. *Pictures of Innocence: The History and Crisis of Ideal Childhood.* New York: Thames and Hudson, 1998.

Hine, Thomas. *Populuxe.* 1st ed. New York: Knopf, 1986.

Hixson, Walter L. *Parting the Curtain: Propaganda, Culture, and the Cold War, 1945–1961.* Houndmills, UK: Macmillan, 1997.

Hoffer, Thomas William. "Nguyen Van Be as Propaganda Hero of the North and South Vietnamese Governments." *Southern Speech Communication Journal* 40 (1974): 20–31.

Hogan, Michael J. *A Cross of Iron: Harry S. Truman and the Origins of the National Security State, 1945–1954.* Cambridge: Cambridge University Press, 1998.

Holl, Jack M. *Juvenile Reform in the Progressive Era: William R. George and the Junior Republic Movement.* Ithaca, N.Y.: Cornell University Press, 1971.

Holland, Barbara. *When All the World Was Young: A Memoir.* New York: Bloomsbury, 2005.

Hoover, J. Edgar. *Masters of Deceit: The Story of Communism in America and How to Fight It.* New York: Holt, 1958.

———. "Who Is to Blame for Juvenile Delinquency?" *Congressional Record,* 83rd Cong., 2nd sess., 1954, A1127.

———. "Youth Communist Target." *Our Sunday Visitor,* 18 January 1959, 1–7.

Howe, Julia Ward. *Reminiscences, 1819–1899.* Boston: Houghton Mifflin, 1899.

Hunt, David. *Vietnam's Southern Revolution: From Peasant Insurrection to Total War.* Amherst: University of Massachusetts Press, 2009.

Humphrey, Hubert. "Hearings before a Subcommittee on Labor of the Committee on Labor and Public Welfare on Communist Domination of Unions and National Security." *Congressional Record,* 82nd Cong., 1st sess., 1952, 75.

———. "The Soviet Education Challenge." *Congressional Record,* 86th Cong., 2nd sess., 1960, 18020.

Ilic, Melanie, Susan Reid, and Lynne Attwood, eds. *Women in the Khrushchev Era.* New York: Palgrave Macmillan, 2004.

Institut Marksizma-Leninizma pri TsK KPSS. *KPSS v rezoliutsiiakh i resheniiakh s" ezdov, konferentsii i plenumov TsK: 1898–1971,* vols. 6–7. Moscow: Izd-vo Polit. Lit-ry, 1954, 1959.

International Conference on Education No. 18. *Public Education in the Soviet Union: Report for 1954–1955.* Geneva: International Bureau of Education, 1955.

Iverson, Robert. *The Communists and the Schools.* New York: Harcourt, 1959.

Jacobson, Lisa. *Raising Consumers: Children and the American Mass Market in the Early Twentieth Century (Popular Cultures, Everyday Lives).* New York: Columbia University Press, 2004.

James, Allison, Chris Jenks, and Alan Prout. *Theorizing Childhood.* Cambridge, UK: Polity Press, 1998.

Javits, Jacob. "Disgracing America." *New York Times,* 3 September 1963, 32.

Javits, Jacob, and Harry Gideonse. "Ideals and Goals of Citizenship Education." *Congressional Record,* 83rd Cong., 2nd sess., 1954, A2478.

Johnson, Priscilla. *Khrushchev and the Arts: The Politics of Soviet Culture, 1962–1964.* Cambridge, Mass.: MIT Press, 1965.

Johnson and Johnson Corporation. "Mommy Always Says You're Safe When You Use Johnson and Johnson." *Life,* 21 March 1949, 63.

Kaganovsky, Lilya. "How the Soviet Man Was (Un)Made." *Slavic Review* 63, no. 3 (Fall 2004): 577–96.

———. *How the Soviet Man Was Unmade: Cultural Fantasy and Male Subjectivity under Stalin*. Pittsburgh, Pa.: University of Pittsburgh Press, 2008.

Kagarlitsky, Boris. *The Thinking Reed: Intellectuals and the Soviet State, 1917 to the Present*. Rev. ed. London: Verso, 1989.

Kahn, Albert. *The Game of Death: Effects of the Cold War on Our Children*. New York: Cameron and Kahn, 1953.

Karpinskii, L. "Prazdnik molodosti." *Iskusstvo kino* 5 (1958): 1.

Kaslow, Florence. "Evolution of Theory and Policy on Inner City Delinquency." *Growth & Change* 4, no. 4 (October 1973): 29–37.

Katz, Milton. *Ban the Bomb*. New York: Praeger, 1986.

Kefauver, Estes. "The Menace of Comic Books." *Congressional Record*, 83rd Cong., 2nd sess., 1954, A3999.

Kelly, Catriona. *Children's World: Growing Up in Russia, 1890–1991*. New Haven, Conn.: Yale University Press, 2007.

———. "Defending Children's Rights, in Defense of Peace: Children and Soviet Cultural Diplomacy." *Kritika: Explorations in Russian and Eurasian History* 9, no. 4 (Fall 2008): 711–46.

———. "A Joyful Soviet Childhood: Licensed Happiness for Little Ones." In *Petrified Utopia: Happiness Soviet Style*, edited by Marina Balina and Evgeny Dobrenko, 3–18. London: Anthem Press, 2009.

Kharkhodin, Oleg. *The Collective and the Individual in Russia*. Berkeley: University of California Press, 1999.

———. "Reveal and Dissimulate: A Genealogy of Private Life in Soviet Russia." In *Public and Private in Thought and Practice: Perspectives on a Grand Dichotomy*, edited by Jeff Weintraub and Krishan Kumar, 333–63. Chicago: University of Chicago Press, 1997.

Khrushchev, N. S. *The Great Mission of Literature and Art*. Moscow: Progress Publishers, 1964.

———. "Vysokaia ideinost' i khudozhestvennoe masterstvo—velikaia sila sovetskoi literatury i iskusstva." *Pravda* 69 (10 March 1963): 4.

Khutsiev, Marlen. "Ia nikogda ne delal polemichnykh fil'mov." In *Kinematograf Ottepeli*, edited by V. Troianovskii et al., 190–96. Moscow: Materik, 1996.

Kincaid, James R. *Child-Loving: The Erotic Child and Victorian Culture*. New York: Routledge, 1994.

Kirschenbaum, Lisa A. *Small Comrades: Revolutionizing Childhood in Soviet Russia, 1917–1932*. New York: RoutledgeFalmer, 2000.

Kline, George. *Soviet Education*. London: Routledge and Kegan Paul, 1957.

Kline, Stephen. *Out of the Garden: Toys, TV, and Children's Culture in the Age of Marketing*. London: Verso, 1993.

Korolev, F. *Razvitie osnovnykh idei sovetskoi pedagogiki*. Moscow: Znanie, 1968.

Kovaleva, L. *Otsy i deti, seriia 11*. Moscow: Znanie, 1963.

Koven, Seth. *Mothers of a New World: Maternalist Politics and the Origins of Welfare States*. New York: Routledge, 1993.

Kozlov, V. *Mass Uprisings in the USSR: Protest and Rebellion in the Post-Stalin Years*. Translated by Elaine McClarnand MacKinnon. Armonk, N.Y.: M. E. Sharpe, 2002.

Kozlov, V., and S. Mironenko, eds. Kramola: Inakomyslie v SSSR pri Khrushcheve i Brezhneve, 1953–1982 gg.: rassekrechennye dokumenty verkhovnogo suda i prokuratury SSSR. Moscow: Materik, 2005.

KPSS [Communist Party of the Soviet Union] Otdel Propagandy i Agitatsii, TsK. Sovetskaia pechat' v dokumentakh: sbornik podgotovlen otdelom propagandy i agitatsii TsK KPSS po soiuznym respublikam. Moscow: Izd-vo Polit. Lit-ry, 1961.

Krupskaia, Nadezhda Konstantinovna. On Education: Selected Articles and Speeches. Moscow: Foreign Languages Publishing House, 1957.

———. Pedagogicheskie sochineniia. Moscow: Pedagogika, 1957.

———. Voprosy kommunisticheskogo vospitaniia molodezhi. Moscow: Pedagogika, 1966.

Kucherenko, Olga. Little Soldiers: How Soviet Children Went to War, 1941–1945. New York: Oxford University Press, 2011.

Kunzle, David. The History of the Comic Strip: The Nineteenth Century. Berkeley: University of California Press, 1990.

Kwon, Heonik. The Other Cold War. Columbia Studies in International and Global History. New York: Columbia University Press, 2010.

Lacy, Mark. "War, Cinema, and Moral Anxiety." Alternatives: Global, Local, Political 28, no. 5, (2003): 611–36.

Ladd, William. On the Duty of Females to Promote the Cause of Peace. Boston: American Peace Society, 1836.

LaFeber, Walter. America, Russia, and the Cold War, 1945–2006. 10th ed. Boston: McGraw-Hill, 2008.

Lakoff, G. "Metaphor and War: The Metaphor System Used to Justify War in the Gulf." Peace Research 23 (1991): 25–32.

LaPierre, Brian. Hooligans in Khrushchev's Russia: Defining, Policing, and Producing Deviance during the Thaw. Madison: University of Wisconsin Press, 2012.

———. "Making Hooliganism on a Mass-Scale: The Campaign against Petty Hooliganism in the Soviet Union, 1956–1964." Cahiers du Monde Russe 47, nos. 1–2 (2006): 349–75.

———. "Private Matters or Public Crimes: The Emergence of Domestic Hooliganism in the Soviet Union, 1939–1966." In Borders of Socialism: Private Spheres of Soviet Russia, edited by Lewis Siegelbaum, 191–210. New York: Palgrave Macmillan, 2006.

Lapp, Ralph. "Fallout—Another Dimension in Atomic Power." New Republic, 14 February 1954, 31.

Latham, Michael. Modernization as Ideology: American Social Science and "Nation Building" in the Kennedy Era. Chapel Hill: University of North Carolina Press, 2000.

Laville, Helen. "'Positive Peace': American Women's Response to the 'Peace Offensive.'" In Cold War Women: The International Activities of American Women's Organizations, edited by Helen Laville, 124–43. Manchester: Manchester University Press, 2002.

Lebedeva, Iu. "Kak zashchishchat'sia ot oruzhiia massovogo porazheniia." Moscow: DOSAAF, 1962.

Ledkovska, Marina. *Russia According to Women: Literary Anthology.* Tenafly, N.J.: Hermitage, 1991.

Leffler, Melvyn P. *For the Soul of Mankind: The United States, the Soviet Union, and the Cold War.* 1st ed. New York: Hill and Wang, 2007.

Lenin, Vladimir Il'ich. *State and Revolution.* New York: International Publishers, 1932.

———. *The Tasks of the Youth Leagues.* 4th rev. ed. Moscow: Progress, 1968.

Levander, Caroline Field, and Carol J. Singley, eds. *The American Child: A Cultural Studies Reader.* New Brunswick, N.J.: Rutgers University Press, 2003.

Lewis, Carolyn Herbst. *Prescription for Heterosexuality: Sexual Citizenship in the Cold War Era.* Chapel Hill: University of North Carolina Press, 2010.

Liebowitz, Samuel. "Judge Liebowitz on Juvenile Delinquency." *This Week,* 15 December 1957, 56–58.

Linden-Ward, Blanche, and Carol Hurd Green. *American Women in the 1960s: Changing the Future.* New York: Twayne Publishers, 1993.

Lipsitz, George. "The Meaning of Memory: Family, Class, and Ethnicity in Early Network Television Programs." *Cultural Anthropology* 1, no. 4 (November 1986): 355–87.

Litchfield, Edward H. "Text of Preliminary Report on Higher Education in the Soviet Union." *Congressional Record,* 85th Cong., 2nd sess., 1958, 13912.

Lotman, Iu. "O Semiosphere." *Sign Systems Studies* 17 (1984): 5–23.

Lotman, Iu., and B. Uspenskii. *The Semiotics of Russian Culture,* edited by Ann Shukman. Ann Arbor: Department of Slavic Languages and Literatures, University of Michigan, 1984.

Lowen, Rebecca S. *Creating the Cold War University: The Transformation of Stanford.* Berkeley: University of California Press, 1997.

MacPherson, Tom. "Soon I Can Vote!" *Boy's Life,* March 1952, 13.

Mastny, Vojtech. *The Cold War and Soviet Insecurity: The Stalin Years.* New York: Oxford University Press, 1996.

Matza, David. *Delinquency and Drift.* New York: Wiley, 1964.

May, Elaine Tyler. *Homeward Bound: American Families in the Cold War Era.* New York: Basic Books, 1988.

May, William. "Who's Running the Show." *Detroit Free Press,* 13 December 1962, 21.

McCardle, Dorothy. "Education Now Power Struggle in Cold War." *Washington Post/Times Herald,* 8 March 1962, C18.

McCartney, James. "It's Ladies Day at the Capitol: Hoots, Howls—and Charm." *Chicago Daily News,* 14 December 1962, 7.

McGrory, Mary. "Peace Strike Explained: 'Nobody Controls Anybody.'" *Washington Evening Star,* 14 December 1962, 8.

McNees, Valerie. "Communism Needs You." *Congressional Record,* 87th Cong., 1st sess., 1961, 76.

Mead, Margaret, and Martha Wolfenstein, eds. *Childhood in Contemporary Cultures.* Chicago: University of Chicago Press, 1955.

Mechling, Jay. *On My Honor: Boy Scouts and the Making of American Youth.* Chicago: University of Chicago Press, 2004.

Merkel', Maia. "Snimaet Vadim Iusov." *Iskusstvo kino* 1 (1963): 104.

Meyerowitz, Joanne, ed. *Not June Cleaver: Women and Gender in Postwar America, 1945–1960.* Philadelphia: Temple University Press, 1994.

Mickenberg, Julia L. *Learning from the Left: Children's Literature, the Cold War, and Radical Politics in the United States.* New York: Oxford University Press, 2006.

Mikhailov, P. A. *Otchetnyi doklad na XI s" ezde komsomola o rabote TsK VLKSM.* Moscow: Molodaia gvardiia, 1949.

Mintz, Steven. *Huck's Raft: A History of American Childhood.* Cambridge, Mass.: Harvard University Press, 2004.

Mitchell, May Niall. "'A Good and Delicious Country': Free Children of Color and How They Learned to Imagine the Atlantic World in Nineteenth-Century Louisiana." *History of Education Quarterly* 40, no. 2 (2000): 123–44.

Mitz, Rick. *The Great TV Sitcom Book.* Expanded ed. New York: Perigee Books, 1983.

Morgan, Robin. *Monster: Poems.* New York: Random House, 1972.

Mundt, Karl. "America's Little Red Schoolhouse." *Congressional Record,* 88th Cong., 2nd sess., 1964, 4089.

Murphy, Marjorie. *Blackboard Unions: The AFT and the NEA.* Ithaca, N.Y.: Cornell University Press, 1990.

Myers, David. *New Soviet Thinking and U.S. Nuclear Policy.* Philadelphia: Temple University Press, 1990.

Nekrasov, V. "Slova 'velikie' i 'prostye.'" *Iskusstvo kino* 5 (1959): 58

Newman, James R. "A Communication." *Washington Post,* 25 September 1961, A13.

Niebuhr, Reinhold. *Moral Man and Immoral Society: A Study in Ethics and Politics.* New York: Scribner, 1960.

Ninh, Bao. *The Sorrow of War: A Novel of North Vietnam.* New York: Riverhead Books, 1996.

Novikova, L. *Iskusstvo i vospitanie novogo cheloveka.* Moscow: Izd-vo Polit. Lit-ry, 1964.

———. "Vospitanie lichnosti v kollektive." *Sovetskaia pedagogika* 40, no. 3 (1967): 109–15.

Nyberg, Amy Kiste. *Seal of Approval: The History of the Comics Code.* Oxford: University of Mississippi Press, 1998.

Ogden, David. "Cold War Science and the Body Politic: An Immuno/Virological Approach." *Literature and Medicine* 19, no. 2 (2000): 241–61.

Oldenziel, Ruth, and Karin Zachmann, eds. *Cold War Kitchen: Americanization, Technology, and European Users.* Inside Technology. Cambridge, Mass.: MIT Press, 2009.

Olich, Jacqueline. *Competing Ideologies and Children's Literature in Russia, 1918–1935.* New York: VDM Verlag, 2009.

Osgood, Kenneth Alan. *Total Cold War: Eisenhower's Secret Propaganda Battle at Home and Abroad.* Lawrence: University Press of Kansas, 2006.

Oshinsky, David. *Polio: An American Story.* Oxford: Oxford University Press, 2005.

Osokina, E. A., and Kate Transchel, eds. *Our Daily Bread: Socialist Distribution and the Art of Survival in Stalin's Russia, 1927–1941.* Translated by Greta Bucher. The New Russian History. Armonk, N.Y.: M. E. Sharpe, 2001.

Ostriakov, Sergei. *Chto trebuet komsomol ot komsomol'tsa.* Moscow: Molodaia gvardiia, 1937.

Papachristou, Judith. "American Women and Foreign Policy, 1898–1905: Exploring Gender in Diplomatic History." *Diplomatic History* 14 (1990): 493–510.

Parry-Giles, Shawn J. *The Rhetorical Presidency, Propaganda, and the Cold War, 1945–1955.* Westport, Conn.: Praeger, 2002.

Pechernikova, I. *Vospitanie poslushaniia i trudoliubiia u detei v sem'e.* Moscow: Uchpedgiz, 1959.

Petrone, Karen. *Life Has Become More Joyous, Comrades: Celebrations in the Time of Stalin.* Bloomington: Indiana University Press, 2000.

Pinnow, Kenneth Martin. *Lost to the Collective: Suicide and the Promise of Soviet Socialism, 1921–1929.* Ithaca, N.Y.: Cornell University Press, 2010.

Pirrung, G. R. "Building the Image of the Scoutmaster." *Scout Executive,* January 1961, 3.

Pollard, T. "The Hollywood War Machine." *New Political Science* 24, no. 1 (March 2002): 121–39.

Prevots, Naima. *Dance for Export: Cultural Diplomacy and the Cold War.* Studies in Dance History. Middletown, Conn.: Wesleyan University Press, 1998.

Primost, J. "Du berger à la bergère." *Le Figaro,* 5 June 1957, 7.

Prokhorov, Alexander. "The Adolescent and the Child in the Cinema of the Thaw." *Studies in Russian and Soviet Cinema* 1, no. 2 (2007): 115–29.

Raleigh, Don. *Russia's Sputnik Generation: Soviet Baby Boomers Talk about Their Lives.* Bloomington: Indiana University Press, 2006.

Randall, Amy E. *The Soviet Dream World of Retail Trade and Consumption in the 1930s: Consumption and Public Life.* New York: Palgrave Macmillan, 2008.

Ravitch, Diane. *Left Back: A Century of Failed School Reforms.* New York: Simon and Schuster, 2000.

Redl, Helen B. *Soviet Educators on Soviet Education.* New York: Free Press of Glencoe, 1964.

Reece, Carroll. "The Institute of Fiscal and Political Education." *Congressional Record,* 84th Cong., 2nd sess., 1955, 1693.

Reid, Susan. "Cold War in the Kitchen: Gender and the De-Stalinization of Consumer Taste in the Soviet Union under Khrushchev." *Slavic Review* 61, no. 2 (2002): 211–52.

———. "Destalinization and Taste, 1953–1963." *Journal of Design History* 10, no. 2 (1997): 177–201.

———. *Khrushchev in Wonderland: The Pioneer Palace in Moscow's Lenin Hills, 1962.* Pittsburgh, Pa.: University of Pittsburgh Press, 2002.

———. "Khrushchev Modern: Agency and Modernization in the Soviet Home." *Cahiers du Monde russe* 47, nos. 1–2 (January 2006): 227–68.

———. "The Meaning of Home: 'The Only Bit of the World You Can Have to Yourself.'" In *Borders of Socialism: Private Spheres of Soviet Russia,* edited by Lewis Siegelbaum, 145–70. New York: Palgrave Macmillan, 2006.

———. "Women in the Home." In *Women in the Khrushchev Era,* edited by Melanie Ilic, Susan Reid, and Lynne Attwood, 149–76. New York: Palgrave Macmillan, 2004.

Richards, Thomas. *The Commodity Culture of Victorian England: Advertising and Spectacle, 1851–1914.* Stanford, Calif.: Stanford University Press, 1990.

Rickover, H. G. *Education and Freedom.* New York: E. P. Dutton, 1959.

Rodino, Peter. "The Boy Scouts of America." *Congressional Record,* 83rd Cong., 2nd sess., 1954, 1150.

Romm, Mikhail. *Montazhnaia struktura fil'ma.* Moscow: Vsesoiuznyi gosudarstvennyi institute kinematografii, 1981.

Rosenthal, Rachel. "Visual Fiction: The Development of the Secular Icon in Stalinist Poster Art." *Zhe: Stanford's Student Journal of Russian, East European, and Eurasian Studies* 1 (Spring 2005): 1–13.

Rudolph, John L. *Scientists in the Classroom: The Cold War Reconstruction of American Science Education.* New York: Palgrave, 2002.

Schlesinger, Arthur. *The Vital Center: The Politics of Freedom.* Cambridge, Mass.: Riverside Press, 1962.

Schrecker, Ellen. *The Age of McCarthyism: A Brief History with Documents.* Boston: Bedford/St. Martin's, 2002.

———. *Many Are the Crimes: McCarthyism in America.* Princeton, N.J.: Princeton University Press, 1998.

———. *No Ivory Tower: McCarthyism and the Universities.* New York: Oxford University Press, 1986.

Scott, James C. *Domination and the Arts of Resistance: Hidden Transcripts.* New Haven, Conn.: Yale University Press, 1990.

———. *Seeing Like a State: How Certain Schemes to Improve the Human Condition Have Failed.* Yale Agrarian Studies. New Haven, Conn.: Yale University Press, 1998.

Sealander, Judith. *The Failed Century of the Child: Governing America's Young in the Twentieth Century.* Cambridge: Cambridge University Press, 2003.

Sherrow, Victoria. *Encyclopedia of Youth and War.* Phoenix, Ariz.: Oryx Press, 2000.

Shields, Amos. "The Men in Your Life." *Scout Executive,* October 1960, 7.

Shimko, Keith L. "Metaphors and Foreign Policy Decision Making." *Political Psychology* 15, no. 4 (1994): 655–71.

Shlapentokh, Vladimir. *Public and Private Life of the Soviet People: Changing Values in Post-Stalin Russia.* Oxford: Oxford University Press, 1989.

Shmakov, S. *Igra i deti.* Moscow: Znanie, 1968.

Siegelbaum, Lewis, ed. *Borders of Socialism: Private Spheres of Soviet Russia.* New York: Palgrave Macmillan, 2006.

Skolnick, Arlene. *Embattled Paradise: The American Family in an Age of Uncertainty.* New York: Basic Books, 1991.

Small, Melvin. *Antiwarriors: The Vietnam War and the Battle for America's Hearts and Minds.* Wilmington, Del.: Scholarly Resources, Inc., 2002.

Smith, Walter Bedell. "Why the Russian People Don't Rebel." *Saturday Evening Post,* 26 November 1949, 22–24.

Smolkin-Rothrock, Victoria. "'A Sacred Space Is Never Empty': Soviet Atheism, 1954–1971." Ph.D. diss., University of California at Berkeley, 2010.

Sovetskii Komitet Detei. "Zhguchaya polemika po voprosam narodnogo obrazovaniia." *O Molodezhi Moskvy,* 21 December 1961, 21.

Spock, Benjamin. *Baby and Child Care*. New York: Pocket Books, 1957.

Stearns, Peter. *Childhood in World History*. New York: Routledge, 2006.

Steedman, Carolyn. *The Tidy House: Little Girls Writing*. London: Virago, 1982.

Stephens, Sharon. "Nationalism, Nuclear Policy, and Children in Cold War America." *Childhood* 4 (1997): 103–23.

Stites, Richard. *Russian Popular Culture: Entertainment and Society since 1900*. Cambridge: Cambridge University Press, 1992.

Students for a Democratic Society. *The Port Huron Statement*. New York: AWOL: The Underground GI Newspaper, 1964.

Symington, James. "Youth, Crime, and the Great Society." *Congressional Record*, 89th Cong., 2nd sess., 1966, 4657.

Suri, Jeremi. "The Cultural Contradictions of Cold War Education: The Case of West Berlin." *Cold War History* 4, no. 3 (April 2004): 1–20.

———. *Power and Protest: Global Revolution and the Rise of Detente*. Cambridge, Mass.: Harvard University Press, 2003.

Sutcliffe, Benjamin M. *The Prose of Life: Russian Women Writers from Khrushchev to Putin*. Madison: University of Wisconsin Press, 2009.

Swerdlow, Amy. *Women Strike for Peace: Traditional Motherhood and Radical Politics in the 1960s*. Chicago: University of Chicago Press, 1993.

Tarkovsky, Andrei. *Sculpting in Time*. London: Bodley Head, 1986.

Taubman, William. *Khrushchev: The Man and His Era*. 1st ed. New York: Norton, 2003.

Timasheff, Nicholas S. *The Great Retreat: The Growth and Decline of Communism in Russia*. New York: Arno Press, 1972.

Tolstoy, Leo. *Detstvo*. Moscow: Russki iazyk, 1990.

Tomilina, N., Stefan Karner, and Aleksandr Oganovich Chubarian, eds. *Prazhskaia vesna i mezhdunarodnyi krizis 1968 goda: Dokumenty*. Moscow: Mezhdunarodyi Fond Demokratiia, 2010.

Tumarkin, Nina. *The Living and the Dead: The Rise and Fall of the Cult of World War II in Russia*. New York: Basic Books, 1994.

Turovskaia, Maia. "Some Documents from the Life of a Documentary Film." *Studies in Russian and Soviet Cinema* 2, no. 2 (2008): 155–65.

Tuttle, William. *Daddy's Gone to War: The Second World War in the Lives of America's Children*. New York: Oxford University Press, 1993.

———. "The Homefront Children's Popular Culture." In *Small Worlds*, edited by Elliott West and Paula Petrik, 143–63. Lawrence: University Press of Kansas, 1992.

U.S. Advertising Council. "What's Nice to Have, Hard to Save, and Essential to Your Future (Besides Money)?" *Saturday Evening Post*, 25 August–1 September 1962, 5.

———. "How to Protect Your Children's Future . . . As You Save for Your Own." *Saturday Evening Post*, 17 March 1962, 91.

U.S. Educational Policies Commission. *The Central Purposes of American Education*. Washington, D.C.: National Education Association, 1961.

U.S. Congress. House. Committee on Un-American Activities. *Communist Activities in the Peace Movement (Women Strike for Peace and Certain Other Groups)*. Washington, D.C.: U.S. Government Printing Office, 11–13 December 1962.

————. Subcommittee on Departments of Labor and Health, Education, and Welfare. *Review of Activities under National Defense Education Act.* Washington, D.C.: U.S. Government Printing Office, 1960.

————. Subcommittee on International Organizations and Movements of the Committee on Foreign Affairs. *Winning the Cold War: The U.S. Ideological Offensive.* Washington, D.C.: U.S. Government Printing Office, 1963.

U.S. Congress. Senate. Committee on Foreign Relations. *Hearings before the Committee on Foreign Relations on the Treaty Banning Nuclear Weapons Tests in the Atmosphere, in Outer Space, and Underwater.* Washington, D.C.: U.S. Government Printing Office, 1963.

————. Internal Security Subcommittee on the Judiciary. *Communist Infiltration in the Test Ban Movement.* Washington, D.C.: U.S. Government Printing Office, 1960.

USSR Academy of Sciences. *70th Anniversary of Stalin's Birth.* Moscow: Akademiia Nauk, 1949.

Varshavskii, Ia. "Nado razobrat'sia." *Iskusstvo kino* 5 (1959): 62–63.

Wachtel, Andrew. *The Battle for Childhood: Creation of a Russian Myth.* Stanford, Calif.: Stanford University Press, 1990.

Wagnleitner, Reinhold, and Elaine Tyler May, eds. *Here, There, and Everywhere. The Foreign Politics of American Popular Culture.* Hanover, N.H.: University Press of New England, 2000.

Wall, Wendy. *Inventing the "American Way": The Politics of Consensus from the New Deal to the Civil Rights Movement.* New York: Oxford University Press, 2008.

Weart, Spencer R. *Nuclear Fear: A History of Images.* Cambridge, Mass.: Harvard University Press, 1988.

Weintraub, Jeff, and Krishan Kumar, eds. *Public and Private in Thought and Practice: Perspectives on a Grand Dichotomy.* Chicago: University of Chicago Press, 1997.

Wertham, Fredric. *Seduction of the Innocent.* New York: Rinehart, 1953.

Westad, Odd Arne. *The Global Cold War: Third World Interventions and the Making of Our Times.* New York: Cambridge University Press, 2005.

Whitfield, Stephen. *The Culture of the Cold War.* Baltimore: Johns Hopkins University Press, 1991.

Williams, William Appleman. *The Tragedy of American Diplomacy.* New York: Norton, 1959.

Wilson, Elizabeth. *Women and the Welfare State.* London: Tavistock Publications, 1977.

Wilson, Sloan. "It's Time to Close Our Carnival." *Life,* 24 March 1958, 36–37.

Wishy, Bernard. *The Child and the Republic: The Dawn of Modern American Child Nurture.* Philadelphia: University of Pennsylvania Press, 1968.

Wittner, Lawrence. *Resisting the Bomb: A History of the World Nuclear Disarmament Movement, 1954–1970.* Stanford, Calif.: Stanford University Press, 1997.

Woll, Josephine. "Mikhail Romm's Ordinary Fascism." In *Picturing Russia: Explorations in Visual Culture,* edited by Valerie Kivelson and Joan Neuberger, 224–29. New Haven, Conn.: Yale University Press, 2008.

————. *Real Images: Soviet Cinema and the Thaw.* Kino, the Russian Cinema Series. London: I. B. Tauris, 2000.

Wylie, Philip. *Generation of Vipers.* New York: Farrar and Rinehart, 1942.

Yeats, Sidney. "Help for a Child or Punishment for a Delinquent." *Congressional Record,* 83rd Cong., 1st sess., 1954, A633.

Yelyutin, Vyacheslav. "Adapting Higher Schools to Contemporary Demands." Translated by Ina Schlesinger. *School and Society* (February 1959): 68–72.

York, Jodi. "The Truth about Women and Peace." In *The Women and War Reader,* edited by Lois Lorentzen and Jennifer Turpin, 19–25. New York: New York University Press, 1998.

Youngblood, Denise. "A War Remembered: Soviet Films of the Great Patriotic War." *American Historical Review* 106, no. 3 (June 2001): 839–56.

Zahra, Tara. *Kidnapped Souls: National Indifference and the Battle for Children in the Bohemian Lands, 1900–1948.* Ithaca, N.Y.: Cornell University Press, 2008.

————. *The Lost Children: Reconstructing Europe's Families after World War II.* Cambridge, Mass.: Harvard University Press, 2011.

Zajda, Joseph. *Education in the USSR.* New York: Pergamon Press, 1980.

Zigler, Edward. "Early Childhood Intervention: A Promising Preventative for Juvenile Delinquency." *American Psychologist* 47, no. 8 (August 1992): 997–1006.

Zorkaia, Naia. *The Illustrated History of the Soviet Cinema.* New York: Hippocrene Books, 1989.

Zubkova, E. *Obshchestvo i reformy, 1945–1964.* Moscow: Rossiia molodaia, 1993.

Zubok, V. M. *A Failed Empire: The Soviet Union in the Cold War from Stalin to Gorbachev.* The New Cold War History. Chapel Hill: University of North Carolina Press, 2007.

Zubok, V. M., and Konstantin Pleshakov. *Inside the Kremlin's Cold War: From Stalin to Khrushchev.* Cambridge, Mass.: Harvard University Press, 1996.

Acknowledgments

I owe a great debt of gratitude to many people for making this book possible. I received financial support from the U.S. State Department as a Fulbright-Hays scholar, the Society for the Historians of American Foreign Relations, the Society for the History of Childhood and Youth, and the Department of Education. I received a number of grants from the University of Texas at Austin, including the Gardner F. Marston Fellowship, the Alice Jane Drysdale Sheffield Fellowship, and a Continuing Education Grant. I also received assistance from the University of Alabama in the form of Research Center Grants, funding from Capstone International, and research provisions from the Department of History.

Several librarians and archivists, across two continents and fourteen archives, were crucial to the success of this project. I owe special thanks to Galina Mikhailovna Tokareva at the Russian State Archive of Socio-Political History, who took me under her wing and gave me access to Pioneer materials. She was herself a Komsomol leader and provided valuable insights during our daily breaks for tea. In the United States, Wendy Chmielewski at the Swarthmore College Peace Collection was very helpful in directing my research, as were Steven Price at the Boy Scouts of America Archive in Irving, Texas, and Yevgeniya Gribov at the Girl Scouts of America Archive in New York City. The archivists running the Vietnam archive in Lubbock, Texas, are also to be commended for their willingness to talk at length with me about digitizing and declassifying documents.

A number of people offered countless hours of careful reading and advice. Joan Neuberger continues to be a role model for professionalism, discipline, and decency in the field. This project would not have been possible without her sound advice and constant encouragement. In the early stages of this project, Josephine Woll, Catriona Kelly, Deborah Field, Charters Wynn, Mark Lawrence, Julia Mickenberg, Mary Neuburger, Karl Brown, Paul Rubinson, and David Oshinsky offered vital feedback.

I relied on the help of my colleagues and friends at the University of Alabama and around the world. I am particularly indebted to Janek Wasserman, who gave thoughtful, line-by-line feedback on the manuscript, along with many hours of challenging conversation. Stephen Bunker, Howard Jones,

Jimmy Mixson, Lisa Lindquist-Dorr, Joshua Rothman, and Kari Frederickson spent many hours coaxing me through this process. George Thompson, our publisher-in-residence, offered useful advice. I also greatly appreciated the assistance of Brett Spencer and Patricia Causey at the University of Alabama libraries. The members of the First International Russian Children's History Colloquium, which met in Paris in the summer of 2012, offered crucial critique before I submitted the manuscript. These include Julie DeGraffenreid, Ann Livschiz, Karl Qualls, Elaine McKinnon, and Jacqueline Olich. The invitation to present the manuscript to the Carolina Seminar at the University of North Carolina proved very rewarding. Once I submitted the manuscript, Jeremi Suri and Jacqueline Olich were generous beyond measure in their careful readings of the manuscript, their suggestions for revisions, and their positive support. I also appreciated the questions and advice that came from friends at crucial points in the revision process: Kate Brown, Paul Hagenloh, Helena Goscilo, Louise McReynolds, Donald Raleigh, Gleb Tsipursky, Emily Baran, Ann Powers, Edward Geist, Zach Levine, Maya Haber, and Sean Guillory. I must especially thank Ann Livschiz, Erik Peterson, and Marcus Witcher, who gave many of their precious hours to ferret out all the little mistakes in the final manuscript that I could no longer see.

At the University of North Carolina Press, I must also thank my editor, Chuck Grench, and his two assistants, Sara Jo Cohen and Lucas Church. My copyeditor, Dorothea Anderson, and production editor, Paul Betz, have been wonderful. Thanks, also, to Odd Arne Westad for placing this book in the New Cold War History series.

To my family I owe my greatest debt. My husband, D.Jay, and our three daughters, Amelia, Sylvia, and Mira, have experienced this book with me. They traveled the world with me. My mother has provided constant encouragement. My father was also an important driving force in this project. He passed away while the book was being written, and I like to think that he was a part of it as well. Finally, I must thank my husband. I could not have accomplished this without him. He was more patient and giving than I could ever have hoped. This book is a testament to his belief in me, and I appreciate it more than words can say.

Index

22; trauma caused by, 37, 161, 163. *See also* Strontium 90; Uranium

Attwood, William, 27

Auden, W. H., 190

Augustus, Ellsworth, 36, 105–6. *See also* Boy Scouts of America

Baden-Powell, Lord Robert, 110, 113. *See also* Boy Scouts of America

Baker, Adelaide, 166

Baldwin, James, 175

Bao Ninh, 197

Barthes, Roland, 8–9

Basin, Anatoly, 123

Bay of Pigs, 119

Beberman, Max, 63

Bedell Smith, Walter, 57

Belafonte, Harry, 175

Belarus, 63

Berlin Airlift, 20–21, 28

Berlin University, 138

Berlin Wall, 119, 169

Bogomolov, Andrei, 134–35. See also *Ivan's Childhood*

Bondarchuk, Sergei, 143

Born, Max, 168

Boys, 10, 237 (n. 58); bodies, 39; killed, 220; and science, 106–8, 241 (n. 42); sexuality of, 86–88; in Soviet film, 127–54; and sports, 104; as symbol for atom bomb, 167; teaching of, 37. *See also* Boy Scouts of America; Girls

Boy Scouts of America, 3–4, 105–20, 231 (n. 65), 232 (n. 7); badges, 37, 108, 110, 114, 231 (n. 69); and civil defense, 36–39, 231 (n. 69); and delinquency, 109; education, 109; and Eisenhower, 110, 241 (n. 52); as international emissaries, 4, 95–96; mobilization of, 36–40, 90; mythmaking, 116–17; racial integration of, 111–13, 241 (nn. 61, 64); science, 106–8; sexuality, 110–11; as substitutes for parents, 109–10; "Thousands for One" campaign, 112;

World Brotherhood Badge, 114. See also *Boy's Life*

Boy's Life (magazine), 106–8, 115, 117, 240–41 (n. 41), 241 (n. 42)

Bovin, Sasha, 139

Bowman Trading Card Company, 29

Bradbury, Ray, 175

Brennan, Terry, 38

Brezhnev, Leonid, 5

Bronfenbrenner, Urie, 60

Brown v. Board of Education, 46

Bulganin, Nikolai, 20

Bulgaria, 78, 102–3, 219

Bykov, Rolan, 144

Cameroon, 50

Capitalism, 2, 5, 14, 24, 81–82, 139, 157, 177, 194, 222–23; appeal of, 58, 28, 30, 113–14; capitalist encirclement and threat of, 20–21, 31, 34–36, 58–59, 71, 77–79, 119, 205, 221; critique of, 26, 43–46, 50, 69, 87, 103–6, 202; cultural, 31; semiotic, 193; symbolic, 223

Cardin Crain, Lucille, 75

Catholic Guild, 76. *See also* Religion

CBS (Columbia Broadcasting System), 18

Central Executive Committee of the People's Revolutionary Party (COSVN), 193, 201, 208–13

Chamberlin, William, 56

Chevy Chase Baptist Church, 55

Chiaureli, Mikhail, 126

Chicago Daily News, 186

Chieu Hoi, 196–97, 200

Childhood, 5, 9–10, 12, 17, 28, 33, 41, 43, 50, 52, 57–58, 99, 111, 120, 124, 215–25, 228 (n. 21); and gender, 40; hooliganism, 77, 81, 84–85, 109; and national identity, 19, 73; and Stalin, 2, 21–24, 97; and atom bomb, 160, 163, 188–89, 191; and the Thaw, 123–24, 129, 130–36, 140, 143, 147, 152; as weapon, 20. *See also* African American children, images of; American children, images of; Capitalism; Children, images of; Consensus; Soviet children, images of; "Other" children, images of

Child labor, 43

Children, images of, 2–3, 5–6, 9–12; as abandoned, 3, 6, 9, 24, 50, 76, 83, 124, 126, 132, 135, 140–49, 159, 191, 224; as affluent, 24–34; ages of, 10; and atom bomb, 22, 37, 64, 108, 139, 153, 160–92, 217, 219; as builders of consensus, 4–5, 8, 11, 23–24, 39, 71–73, 79–80, 92–93, 96–97, 106, 113, 120; as commodities, 9–10; as consumers, 4, 24–34, 57, 72, 80, 82, 87, 89, 175, 202; as contained, 4, 12, 18–19, 22, 32–35, 39–42, 92–97, 106, 149, 190, 197, 210, 218; depravity and suffering of, 6, 31, 44–58, 82–83, 214; as destroyers of consensus, 6, 13; as emissaries of peace, 4, 94–120; historical, 2, 19; as idealized, 3, 19, 17–41; importance of in 1950s, 9, 18; as mobilized for peace, 4; as mobilized for war, 3, 34–39, 94; Mormon, 69; as myths, 8, 22, 23–24, 41, 55, 69, 116–17, 124, 126, 132, 154, 207, 211–13; Native American, 69; Pacific Islander, 69; as partisans, 57, 116–17; as protected, 5; semiotics and, 8–9, 33, 52, 120, 151, 193–94; and sexuality or gender, 13, 38–40, 65, 72, 80, 82, 86–88, 104, 110–11; shared Soviet and American uses of, 5, 8, 11–12, 24, 31, 34, 40–43, 58–60, 67–73, 79–80, 89–96, 117–20, 160–62, 190–94, 214–25; as soldiers, 51, 196; as subversive of status quo, 9, 69–70, 119–20, 123–26, 158–59, 160–92, 193–94, 95, 214–25; as symbols of death, 10, 135–36, 140, 165–68, 178, 191, 213, 225; in the Thaw, 123–59; as Third World supporters, 2, 5, 7, 41, 50–51, 62, 69, 78, 100, 104–5, 114–17, 199–200, 208–10; as threatened by the state, 123–59, 160–62, 187; in

Vietnam, 193–214; visual and rhetorical reproduction of, 7, 10. *See also* African American children, images of; American children, images of; Boys; Boy Scouts of America; Civil defense; Consensus; Education; Girls; Girl Scouts of America; Hooliganism; Juvenile delinquency; "Other" children, images of; Pioneers; Soviet children, images of; Thaw film, images of children in; Threatened children, images of; United Nations; Vietnamese children, images of

Children's Bureau, 95

Children's Crusade against Communism, 29

Children's Day, 56

Children's labor schools in the Soviet Union, 55

Child-saving, 24

Chile, 50

China, 57, 86, 208

Christianity. *See* Religion

Christian Science Monitor, 56

Circus (*Tsirk*), 46

Civil defense, 34–39, 44, 162–63, 172, 192, 231 (n. 68)

Civil Rights Act, 189

Civil rights movement, 112; Soviet coverage of, 46–51. *See also* African American children, images of

Clark, Edward, 55

Clark, Joseph, 63

Cleaver, Beaver, 1

Comics, 88–89

Committee for a Sane Nuclear Policy (SANE), 6, 13, 161–76; and civil defense, 162–63, 172; Dentists' Committee, 174; Public Information Committee, 169–70

Committee on Youth Fitness, 87

Communism: as alternative to capitalism, 5; and fascism, 55; theories on children, 52; threat of, 10, 39, 72–75

Communist Manifesto, The, 43

Conniff, Frank, 57

Consensus, 4, 12, 215–17, 219, 221–25; collapse of, 6–7, 43, 59, 70, 95, 124–28, 144, 149, 161, 182, 188–89, 192–94, 208, 214; construction of, 5, 8, 11, 23–24, 39, 71–73, 79–80, 92–93, 96–97, 106, 113, 120; consumerism and, 24–25, 27, 31–34; Girl Scouts, 40; and the "Other" child, 43, 57–59, 69; and Stalin, 39

Consumerism, 4–5, 24–34, 39, 57, 175, 202, 230 (n. 35)

Containment, 1, 4, 7, 12, 17–18, 19, 21–22, 32–35, 39–42, 72–73, 92–97, 106, 118, 120, 123, 149, 190, 197, 210, 218; as American policy, 18, 33; and NSC-68, 18; as Soviet policy, 35

Cooper Union College, 165

Coplon, Judith, 60

COSVN (Central Executive Committee of the People's Revolutionary Party), 193, 201, 208–13

Cousins, Norman, 162, 164–66, 168–69, 175

Creative Playthings, Inc., 33

Crusade for Children, 52, 56

Cuba, 94, 119

Cushing, Richard, 106, 240 (n. 37)

Czechoslovakia, 20, 103, 116–17, 219–20, 224

Daisy spot, 189–91, 249 (n. 110)

Danelia, Georgy, 140–43

David and Bathsheba, 189

Day of Soviet Youth, 94

Delinquency. *See* Juvenile delinquency

Derthick report, 61–62, 67

Détente, 7

Dewey, John, 60

Disneyland, 22

Doctor's Plot, 77

Dodd, Thomas, 168

DOSAAF. *See* Volunteer Society for Cooperation with the Army, Aviation, and Fleet

Douglas Aircraft Company, 28

Doyle, Clyde, 185

Doyle, Dane, and Bernbach, 189

Drier, Alex, 89

Dr. Strangelove or: How I Learned to Stop Worrying and Love the Bomb (1964), 125

Duck and Cover, 38

Dylan, Bob, 218

Education, 3, 9, 33, 44–45, 59–69, 89, 118–19, 161, 166, 168, 175, 181, 215, 222, 233 (n. 43); African American, 47; and American juvenile delinquency, 82–84; Artek and, 103–5; Boy Scouts and, 109; communist threat in American, 10, 72–75; creativity in, 39, 59–60, 64–65, 67, 100; in crisis, 59; Derthick report and, 61; Dewey and, 60; exchanges, 118, 202; Fulbright and, 61; funding, 43; impact of Cold War on, 59–69; Internats, 66; Khrushchev and, 26, 59, 64, 124; and Komsomol, 65, 67; life-adjustment, 60, 62, 63, 65; Litchfield report, 61–62; New Math, 63; progressivist, 63, 69; reforms, 59, 63–69; science and, 4, 37, 60–62, 65, 108; in Soviet film, 155; Soviet history of, 51–52; Soviet hooliganism and, 99–100; Soviet shortages in, 62–63; Soviet urban schools, 65; Stalinist, 4, 60, 63–67. *See also* Child-saving; "Other" children, images of

Educational Reviewer (newsletter), 75

Efremov, Oleg, 144

Eisenhower, Dwight D., 23–24, 33, 58, 87, 118, 165, 168, 229 (n. 18); and Boy Scouts, 110, 241 (n. 52); Emergency Fund for the Arts, 118

Engels, Friedrich, 43

England, 113, 180

Ermler, Fredrikh, 126

Evers, Medgar, 205

Ewing, Oscar R., 27

Music, 33, 43, 66, 81, 101, 144, 151, 158, 200; rock-n-roll, 45, 84
My Lai, 194, 218
Myrick, Norman, 175–76

Nagy, Imre, 119
National Broadcasting Corporation (NBC), 89, 189
National Catholic Guild, 75
National Citizens' Commission for Public Schools, 62
National Committee on War Tensions in Children, 163
National Council for American Education, 75
National Defense Education Act, 63, 108
National Education Association, 59
National Interracial Service, 112
National Liberation Front (NLF), 193, 198, 200–201, 208–10, 212–13
National Urban League, 112
Nazis, 3, 21, 56, 117, 121, 137–39. *See also* Hitler, Adolf
Neel, James V., 173
Neizvestny, Ernst, 158
Nekrasov, Victor, 129–30
Neuberger, Maurine, 187
Newman, James R., 160–61
New Math Movement, 63
New York City Police Department, 84
New York Times, 111, 164, 170, 174, 176
Nguyen Van Be, 210–13
Nguyen Van Ty, 94
Niebuhr, Reinhold, 41, 232 (n. 84)
Night of the Dragon (1964), 198–99, 200, 210
Nigeria, 104
Nixon, Richard M., 32
NLF. *See* National Liberation Front
North Vietnamese Army (NVA), 195, 200, 205
Novikova, Lydia, 66, 67
Novocherkassk, 80
Novyi mir, 27
NSC-68, 18

Nuclear Test Ban Treaty, 161, 164–66, 174, 176–77, 180, 183, 187, 189
NVA (North Vietnamese Army), 195, 200, 205

One Day in the Life of Ivan Denisovich, 123
Operation Ranch Hand, 206
Ordinary Fascism (Obykhnovennyi fashizm), 136–40
Ostriakov, Sergei, 43
"Other" children, images of, 13, 41, 42–70; American children as, 42–50, 59; complications with, 42, 70; as counter-ideals, 42; enviable, 42–43, 58; postcolonial children as, 50; Soviet children as, 42, 51–59; uses of, 42–43, 51–52, 59. *See also* African American children, images of; American children, images of; Soviet children, images of

Papanek, Jan, 20
Paradzhanov, Sergei, 143
Parenting, 9, 53, 170, 175, 215; bad, 13, 72, 81–86, 90–92, 118, 119, 166, 244 (n. 47); good, 30. *See also* Fatherhood; Motherhood
Parents' Magazine, 9, 215
Pauling, Linus, 165, 169, 183
Peace Corps, 95, 118
Peaceful competition, 5
Pechernikova, Irina, 81
Penn, Arthur, 175
People-to-People Program, 95
Pepper, Claude, 84
Philmont camp, 38, 231 (n. 74)
Phlaum, George, 76
Pickett, Clarence, 168, 175
Pioneers, 3–4, 17, 20, 37–38, 43–44, 49, 81–82, 109, 119–20, 125, 140–41, 143; as affluent youth, 24; camps, 25, 46, 52, 100–105, 113–15, 150–58, 203, 239 (n. 17), 241 (n. 25); and education, 66; and film, 144–47, 155–58, 202–3, 244

Twain, Mark, 75
Twentieth Party Congress of the Communist Party of the Soviet Union, 64
Twenty-second Party Congress of the Communist Party of the Soviet Union, 25
Two Fedors (Dva Fedora, 1958), 127–30

Uganda, 104
Ukraine, 52, 55, 129
Ulbricht, Walter, 169
UNESCO. *See* United Nations Educational, Scientific, and Cultural Organization
United Nations, 9, 20, 28, 56–57, 75, 217, 252 (n. 50); and The Declaration on the Rights of the Child, 9, 57
United Nations Educational, Scientific, and Cultural Organization (UNESCO), 52, 234 (n. 69)
U.S. Atomic Energy Commission, 164, 166, 178
U.S. Commission on Civil Rights, 111
U.S. Congressional Record, 53, 233 (n. 48)
U.S. Department of Defense, 63
U.S. Department of Education, 63, 233 (n. 43)
U.S. Information Agency, 105, 174, 198
U.S. Joint Public Affairs Office (JUSPAO), 193–201, 203–4, 207, 212–13; family appeal, 196; fear appeal, 196
U.S. Postal Service, 75
U.S. Public Health Service, 178
U.S. Savings Bonds, 28–29
U.S. Senate Committee on Atomic Energy, 160, 164, 166, 178
U.S. State Department, 18, 20, 35, 47, 105, 114, 118
Uranium, 56
Ut, Nick, 218

Vancouver Sun, 187
Vassiliev, Oleg, 123
Vatolina, Nina, 21–22, 97
Venice Film Festival, 130

Vietnam, 2, 13, 23, 100, 115, 188, 193–214. *See also* Vietnamese children, images of
Vietnamese children, images of, 1, 6, 10, 13, 94, 116, 193–214; as contained, 197, 210; as recipients of American care, 193–201; as recipients of Soviet care, 193, 201–8; as revolutionaries, 193, 208–13; as victims of Americans, 193, 205–7; as victims of North Vietnamese, 195; as victims of Soviets, 193, 199. *See also* Soviet State Service for Televisions and Radio; U.S. Joint Public Affairs Office
Virgin Lands. *See* Khrushchev, Nikita: Virgin Lands project
Vladimirsky, Boris, 21
Voice of America, 29, 118, 194
Voice of Freedom, 194
Volunteer Society for Cooperation with the Army, Aviation, and Fleet (DOSAAF), 98, 230 (n. 57), 231 (n. 60–62). *See also* Civil defense; Local Anti-Air Defense
Vysotsky, Vladimir, 220–21

Wallace, George, 204
Wall Street Journal, 56
War on Poverty, The, 189
Warsaw Pact, 20
Washington Evening Star, 186
Washington Post, 160, 184
Washington Star, 178, 179
Welcome, or No Trespassing (Dobro pozhalovat', ili postoronnim vkhod vospreshchen, 1964), 150–58
Wertham, Fredric, 88–89
White Plains Reporter, 182
Wilson, Dagmar, 178 81, 186, 218
Wilson, Sloan, 62
Women, 3, 26, 146; American, 90, 104; in film, 126, 146; Russian, 32, 38, 61. *See also* Women Strike for Peace
Women Strike for Peace (WSP), 6, 13, 161; critique of U.S. and Soviet

foreign policy, 161; mobilization of children, 161

Woolley, Helen Thompson, 86

Wordsworth, William, 19

World Jamboree, 114–17. *See also* Boy Scouts of America

World Scouting, 113–17; World Friendship Fund, 114. *See also* Boy Scouts of America

World War I, 2

World War II, 1; American wealth from, 27; Soviet destruction from, 17, 52; in Soviet film, 123–40; Soviet recovery from, 5, 20–21; Soviet sacrifice in, 18

Wright, Marlon, 111–12

WSP. *See* Women Strike for Peace

Wylie, Philip, 81, 85, 89

Yates, Sidney, 84

Yevtushenko, Evgenii, 123

Young Men's Christian Association (YMCA), 37, 40, 90

Young Men's Jewish Council, 84

Zarkhi, A. G., 155

Zhiltsova, Svetlana, 18, 38, 71, 80, 217

Zhukov, Nikolai, 27

Zoll, Allen, 75

Zorthian, Barry, 195, 249 (n. 3)

Zoshchenko, Mikhail, 123

The New Cold War History

Margaret Peacock, *Innocent Weapons: The Soviet and American Politics of Childhood in the Cold War* (2014).

Austin Jersild, *The Sino-Soviet Alliance: An International History* (2014).

Piero Gleijeses, *Visions of Freedom: Havana, Washington, Pretoria, and the Struggle for Southern Africa, 1976–1991* (2013).

Lien-Hang T. Nguyen, *Hanoi's War: An International History of the War for Peace in Vietnam* (2012).

Tanya Harmer, *Allende's Chile and the Inter-American Cold War, 1970–1973* (2011).

Alessandro Brogi, *Confronting America: The Cold War between the United States and the Communists in France and Italy* (2011).

Gregg Brazinsky, *Nation Building in South Korea: Koreans, Americans, and the Making of a Democracy* (2007).

Vladislav M. Zubok, *A Failed Empire: The Soviet Union in the Cold War from Stalin to Gorbachev* (2007).

Stephen G. Rabe, *U.S. Intervention in British Guiana: A Cold War Story* (2005).

Christopher Endy, *Cold War Holidays: American Tourism in France* (2004).

Salim Yaqub, *Containing Arab Nationalism: The Eisenhower Doctrine and the Middle East* (2003).

Francis J. Gavin, *Gold, Dollars, and Power: The Politics of International Monetary Relations, 1958–1971* (2003).

William Glenn Gray, *Germany's Cold War: The Global Campaign to Isolate East Germany, 1949–1969* (2003).

Matthew J. Ouimet, *The Rise and Fall of the Brezhnev Doctrine in Soviet Foreign Policy* (2003).

Pierre Asselin, *A Bitter Peace: Washington, Hanoi, and the Making of the Paris Agreement* (2002).

Jeffrey Glen Giauque, *Grand Designs and Visions of Unity: The Atlantic Powers and the Reorganization of Western Europe, 1955–1963* (2002).

Chen Jian, *Mao's China and the Cold War* (2001).

M. E. Sarotte, *Dealing with the Devil: East Germany, Détente, and Ostpolitik, 1969–1973* (2001).

Mark Philip Bradley, *Imagining Vietnam and America: The Making of Postcolonial Vietnam, 1919–1950* (2000).

Michael E. Latham, *Modernization as Ideology: American Social Science and "Nation Building" in the Kennedy Era* (2000).

Qiang Zhai, *China and the Vietnam Wars, 1950–1975* (2000).

William I. Hitchcock, *France Restored: Cold War Diplomacy and the Quest for Leadership in Europe, 1944–1954* (1998).